CHRISTOPHER SMART
AND THE
ENLIGHTENMENT

CHRISTOPHER SMART
AND THE
ENLIGHTENMENT

Edited by Clement Hawes

St. Martin's Press
New York

ISBN 0-312-21369-7

Library of Congress Cataloging-in-Publication Data

Christopher Smart and the Enlightenment / edited by Clement Hawes.
   p. cm.
  Includes bibliographical references and index.
  ISBN 0-312-21369-7
  1. Smart, Christopher, 1722-1771—Criticism and interpretation.
  2. England—Intellectual life—18th century. 3. Enlightenment—
England. 4. Poetics. I. Hawes, Clement.
PR3687.S7Z627 1999
821'.6—dc21   98-48374
                                                              CIP

Design by Orit Mardkha-Tenzer

First edition: May, 1999
10 9 8 7 6 5 4 3 2 1

Contents

Acknowledgments

THIS PROJECT WAS born out of a conversation with Jim Thorson and Todd Parker, whom I wish to thank for galvanizing me into action. The idea could not have come to fruition without the generously engaged and creative support of Karina Williamson. I have also benefited throughout the editing process from the helpful guidance of Greg Clingham, Betty Rizzo, Linda E. Merians, and Tom Keymer. I am grateful to all of the contributors, who have been enthusiastic and unselfish collaborators in our joint venture. I would also like to thank Maura Burnett, whose wise suggestions have greatly eased the task of preparing this volume.

Last but not least, I am grateful for the intellectual partnership I share with Mrinalini Sinha. This book bears the mark of many specific and substantial suggestions by her; but there is a more intangible level of conversational exchange—an editing by osmosis—that may be her most profound contribution to the project.

List of Abbreviations

All quotations from Christopher Smart, unless otherwise noted, are from *The Poetical Works of Christopher Smart*, eds. Karina Williamson and Marcus Walsh, 6 vols. (Oxford: Clarendon Press, 1980-1996), hereafter referred to as *PW*. Quotations from *Jubilate Agno* are noted in the text by alphabetized fragment and line number. Quotations from the Bible are from the Authorized Version.

Bond	*Jubilate Agno*, ed. W. H. Bond (London: Rupert Hart-Davis, 1954).
Boswell's *Life*	James Boswell's *The Life of Samuel Johnson, LL.D.*, ed. G. B. Hill, revised by F. Powell, 6 vols. (Oxford: Clarendon Press, 1934-50).
Devlin	Christopher Devlin, *Poor Kit Smart* (London: Rupert Hart-Davis, 1961).
ELH	*Journal of English Literary History*
Gent. Mag.	*Gentleman's Magazine*
Guest	Harriet Guest, *A Form of Sound Words: The Religious Poetry of Christopher Smart* (Oxford: Clarendon Press, 1989).
Hartman	Geoffrey H. Hartman, "Christopher Smart's 'Magnificat': Towards a Theory of Representation," in his *The Fate of Reading and Other Essays* (Chicago: University of Chicago Press, 1985), 74-98.
Hawes	Clement Hawes, *Mania and Literary Style: The Rhetoric of Enthusiasm from the Ranters to Christopher Smart* (Cambridge: Cambridge University Press, 1996).
Letters	*The Annotated Letters of Christopher Smart,* eds. Betty Rizzo and Robert Mahony (Carbondale: Southern Illinois University Press, 1991).
Midwife	*The Midwife; or, the Old Woman's Magazine* (1750-1753). 3 vols. (1751-53).
Newton's *Principia*	Sir Isaac Newton, *Philosophiae Naturalis Principia Mathematica* (London: Reg. soc., 1687).

PMLA	*Publications of the Modern Language Association*
Sherbo	Arthur Sherbo, *Christopher Smart: Scholar of the University* (Lansing: Michigan State University Press, 1967).
Stead	*Rejoice in the Lamb: A Song from Bedlam*, ed. William Force Stead (London: Jonathan Cape, 1939).

Permissions

BENJAMIN BRITTEN
Excerpts from *Rejoice in the Lamb* from an article entitled "Benjamin Britten's *Rejoice in the Lamb:* Figural Invention, 'Impression' and the Open Text" by William Kumbier are reprinted with the permission of Boosey & Hawkes for non-exclusive world rights in the English language.

GAY CLIFFORD
7 lines from "Happiness" (p. 179) in *Poems by Gay Clifford* (Hamish Hamilton, 1990) poems copyright © Gay Clifford, 1990. Reprinted by permission of Penguin Books Ltd. for non-exclusive world rights in the English language.

DONALD DAVIE
Lines from "The Creature David" from *To Scorch or Freeze* by Donald Davie are reprinted with the permission of Doreen Davie for non-exclusive world rights in the English language.

ALLEN GINSBERG
Lines from *Howl* from *Collected Poems, 1947-1980* by Allen Ginsberg are reprinted with the permission of HarperCollins Publishers for non-exclusive world rights in the English language. Copyright © 1984 by Allen Ginsberg.

ANTHONY HECHT
Lines from "Divination by a Cat" are reprinted with the permission of Anthony Hecht for non-exclusive world rights in the English language.

EDWARD HIRSCH
Lines from "Wild Gratitude" from *Wild Gratitude* by Edward Hirsch. Copyright © 1985 by Edward Hirsch. Reprinted by permission of Alfred A. Knopf, Inc. for the United States and elsewhere throughout the world in the English language.

GALWAY KINNELL
Excerpt from "The Porcupine," from *Three Books.* Copyright © 1993 by Galway Kinnell. Previously published in *Body Rags* (1965, 1966, 1967). Reprinted by permission of Houghton Mifflin Company. All rights reserved.

Introduction

CLEMENT HAWES

The Lord increase the Cambridge collection of fossils.
—Jubilate Agno

CHRISTOPHER SMART AND THE ENLIGHTENMENT is a collection of commentaries on Christopher Smart that engages with more general problems of historical periodization in current cultural studies and literary theory. It provides a reappraisal of the work of Christopher Smart—too long "the invisible man of literary history," as Karina Williamson remarks in Chapter 12—and of his impact on contemporary literature. It also provides, through the work of Smart, a fresh understanding of Smart's moment and milieu in all their heterogeneity. Through the lens of a finely historicized approach to Smart's challenging *oeuvre*, this collection of essays points to a more subtle eighteenth century than is often found in the literary periodizations of certain widely cited cultural historians and literary theorists.

Christopher Smart and the Enlightenment represents the first effort to bring together in one volume current developments in the field of Smart studies. In recent years there has been considerable interest in Smart. The completion in 1996 of the Oxford edition of Smart's works (edited by Karina Williamson and Marcus Walsh) has finally made his complete *oeuvre* available in a standard edition. This six-volume scholarly edition has been supplemented, moreover, by an affordable Penguin paperback volume of Smart's *Selected Poems* (also edited by Williamson and Walsh) and by an annotated edition of Smart's correspondence (edited by Betty Rizzo and Robert Mahony). There has been also a sustained burst of important new critical work on Smart over the past couple of decades. This scholarship has served both to establish his canon and to place his poetry in a great variety of fresh contexts, marking a significant maturation of Smart studies. The current collection builds upon this foundational work. The volume contains new and unpublished essays by a distinguished group of scholars, many of whom have themselves made crucial contributions to the current consolidation of Smart scholarship. *Christopher Smart and the Enlightenment* thus makes a substantial addition to the existing scholarship on Smart.

An important theme of the volume, furthermore, is to highlight the markedly transitional quality of the eighteenth-century moment in regard to the Enlightenment project. It is precisely the historical specificity of the eighteenth century's liminality that tends to get erased in the reified versions of the Enlightenment circulating widely in many texts of literary history and theory. "A long time ago we fell into an obscure disaster known as Enlightenment"—so begins Terry Eagleton's droll caricature of such periodizations—"to be rescued around 1972 by the first lucky reader of Ferdinand de Saussure."[1] The eighteenth-century has in fact been uniquely pivotal for defining historical breaks. Indeed, the last two decades of literary scholarship have frequently revolved around the various legacies of the Enlightenment. The debates over these legacies include not only the highly polemical attempt to define a "new eighteenth century" but, perhaps even more crucially, a lingering set of definitional conundrums about "modernity" and "postmodernity." For it is above all as the originary moment of the Enlightenment that the eighteenth century has figured so centrally in these debates: a "modernity," largely defined by continental theorists such as Jean François Lyotard and Michel Foucault, that often connotes far more than a chronological epoch. The eighteenth-century moment, then, often assumed to epitomize "classical modernity,"[2] continues to serve as a handy whipping-boy for contemporary thinkers bent on staking their own claim to effect a clean and emancipatory break with an oppressive modernity. It is seldom noticed, moreover, how this thoroughly Francocentric model—one that frames the Enlightenment as "a clash between the apostles of reason and the clerical defenders of tradition"[3]—distorts the very different trajectory of the Enlightenment as it evolved in Britain and elsewhere. It is precisely by compelling a more complex, nuanced, and messily contingent definition of the actual eighteenth-century moment—and thus serving to refine our contemporary debates—that a current focus on Smart is so valuable.

The essays collected here, written by individual authors and representing a wide range of approaches, are unified by the attempt to situate their individual readings of Smart in the context of current debates that bring out the transitional nature of the eighteenth century. The life and work of Smart are indeed almost uniquely germane to our understanding of the place and implication of the Enlightenment within the more general study of the eighteenth century. Because of Smart's own extraordinarily liminal status vis-à-vis certain key features of the Enlightenment—above all, "modern" encroachments on the sacred and on a high-cultural literary tradition—he can be said to encapsulate some of the constitutive contradictions of his age. Such a focus on Smart highlights the urgent necessity of historicizing our approach to certain theoretical issues.

Moreover, the life and work of Christopher Smart provide an especially useful opportunity to bring a more densely historicized complexity to the familiar antinomies—such handy binary oppositions as "tradition" and "modernity"—that seem to arise almost automatically whenever one discusses the impact of the Enlightenment on the eighteenth century. The volume addresses the following aspects of the Enlightenment project as they are manifest in, and through, the work of Christopher Smart:

1. *the dynamics of secularization*, or what Max Weber calls "disenchantment"[4]: the enabling and disabling impact on literary culture of an increasingly autonomous rationality;
2. *the emergence of the "author-function"* based on authorial claims to autonomy. This involves, on the one hand, the gradual transition from a patronage-based culture of aristocratic belles-lettres to a "modern" market-driven popular culture; and, on the other, the negotiation of originality in relation to normative definitions of madness and sanity; and
3. *the teleological nature of literary-historical periodization* as it has influenced our subsequent constructions of the eighteenth-century moment: a telling index of the monolithic way in which the Enlightenment now figures in debates about modernity.

Each of these broad themes constitutes the basis for a cluster of related essays in this book.

The fluid and shifting boundaries of "tradition" and "modernity" in the eighteenth century involve, above all, what Robert Markley terms "the origin myths of modern science"[5]: for the autonomous rationality aimed for, and claimed, in scientific discourse did not suddenly spring forth at birth as a fully developed alternative epistemology. Markley discerns instead a prolonged "crisis of representation" in the efforts of post-Restoration intellectuals, such as scientist Robert Boyle, to mediate between the language of physics (which purported to describe the merely contingent and fallen world of matter) and that of metaphysics (which purported to describe the ideal and eternal order of Christian theology).[6] The two languages often deeply interpenetrated, as Markley argues, each bearing ineradicable traces of its inscriptions and reinscriptions by the other, in ways that defy easy compartmentalization into, say, "emergent science" versus "residual theology." In *The Christian Virtuoso* (1690), for example, Boyle contends that it is the scientist alone, because he most precisely understands the creation's excellence, who can give God adequate praise.[7]

In any case, the full meaning of Smart's use of science, which may reflect his ties to freemasonry,[8] remains to be settled. *Jubilate Agno* (written 1759-63) takes up all sorts of topics current in eighteenth-century natural history and science: Newtonian optics, depth-of-field perception, capillary attraction, magnetism, the mysteries of bird migration, methods for computing longitude at sea, and so on. And Donald Davie, indeed, suggests that only "the merest arrogant prejudice" would deny that Christopher Smart, as an avid student of "the most advanced thought of [his] time," was "of the Enlightenment" and that his poems are "products of the Enlightenment."[9] Yet critics continue to debate whether Smart's selective antipathy to a major Enlightenment icon, Sir Isaac Newton—his fellow freemason and Cambridge luminary—implicates him in a retrograde obscurantism. On the one hand, the intellectual respectability of Smart's "immaterialist" positions has been urged by Donald Greene, who invokes the idealist philosopher George Berkeley as a source for Smart's doctrines.[10] On the other, Smart has been described as stubbornly backward-looking by the physician William Ober: as "[throwing] down the gauntlet to science."[11] Such a framing of the debate seems to ignore the fact that Newton himself—"the last of the magicians," as John Maynard Keynes said in 1942—had strong hermetic interests in alchemy and astrology, and in biblical chronology, prophecy, and eschatology.[12]

Further research has suggested that Berkeley's influence on Smart was negligible in comparison with that of eighteenth-century physico-theologians such as John Hutchinson and his redactor, Robert Spearman.[13] Physico-theology, a resilient phenomenon that flourished more in Britain than on the Continent, persisted well into the nineteenth century.[14] It was a discourse that depended, above all, on a "divine analogy" between the physical and the metaphysical: an analogy that, in Earl Wasserman's words, "gives philosophical validity to art and figurative language."[15] Physico-theology should be understood in this context as a profoundly liminal discourse. It was, in Markley's words, "the quest for a single system of representation that articulates its equally strong commitments to experimental philosophy and to theology."[16]

The crisis of representation described by Markley compelled a heightened self-reflexivity about written language more generally. Ideas about the nature and function of *writing*, as Nicholas Hudson demonstrates, had shifted during the seventeenth century, gradually moving from a hieratic focus on the arcane significance of sacred glyphs toward that utilitarian cultivation of transparency that permitted the development of a vernacular public sphere. Indeed, by Smart's mid-eighteenth-century moment, this demystification, and the ascendancy of print culture it represented, had begun to produce a certain backlash against writing in favor of speech. With this backlash came a corresponding resuscitation of divine-origin theories of letters. Such theories were part of a broader attempt during the second half of the eighteenth century, as Hudson argues, "to combine traditional ideas about natural origins of writing and speech with a basically modern and scientific understanding of the world."[17]

Smart perfectly illustrates the complexity, highlighted in this account, of disentangling the modern from the traditional in the eighteenth-century context—so much so that his work compels a rethinking of such oppositions. For Smart, in particular, seems to exemplify the habitual strategy of straddling such oppositions. What is so productive about this habit, moreover, is that it produces—within the single cultural space of Smart's work—the simultaneous critique both of tradition and of modernity. Such critiques are more profound rather than less in arising from within. It is indeed precisely because so much of Smart's work is immanent to the Enlightenment, and engaged with its potential, that his selective "counter-Enlightenment" tactics are so resonant. And it is thus from within the liminality of an emergent modernity, still embedded within the logic of multiple traditions, that one can find the most subtly telling critiques of modernity.

PART I: BETWEEN SECULAR AND SACRED

Part I of *Christopher Smart and the Enlightenment* gathers essays dealing with Smart's commitment to religious genres, from sacred lyrics to parables: genres that foreground the intricacy of literary mediations between the worldly and the sacred. The question motivating all of the essays in this part, then, is how the poetry of Smart attempts to mediate between a desacralizing modernity and his own sense of vocation as a religious poet. Taken as a whole, the essays clustered in this section present a Smart who seems to skate back and forth across the antinomies of secular and sacred with a confounding alacrity.

Smart's poetics negotiate in complex ways with the "disenchanting" impact of both the new public sphere, based on print culture, and the project of scientific empiricism. These developments exerted special pressure, above all, on the status of figurative language. Classical empiricism, as Jules David Law argues, was constituted by "a strategic tension between figurative and literal usages in empiricist writing, a tension related—though not reducible—to the tension between verbal and visual models of experience."[18] On the one hand, empiricism deployed its own set of founding tropes. Law lists such optical metaphors as "surface," "depth," and "reflection." All of these are closely linked, as he notes, to John Locke's attempt to explain the impact of sensory data on the mind,[19] which the famous trope of the tabula rasa imagines in terms of a writing apparatus. On the other hand, empiricism also launched attacks, in the name of things visible and verifiable, on the distorting effects of rhetoric and figuration. So Thomas Hobbes redefined tropes as a mere abuse of language; and so Locke attacked figurative language as a "perfect cheat" whose sole purpose is "to insinuate wrong *Ideas*."[20] And it was precisely the embattled and doubtful status of figurative language that led to Samuel Johnson's strong reservations about the entire genre of sacred poetry.[21]

Smart's own understanding of figuration—notably, the poetics of what he himself terms *Impression*—thus serves to bring into focus the Enlightenment's impact on language and rhetoric. According to a passage in the preface to his verse translation of Horace (1767), Smart subscribes to a poetic doctrine based on moments of heightened emphasis that produce a quasi-divine forcefulness and immediacy: "*Impression* then, is a talent or gift of Almighty God, by which a Genius is impowered to throw an emphasis upon a word or sentence in such wise, that it cannot escape any reader of sheer good sense, and true critical sagacity. This power will sometimes keep up thro' the *medium* of a prose translation; especially in scripture, for in justice to truth and everlasting preeminence, we must confess this virtue to be far more powerful and abundant in the sacred writings" (*PW*, v: 6-7). An anticipatory explication of this doctrine, as various critics have noted, appears in *Jubilate Agno*: "*For my talent is to give an impression upon words by punching, that when the reader casts his eye upon 'em, he takes up the image from the mould which I have made*" (B404). One notices, first of all, that Smart here claims as his own what he later admired in scripture and in Horace. One notes too the elaboration of a metaphor from type-founding in which the reader *casts* the image that Smart has "impressed" into the mold of his language: an artistic medium that he seems to imagine in peculiarly plastic terms (see Chapter 8).

Smart's highly sedimented notion of *impression* depends on a "violent imprinting" metaphor derived from the technology of print culture, and it condenses a great number of themes and issues around origins, copying, mechanical reproduction, novelty, sensory perception, and memory. If the term ultimately derives from Locke's usage, it probably does so antithetically: for Locke himself uses *impression* mostly to describe the views of those, like René Descartes, and Smart himself (see Chapter 2), who insisted that ideas could be innate.[22] And though *impression* was a broadly circulating term among the intelligentsia of the earlier eighteenth century,[23] it names for

Smart a very special term of art. As the numerous discussions of the term below suggest—see especially Chapter 6—*impression* encapsulates a great deal about the ensemble of techniques that makes up the insignia of Smart's poetic practice.

Offering a compelling entry into the nature and significance of Smart's figurative turnings is Marcus Walsh's chapter, "'Community of Mind': Christopher Smart and the Poetics of Allusion." This essay launches a fresh discussion of Smart's poetics through a rhetorical analysis focusing on the significance to literary history of his charged and peculiarly taut practice of allusion: "the characterizing figurative method of [his] later religious verse." As Walsh demonstrates, Smart's poetics in such works as his *Hymns and Spiritual Songs* and "Song to David" often depends upon a figurative compression that made his verse vulnerable, in its reception, to changes in the degree to which a modernizing public culture shared his knowledge and understanding of Scripture. This assertively figurative technique—itself another refraction of literary modernity—relies on the use of complex and telescopically condensed allusions to a typological understanding of scripture. Such concentrated allusions work as pleasure-giving tropes in their own right, beyond their immediate and local effects, and thus become the vehicles for larger structures of sacred meaning. Their arresting power of verbal concentration, however, which invites a serious comparison of Smart's figures to the wit of metaphysical conceit, interferes with the transparency of his poetic texture. Smart's scriptural allusions thus tested—sometimes severely—the possible community of mind between poet and reader in the noisy, distracting, and heterogeneous print culture of eighteenth-century Britain. Smart's uses of allusive techniques, indeed, can be seen as hopeful or wistful "acts of filiation": appeals to a particular community of like-minded Anglican readers whose learning Smart may have simply overestimated. By the same token, the restoration of intellectual community in the present often requires the mediation of an editor, making Smart, as Walsh puts it, "one of the most annotatable of poets."

A second angle for exploring the historically shifting boundaries of the sacred through Smart is by way of his response to the Enlightenment's disenchanting pressure on the written word. In his logological analysis, á la Kenneth Burke, Edward Katz explores the nature of *Jubilate Agno* as a prophetic reassertion of the verbal as a sacred medium. In Chapter 2, "'Action and Speaking are One': A Logological Reading of Smart's Prophetic Rhetoric," Katz shows how Smart seeks to purify language, to recover its sacred character, and harness it to a sacred vocation. Smart's prophetic poem thus operates against the "official names" that secured a normative consensus: the public sphere at its most smugly inert. In making himself the vehicle for this profoundly negating vision, the poet-prophet must authorize his own written voice through a rhetoric of cathartic identification. Smart thus positions himself as a scapegoat whose mediating sacrifice opens up a space of redemption for a reader mired in workaday secular concerns. The prophet in his zeal must risk all and assume the stigmatized identity of fool or madman. This stigmatized identity provides, for the reader, a cathartic sense of participation in communal concerns that are simultaneously aesthetic and spiritual. Indeed, the connective and negating powers of language merge for Smart with divine creativity, and approximate, in pure form, the wordless beauty of music. *Jubilate Agno* thus mediates the sacred by unveiling what Kenneth Burke terms the "motive toward perfection" intrinsic to the use of language as such.[24]

The interaction between Smart's sacred poetics and a child-oriented literary genre is the point of departure for Mark Booth's chapter, "Syntax and Paradigm in Smart's *Hymns for the Amusement of Children.*" This is a work that Smart produced in 1770—a scant few months before his death, at age forty-nine, in debtor's prison. It was to be his last work. Along with Charles Wesley's *Hymns for Children* (1763), it was one of only two volumes of its kind—devotional poetry for children—since Isaac Watts's *Divine Songs for Children* (1715). In probing the significance of the *Hymns for the Amusement of Children,* Booth sets out to answer an apparently simple question: namely, why these apparently unassuming poems, ostensibly designed to "amuse" children, are at first glance often more teasing than plain, even for adult readers. Booth pursues this question by reviving a structuralist model that maps the double articulation of discourse along the intersecting axes of word-selection and syntactic combination. By analyzing a pronounced tension in Smart's hymns between the progressive flow of syntax and an arresting crosscurrent of similitudes, Booth arrives at a new vantage point for viewing Smart's poetics of *impression* and *punching.* Smart's metaphor points to the way his poetic effects of rapture and exaltation operate, even in *Hymns for the Amusement of Children,* through a controlled violence toward the flow of syntax. It is, as Booth suggests, as though something "from another dimension" *hits* the words in the line on the page. The achieved result, according to Booth's persuasive reappraisal of the *Hymns,* is a special poetic language that cuts diagonally athwart discursive values generally ascribed to the Enlightenment: "the language of individual voice, rational thought, and practical business."

Smart's partial and selective embrace of "Enlightenment" ideals and language constitutes a fourth point of entry into the topic of boundaries between the secular and the sacred. For another "Enlightenment" tendency in Smart's work might be seen in the democratizing logic by which he recasts the genre of the parable. The parable is a genre whose indirect language, as Todd Parker argues in Chapter 4, "Smart's Enlightened Parables and the Problem of Genre," had traditionally served to guard esoteric pearls of wisdom from the uncouth multitudes. Obliquity was a means to screen out unworthy auditors: those who did not, as Jesus puts it, have ears to hear. Parker demonstrates that *The Parables of Our Lord and Saviour Jesus Christ* (1768) is informed by an anti-elitist attitude whose leveling import is simultaneously epistemological and political: "a determination to accommodate his genius to the lowest common denominator." As Parker persuasively argues, what has often been dismissed as mere aesthetic impoverishment—Smart in a pedestrian vein—needs to be seen afresh as a radical poetic experiment motivated by the drive for all-inclusive communication. In working toward the seemingly oxymoronic ideal of a transparent parable, Smart accommodated his poetic project to the ruthlessly streamlined discursive norms of a modern print-based public culture. To see a brilliant and learned poet deliberately jettison the hard-won cultural capital that served to mark his originality: that, then, according to Parker, is the risk-taking drama behind *The Parables of Our Lord and Saviour Jesus Christ*. Smart's act of poetic accommodation is thus a willing, and somewhat uncanny, self-emptying gesture. And indeed, when Parker shows that Smart goes so far in the *Parables* as to renounce his signature poetics of *impression*, we verge on the recognition of something like a poetic *kenosis*.[25] Thus do Smart's "enlightened" parables—spookily devoid of ego, perhaps, but by no means deficient in skill or care—attempt to carve out a space for poetic traffic between modernity and the sacred.

A final "Enlightenment" aspect of Smart's work can be traced in his intricate negotiations with the early discourses of natural history. Eric Miller's chapter, "Taxonomy and Confession in Christopher Smart and Jean-Jacques Rousseau," explores Smart's symbiotic engagement with those very taxonomic systems, such as the binomial nomenclature devised by the great Swedish botanist Carolus Linnaeus, whose precise, severely neutral, and systematic character is often taken to typify the Enlightenment. And while Smart's attitude toward names and signifiers might seem at first resolutely "premodern"—a denial, in effect, of their imbrication in a system of humanly crafted linguistic conventions—the remarkable idiosyncrasy with which he exploits verbal patterns points to a "modern" freedom, as well as to a modern anxiety, in his memoir-like literary practice. *Jubilate Agno*, that is to say, is a work that *comes after* the Enlightenment's purgatorial and disenchanting assault on ancestral lore about the creatures.[26] Smart fills the resulting chasm between science and traditional natural history with a confessional mode that can be instructively compared with Jean-Jacques Rousseau's personal apologetics: both "recruit natural history," albeit divergently, "to sponsor the arguments of their all-too-human histories." Reading Smart's celebrated disquisition on Jeoffry the cat as "an intimate field-guide entry," Miller demonstrates how the poet creates a "dynamic collage" precisely by assimilating scientific document and legendary fable to personal observation. Smart thus produces a poetic model of experience that could be said to combine archaic cultural themes with elements that are proleptic and anticipatory. In precisely this combination, moreover, he parallels Linnaeus himself, as Miller argues: for the botanist and the poet share a tendency simultaneously to fall behind *and* advance beyond the conceptions of their immediate contemporaries.

Miller's explicit parallel is foreshadowed in Edith Sitwell's poem "The Two Loves" (1945), which links Smart with Linnaeus (see Chapter 12, 243). Both were worshipers; and both, indeed, were shaped by the special dynamics of eighteenth-century physico-theology. As Lisbet Koerner points out, Linnaeus, a Lutheran parson's son, was well read in the works of British physico-theologians such as Boyle, William Derham, and John Ray, from whom he derived his notion of a divine economy or homeostasis in nature. Most interestingly, perhaps, he fashioned himself, in Koerner's words, as a "second Adam": an identity "nicely illustrated in the frontispiece to the 1760 Lange edition of *Systema naturae*, where, collapsing time, he at once names the animals and writes the *Systema*."[27] The intersection in Linnaeus between the modern and the premodern thus involves the project of physico-theology he shares with Smart. This telling parallel exemplifies the way that Part I serves to complicate overly unilinear accounts of the rupture represented by the Enlightenment. In the end, as Harriet Guest has argued, the strains in Smart that seem more metaphysical than empirical do not necessarily distance him from the natural philosophy of the eighteenth century.[28]

And indeed, in the Smart who emerges by the end of Part I, the sacred and the secular cannot be said to coexist as discrete rungs on an evolutionary ladder of historical "progress." Rather, each category is made to continually rework the other in a cross-hatched, zigzag pattern that points in many directions simultaneously. For Smart, what often counts about scientific language is its potential as spiritual emblem: thus, as Guest points out, the scientific quest for a means of determining longitude at sea gets absorbed into the familiar figure of the Christian's life as a voyage.[29] This example suggests a poetic *appropriation* of science for otherworldly ends. Such appropriations, as Mark Greenberg argues, constitute a broad eighteenth-century pattern whereby poets such as James Thomson worked poetic transformations on the raw materials of scientific discoveries.[30] Following Markley's more dialectical account, however, it should also be noted that such appropriations are likely to reinscribe aspects of the language of science—its encyclopedic character, its systematic and technical nomenclature, and perhaps even its passionate observation of the creatures of this world—into the texture of poetic and religious tradition. And so Christopher Smart—"number[ing] the streaks of the mollusc," as Donald Davie puts it (see Chapter 12, 248)—could be said to have "botanized" the genre of devotional poetry, which he created from the languages of field guides, horticultural manuals, and pharmacopeias; and from textbooks on geology, optics, zoology, and mineralogy.

SECTION II: AUTHORSHIP IN TRANSITION

The title of this section is intended to evoke recent historical work on the conditions surrounding the emergence and consolidation of vernacular literary authorship. Roger Chartier's work demonstrates that the emergence of the "author-function," as Michel Foucault has termed it, long predates the modern age: indeed, it altogether predates print culture (and its system of assigning literary property), reaching back to the fourteenth century and the end of the manuscript age. Kevin Pask's recent work on the history of the "life-of-the-poet" genre confirms Chartier's modification of Foucault's chronology.[31] The supposed break that Foucault had vaguely located in the seventeenth or eighteenth century[32] has been recast by Chartier as occurring around Smart's moment, in the latter half of the eighteenth century, in somewhat different terms: "Thus, in the latter half of the eighteenth century a somewhat paradoxical connection was made between a desired professionalization of literary activity (which should provide remuneration in order for writers to live from their writings) and the authors' representation of themselves in an ideology of literature founded on the radical autonomy of the work of art and the disinterestedness of the creative act."[33] It is precisely during the mid-eighteenth century, then, as Brean S. Hammond observes, "that individual careers and texts, and literary genres, are most obviously striated by profound changes in the underlying geology of authorship."[34] The assertion of this emerging sense of autonomy, through the elaboration of "originality" and "genius" as aesthetic categories, is, of course, precisely what leads to dilemmas around the relation between the self-maximizing singularity of individual talent, as T. S. Eliot once put it, and a tradition largely founded on notions of continuity. As Pask argues, it was precisely the eighteenth-century bourgeois public sphere, with its drive to make public the hitherto private and domestic, that permitted a new heroicization of the poet as such: a biography-based heroicization founded precisely on arduously achieved singularity.[35]

Dustin Griffin's work, meanwhile, has established the strong persistence of patronage throughout the eighteenth century, and, as a result, the existence of "overlapping" economies of patronage *and* marketplace.[36] Smart's quest for patronage was indeed central to his vocational sense of working within a determinate classical tradition. He dedicated his *Poems on Several Occasions* (1752) to the Earl of Middlesex, signing up more than 700 subscribers for the same volume, and successfully courted patronage from the Earl of Northumberland with a flattering ode.[37] Yet Smart, superbly trained inheritor of the classical legacy that he was, also immersed himself neck-deep in the emerging market-based culture whose commercial imperatives were insistently transgressing older generic traditions.

The Smart we retrieve from the past thus may depend upon the particular moment in his career that we choose to scrutinize. At one moment, we see him penning award-winning religious odes for Cambridge's Seatonian Prize: an annual literary "premium," won by Smart five times between 1750 and 1756, which illustrates how new institutions had begun to assume patronal functions.[38] Overlapping with this moment, however, is the Grub Street tableau in which Smart appears as an overtaxed hack in the stable of his father-in-law, publisher John Newbery, who was also "the first great entrepreneur of children's literature" (see Booth, Chapter 3). In that snapshot, Smart appears frenetically peddling such burlesque ephemera as "The Old Woman's Oratory" in the competitive Grub Street marketplace under a protean variety of extravagant pseudonyms, from "Ebenezer Pentweazle" to "Zosimus Zephyrus." The most famous of these personae is the gossipy midwife, Mother Midnight. Like Delarivier Manley's narrator "Mother Nightwork," to which Smart acknowledges an imaginative debt,[39] Mother Midnight represents unofficial tale-telling and creative fecundity. In another sense, of course, Mother Midnight also represents an author in thrall to market imperatives. And it is to this market-driven phase of Smart's career that the famous astronomer/surveyor Charles Mason alludes in Thomas Pynchon's *Mason & Dixon*, speculating that "Perhaps too many damn'd *Gothickal Scribblers* about, far too many's what did for Mr. Smart. . . ."[40]

At a later moment (1759-63) we see Smart writing inspiration-based sacred poetry in the involuntary privacy of a madhouse cell. And it is this latter setting, indeed—where Smart often figures as a saintly martyr to the heartless depredations of "Enlightenment rationality"—that has largely served to frame his literary reputation for the last two centuries. The subsequent mythologizing of Smart's life in terms of madness, indeed, illustrates almost too neatly Pask's conclusion about the life-of-the-poet genre: "The 'sensibility' of the artist . . . reflects the admission of the artist's life-narrative to modern capitalist society as the residual site of aristocratic excess and saintly self-sacrifice."[41]

One last snapshot: in 1770, very near the end, we see Smart in debtor's prison producing an innovative kind of children's literature for his brother-in-law Thomas Carnan, Newbery's stepson. Smart's *Hymns for the Amusement of Children,* like Mary Wollstonecraft's *Original Stories from Real Life* (1788) and Maria Edgeworth's *Popular Tales* (1801), were written for that "newly emergent children's book market" that Alan Richardson describes in connection with the educational history of the later eighteenth century.[42] This final work closes a truly extraordinary career that prompts many questions about the exact negotiations, in Smart's own practice as a writer, between such overlapping but discrepant contexts. Part II thus gathers essays highlighting the historical dimension of Smart as an author in relationship to the transitional nature of his career. It is a liminality manifest not only in the tensions between professionalism (geared to an anonymous public) and patronage (geared to a coterie), but also in conflicts as regards social and literary norms. The critical essays collected in this section thus bring together questions about such topics as madness and authorship, and about individual agency and responsibility in relation to the social contract represented by literary genres.

A central issue opened up anew by the rubric of authorship is the relation of Smart's career to the strict hierarchy of literary genres within which he worked. Several chapters in this section are thus concerned with Smart's struggle to define himself through the kinds of writing he produced. Several of these chapters, moreover, serve as a salutary corrective to the tendency to read Smart only on the basis of one or two of his best-known works. Betty Rizzo's essay, "Christopher Smart's Poetics," usefully reminds us of Smart's profound interest in classical models that would have appealed especially to a "polite" audience. Not least among these venerable patterns was the *rota Virgilii,* or Virgil's wheel, by which the unfolding of a poet's career was mapped according to progress along a prescribed sequence of genres from apprentice-work genres (pastoral and georgic) to the lofty and oeuvre-crowning genre of epic.[43] Smart deliberately embarked on a course of self-preparation that involved, among other apprentice labor, imitation by way of abbreviation: a practice of formal miniaturization. And indeed, early and late, a constant feature of Smart's poetic signature was his highly cultivated genius for expressive condensation, or *brevitas.* Such *brevitas,* indeed, is linked closely to Smart's doctrine of *impression*: "the key," in Rizzo's phrase, "to his self-fashioning as an author." Brevity is a figure well-represented in the tradition of classical rhetoric, but characteristically overlaid in Smart with a more contemporary layer of implications. As he gained in confidence and maturity, however, Smart increasingly abandoned a "modest" brevity of form in favor of "comprehension." "Comprehension" implied instead a breadth, capaciousness, and thoroughness befitting an author whose elevated ambitions probably included the laureateship. Smart's quest for strength of *impression* through brevity thus seems to have gradually evolved into a formal emulation of God's creative abundance. Hence a generic affinity in the later Smart with encyclopedic forms addressed to the public at large: for one consequence of the "comprehension" ideal is the systematic codification of miscellaneous knowledge. And hence a mature Smart who is, perhaps, brother under the skin to Denis Diderot.

For Lance Bertelsen, the crucial point about the overlapping economies of bookseller and patron is precisely their tremendous relativizing effect on each other's constructions of authorship. In Chapter 7, "'Neutral Nonsense, neither false nor true': Christopher Smart and the Paper War(s) of 1752-53," Bertelsen focuses on Smart's antics and motives in a well-publicized satirical skirmish between Henry Fielding and John Hill. This was a commercially driven "paper war" in which Smart, author of the mock-epic poem, *The Hilliad* (1753)—the war's "loudest broadside"—appeared in a protean variety of personae and contexts. Indeed, Smart's madcap persona of Mary Midnight eventually became, as Bertelsen writes, "a kind of pervasive referent, almost an atmosphere." The much-ballyhooed "war," as Bertelsen argues, is an episode ideally suited for exploring the "schizophrenic" world of eighteenth-century commercial publishing: a world where contentious publication actually functioned as part of a symbiotic, sales-generating system. Hence the possibility of an "underlying neutrality" between the supposed antagonists—something like the hyperbolically ferocious relations, perhaps, between the posturing combatants in contemporary championship wrestling. What the paper war makes visible, in historically emergent form, is a public culture of hype and puffery in which, as the quintessentially modern dictum has it, there can be no such thing as bad publicity. The proliferation of such pseudonyms and performed identities as Smart's Mary Midnight made authorship in this commercialized environment a remarkably changeable, and exchangeable, role. Grub Street authorship was perhaps more akin to the frothiness of popular celebrity than to the sponsored dignity of patronage-based authority.[44] The transgressive antics performed by the mutably wrangling "stars" of this quasi-magical "nonsense" world, however, can also be seen as the "importation into the 'Enlightenment' world of eighteenth-century journalism" of "the carnivalesque elements of a far older and murkier popular tradition": a resourceful tapping of archaic cultural strata that unmistakably lends to Mother Midnight, for example, an archetypal resonance.

Immersed as he was in the force field of commercial pressures and opportunities surrounding eighteenth-century authorship, Smart continually confronted philosophical issues involving the nature of artistic representation as such. His attempt in *Jubilate Agno* to work through the issues around classical notions of mimesis and enunciation, as Fraser Easton demonstrates in Chapter 8, serves to illuminate the terms in which he understood his poetic art. In "'Mary's Key' and the Poet's Conception: The Orphic versus the Mimetic Artist in *Jubilate Agno*," Easton unpacks the potential complexity inherent in the concept, from Smart's hymn on "The Annunciation of the Blessed Virgin," of singing "in Mary's key." Easton demonstrates that it is necessary to reconsider a familiar set of linked oppositions in Smart—of Orphic to mimetic, origin to copy, primary creation to secondary repetition, animating voice to static image—in relation to the sexual implications of Plato's ontological critique of art. Both the Orphic and the mimetic, from this perspective, are vulnerable to what Philippe Lacoue-Labarthe terms *depropriation*: the loss, through doubling, of proper being. Easton examines the issue of depropriation in relation to a "matrix" of sexually inflected metaphors in Smart's artistic theory and practice—especially as regards enunciation—and thus resituates the notion of Smart's Orphic understanding of his poetic vocation. Easton argues that Smart defines his own poetic role as a second Mary, author of the lyrical Magnificat, no less than as a second David. As the self-conscious "bearer" of a material enunciation, moreover—a lyrical discourse embodied in sound and rhythm—Smart is somewhat less the mystical metaphysician than is often supposed. And despite a certain "testosterone blare" surrounding Smart's prophetic disquisition about "male degeneration," the "key" of Mary's fecund womb ultimately figures in his work as a positive and creative example of depropriation: a quickening "release," as Easton puts it, "from art as copying. . . ." Indeed, Easton demonstrates that a marked sexual ambivalence lies at the root of Smart's contrast between Orphic and mimetic art, which overlap in the notion of art as *conception:* both imaginative head-birth and carnal reproduction, both genesis and simulacrum.

Thomas Keymer uses the rubric of authorship in order to provide a fresh take on the theme of madness in Smart studies. Modern authorship itself, as noted earlier, was partly constituted through the writing of authors' lives. As Keymer demonstrates in Chapter 9, Samuel Johnson's *obiter dicta* about Smart, his friend and fellow professional writer, thus offer a special vantage point from which to reconsider the significance of Smart's writing career: both to Johnson, who feared madness in himself, and to a posterity attempting to make sense of Smart's trajectory. "Johnson, Madness, and Smart," through a subtle recontextualization of these familiar gleanings, begins to reconstruct a hypothetical biographical preface whose absence we can only regret: Johnson's *Life of Smart*. Though Johnson never wrote such a text for his *Lives of the English Poets* (1779-81)—a refusal whose motives can only be guessed at—he did ruminate aloud about the plight of Smart. As Keymer demonstrates, Smart's confinement provided a personally resonant occasion for Johnson's conflicted musings as regards the prevailing discriminations between the mad and the sane. Such musings, indeed, far from reflecting a triumphalist rationality, instead reveal Johnson's own troubled and sometimes deeply empathetic vulnerability. And though Johnson is not quite a brother to Michel Foucault, his observations on the arbitrariness of Smart's confinement demonstrate the capacity of "Enlightenment reason" to reflect critically on the constructed nature of such discriminations. Indeed, what Johnson can teach us about Smart's mode of authorship turns out to be as applicable to twentieth-century literary criticism as to eighteenth-century habits of diagnosis and confinement: that in both his life and his writings Smart is better seen as a disrupter of decorums than as categorically "mad." To continue reading the deviant poetry as "mad," then, is to replicate at a critical level the crude and arbitrary eighteenth-century diagnosis of his deviant conduct.

In Chapter 10, I address the question of Smart's authorship by way of current scholarly attention to the making of the bourgeois public sphere in eighteenth-century Britain.[45] In "The Utopian Public Sphere: Intersubjectivity in *Jubilate Agno*," I attempt to understand the altered subjectivity expressed in Smart's poem in relation to the specifically eighteenth-century configuration of public-private relations. The exorbitant subjectivity of the *Jubilate,* in this view, both draws upon and extends the "associational individualism" characteristic of the emerging public sphere of eighteenth-century Britain. Indeed, that more permeable mode of individualism provides the specific background for Smart's utopian reconfiguration of public and private spheres. The utopian achievement of the *Jubilate*—its ability to traverse between public and private in ways that perturb the boundaries between them—is thus more particular to its historical moment than is often acknowledged. This reading also offers a new take on Smart's well-known sublimity, usually understood either as a matter of religious fervor, on the one hand, or of madness, on the other. Smart's celebrated "visionary madness" now appears as thoroughly immanent to the Enlightenment—as, indeed, an *alternative modernity*—of which the most compelling import is precisely to furnish the seeds of other possible lines of development, other trajectories, from the eighteenth century to the present. Part II is thus organized so as to illustrate the complexity of Smart's relationship to authorship. Here again Smart's simultaneous trafficking with traditional and modern notions of authorship cannot be adequately understood according to a unidirectional evolutionary model. As a writer, Smart is both professionally and prophetically motivated; as a thinker he is at once attuned to the ordering power of comprehensive intellectual systems and a disruptive jammer of such systems; as an artist working in a verbal medium, he is simultaneously mimetic and profoundly antipictorial; and as a stylist addressing an imagined readership, he is both humbly transparent and "problematically esoteric or uncommon" (see Chapter 2). Such dizzying complexity points to the potential of new genealogies—beginning in the very cradle of modernity itself—for currently flourishing themes of resistance to the disciplining and normalizing force of the modern.

PART III: PARLEYING WITH THE EIGHTEENTH CENTURY

Part III of *Christopher Smart and the Enlightenment* deals with the artistic use and re-creation of Smart. Like a number of contemporary and avowedly intertextual "returns to the eighteenth century,"[46] the twentieth-century recycling of Smart's poetic achievement is a phenomenon with broader historical and cultural implications: it amounts, in its entirety, to an elaborate exchange between the eighteenth and the twentieth centuries. The very fact that Smart continues to have such a significant currency—that he circulates far and wide in certain twentieth-century contexts—highlights the necessity for rethinking the place of the eighteenth century in contemporary literary culture. Hence the insistence in *Christopher Smart and the Enlightenment* on an eighteenth-century moment that deserves to be understood in terms of its own chiaroscuros, its own priorities and possibilities.

In the late nineteenth century, Robert Browning's celebratory emphasis on the unique achievement of "A Song to David" produced an excessively narrow view of Smart's poetic achievement. Since the belated publication of *Jubilate Agno* in 1939, under the editorial title of *Rejoice in the Lamb: A Song from Bedlam*, the breadth of Smart's achievement has gradually come back into focus. And the *Jubilate* in particular has been revived in an amazing variety of contexts, from Beat poetry to the important choral setting by Benjamin Britten of *Rejoice in the Lamb*. *Jubilate Agno* has indeed unmistakably joined "A Song to David" as one of the twin keystones of Smart's poetic edifice.

Britten's brilliant setting of the *Jubilate*, moreover, as William Kumbier demonstrates in Chapter 11, yields certain analogies both to eighteenth-century musicology and to Smart's own doctrine of *impression*. In "Benjamin Britten's *Rejoice in the Lamb*: Figural Invention, 'Impression,' and the Open Text," Kumbier argues that Britten's setting of Smart's work "represents" the poem in at least two ways. One is through virtuoso mimetic effects, of considerable interest in themselves, whereby particular musical figures of melodic rising, falling, cycling, and so on are directly sparked by particular verbal themes. The second and more crucial representation of Smart's poem, however, is through a more global process of musical invention: through "[the] creation of a pervasively figured musical text." Britten's "metamimetic" musical tropes, then, are not limited to merely locally appropriate special effects, but extend in *Rejoice in the Lamb* to a full-fledged interpretation of the poem's more cosmic concerns with harmony and dissonance, echo and resonance, sound and resounding—and, of course, magnification. Britten's *Rejoice in the Lamb* thus foregrounds conventional devices of eighteenth-century musical rhetoric as a sort of launching pad for its own intertextual engagement with the very moment in musical history when music began to spring loose from the burden of "imitating" a verbal text. Smart's moment, indeed, as Kevin Barry demonstrates, was one that increasingly located the significance of music precisely in the peculiar *emptiness* of its signifiers—and, therefore, "in the act of listening, in the energy of mind which its emptiness provokes."[47] And so it makes perfect sense to juxtapose, as Kumbier's reading of Britten's musical homage encourages us to do, two great masters of an art that is intricately braided, polyphonic, and playfully self-referential: Christopher Smart and Johann Sebastian Bach.

It is fitting that this volume, which opens with a study of Smart's allusive intertextuality, should be capped with a substantial study of Smart's life and oeuvre as the generative basis for later acts of intertextual affiliation. And indeed, the tracing of Smart's twentieth-century presence enables Karina Williamson to rewrite a significant chapter of literary history. In "Surfing the Intertext: Smart among the Moderns," she establishes a poetic dialogue that scholars of twentieth-century poetry can no longer afford to ignore. Among other discoveries, she is able to describe a series of distinct waves in the trajectory of Smart's reputation and influence, from the mid-nineteenth century to the present moment, in which one can see that Smart's frequently anthologized "My-Cat-Jeoffry" sequence has now spawned a new poetic genre all its own. The sheer variety of the engagements with Smart is dazzling. A British wave of Smartian intertextuality includes poets as varied as Edith Sitwell, Peter Porter (an expatriate Australian), and Donald Davie: the latter who characteristically refuses to pit Smart over and against Enlightenment rationality. Most crucially, perhaps, Williamson's chapter maps out the ramifications of Smart's re-entry into the poetic mainstream in the 1950s, which demonstrably contributed to the character of a strong poetic flowering—an "American Moment," as one critic has it—during that decade. The widespread discovery of *Jubilate Agno* in the 1950s, as Williamson shows, was a catalyst in the revival and reshaping of Walt Whitman's long-line verse, making available for use—even to poets who may not have in not have known its source in Smart—a new rhetoric and tonality. The profound impact of *Jubilate Agno* on Allen Ginsberg's *Howl*, a poem that explicitly identifies with a numinous madness, is typical of a generational appropriation that was both broad and deep, on the one hand, and frequently bound up with issues of rationality, on the other. Nevertheless, such appropriations form an intertextual pattern that cannot be comfortably reduced to the postmodern claim to have broken, for once and for all, with the Enlightenment. For if twentieth-century poets have found in Smart the compelling resonance of a "subversive rhetoric," the fact remains that the daringly experimental edge of that rhetoric derives precisely from the specific possibilities inherent in Smart's eighteenth-century moment. To parley with Smart, then, is not merely to honor the exceptional poetry of madness in an age of prose: it is, rather, to reopen a dialogue with the eighteenth century.[48]

To be sure, it appears that in some of twentieth-century poets mentioned earlier the valorization of Smart's madness does indeed sound a familiar anti-Enlightenment theme: "breaking/through to the other side of reason," as Jeremy Reed has it.[49] Yet Smart's current resonance also depends on aspects of the Enlightenment ethos that are seldom recognized as such. It is worth recalling how quintessentially "modern" the propensity to ascribe personality to domestic animals really is. For Gay Clifford, Gavin Ewart, Erica Jong, and Susan Fromberg Schaeffer, the variation on a Smartesque theme concerns precisely this—the *individuation* of a pet: respectively, Clifford's cat Thisbe (who has the art of lying all over words),[50] Ewart's cat Matty (who resists the Devil and is completely neuter),[51] Jong's democratic dog Poochkin (who believes all smells are equal before God),[52] and Schaeffer's cat Thomas (who comes forth like a soldier to do battle with a bug).[53] The cultivation of such personalized attachments reflects the extent to which we inherit the Enlightenment's popularization of pet-keeping and its corollary attitude of "benevolence" toward animals.[54] For Edward Hirsch, too, it is a particular cat, Zooey, that enables him to comprehend the nature of Smart's "wild gratitude," even as he duly measures its apparent cost in terms of a "sad religious mania."[55] It can be no surprise, then, that Smart has a certain profile as well in the middlebrow subgenre of "pet discourse"—that is, anthologies, literary companions, and coffee-table books—in which the feline "Tribe of Tiger" figures prominently.[56] It seems doubtful that current theories calling for a wholesale repudiation of "Enlightenment rationality" can do full justice to this particular constellation of eighteenth-century discourses.

It is thus fitting that cat-companion Jeoffry make a cameo appearance as well in the contemporary verse-epistle—appearing here for the first time—which adds a poet's commentary to the parleying theme with which the volume closes. Amittai F. Aviram's "Epistle of Mrs. Frances Burney to Dr. Samuel Johnson Regarding the Most Unfortunate Mr. Christopher Smart" imagines Smart's celebrated cat "purring loudly as a Drunk might snore" while the poet himself recites aloud from *Jubilate Agno*. Aviram's poetic envoi alludes to issues of historical periodization first of all through the voice of a junior member of Johnson's circle, Frances Burney. Within that couplet-based frame, then, one finds a more teasingly evocative meditation on the encounters that constitute literary history, in the form of Burney's enigmatic anecdote about a member of the next poetic generation: a boy—one of Smart's Latin students—whose melancholy song revolves around various paradoxes of illumination. Burney, whose encounter with Smart in debtor's prison (1768) is imaginatively telescoped with his sojourn some five years before in Mr. Potter's madhouse, also offers her own speculations about Smart's difficulties. To what extent, she muses to Johnson, can the beguilingly "pagan" art of poetry—ever dependent on "wanton Words"—be an adequate vehicle for a religious faith in things unseen?

Aviram's poem joins a well-established tradition: for it is indeed above all in poetic circles that Smart's twentieth-century impact has been registered. The annotated checklist that provides a bibliographical supplement to Karina Williamson's chapter—"Twentieth-Century Poetic Encounters with Christopher Smart"—thus concisely documents a stunning fact: that the list of distinguished poets who have "parleyed," as it were, with Smart includes W. H. Auden; Edmund Blunden; Louise Bogan; Gay Clifford; Wendy Cope; Donald Davie; James Dickey; Gavin Ewart; Robert Frost; Allen Ginsberg; Edward Heath-Stubbs; Anthony Hecht; Edward Hirsch; Ralph Hodgson; John Hollander; Erica Jong; Galway Kinnell; Eli Mandel; W. S. Merwin; Marianne Moore; Norman Nicholson; Peter Porter; Jeremy Reed; Theodore Roethke; Susan Fromberg Schaeffer; Delmore Schwartz; Anne Sexton; Edith Sitwell; Joseph Stroud; Mona Van Duyn; Mac Wellman; and John Williams. The widespread recognition of Smart as the quintessential poet's poet is a crucial barometer of his increasing importance. Twentieth-century poets—and nowhere more than in North America—have already engaged in a far deeper and more productive dialogue with Smart than is commonly recognized. These poets have in fact already elevated Smart into a canonical figure far above his alleged status as a minor poet. More crucially, perhaps, they have made Smart readily available to us, as never before in all of literary history. As we read Smart's work now, with the hindsight of our moment, it is essential that our critical discourse also register how much of our poetic moment derives from his: how much of Smart, indeed, has already entered into the metabolism of our poetic traditions.

The sheer variety of commentaries gathered in this volume foregrounds the significance of Smart studies for the understanding of literary history more generally. The will to transgress represented by Smart—the subversive resonance noted by several of the contributors to this volume—cannot easily be pigeonholed. Is Smart a cultural conservative, desperately holding out against the deluge of modernity? Or is he himself precisely a modernizing leveler of the inherited distinctions of the past? Is it even possible to decide? The dialogue documented in Part III between the eighteenth and twentieth centuries is in fact predicated, however unconsciously, on the sheer undecidability of this question. For it is precisely by embodying modernity while simultaneously exceeding it that Smart most matters to us now. His work constitutes not only an invaluable challenge to the reigning *doxa* of literary-historical periodization, but also an indispensable site for the immanent critique of modernity.[57] If we allow ourselves to imagine Smart afresh—neither as a Romantic genius regrettably trapped in the historical antechamber of the "pre-Romantic," nor as a mere martyr to the birthpangs of a brutal modernity—then he can represent one important site from which a necessary rethinking of literary history can take place. The most crucial element of this new space would be the refusal to suppress that quality of historical liminality that is so often foreclosed by received characterizations for the eighteenth-century moment: a moment whose assigned role in the pageant of cultural memory has been seen either as the modest harbinger to the desirable and fulfilling consummation of a later, nineteenth-century version of modernity, or as the grim origin and essence of a modernity now viewed, in the late twentieth century, as a discredited and ravaging scourge. It may well be that only a critical reappropriation of eighteenth-century modernity, based on substantial engagement with figures such as Smart, can enable even a modest outflanking of this reductionist orthodoxy amongst many literary theorists. In proposing to study Smart thus, *Christopher Smart and the Enlightenment* bears on a range of issues also germane to the writing of the cultural history of our own late-twentieth-century juncture. In highlighting contingency and liminality, the volume presents an eighteenth-century moment that challenges, rather than reinforces, many of the constitutive mythologies of our own moment.

NOTES

I wish to thank Greg Clingham and Mrinalini Sinha for their perceptive suggestions about earlier versions of this introduction.

1. Terry Eagleton, *The Illusions of Postmodernism* (Oxford: Blackwell, 1996), 23.
2. See Michel Foucault, *Madness and Civilization: A History of Insanity in the Age of Reason*, trans. Richard Howard (N.Y.: Vintage Books, 1965); and *The Order of Things: An Archaeology of the Human Sciences* (N.Y. Vintage Books, 1970).
3. John Gascoine, *Cambridge in the Age of the Enlightenment: Science, Religion and Politics from the Restoration to the French Revolution* (Cambridge: Cambridge University Press, 1989), 3.
4. See Max Weber, "Science as a Vocation," in *On Charisma and Institution Building*, ed. S. N. Eisenstadt, trans. H. H. Gerth (Chicago, IL: University of Chicago Press, 1968), 298. The German term translated by "disenchantment" is *Entzauberung*.
5. Robert Markley, *Fallen Languages: Crises of Representation in Newtonian England, 1660-1740* (Ithaca, NY: Cornell University Press, 1993), 260.
6. Ibid., 7.
7. See the Lilly Library exhibiton catalogue *Newton and the Scientific Revolution*, prepared and described by Richard S. Westfall (Bloomington: Indiana University Press, 1987), 65.
8. See Marie Roberts, *British Poets and Secret Societies* (Totowa, NJ: Barnes and Noble Books, 1986), 10-51.
9. Donald Davie, "Enlightenment and Dissent," in *Dissentient Voice: The Ward-Phillips Lectures for 1980 with Some Related Pieces* (Notre Dame: University of Notre Dame Press, 1982), 22.
10. See D. J. Greene, "Smart, Berkeley, the Scientists and the Poets," *Journal of the History of Ideas,* 14, no. 3 (1953): 327-52.
11. William Ober, *Boswell's Clap and Other Essays: Medical Analyses of Literary Men's Afflictions.* 1979. (N.Y.: Perennial Library, 1988), 179.
12. See Charles Webster, *From Paracelsus to Newton: Magic and the Making of Modern Science* (Cambridge: Cambridge University Press, 1982); and Michael White, *Isaac Newton: The Last Sorcerer* (Reading, MA: Addison-Wellesley, 1997).
13. Karina Williamson, "Smart's *Principia*: Science and Anti-Science in *Jubilate Agno*," *Review of English Studies,* 30, no. 120 (1979): 409-22; and

"Smart and the Hutchinsonians," appendix to *The Poetical Works of Christopher Smart*, 6 vols., eds. Karina Williamson and Marcus Walsh (Oxford: Clarendon Press, 1980-1996), I: *Jubilate Agno*, 131-32.

14. See John H. Brooke, "Why Did the English Mix Their Science and Their Religion?" in *Science and Imagination in XVIIIth-Century British Culture*, ed. Sergio Rossi (Milano: Edizione Unicopli, 1987), 57-78.

15. Earl R. Wasserman, "Nature Moralized: The Divine Analogy in the Eighteenth Century," *English Literary History*, 20, no. 1 (1953): 47.

16. Markley, *Fallen Languages*, 7.

17. Nicholas Hudson, *Writing and European Thought, 1600-1830* (Cambridge: Cambridge University Press, 1994), 84.

18. Jules David Law, *The Rhetoric of Empiricism: Language and Perception from Locke to I. A. Richards* (Ithaca, NY: Cornell University Press, 1993), 50.

19. Ibid., 64.

20. Thomas Hobbes, *Leviathan*, eds. Richard E. Flathman and David Johnston (New York: W. W. Norton & Co., 1997), 21; John Locke, *An Essay Concerning Human Understanding*, ed. Peter H. Nidditch (Oxford: Clarendon Press, 1975), 508. See also Robert E. Stillman, "Hobbes's *Leviathan*: Monsters, Metaphors, and Magic," *ELH*, 62, no. 4 (1995): 791-819.

21. See Samuel Johnson, "Waller," *Lives of the English Poets*, ed. George Birkbeck Hill (Oxford: Clarendon Press, 1905), I: 292.

22. See Locke, *Essay* I: ch. 2, 49-50. For more on the terminology of "impression" and "imprinting" in Locke, see William Walker, *Locke, Literary Criticism, and Philosophy* (Cambridge: Cambridge University Press, 1994), 34-41.

23. John Dennis, for instance, suggests in his preface to *The Grounds of Criticism in Poetry* (1704) that religion "has need of Poetry to make its utmost Impression upon the Minds of Men." See his preface to *The Grounds of Criticism in Poetry*, in *The Critical Works of John Dennis*, ed. Edward Niles Hooker, 2 vols. (Baltimore, MD: Johns Hopkins Press, 1939), I: 325.

24. See Kenneth Burke, *The Rhetoric of Religion: Studies in Logology* (Berkeley: University of California Press, 1961), 296-316.

25. The theology of *kenosis*, which refers to the heavenly Christ's emptying himself of divinity in order to assume, on earth, "the form of a servant" and "the likeness of men" is based on Paul's Epistle to the Philippians, 2: 7.

26. See Keith Thomas, *Man and the Natural World: A History of the Modern Sensibility* (N.Y.: Pantheon Books, 1983), 51-91.

27. Lisbet Koerner, "Purposes of Linnaean Travel: A Preliminary Research Report," in *Visions of Empire: Voyages, Botany, and Representations of Nature,* eds. David Philip Miller and Peter Hanns Reill (Cambridge: Cambridge University Press, 1996), 124-25.

28. Harriet Guest, *A Form of Sound Words: The Religious Poetry of Christopher Smart* (Oxford: Clarendon Press, 1989), 203.

29. Guest, 233.

30. Mark L. Greenberg, "Eighteenth-Century Poetry Represents Moments of Scientific Discovery: Appropriation and Generic Transformation," in *Literature and Science: Theory and Practice,* ed. Stuart Peterfreund (Boston: Northeastern University Press, 1990), 115-37. See also Marjorie Hope Nicolson, *Newton Demands the Muse: Newton's Opticks and the Eighteenth-Century Poets* (Princeton, NJ: Princeton University Press, 1946).

31. Kevin Pask, *The Emergence of the English Author: Scripting the Life of the Poet in Early Modern England* (Cambridge: Cambridge University Press, 1996).

32. Michel Foucault, *Language, Counter-Memory, Practice: Selected Essays and Interviews by Michel Foucault,* ed. Donald F. Bouchard (Ithaca, NY: Cornell University Press, 1977), 126.

33. Roger Chartier, *The Order of Books: Readers, Authors, and Libraries in Europe between the Fourteenth and the Eighteenth Centuries,* trans. Lydia G. Cochrane (Stanford, CA: Stanford University Press, 1994), 37.

34. Brean S. Hammond, *Professional Imaginative Writing in England, 1670-1740* (Oxford: Oxford University Press, 1997), 5-6.

35. Pask, *The Emergence,* 141-66.

36. Dustin Griffin, *Literary Patronage in England, 1650-1800* (Cambridge: Cambridge University Press, 1996), 10.

37. Ibid., 259.

38. Ibid., 277.

39. See Paula McDowell, *The Women of Grub Street: Press, Politics, and Gender in the London Literary Marketplace 1678-1730* (Oxford: Clarendon Press, 1998), 249-50.

40. Thomas Pynchon, *Mason & Dixon* (N.Y.: Henry Holt, 1997), 117.

41. Pask, *The Emergence,* 170.

42. Alan Richardson, *Literature, Education, and Romanticism: Reading as Social Practice, 1780-1832* (Cambridge: Cambridge University Press, 1994), 154.

43. See Ernst Robert Curtius, *European Literature and the Latin Middle Ages,* trans. Willard R. Trask (Princeton, NJ: Princeton University Press, 1973), 231-32.

44. See Frank Donoghue, *The Fame Machine: Book Reviewing and Eighteenth-Century Literary Careers* (Stanford, CA: Stanford University Press, 1996), 56-85.

45. See especially Jürgen Habermas, *The Structural Transformation of the Public Sphere: An Inquiry into a Category of Bourgeois Society*, trans. Thomas Burger, with the assistance of Frederick Lawrence (Cambridge, MA: MIT Press, 1989); Terry Eagleton, *The Function of Criticism from the Spectator to Post-Structuralism* (London: Verso, 1984); Geoffrey Hartman, *Minor Prophecies: The Literary Essay in the Culture Wars* (Cambridge, MA: Harvard University Press, 1991); and Joan B. Landes, "The Public and the Private Sphere: A Feminist Reconsideration," in *Feminists Read Habermas: Gendering the Subject of Discourse*, ed. Johanna Meehan (N.Y.: Routledge, 1995), 91-116.

46. See Clement Hawes, "Leading History by the Nose: The Turn to the Eighteenth Century in *Midnight's Children*," *Modern Fiction Studies,* 39, no. 1 (Spring, 1993): 147-68; Amy J. Elias, "The Postmodern Turn on(:) the Enlightenment," *Contemporary Literature* 37, no. 4 (Winter, 1996): 533-58; Donna Heiland, "Historical Subjects: Recent Fiction about the Eighteenth Century," *Eighteenth-Century Life* 21, n.s. no. 1 (Feb., 1997): 108-122; and *Questioning History: The Postmodern Turn to the Eighteenth Century*, ed. Greg Clingham (London: Associated University Presses, 1998).

47. Kevin Barry, *Language, Music and the Sign: A Study in Aesthetics, Poetics and Poetic Practice from Collins to Coleridge* (Cambridge: Cambridge University Press, 1987), 65.

48. For an elegant analysis of the urgent need for such a historical dialogue, see Greg Clingham's "The Question of History and Eighteenth-Century Studies," Introduction to *Questioning History: The Postmodern Turn to the Eighteenth Century*, ed. Greg Clingham (London: Associated University Presses, 1998), 11-17.

49. Jeremy Reed, "Christopher Smart in Madness," in *By the Fisheries* (London: Jackson Cope, 1984), 12.

50. Gay Clifford, "I Will Consider My Cat Thisbe," *Poems by Gay Clifford* (London: Hamish Hamilton, 1990), 100.

51. Gavin Ewart, "Jubilate Matteo," *Selected Poems 1933-1993* (London: Hutchinson, 1996), 105.

52. Erica Jong, "Jubilate Canis," in *At the Edge of the Body* (N.Y.: Holt, Rinehart and Winston, 1979), 40.

53. Susan Fromberg Schaeffer, "Jubilate Agno: Thomas Cat," *The Bible of the Beasts of the Little Field* (N.Y.: E. P. Dutton, 1980), 62.

54. For a thorough discussion of this shift, see Keith Thomas, *Man and the Natural World: Changing Attitudes in England 1500-1800* (London: Allen Lane, 1983), 92-191. For the popular tradition of torturing cats, see Robert Darnton, "Worker's Revolt: The Great Cat Massacre of the Rue Saint-Séverin," in *The Great Cat Massacre and Other Episodes in French Cultural History* (N.Y.: Basic Books, 1984), 75-106. For pet-owning as available to the middling classes first in Smart's moment, see Harriet Ritvo, *The Animal Estate: The English and Other Creatures in the Victorian Age* (Cambridge, MA.: Harvard University Press, 1987), 84-85.

55. Edward Hirsch, "Wild Gratitude," in *Wild Gratitude* (N.Y.: Alfred A. Knopf, 1986), 17.

56. For a few examples among many, see Mildred Kirk, *The Everlasting Cat* (N.Y.: Galahad Books, 1977); *The Book of Cats*, eds. George Macbeth and Martin Booth (New York: Penguin, 1979); Clare Boylan, *The Literary Companion to Cats: An Anthology of Prose and Poetry* (London: Sinclair-Stevenson, 1994) and *The Literary Cat: Quips, Quotes, and Observations* (Philadelphia: Running Press, 1990). The title of Elizabeth Marshall Thomas's *The Tribe of Tiger: Cats and Their Culture* (New York: Simon and Schuster, 1994) comes from *Jubilate Agno*.

57. For more on the Enlightenment's capacity for immanent critique, see Clement Hawes, "Johnson and Imperialism," in *The Cambridge Companion to Samuel Johnson*, ed. Greg Clingham (Cambridge: Cambridge University Press, 1997), 114-126; and "Singing the Imperial Blues: The Scriblerians after Wole Soyinka," in *Questioning History: The Postmodern Turn to the Eighteenth Century*, ed. Greg Clingham (London: Associated University Presses, 1998), 139-59.

PART I

BETWEEN SECULAR AND SACRED

CHAPTER 1

"Community of Mind": Christopher Smart and the Poetics of Allusion

Marcus Walsh

JAMES BOSWELL RECORDS that when John Wilkes censured quotation as a pedantic practice Samuel Johnson firmly replied, "No, Sir, it is a good thing; there is a community of mind in it. Classical quotation is the *parole* of literary men all over the world."[1] Allusion, like quotation (which is a particular form of allusion), depends upon community of understanding, assumed, achieved, exploited, manipulated, failed. Poetry operates within a spectrum of allusive familiarity. At one extreme there is writing that makes virtually no use of allusion, or alludes in ways that are entirely and readily recognizable to a very wide readership. (This is a hermeneutic aspect of that kind of unchallenging and routine literature that Hans Robert Jauss terms "culinary.")[2] At the other extreme, there is the esoteric or hermetic, writing whose allusions may be understood only by a small group, perhaps a group of one. Allusion therefore has a sociopolitical dimension, which varies according to what is alluded to, and how, and why. This might be brought into focus by substituting for "classical quotation," in Johnson's reply to Wilkes, the phrase "biblical quotation." Classical learning was a field significantly restricted even in Johnson's phrase to the lettered and the masculine. Knowledge of the Scriptures was available, in principle, to a wider and more mixed audience.

An allusion, in Johnson's *Dictionary* definition, is "that which is spoken with reference to something supposed to be already known, and therefore not expressed." The political or cultural problematic of allusion as a method is summed up in Johnson's "supposed to be already known": supposed by whom? known by whom? This same essential point is made in an illuminating recent study of allusion by Michael Leddy: ". . . allusion-words typically describe a reference to a certain kind of entity or event, namely cultural material that is shared to some limited extent, neither highly personal nor so well known as to be 'too' obvious. . . . Allusion then is predicated upon the possibility that some will catch the point while others will (or would) miss it; even when an allusion seems obvious, the fact that there is pleasure in recognition presupposes that an allusion is not all that obvious, not to everyone."[3] Allusions, precisely, are shared "to some limited extent." They offer a resistance to understanding. They are available to some readers but not to all. They involve an Aristotelian pleasure of recognition, but also create a fortunate or unfortunate possibility of exclusion. Thus authors may through allusion select their own readership, and refuse admission to others; in Jonathan Swift's famous autobiographical claim, for instance, that "To steal a hint was never known, / But what he writ was all his own," are two lines and several ironies recognizable only to those who remembered a couplet from John Denham.[4]

Though satirists may bend or subvert its procedures, allusion nonetheless normally depends on common understanding. Where there is communion between author and reader, the text alluded to, as John Hollander has put it, "is part of the portable library shared by the author and his ideal audience."[5] There are times and circumstances when the constitution of that library, however, and the identity or even the existence of that ideal audience, become uncertain. Allusion as a mode becomes problematic, or critical, when the community of understanding becomes fissured or entropic.

The problem of allusion, in fact, in one of its dimensions, is a problem of history and modernity.[6] In a key discussion, published just two years later than *The Waste Land*, I. A. Richards acknowledged that allusions "are a normal and regular part of the resources of all poets who belong to the literary tradition," and have "a fit and justifiable place in poetry," but nonetheless pointed out the difficulties raised for allusion by the increasing knowledge, and fragmentation and specialization of knowledge, typical of the modern condition:

> the difficulty [allusion] raises is merely a special instance of a general communicative difficulty. . . . All the thought and feeling of recent man goes on in terms of experience which is much more likely to be special and peculiar to the individual, than, let us say, the experience of medieval man . . . the people for whom the poet writes . . . inevitably build up their minds with far more varied elements than has ever been the case before. And the poet . . . does the same. It is hard, and, in fact, impossible, to deny him his natural and necessary resources on the ground that a majority of his readers will not understand.[7]

The effect of this change is a narrowing, as Richards puts it, of "the range of the artist's communication." Allusion may become more and more restricted to the individual or the coterie, in the worst case bringing about, both in the writer and the privileged audience, "a sense of superiority over others which is trivial and mean."[8] Yet in *The Waste Land*, a poem that raises such problems especially acutely, Richards recognizes that allusion is a necessary, an enabling technique. "Allusion, in Mr. Eliot's hands is a technical device for compression"; a device, that is, by which Eliot is able to write, in a relatively short poem, what would otherwise have required the compass of an epic.[9]

In this chapter, I set out to examine some aspects of Smart's poetics of allusion. Like other post-Augustan poets, and notably William Collins and Thomas Gray, Smart faced a problem of modernity. With different things to say than a previous generation, Smart and his contemporaries needed "a style of writing for themselves" (to borrow T. S. Eliot's dictum) "suited to the matter they wanted to talk about and the way in which they apprehended this matter."[10] In search of such an answerable style they explored a wide variety of different forms and languages. For Smart, allusion became an essential, even a characterizing, rhetorical device. It gave him scope for a distinctive play of verbal wit, and allowed him the concise expression of conceptual riches. It served him as a vehicle not only for poetic effect, but also for meaning. It offered him the possibility at least of a community of mind with his readers.

The resistance of many Augustan poets and poetic theorists to allusion was part of their more general distrust of metaphoric modes. In one of the best-known accounts of this issue in recent years, Irvin Ehrenpreis has explained why this makes "Augustan" writers particularly strange to modern critics: "It is because the so-called Augustans seldom trusted allusion or connotation, imagery or allegory alone to convey their meaning, because they normally made explicit any doctrine they wished to inculcate, that the fathers of modern criticism could so easily ignore other features of their work. . . . [T]he whole modern idea of poetry would have puzzled the Augustans. What most critics prize today is suggestion, allusiveness, implicit meaning."[11] Early eighteenth-century poetic theorists did not have a recognizably modern attitude to figurative and allusive modes of expression. Their distrust of the "abuse of words" owed something to John Locke, who entirely rejected "*figurative Speeches*, and allusion in language" from writings which aimed at truth and knowledge, and allowed them only the most grudging admission to "discourses, where we seek rather Pleasure and Delight."[12] Joseph Addison, Alexander Pope, and others attacked all forms of what they judged to be false verbal wit, and especially the pun, a type of verbal play that has historically been thought nearly related to allusion.[13] Elaborate and far-fetched metaphors were for the most part suspected, and the more explicit and discursive simile was regarded by many as a more appropriate figure for illustrating and amplifying meaning. Addison's *Spectator* papers on the Pleasures of the Imagination, in emphasizing the imaginative preeminence of the sense of sight, influenced many poets and critics towards the potentially visual simile, and away from the more verbal metaphor. Samuel Johnson stated an established eighteenth-century view in defining the simile in his *Dictionary* as "a comparison by which anything is illustrated and aggrandized," and in requiring it "to exhibit, independently of its references, a pleasing image." The compression of the metaphor, in which literal and figurative meet in the same words, by contrast involves a danger that the real can be confused with the imagined, the verbal figure replacing the thing described, which it should clarify, and to which it should remain subservient. Johnson's celebrated criticism of the opening lines of Thomas Gray's *Progress of Poesy* is based on precisely the same ground as that on which Gray himself had thought to justify them; that is, the uniting of tenor and vehicle. Johnson's most explicit challenge to metaphorical modes appears in the *Life of Cowley*, where he denies that the metaphysical poets practiced poetry as an Aristotelian mimetic art, for "they neither painted the forms of nature, nor represented the operations of intellect." In their descriptions, "they looked out not for images, but for conceits." Johnson's attack on the metaphoric in the *Life of Cowley* most specifically targets the potential obscurities of the referential and allusive in his insistence that "every piece ought to contain within itself whatever is necessary to make it intelligible," an anti-modern demand parallel to Richards's distrust of Eliot's allusiveness.[14]

A number of mid-century developments in aesthetics and literary historiography, however, sponsored attitudes more hospitable to the figurative and verbal in general, and the allusive in particular. It is now well established that a significant influence on Smart was Robert Lowth's account, and approval, in his *De sacra poesi Hebraeorum praelectiones* (1753), of the characterizing ellipses, parallelisms, and vividly immediate figures of the Hebrew poetry. In Chapter 6, Betty Rizzo suggests that Richard Hurd's essay *On Poetical Imitation* might have inspired Smart's poetic applications of conciseness and *energia* (see below, 121). Also significant for Smart's more metaphoric mode of poetry is Edmund Burke's reasoned denial, in his *Philosophical Enquiry into the Origin of our Ideas of the Sublime and Beautiful*, that poetry is primarily or necessarily a visually mimetic art. Poetry is an art of imitation only so far as it "describes the manners and passions of men which their words can express." Burke insists that descriptive (that is, nondramatic) poetry "operates chiefly by *substitution*," words having "no sort of resemblance to the ideas for which they stand." Burke's account stresses the verbal dimension, and imposes no duty of creating images: ". . . if poetry gives us a noble assemblage of words, . . . associated in any natural way, they may be moulded together in any form, and perfectly answer their end. The picturesque connection is not demanded; because no real picture is formed."[15]

Burke's understanding of this issue is by no means directly opposed to that of Johnson, who knew that words do not resemble things, and (despite his own metaphors of painting, illustration, and imaging) did not confine figurative language to the visual. Nonetheless, Burke's different emphasis is in tune with a project shared by a number of poets writing in the 1740s and later to find significantly new poetic languages and new poetic models.

Smart's poetry is characterized, especially after the madhouse years, by nonvisual modes, the conceit, the pun, the metaphor, and the allusion. His clearly avowed poetic exemplars were the Scriptures, particularly the Old Testament, and Horace; but in his exploitation of the resources of verbal wit there are affinities too with English poetry of the preceding century. Even from the outset of his poetic career Smart was one of the most rhetorically self-conscious of poets. At the age of thirteen he is to be found writing in an ostentatiously conceited seventeenth-century manner in his verses "To Ethelinda, On her doing my Verses the honour of wearing them in her bosom":

> Oft thro' my eyes my soul has flown,
> And wanton'd on that ivory throne:
> There with extatic transport burn'd,
> And thought it was to heav'n return'd.
> Tell me, is the omen true,
> Shall the body follow too?[16]

Similarly, distinctly metaphysical tendencies survive into the religious verse of his maturity. In his Nativity hymn, for instance, Smart explores a tradition of paradox that he might have found in Robert Southwell or Richard Crashaw:

> O the magnitude of meekness!
>   Worth from worth immortal sprung;
> O the strength of infant weakness,
>   If eternal is so young![17]

And Smart exploits the resources of the pun repeatedly: the typological resonances of "the dreadful cross / That happen'd by a tree," for example; the architectural as well as the geographical implications of placing St John "in the church her southern isle"; the double assertion of Luke's divine inspiration and painterly skill in the claim that his gospel is the product of "a master's hand." In these instances, as so often, paronomasia and allusion are inextricably interlinked.[18]

And indeed the characterizing figurative method of Smart's later religious verse is allusion. Smart uses many kinds of allusion, from the most transparent and signposted, to the most covert. There is little that is surprising, or disturbing to the community of mind between poet and reader, of course, in allusion to well-known and obviously appropriate texts. This was a staple method of eighteenth-century hymnody, a poetry more than any other shared and communal, whose allusive world was (with some important and significant exceptions) bounded by a relatively restricted stock of scriptural instances. Smart, particularly in his *Hymns and Spiritual Songs* and *Hymns for the Amusement of Children*, certainly used just such overt and direct allusiveness. Typical moments are the characterization of plain English Protestant Christians as "the sons of YEA and NAY," or his appeal to Christ to keep our hearts "Innocent as doves . . . / But as serpents wise," in his hymns on St Peter and St Luke.[19] More distinctive are two hymns whose symmetrical structures are built on insistent and evident allusion: the accounts of Old Testament and New Testament miracles in "Conversion of St Paul," and the series of citations of Christ's miracles in "The Crucifixion of our Blessed Lord."

Smart's community with his reader is soon tested, however. Even a clearly signposted allusion may pose problems. Insisting on a theological issue to which he was himself deeply committed, Smart tells us that "The Trinity is plain, / So David's psalms maintain," but this line in the hymn for Trinity Sunday seems to depend on a typological interpretation of a by-no-means obvious verse:

> By the word of the LORD were the heavens made; and all the host of them
> by the breath of his mouth" (Psalms: 33: 6).

Nor are all his allusions straightforwardly scriptural. In the same hymn, the apostrophe to the Trinity as "THREE! of blest account / To which all sums amount" seems to be a reference to Pythagorean number theory, and particularly the *tetractys*.[20] Other expressions depend, both for poetic resonance and, frequently, for verbal understanding, on a reader equipped with both classical and vernacular literature. The sun is referred to in *A Song to David* by its "saffron robe," which readers of Ovid, for instance, would recognize as an attribute of Aurora.[21] In "The Annunciation of the Blessed Virgin," the praise of God by the "high strains on golden wire" of seraphic instruments is perhaps an enriching echo of lines in Milton's "At a Solemn Music," in which the "bright seraphim" blow their trumpets, and the cherubs "Touch their immortal harps of golden wires." So too the characterization of David as "bright effluence of exceeding grace" perhaps profitably recalls, in its christological implications, Milton's invocation to the "holy Light" as "bright effluence of bright essence increate" in the exordium of the third book of *Paradise Lost*.[22] There seems to be a more deliberate and significant response to the elder poet in Smart's Nativity hymn, where he invites us to see how "Nature's decorations glisten / Far above their usual trim"; here a verbal echo rebuts the assertion of Milton's "On the Morning of Christ's Nativity" that nature, in awe to the newborn Christ, "had doffed her gaudy trim."[23]

More elaborately than this, however, allusion becomes in Smart a regular exercise of wit, generating metaphors that articulate meaning, and shape the structure of both his shorter and his longer lyrics. In the "Adoration" passage of *A Song to David*, for instance, we encounter what appears to be an almost naïve passage of natural description:

> For ADORATION, in the dome
> Of Christ the sparrows find an home;
>   And on his olives perch:
> The swallow also dwells with thee,
> O man of God's humility,
>   Within his Saviour CHURCH.
>   (*Song to David*, 421-26)

But, in these lines, Smart maintains his hero's typological presence through covert allusions to verses of the Psalms in which David likens himself to "a green olive tree in the house of God," and tells how "the sparrow hath found an house, and the swallow a nest for herself, . . . even thine altars, O LORD of hosts" (52: 8; 84: 3). In his Circumcision hymn, more complexly, Smart summons to the chorus of praise of Christ, along with other natural emblems of purity, "the famous tree, / Whose name is chastity." The allusion is signposted, and not in itself difficult to identify; Smart has in mind the "*Vitex: sive Agnus castus*. The chaste tree," to be found in Pliny or Gerard. The *vitex*, appropriately to the religious implications of the circumcision as a purification rite, is symbolic of sexual continence; as Gerard puts it, "*Agnus Castus* is a singular medicine . . . for such as would willingly live chaste, for it withstandeth all uncleanness, or desire to the flesh." But there are other associations, less obvious, less direct, yet fundamental to the thematic movement of Smart's hymn, whose two heroes, Christ and Abraham, are identified in the tree's Latin name, *Agnus castus*, and in its English name, "Abraham's balm."

And the word *tree* may conceivably also suggest, as it does elsewhere in Smart's writings, Christ's cross.[24]

If such compressed, suggestive, multiple, punning, *figurative* uses of allusion were merely local they would be sufficiently striking. Allusion, however, becomes more elaborated, more extended, and more personal in several metaphoric complexes to be found in his later religious poetry. In the "Seven Pillars" passage of *A Song to David*, for instance, and at a number of points in his *Translation of the Psalms of David*, Smart exploits an imagery of arches, vaults, and pillars, depicting the earth supported on its own pillars beneath "th'etherial arch" of the heavens, and drawing perhaps on cabalistic and more probably on Hutchinsonian sources.[25] Elsewhere, he plays a number of variations on the metaphor of the breath or perfume of the creation as praise of God, a figure common in seventeenth- and eighteenth-century religious poetry.[26]

One of the most remarkable instances of Smart's telescoped allusive image-systems may be found in the second hymn of his cycle for the church year, "Circumcision." In this poem a list of the purest things of nature— swans, rose, and lily, the tree of chastity, and "the brilliants of the mine"— are invited to join in one of Smart's signature choruses of adoration. Smart's figuring of the object of that adoration in the ten concluding lines of the hymn demonstrates both the intellectual and imaginative richness, and the potential difficulty, of his allusive method:

> All, all the praise of Jesus sing,
> The joy of heav'n and earth,
> And Christ's eternal worth,
> The pearl of God, the Father's ring.
>
> Let elegance, the flow'r
> Of words, in tune and pow'r,
> Find some device of cleanest choice
> About that gem to place —
> "This is my HEIR of GRACE,
> "In whose perfections I rejoice."
>
> (*Hymns and Spiritual Songs*, 2. 45-54)

The "pearl of God" is of course an allusion to a scriptural image well known to most readers, the "pearl of great price" of Matthew 13: 45-6: "the kingdom of heaven is like unto a merchant man, seeking goodly pearls: / Who, when he had found one pearl of great price, went and sold all that he had, and

bought it." The pearl of price is emblematic of salvation, and regularly iden-
tified with Christ.[27] What, however, is "the Father's ring," and why is it as-
sociated with the pearl and with "Christ's eternal worth"? The phrase,
obscurity in apposition with the familiar, requires interpretation, and forces
the reader to seek out an allusion. The meaning of "the Father's ring" seems
in fact to derive from a very much less obvious biblical source, the Messianic
prophecy of Haggai 2: 23:

> In that day, saith the LORD of hosts, will I take thee, O Zerubbabel, . . . and
> will make thee as a signet: for I have chosen thee.

In his paraphrastic explanation of this verse, Edward Wells (like other scrip-
tural commentators) makes Haggai's reference to the Messiah explicit:
"Zorobbabel, of whom Christ is to descend or be born: Which thy Offspring
I will make as my Signet."[28] Smart certainly knew this prophecy, and would
allude to it more directly in his verse paraphrase of the Psalms:

> Thou art an everlasting king,
>   In endless glory crown'd;
> Truth is the signet of thy ring,
> And thy dominion takes a swing
>   From alpha—from omega—round.
>   (*A Translation of the Psalms of David*, 145: 61-65).

In this stanza, Smart characteristically combines Old Testament with New
Testament allusion, applying the words of the Psalm ("Thy kingdom is an
everlasting kingdom: and thy dominion endureth throughout all ages")[29] to
Christ, who is alpha and omega, the beginning and the ending (Revelation,
1: 8). Haggai's prophetic metaphor is given an evangelical development:
Christ, who is the truth (John 14: 6), is not only the Lord's signet, but specif-
ically the signet stone in the ring of the Father. The conceit finds a somewhat
different setting and development in Smart's Circumcision hymn, where the
pearl of great price is identified with the "gem" of God's ring.[30] Smart here
has in mind not only a signet ring, but a posy-ring, bearing a brief motto or
"device" on its inner circumference or, as here, about its stone. The two-line
"device" itself is not so much allusion as marked near-quotation, of
Matthew 3: 17, the words of the Father following Christ's baptism by St.
John: "This is my beloved Son, in whom I am well pleased." Smart's mod-
ification of the Father's words, most appropriately in this "cleanest" of mot-
toes in a hymn on the Circumcision, stresses Christ's "perfections." Equally

pertinently, it also draws evangelical attention to Christ's role as the Father's "HEIR of GRACE."

Allusion is intentional, and surely Smart intended the resonant allusive play of these lines. Some of Smart's allusions here—certainly the pearl of price—must have been apparent to even a casual eighteenth-century reader, and must be apparent to a modern one. Some—in particular the likely echo of Haggai—may very well not be apparent. Here, as ever, allusion tests the community of mind between poet and reader. The relation of allusion and meaning, or understanding, is further tested however, and further illuminated, by the recurrence of the figures and ideas of these ten lines, with other associated ideas, in a rich and significant variety of combinations elsewhere in Smart's late religious verse.

For instance, the appeal in the Circumcision hymn to a personified "elegance" to find in the "flow'r of words" an appropriate "device" for the ring might seem a trite enough use of the well-worn image of "flowers of rhetoric," yet the metaphor does not lie dead in Smart's hands. There is a resonant though partly articulated internal doubleness in the unspoken quibble on a "posy" of flowers and the poetic "posy" of a ring. Probably too there is a reticent pun on "gem," which is both a precious stone, and a flower bud; the equivocation continues both of the two main conceits of the stanza. More profoundly, Smart gives his floral metaphor a spiritual and Christian turn which chimes with other expressions of his sense of the spiritual and divinized nature of language itself:

> For elegant phrases are nothing but flowers.
> For flowers are peculiarly the poetry of Christ.
> (Jubilate Agno, B505-6.[31])

Less familiarly, in a number of places Smart plays a bewildering series of allusive exercises on figurative associations of the pearl of great price, God's ring, and precious stones. Gems have symbolic and spiritual senses everywhere. In his Hymn on Easter Day, Smart links the "pearl of price" with the "stone of lucid white" (Hymns and Spiritual Songs, 11. 29-30). His own (rare) footnote ensures that the reader does not miss the allusion to Revelation 2: 17, the Spirit's promise of the white stone as a sign of salvation: "To him that overcometh will I give to eat of the hidden manna, and will give him a white stone, and in the stone a new name written." This same combination of scriptural emblems of salvation appears in Smart's celebration of the preciousness of "alba's blest imperial rays, / And pure cerulean pearl" in A Song to David (lines 485-86).[32] There is a more complex figurative exercise upon this and related scriptural texts in one of the more extraordinary pairs of lines in the *Jubilate*:

> Let Machir rejoice with Convolvulus, from him to the ring of Saturn, which is the Girth of Job; to the signet of God—from Job and his daughters BLESSED BE JESUS.
> *For there is a blessing from the* STONE *of* JESUS *which is founded upon hell to the precious jewell on the right hand of God.*
> <div align="right">(<i>Jubilate Agno</i>, B31).</div>

Here, once more, the "stone of Jesus" is linked with the signet ring of God, and with the precious jewel that, in Smart's imagination, it bore. It is linked, too, both with Christ as the corner stone of the true faith (Acts 4: 11; 1 Peter 2: 6), and with Christ as the "living stone," to whom the "newborn babes" of the New Covenant come as "lively stones," so making up the "spiritual house" of Christ's followers (1 Peter 2: 2, 4, 5).

These reciprocations of allusion in Smart's writing provide contexts within which such passages as the concluding stanzas of the Circumcision hymn may be read; and these contexts provide not merely enrichment, but meaning. Particularly, they enable us to understand the Circumcision hymn as part of Smart's project of poetic evangelism. The Circumcision was of course the mark of the first covenant, by which God's chosen were identified; the complex figures and references of these concluding lines make the typological connection with Christ's new covenant of grace, in covert and indirect as well as in obvious ways. It seems, from a number of passages in Smart's writings, that he understood the Father's ring as the signet with which those saved by Christ are "sealed" and identified. A key biblical verse is from the second book of Timothy: "the foundation of God standeth sure, having this seal, The Lord knoweth them that are his."[33] The allusion is not made in the Circumcision hymn, but the figure of the signet ring functioning as God's seal appears in "Truth," one of Smart's *Hymns for the Amusement of Children*, and the association of God's ring with election is made in Smart's hymn on St. Bartholomew, where Sincerity is figured as wearing "the precious ring that holds / Each jewel of the tribes," with a likely allusion to the "breast-plate of judgment" of Aaron, in which are set twelve jewels with "the names of the children of Israel, . . . like the engravings of a signet."[34]

The concluding stanzas of Smart's Circumcision hymn are forged out of a sequence of emblematic metaphors: the Father's signet ring with its precious stone or priceless pearl, the device or posy inscribed about the stone, the flowers of poesy of which these stanzas are themselves an instance. This intense concentration of interconnecting figures is reminiscent of the metaphysical conceit, the "telescoping of images and multiplied associations" that T. S. Eliot finds in John Donne's "The Relique," and in some Jacobean dramatists.[35] Such "telescoping" is not only metaphoric, but allusive, bringing together "images" and "associations." Allusion, when used with the complexity and frequency with which it appears in Smart, is metaphoric in itself, creating levels of imaginative suggestion around literal meaning, and indeed replacing literal meaning, with just such a metaphorical logic as Johnson found so disturbing in the poetry of Gray. The verbal play however does serious work: an elaborated process of allusive association makes Smart's essential typological point, that the Circumcision as the sign of God's first covenant foreshadows Christ's second covenant of grace.

The Scriptures, in a Protestant and more especially, it can be argued, in an evangelical or typological understanding, provide Smart with authority and a voice. Tom Keymer has shown how Smart derives in *Jubilate Agno* a personal authority in his "jeopardy" from David and Job's descriptions of their own sufferings.[36] For the more impersonal published religious verse, the *Song to David* and especially the *Hymns and Spiritual Songs*, the Bible provides the extensive and familiar materials of a body of belief shared, Smart thought, with his readership. Quotation and allusion are intended as acts of filiation, statements of community and communal identity.

Yet Smart's published verse nonetheless has seemed less than straightforwardly accessible both to contemporary and to recent readers. Allusion is a matter of meaning; missed allusion must lead to partial understanding. Gérard Genette defines allusion, precisely, as "an enunciation whose full meaning presupposes the perception of a relationship between it and another text, to which it necessarily refers by some inflections that would otherwise remain unintelligible."[37] In many cases, perhaps in most, allusion may contribute to some aspect of literary value, to "emotional aura" (as I. A. Richards claims it does in the case of Eliot), or to "richness of effect" (such as Roger Lonsdale finds in Gray's evocation of earlier classical and English descriptions in his "Ode on the Spring").[38] Allusion, however, clearly in Eliot and in Gray, and certainly in Smart, also carries a dense and powerful semantic charge. George Steiner's account of "difficult" poetry exactly describes the character of Smart's writing: ". . . the language of the poem implicates a surrounding and highly active context, a corpus . . . of supporting, echoing, validating, or qualifying material whose compass underwrites its own concision. The implication is effected by virtue of allusion, of reference to."[39] The surrounding context of Smart's later Christian poetry, the context that enables his tautly compact expression and validates his meaning, includes his own writings in general, and a world of literary reference, but it is constituted primarily by the Bible. The difficulty of Smart's allusiveness is brought about in large part by the nature of his use of Scripture, by his "concision," by his resort to unfamiliar texts, and his frequently covert or implied reference to familiar ones. This makes necessary what Steiner calls "the homework of elucidation"; it makes Smart, as it makes Gray, one of the most annotatable of poets. The scholarly labor of the editor has always sought to recover lost contexts, to identify and draw the reader's attention to (as Thomas Newton put it, in 1749) "such passages as we may suppose the author really alluded to, and had in mind at the time of writing."[40] The editor in fact seeks to reconstruct the "community of mind" that existed between the author and original audience.

There are cases, however, where the community of mind between author and original audience was itself incomplete, whether because the author chose to write for intimates or *adepti*, or more simply misjudged the knowledge of his readers. The poems of Smart and Gray represent somewhat different versions of such an imperfect community. Certainly the works of both men seemed difficult and obscure to contemporaries. The *Monthly Review*, discussing Smart's *Ode to the Earl of Northumberland* (1764), complained that "there is in the later productions of Mr. Smart, a *tour* of expression, which we many times are at a loss to understand." Boswell thought *A Song to David* "a very curious composition, being a strange mixture of *dun obscure* and glowing genius at times." Samuel Johnson's difficulties with Gray were shared by many readers of the two great *Odes*. Gray reports his friend Bedingfield overhearing at York races "three People, whom by their dress & manner he takes for Lords, say, that I was impenetrable & inexplicable, and they wish'd, I had told them in prose, what I meant in verse." I. A. Richards would note the common stricture of many critics of *The Waste Land* about the necessity of notes, and suggest that "a more reasonable complaint would have been that Mr Eliot did not provide a larger apparatus of elucidation." Gray was as reluctant as Eliot to provide his own explanatory glosses, and as willing to leave comprehension or incomprehension to the reader's own resources. In connection with the publication of *The Bard* he sturdily maintained, in a letter to Walpole: "I do not love notes, though you see I had resolved to put two or three. They are signs of weakness and obscurity. If a thing cannot be understood without them, it had better be not understood at all." Yet it is clear from this letter, and from others, that Gray wanted and expected to be understood, and was irritated not to be understood. The Sister Odes were intended (as their Pindaric motto boasts) to be "vocal to the intelligent alone," but vocal nevertheless, if only to a chosen few.[41]

There is no apparent use of a coterie or esoteric language in Smart's published verse, with the possible exception of his occasional uses of Hutchinsonian thinking. Allusion may in principle operate as a private code or idea system, but Smart seems to have used allusion as a vehicle of intended and sharable sense. Holy Scripture is the target text of most of the allusion in his later religious poetry, and no doubt he thought scriptural allusion to be a language he shared with his readers. There are many reasons why that intended community of mind worked less easily or completely than Smart expected. One, no doubt, was that even his published work was (to use I. A. Richards's terms) the product of thought and feeling special and peculiar to himself as an individual—a modern condition he shared in varying degree with William Collins and Thomas Gray among others. The *Song to David* and *Hymns and Spiritual Songs* grind a good many of Smart's personal theological axes, especially of a typological and evangelical kind. More generally, it is arguable that Smart's dependence on and appeal to Scripture made his verse vulnerable in its reception to that incipient breakdown in shared knowledge and understanding of the Bible, especially of typological understandings of the Bible, which has been termed, by Hans Frei, the "eclipse of biblical narrative."[42] Eighteenth-century congregational hymn writers, from Isaac Watts to Augustus Toplady, from John and Charles Wesley to John Newton, could ensure communication with their rather well-defined audiences by a relatively restricted range of scriptural references and *topoi*, and a poetic style for the most part relatively direct and simplified. Smart's communication with his own chosen, Anglican, audience, was very much less immediate, or recognized, or accepted. Smart's verse is significantly distinguished from the Independent or Wesleyan or Evangelical hymnody by a number of its stylistic and rhetorical features, among them, as I hope to have shown, the intense compression, brevity, self-referentiality, and occasional frank obscurity of his methods of scriptural allusion. Above all, perhaps, Smart's allusiveness derives from and is informed by an astonishing level of personal involvement with and recall of the Scripture text, which very few readers then, or now, could hope to match. Smart's is a poetry that does not always "contain within itself whatever is necessary to make it intelligible," except for a reader as learned, as committed, and as verbally intelligent as Smart himself. There is every possibility that Smart may have overestimated the learning, and especially the biblical learning, of his readership; that he had misconceived, in fact, the community of mind within which he might have operated.

NOTES

1. James Boswell, *The Life of Samuel Johnson, LL.D.*, ed. George Birkbeck Hill, rev. and enlarged L. F. Powell, 6 vols. (Oxford: Oxford University Press, 1979), 4: 102.
2. Hans Robert Jauss, *Toward an Aesthetic of Reception*, trans. Timothy Bahti (Brighton: Harvester, 1982), 25.
3. Michael Leddy, "Limits of allusion," *British Journal of Aesthetics* 32 (1992): 111-12.
4. Jonathan Swift, "Verses on the Death of Dr Swift, D. S. P. D.," in *Jonathan Swift: The Complete Poems*, ed. Pat Rogers (London: Penguin Classics, 1989), 493, ll. 317-18. The lines are borrowed from John Denham's "On Mr. Abraham Cowley," ll. 29-30; see *The Poetical Works of John Denham*, second edition, ed. Theodore Howard Banks (North Haven: Archon Books, 1969), 150.
5. John Hollander, *The Figure of Echo: A Mode of Allusion in Milton and After* (Berkeley: University of California Press, 1981), 64.
6. As Peter Hughes, among others, has noted. See his "Allusion and Expression in Eighteenth-Century Literature," in *The Author in his Work*, eds. Louis L. Martz and Aubrey Williams (New Haven and London: Yale University Press, 1978), 298.
7. I. A. Richards, "The Allusiveness of Modern Poetry," in *Principles of Literary Criticism* (London: Routledge and Kegan Paul, 1960), 216, 218-19. *Principles* was first published in 1924.
8. Ibid., 215, 217-18.
9. See Richards's appendix, "The Poetry of T. S. Eliot," ibid., 290-91.
10. From Eliot's introductory essay to Johnson's *London* and *Vanity of Human Wishes* (1930), in *Selected Prose*, ed. John Hayward (Harmondsworth: Penguin, 1953), 155.
11. Irvin Ehrenpreis, *Literary Meaning and Augustan Values* (Charlottesville, VA.: University Press of Virginia, 1974), 4-5, 6.
12. John Locke, *An Essay Concerning Human Understanding*, ed. Peter H. Nidditch (Oxford: Clarendon Press, 1975), Book 3, ch. 10, para. 34.
13. See, notably, Joseph Addison, *Spectator* 61, in Joseph Addison and Richard Steele, *Selected Essays from "The Tatler," "The Spectator," "The Guardian,"* ed. Daniel McDonald (N.Y.: Bobbs-Merrill Company, Inc., 1973), 216-20; Alexander Pope, *The Art of Sinking in Poetry: A Critical Edition*, ed. Edna Leake Steeves (N.Y.: King's Crown Press, 1952), ch. 10.

14. Samuel Johnson, *Life of Pope*, in *Lives of the English Poets*, ed. George Birkbeck Hill, 3 vols. (Oxford: Oxford University Press, 1905), vol. 3: 229; *Life of Gray*, in *Lives*, vol. 3: 436; *Life of Cowley*, in *Lives*, vol. 1: 19, 33, 35-36.

15. Edmund Burke, *A Philosophical Enquiry into the Origin of our Ideas of the Sublime and Beautiful*, ed. J. T. Boulton (Oxford: Blackwell, 1987), 171, 172-3. First published in 1757, Burke's *Enquiry* was revised and expanded in 1759. For evidence of Smart's knowledge of this part of the *Enquiry*, see my editorial note on *A Song to David*, ll.19-21, in *PW, ii*: 430.

16. *PW*, iv: 3. For a more mature, elaborated, and comic instance of the conceit see, for example, "On Seeing Miss H— P—t, in an Apothecary's Shop" (*PW*, iv: 108- 9).

17. *Hymns and Spiritual Songs*, 32, ll. 9-12, in *PW*, ii: 88. See my note on these lines in *PW*, ii: 424-25.

18. *Hymns,* 10, ll. 92-3, in *PW*, ii: 51; 23, l. 30, in *PW* ii: 77; 25, l. 25, in *PW* ii: 79.

19. *Hymns*, 20, ll. 28-9, in *PW*, ii: 72 (compare Matt. 5: 37); 25, ll. 39-40, in PW, ii: 80 (compare Matt. 10: 16).

20. *Hymns*, 16, ll. 49-50, in *PW*, ii: 64; 16, ll. 13-14, in *PW*, ii: 63. See my notes in *PW*, ii: 398, 399.

21. *Song*, 202; compare with Ovid, *Ars amatoria*, 3 (Loeb Classical Library, 2nd ed., 1979), ll. 179-80.

22. *Hymns*, 9, ll. 37-40 in *PW*, ii: 47; John Milton, "At a Solemn Music," ll. 10-13 in *Complete Poems and Major Prose*, ed. Merritt Y. Hughes (N.Y.: The Odyssey Press, 1957), 81-82; *A Song to David*, l. 22, in *PW*, ii: 129; Milton, *Paradise Lost*, in Hughes, Book 3, l. 6, 257.

23. *Hymns,* 32, ll. 21-2; Milton, "On the Morning of Christ's Nativity," in Hughes, ll. 32-33, 43.

24. *Hymns*, 2, ll. 40-41, in *PW*, ii: 36; Pliny, *Natural History*, 7: Books 24-27, tr. W. H. S. Jones (Loeb Classical Library, 1956), 47-8. John Gerard, *Herbal*, ed. Thomas Johnson (1633), 1388. For other instances of this kind of covert structural allusion, see Smart's linking of the Glastonbury thorn with the rod of Aaron in the phrase "blest Mosaic thorn" (*Hymns and Spiritual Songs*, 32, ll. 29-32, in *PW*, ii: 89); or his reference to gold and silver fish as "crusions" and "silverlings," a choice of terms and spellings that pun on coinage (*A Song to David*, 340-42, in *PW*, ii: 140.)

25. I discuss the sources and uses of this image-system in *PW*, ii: 148-49; *PW*, iii: *A Translation of the Psalms of David*, xviii-xix; and in "Smart's Pillars and the Hutchinsonians," *Notes and Queries* n.s. 33 (1986), 67-70.

26. For instance, in *Hymns*, 1, l. 25; and 13, l. 4, in *PW*, ii: 34, 57; *Jubilate Agno*, B208; *A Song to David*, 403-8, 427-44, in *PW*, ii: 143, 144; and *Hannah*, II, l. 30, in *PW*, ii: 172.

27. See Matthew Henry's comment on this verse in his *Exposition of all the Books of the Old and New Testament*, 6 vols. (1721, 1725).

28. Edward Wells, *An Help for the More Easy and Clear Understanding of the Holy Scriptures*, 6 vols. (1716-28). Wells supplies the necessary cross-reference to Matt. 1: 12, 13.

29. Smart's *Translation* was based on the Psalter in the Book of Common Prayer; this is 145: 13.

30. The metaphor is not, as it might seem to a modern reader, the result of a naïve mistake in natural history; it was possible in Smart's time to think of pearls as gemstones. Matthew Henry, in his comment on Matt. 13: 45-6, tells us that Jesus Christ "is a *Pearl of great Price*, a jewel of inestimable value"; and in his *Dictionary* Samuel Johnson cites John Hill to the effect that pearls are "esteemed of the number of gems by our jewellers."

31. Flowers are also associated by Smart with harmony or tunefulness, as (metaphorically) in the Circumcision hymn: see, for example, *Jubilate Agno*, B508; *Hymns and Spiritual Songs*, 12, 7-8, in *PW*, ii: 55.

32. Elsewhere in this poem it is the jasper that seems to be briefly imaged not only as the likeness of God, as in the vision of St. John (Revelation 4:3), but as God's "stamp" (*Song*, 154, in *PW*, ii: 134).

33. 2 Tim. 2: 19. There is a similar use of the image of the seal of salvation at Rev. 7: 2-4 .

34. *Hymns for the Amusement of Children*, 10: 11, in *PW*, ii: 335; *Hymns and Spiritual Songs*, 22: 11-12, in PW, ii: 75. Aaron's breastplate is described in Exodus, 28: 15-21. In a further variation on this metaphoric theme, "sincerity" is imaged in the *Jubilate* as "*a jewel which is pure and transparent, eternal and inestimable*" (B40)— like Christ, who is the truth, eternal, and without price.

35. T.S. Eliot, "The Metaphysical Poets," in *Selected Prose of T. S. Eliot*, ed. Frank Kermode (N.Y.: Harcourt Brace Jovanovich, 1975), 60.

36. In Thomas Keymer's "Presenting Jeopardy: Language, Authority and the Voice of Smart in *Jubilate Agno*," in *Presenting Poetry: Composition, Publication, Reception*, eds. Howard Erskine-Hill and Richard A. McCabe (Cambridge: Cambridge University Press, 1995), 97-116.

37. Gérard Genette, *Palimpsests: Literature in the Second Degree*, trans. Channa Newman and Claude Doubinsky (Lincoln and London: University of Nebraska Press, 1997), 2.

38. Richards, *Principles*, 290; Roger Lonsdale, ed., *The Poems of Thomas Gray, William Collins, Oliver Goldsmith* (London: Longmans, 1969), 48.
39. George Steiner, "On Difficulty," in *On Difficulty and other Essays* (Oxford: Oxford University Press, 1978), 22.
40. Thomas Newton, ed., *Paradise Lost,* 2 vols. (London, 1749), I. sig. a4^V.
41. *Monthly Review* 31 (1764): 231; *Letters of James Boswell*, ed. C. B. Tinker (Oxford: Oxford University Press, 1924), 39; Richards, *Principles*, 219 n.; Gray, letters to Thomas Wharton, 7 October 1757, and to Horace Walpole, 11 July 1757, in *Correspondence of Thomas Gray*, eds. Paget Toynbee and Leonard Whibley, with corrections and additions by H. W. Starr, 3 vols. (Oxford: Oxford University Press, 1971), 532, 508. Compare Gray's letter to Beattie, about the notes provided in the 1768 edition of his poems (*Correspondence*, 1002). For a compelling recent study of Gray's uses of allusion, see Robert F. Gleckner, *Gray Agonistes: Thomas Gray and Masculine Friendship* (Baltimore: Johns Hopkins University Press, 1997).
42. Hans Frei, *The Eclipse of Biblical Narrative: A Study in Eighteenth and Nineteenth-Century Hermeneutics* (New Haven, CT: Yale University Press, 1974).

CHAPTER 2

"Action and Speaking Are One": A Logological Reading of Smart's Prophetic Rhetoric

EDWARD JOSEPH KATZ

IN HIS STRANGE AND strangely delightful poem *Jubilate Agno,* Christopher Smart presents himself as one called upon to do for humankind the good work of praising God and laying out his plan for the created universe. In fact, Smart argues,

> . . . it is the business of a man gifted in the word to prophecy good.
> FOR *it will be better for England and all the world in a season, as I prophecy this day.* (C57-58)

Elsewhere, I have discussed how Smart "establish[es] a poetics of prophecy as hermeneutic, as a way of interpreting the self in its relation to the world and to God."[1] Implicit in the *Jubilate* is Smart's insistence that the poet's "business"—precisely because he is "gifted in the word"—must be to serve as the voice of redemption for a troubled world, as a means of salvation for a stained humanity. Through his suffering, the poet-prophet can open our eyes to the Divine, can help us to hear the music of God's "heavenly harp in sweetness magnifical and mighty" (A41). Smart's redemptive mission as the poet-prophet can be best understood as a sort of cathartic enterprise, in which, as Kenneth Burke argues, "the victim is a scapegoat, being symbolically or ritually laden by the victimizer with the guilt of the victimizer."[2] Burke's formulation here demonstrates that the poet-prophet allows us to see God because he enables us to see ourselves—as agents of a tragic drama of moral blindness, of a turning-away from the world and the Word.

Burke's theory of dramatism and his conceptions of both victimage and cathartic poetry clarify in precise terms the apocalyptic nature of *Jubilate Agno.* As laid out in *The Grammar of Motives,* dramatism offers a means of reading into the symbolic action of language; it provides a method for rhetorically constituting the subject of discourse, in order to study how language enacts its meaning. If dramatism represents, as William H. Rueckert argues, "a systematic vision of man and the drama of human relations," then Burke's later trajectory shifts toward a theory of the subject grounded in the structure of theology.[3] Thus, in *The Rhetoric of Religion*, Burke describes his project as an exploration in "logology," or "studies in word-about-words," the primary focus of which will be to investigate man's "relationship to the *word* 'God'"; he goes on to define theology as "preeminently *verbal* . . . [as] *words* about 'God.'"[4] Smart's *Jubilate* is profoundly theological—it is "words about 'God'"—and it limns for its reader the way in which the words of the poet can transform one's sense of self and moral responsibility. The prophetic language of the *Jubilate* brings us nearer to what Burke understands as "the Aristotelian concept of 'entelechy' . . . an aim contained within the entity":[5] that is, through Smart's poetry of catharsis, we share in what amounts to "the motive toward perfection that is intrinsic to language."[6] For Smart, then, the poetic *Logos* potentially opens us up to the perfect and transforming divine *Logos*. Through the catharsis of the poet-prophet, we too can find a transcending relief, a sublime moment that at once compels us to acknowledge, and releases us from, our participation in the tragedy of our human condition. Thus, in the *Jubilate*, Smart reveals to us that the rhetoric of the poet-prophet is one that allows us to re-envision our own purpose in the world, our own *telos*, so that we may participate in the redemptive mission that lies beyond the narrow confines of the self.

Smart's *Jubilate* comes to the reader in all its strangeness because its utterances do not seem to operate in the way that poetic language typically does. The reader confronts the page of prophetic poetry unsure of reference and allusion, unable to ascertain with anything more than "provisional certainty" the symbol's range of content. Often, we are unsure, radically, what it is the poet intends, even though we are most often quite sure of what he moves toward in the way of general meaning. A consideration of the textual commentary for the standard edition of Smart's poem presents interesting challenges in this light. His allusions to various occult traditions, mostly found in Fragments B296-694 and C, obscure as much as they illumine. Extensive glossing of proper names, animals, plants, intricate cross-references, and so on, suggests a specificity of intention that one can never determine. The poet's use, for example, of the Linnaean binomial system for identifying plants and animals demonstrates an acquaintance with emerging, but still unfamiliar, scientific developments; thus, Smart's "naming" serves as a way to defamiliarize phenomenal experience. Here, as elsewhere, the reader begins tracing out the various hermeneutic threads, only to have them collapse or lead nowhere in particular. Smart's language, the prophetic "naming" of his vision of the world, erects obstacles to the way meaning conventionally comes to the reader; his naming of things in the world, his construction of prophetic content, is problematically esoteric or uncommon, as is the case in much prophetic work.

In *Language and Symbolic Power,* Pierre Bourdieu helps clarify the dynamics of the *Jubilate,* arguing that the creation of meaning is in fact a "symbolic struggle for the production of common sense or, more precisely for the monopoly of legitimate *naming* as the official—that is, explicit and public—imposition of the legitimate vision of the social world."[7] What is at stake, then, is a writer's power to establish the terms for "common sense," or a communal apprehension of meaning. Bourdieu notes that "official naming" is "a symbolic act of imposition which has on its side all the strength of the collective, of the consensus, of common sense, because it is performed by a delegated agent of the state" or institution; such writers are authorized by a source of power prior to them that exists in the world, such as a church, a government, an academy. Against these writers of the orthodoxy, there is a second class of authors, whose namings arise out of their particular view of the world. As such, Bourdieu observes, their namings are self-reflexive and therefore cannot gain the status of authoritative meaning. These are the writers whose visions of the world are too unlike those that derive from conventional perspectives, that arise out of entirely "uncommon" or idiosyncratic viewpoints. This class of author includes those who stand beyond the boundary of the acceptable or "official" paradigm. No source of power (existing in the world) stands prior to their act of naming—these authors might be the mad and the outcast, but they might also be the writers of conscience who feel the need to invent a new, unauthorized language to convey their meaning. The prophet's dilemma is to authorize the unauthorized, to become himself an authority, when behind him there stands no source of power, no authorizing discourse, to which he can appeal. There are, of course, writers who do accomplish this: William Blake, for example, in his prophetic mythology, or Walt Whitman throughout *Song of Myself,* or William Butler Yeats in *A Vision.* Writers who adopt a prophetic stance, then, bring us over to their way of naming, they carry us across the threshold of the authorized and accepted, into a new way of seeing. And in doing so they enact a drama of transcendence.

How are we to understand this drama, which is specifically a drama of naming? In *The Rhetoric of Religion,* Kenneth Burke argues that language is "a species of action: 'symbolic action,'" and he makes the following distinction:

> I would set "Dramatism" against "Scientism." In so doing, I do not necessarily imply a distrust of science as such. I simply mean that language in

particular and human relations in general can be most directly approached in terms of *action* rather than in terms of *knowledge* (or in terms of "form" rather than in terms of "perceptions"). . . . Either approach ends by encroaching upon the territories claimed by the other. But the *way in* is different, Dramatism beginning with the problems of act, or form, and Scientism beginning with problems of knowledge, or perception.[8]

Burke provides a way of understanding the text of the author whose naming is not reducible to certain knowledge. His idea of dramatism "is based on the obvious *empirical* distinction all men make between their approach to 'people' and their approach to 'things.' 'People' are entities capable of 'symbolic action'; to varying degrees they can be addressed, 'reasoned with,' petitioned, persuaded. 'Things' can but move, or be moved."[9] Dramatism extends to all verbal activities of humankind and is central to his "empirical definition" of man as the "symbol-using animal." In this formulation, Burke demonstrates his critical preference for what can be observed to operate in the text, rather than what might be supposed to operate there. And for a work such as Smart's, this distinction is especially crucial, for so often our knowledge of the text is so open to doubt and revision.

The discourse of dramatism offers further useful distinctions for apprehending the poet- prophet and what he enacts in his text. The dramatistic focus on action "involves *character,* which involves *choice;* and the form of choice attains its perfection in the distinction between Yes and No (between *thou shalt* and *thou shalt not*)."[10] Burke clarifies for us the concept of the poet- prophet as an essentially dramatistic character, using his peculiar language to enact ethical moments, to say "no" to the world that fails itself. In "The Twelve Prophets," Herbert Marks writes that prophetic rhetoric evinces the "ecstatic fury of the negative," which takes aim at iniquity so as to level and annihilate it. The prophet articulates the pathology of the forbidden as it afflicts him and passes judgment upon it.[11] Smart's poet-prophet allows the reader a way to participate in his ecstatic fury, in his act of negation. As the poet "names" the catastrophe about him, he casts the reader as witness to the prophetic agon and so the reader shares in the drama of prophetic condemnation, experiences its persuasive force.[12]

In considering how Smart evokes prophetic language, it is useful to consider prophets and prophetic poetry more generally as we think about the *Jubilate*. Robert Alter, in *The Art of Biblical Poetry,* distinguishes several important qualities of prophetic verse, chief among them its vocative force, its enactment of calling out to the listener in direct address, for the purpose of persuasion. In his discussion of this feature in nonprophetic poetry, as we find it in the Psalms, for example, "the vocative is invariably from man to God, [and] the one addressed is really not an object of rhetorical manipulation."[13] In the prophetic form, and especially as Smart deploys it, the vocative force of speech arises with the potential of rhetorical persuasion, and this occurs in more than one direction. In the opening lines of Fragment A, the poet-prophet calls out to humankind, as he himself has been called:

> Rejoice in God, O ye Tongues: give the glory to the Lord, and the Lamb.
> Nations, and languages, and every Creature, in which is the breath of Life.
> Let man and beast appear before him, and magnify his name together. (A1-3)

This invocation, which recollects for us the vision of the redeemed in Revelations 7:9-10, commands us to rejoice and give glory to God, and to understand that all creation is the breath of divine spirit. Then there is the prophet's call for Christ to give him the power of the artist to praise: *"For I pray the Lord Jesus to translate my Magnificat into verse and represent it"* (B43). So the prophet's vocative role is to address God for humankind and for himself as God's voice on earth; his calling is to bring us before God, and to bring God before himself so that he may represent for us God's powerful mercy.[14] And finally he petitions God as an intercessor, so that God might care for us in our time of need, as he does in the following lines for his children:

> Let Ibhar rejoice with the Pochard—a child born in prosperity is the
>   chiefest blessing of peace.
> *For I bless God from my retreat at* CANBURY, *as it was the place of the na-*
>   *tivity of my children.*
> Let Elisha rejoice with Cantharis—God send bread and milk to the chil-
>   dren.
> *For I pray God to give them the food which I cannot earn for them any oth-*
>   *erwise than by prayer.* (B75-76)

The vocative nature of prophetic poetry, to return to Burke, allows us to see the poet-prophet more clearly in dramatistic terms, as a character or agent, whose calling or purpose is always foregrounded, always about choice and therefore, symbolically, always ethical, even if the meaning of the prophetic utterance itself is only dimly grasped in its literal sense.

Since prophetic discourse comes to us in the form of vocation, we must examine the matter of the poet's auditors. As opposed to other forms of biblical language, Alter observes, prophetic poetry "is devised as a form of direct address to a historically real audience."[15] But for Alter, this is complicated by the fact that "it is not, in formal terms, the prophet who is speaking but God who is speaking through the prophet's quotation." In other words, even though the prophet's audience is historical, his "prophetic poetry is represented speech rather than historical speech." Even if, to borrow from Burke, we are to imagine the scene of Smart's prophetic expression to be eighteenth-century London, we must see that "the form of the speech exhibits the historical indeterminacy of the language of poetry."[16] This, partly, is what Smart captures when he writes, *"For I am the Lord's News-Writer—the scribe-evangelist"* (B327). In *Mania and Literary Style,* Clement Hawes explains that in the tropes of "news-writing" and "scribe-evangelism"—which recuperate the low literary form of journalism by attaching it to the godly work of spreading the Word—Smart's poetry "mediates between popular and elite concepts of cultural authority: it claims the alternate authority of divine inspiration for something relegated to the cultural margins" (Hawes, 135). The prophet is a human being writing to other human beings; his language is the language of humanity, but it is filled with something more, and so it seems strange to his auditor. As both Alter and Hawes observe, the poet-prophet sees himself as a vehicle for divine meaning, a bridge between God and the world. This desire to cross thresholds, spiritual and moral, operates out of the poet's position on the margins of culture; and the historical indeterminacy of prophetic discourse gives it power as symbolic action. The prophet's speech, as an ethical act, is now authorized, or validated, by the universally applicable nature of its status as symbolic action.

The paradox of the historically particular audience and historically indeterminate speech reveals itself especially in the poem's difficulty for the modern reader. For example, the pairing of biblical names with "unclean" creatures, as Karina Williamson comments in her introduction to the poem, refers to the superiority of the Christian ethos to Jewish law, as Smart concludes the series with an association to Peter's baptism of the "unclean" Gentile: "Let Cornelius with the Swine bless God, which purifyeth all things for the poor."[17] Such broad movements in the poem are easy to interpret, but within an individual thematic constellation specific associations are more difficult to account for. Thus, Smart pairs Tobias with his dog in blessing Charity (from the Book of Tobit), as an expression of the centrality of faith, vigilance, and friendship to the Christian life (A56). But in the next line he has Anna, Tobias's mother, "bless God with the Cat," without offering any means to ascertain the local, internal association. The same sort of thing happens, in Fragment D, when Smart uses names taken out of periodical obituary lists.[18] At times, names seem chosen for the intention of punning or word association, but the dramatistic purpose of Fragment D is to effect temporally a change of scene, to bring the prophetic discourse again into the modern world in a new way. Viewed dramatistically, Smart's prophetic speech crosses time to join the naming of the past with signs of the present; thus, when we observe with Alter that prophetic poetry is historically indeterminate, what we are saying is that it is trans-historical and therefore symbolically expresses the idea of the universal: the scene of Smart's discourse is both the age of biblical prophets *and* the age of Enlightenment—it is then *and* now. The trans-historical quality of the prophet's rhetoric engenders its power, as symbolic action, to move readers.[19]

In the *Jubilate,* then, the meaning of a passage often places itself in tension with meaning at the level of the line. The closer we approach to the line and its significance, the further we move away from the poem's symbolic action, which recedes under the cloud of the line's indeterminacy. But even dynamics such as the one Smart shapes here possesses a dramatistic purpose if considered as symbolic action. For this tension gives Smart's prophetic verse the rhetorical quality of what Alter calls "oracular vision."[20] In the Bible, the prophet's visions are the translated speech of God, directed through the prophet to his audience. These visions, Alter points out, frequently involve significant narration and inspired interpretation, often having to do with working out the meaning of natural or supernatural catastrophe in the context of mankind's sinfulness. In Smart's formulation of this rhetorical feature, the strangeness and obscurity of associations within the line or between two or more specific lines represent symbolically the oracular quality of divinely inspired vision; it portrays the otherness of divine speech, offers a literary simulation of ecstatic utterance.

God's scribe, in his ecstatic strangeness, exists on the social, cultural, and political margins. In a powerfully historical illustration of this stance on the boundary, Hawes documents "Smart's dialogue with an evangelical enthusiasm" whose rhetoric occupied the borders of official Anglicanism.[21] Smart's religious interests included reform of the liturgy, a fascination with street-preaching, a desire to engage faith as an expression of both deep personal experience and immediate political concern.[22] For Smart, the poet-prophet serves a sacrificial role: "*For I have adventured myself in the name of the Lord, and he hath mark'd me for his own*" (B21). The poet has the sign of God upon him: he is singled out as the heterodox. His willingness to "*be called a fool for the sake of Christ*" (B51) rhetorically clarifies his status as reformer, when viewed from the vantage of normative Anglican belief: to the orthodox, reformers can only be fools who fail to understand truth.

And yet, the prophet's impulse to transform is his vocation. He has been graced to understand the calling of God and for this offers praise:

> *For I bless the thirteenth of August, in which I had the grace to obey the voice of Christ in my conscience.*
>
> *For I bless the thirteenth of August, in which I was willing to run all hazards for the sake of the name of the Lord.* (B49-50)

The poet's hunger "to run all hazards" casts him as God's warrior. Here, the effect of the rhetoric is to align the reader with the prophet in a common desire to "obey the voice of Christ," to rise to the demands of conscience. In rhetorical moments such as these, Smart transforms the *Jubilate*'s strangeness of phrasing and structure: as we saw earlier, the opacity of the poem's language is itself a symbolic act, one that acquires power for the prophetic work. The poem is not of this world, its language argues; the force of the prophet's vision is the force of God. And the reader must move beyond the orthodox reference points that condition his understanding of divine truth.

The language of the *Jubilate,* then, enacts its meaning in part by rhetorically structuring perspective into its argument. The poet-prophet understands that to the world, whose ideas are shaped by convention, his words ring of madness:

> *FOR I pray the Lord JESUS that cured the LUNATICK to be merciful to all my brethren and sisters in these houses.*
>
> *For they work me with their harping-irons, which is a barbrous instrument, because I am more unguarded than others.* (B123-24)

The *Let* phrases that accompany these lines, as Williamson observes in her editorial notes to the *Jubilate,* form the introduction of a series of names from the New Testament, beginning with the twelve apostles whose names are linked with various fishes, as an expression of Christ's exhortation to Peter and Andrew, in Matthew 4:19, to "Follow me, and I will make you fishers of men." In imitation of Christ, the prophet Smart will also become a fisher of men, but he knows that, like Christ himself, he presents to us a new paradigm to stand against the old. His prophetic work is one of regeneration, of renewal, but he knows that others will see it as lunacy. Smart reinforces this matter of perspective, of the old over against the new, in the image of the "harping-iron," which is connected the act of fishing in its association with the Whale in the *Let* phrase of B124, but also to modern methods of treatment Smart encountered in the asylum.[23] Two arguments, then, are conflated into one rhetorical operation: first, the prophet stands out against others in the strangeness of his perceptions about the world; and, second, in his reference to the technology of the madhouse, he opposes the modern world generally and applied science in particular, which are both characterized as barbaric.

Smart modifies his critique of modernity in the lines cited earlier by way of stressing his attitude toward the cruelty he encounters. The poet-prophet reveals that he is "unguarded" in offering his experience to us, sincere in helping us to understand his pain and how it brought him to his prophetic critique.[24] Elsewhere, too, he comments on the power and virtue of honesty, sincerity, and purity (B25, B40, B287-88). For the poet-prophet, who by definition stands on the edge of human affairs, authority rests upon maintaining an honesty in the face of a fallen and hostile world, a harmonizing sincerity in the face of divisiveness and hypocrisy:

> Let Shelumiel rejoice with Olor, who is of a goodly savour, and the very
> look of him harmonizes the mind.
> *For my existimation is good even amongst the slanderers and my memory*
> *shall arise for a sweet savour unto the Lord.* (B3)

Williamson's gloss on these lines explains that Shelumiel was one of the princes who made burnt offerings to God at the dedication of the altar (Numbers 7:36) and that the Old Testament formula describes such offerings as "of a good (sweet) savour." The passage is about sacrifice and reputation ("existimation") bringing to the individual status among others. The prophet stands out as authoritative and good, even to those whose desires and agendas contravene his own. And his sacrifice brings forth intellectual and moral harmony out of the division and decadence of modernity.

The operation of the prophetic discourse in the *Jubilate* is associative, then, in that the poet approaches the object of his critique from within multiple, and often ostensibly divergent, contexts. For instance, Smart spends much of his prophetic energy, as did his Old Testament forebears, in attacking the property-oriented materialism of his time:

> Let Lazarus rejoice with Torpedo, who chills the life of the assailant
> through his staff.
> *For Charity is cold in the multitude of possessions, and the rich are cov-*
> *etous of their crumbs.* (B154)

Material wealth numbs us to the pain of the poor and traps us in the desire for increase. In casting our lot with the world of things, we are choosing the fallen, the "sinking object"; we are choosing impermanence and death:

> *For avaricious men are subtle like the soul seperated from the body.*
> *For their attention is on a sinking object which perishes.* (B336-37)

These lines equate acquisitive desire with man's fallen or dualistic nature, an association reinforced by the reference to subtlety, which takes us back to the serpent of Genesis 3:1 and the fracture of Edenic unity.

The poet-prophet extends his assault on modernity by calling into question a materialism of a different order, that is, the foundations of a materialist understanding of nature, as advanced in Newton's *Principia* (1687). In the For lines of B160-63, Smart rewrites the first five of Newton's principles:

> *For MATTER is the dust of the Earth, every atom of which is the life.*
> *For MOTION is as the quantity of life direct, and that which hath not motion, is resistance.*
> *For Resistance is not of GOD, but he—hath built his works upon it.*
> *For the Centripetal and Centrifugal forces are GOD SUSTAINING and DIRECTING.*

The critique of materialism in these lines opposes classical and Christian idealism to the mechanistic worldview arising out of the scientific revolution. It is a critique of the materialistic worldview that produced the sort of medical treatment we saw Smart vilify earlier, which addresses the mind as though it were a thing to be reshaped. Of course, Newton believed that his mechanistic universe involved God and his divine will. But for Smart, Newtonian materialism represents a retreat from God's presence in the world, a rejection of his efficacy in nature. In the lines earlier, the poet-prophet assumes the role of the Lord's interpreter, reinscribing the principles of modern material science with the sustaining and directive power of the Divine. Likewise, Smart censures Locke's model of the mind and his insistence that there are no innate ideas in the mind[25]: "*For Lock supposes that an human creature, at a given time may be an atheist i.e. without God, by the folly of his doctrine concerning innate ideas*" (B396). Here, the poet charges that Lockean psychology—that is, the modern understanding of mind—carries with it, by logical extension, an abandonment of God.

In such passages, Smart views the poet as the last line of defense against the cumulative and encroaching decadence of natural philosophy. The prophet-warrior derives his power from God's Word:

> *For the word of God is a sword on my side—no matter what other weapon a stick or a straw.* (B20)
> *For I have the blessing of God in the three POINTS of manhood, of the pen, of the sword, and of chivalry.*

> *For I am inquisitive in the Lord, and defend the philosophy of the scripture*
> *against vain deceit.* (B129-30)

As Williamson notes in her commentary to B130, Smart aligns himself with Paul's admonition, in Colossians 2:8, to shun "the tradition of men" and "the rudiments of the world," in favor of Christ. After the manner of St. George, with the "whole armour" of the Lord upon him (B95), the poet views himself literally as the bearer of Christ, slaying the dragon of atheism and false doctrine: "*For CHRISTOPHER must slay the Dragon with a PHEON's head*" (B58).

Whether engaging his agent-role as defender or as madman, the poet-prophet shapes his verse out of what Alter identifies as a "rhetoric of entrapment," in which the prophet's listeners are caught up in their guilt.[26] Alter observes that, in prophetic poetry of the Old Testament, this entrapment is suggested by observable patterns involving constellations of images and keywords signifying "sin and its metaphorical equivalents (sickness, defilement) and for destruction (burning, overthrowing, and elsewhere, smashing, shattering, rending, and so forth)." This rhetorical patterning creates a structure of "thematic intensification" that overtakes the listener or reader. Smart extends this rhetorical structure by placing himself within the boundaries of entrapment:

> Let Elizur rejoice with the Partridge, who is a prisoner of state and is proud
> of his keepers.
> *For I am not without authority in my jeopardy, which I derive inevitably*
> *from the glory of the name of the Lord.* (B1)

Commenting on these and the following lines, Karina Williamson writes, "In the FOR verses, Smart takes on the mantle of an OT prophet, in captivity, like Ezekiel, looking forward, like Isaiah, in time of war to peace and salvation through Christ." The term *jeopardy,* she notes, commonly assumes in Smart's work the meaning of "captivity."[27] The poet places himself in a sympathetic relation to his audience: both are imprisoned, though the meaning of this fact may be different for each of them. For Smart, even more than for the prophets of the Old Testament, the rhetoric of entrapment forms the basis for common feeling between the prophet and humankind. He can speak with the knowledge of his auditors' suffering, or can take them by surprise because he understands the blinding power of temptation. Still more, the rhetoric of entrapment in the *Jubilate* reaches out to God, as well, where, in an echo of Mark 3:21, Smart identifies his condition with that of Christ: "*For I am under the same accusation with my Saviour—for they said, he is besides himself*" (B151). Accused with his Savior, Smart joins him on the margins. As the multitude come forth to lay hold of Christ, so too, in effect, they lay hold of his scribe, his witness to humanity. Both Christ and his prophet are beside themselves, divided from those about them, and it is the prophet's task to bridge the gap. Against the sinking objects and empty doctrine of modern world, the poet-prophet asserts, *"I wish to God and desire towards the most High, which is my policy"* (B156).

A dramatistic reading of the *Jubilate* centers on the symbolic action of the prophet confronting what he evokes as an increasingly secular, and therefore fallen, modern world. The scene he encounters has placed both him and his God under "the same accusation"; it is a world that, in its deepest philosophical and material structures, responds to prophetic concern by declaring it needs neither God nor prophet. The rhetoric of the prophet's verse shows him symbolically coming to his spiritual responsibility through pain and confusion in his madness, through sacrificial desire and confidence as he puts on the armor of the Lord. Prophetic rhetoric compels us to acknowledge the poet's sacrifice, his zeal to risk himself, "to run all hazards for the sake of the name of the Lord" (B50). Because his speech is dramatistic in its conception—because, in Smart's words, *"Action and Speaking are one"* (B562)—it symbolically represents or enacts the sacrifice he willingly assumes.

The symbolic meaning of the sacrificial victim is central to understanding Smart's idea of the poet-prophet and it is most clearly approached in its formal features through Kenneth Burke's conception of victimage and poetic catharsis. In *Language as Symbolic Action,* Burke defines catharsis in terms of purification and the role of the victim, for it "involves fundamentally purgation by the imitation of victimage." Burke finds "our paradigm for catharsis" in "a play that produced in the audience a unitary tragic response regardless of personal discord."[28]

In the *Jubilate,* the uniqueness of his discourse, the idiosyncrasy of the language he deploys, seems to express the poet's isolation from those around him and to evoke the radical individualism of his project. Smart wants to counter the rationalist and empirical ethos of his time with an enthusiastic rhetoric.[29] The poet-prophet himself is this cathartic agent and his symbolic act is to create a bond, a dialogical connection, between himself and the reader in order to bring the reader across the abyss to God. The scene of his action is no longer eighteenth-century London at all, but the field of the poet's and the reader's respective spiritual battles, the divided world of their *agon.*[30] In Burke's words: "Viewed as a sheerly terministic, or symbolic function, that's what transcendence is: the building of a *terministic bridge* whereby one realm is *transcended* by being viewed *in terms of* a realm 'beyond' it."[31] Victimage, for Burke, is the "principle of transformation" that symbolically makes transcendence possible; and this principle, operating in terms of a "beyond," serves in ways similar to "the 'priestly' function, in that it pontificates, or 'builds a bridge' between disparate realms. And insofar as things here and now are treated in terms of a 'beyond,' they thereby become infused or inspirited by the addition of a *new or further dimension.*"[32] As words about God, the prophetic discourse in *Jubilate* builds a bridge between heaven and earth: by engaging the poet's experience the reader dramatistically "crosses over" from a spiritually troubled and morally fraught condition to one of harmony.

Smart symbolically renders the drama of sacrificial victimage, through his dual status as the mad prophet who suffers and as the warrior-prophet who adventures all; and through his role as scribe for God qua artist-agent, he becomes a vehicle for transcendence. At several points in the *Jubilate,* Smart describes God as an artist or musician:

> Let David bless with the Bear—The beginning of victory to the Lord—to the Lord the perfection of excellence—Hallelujah from the heart of God, and from the hand of the artist inimitable, and from the echo of the heavenly harp in sweetness magnifical and mighty. (A41)

> *For god the father Almighty plays upon the harp of stupendous magnitude and melody.*
> *For innumerable Angels fly out at every touch and his tune is a work of creation.*
> *For at that time malignity ceases and the devils themselves are at peace.*
> (B246-48)

The music and word ("Hallelujah") of God, which come from his power ("hand") and from his feeling ("heart") for creation, themselves become an ordering principle ("melody"). Smart describes divine art in the language of the enlightenment sublime as "of stupendous magnitude," "in sweetness magnifical and mighty": it is efficacious and transformative, for it stifles evil and subdues the wicked. God's art, his voice and his Word, are in fact creation itself.

The poet-prophet shares in the divine power of the Word, because *"my talent is to give an impression upon words by punching, that when the reader casts his eye upon 'em, he takes up the image from the mould which I have made"* (B404). In the note to this line, Karina Williamson observes that Smart, in his introduction to *The Works of Horace* (1767), considers "impression" to be a talent bestowed on the poet by God, whereby ideas can be powerfully and accurately conveyed to the reader.[33] But, interestingly, the images of impression, punching, and molding also appear in the discourse of Lockean associationism, particularly as they relate to sense perception.[34] Smart claims the power to shape our minds like his, with the proviso that such power arises not merely out of similarities in the way individuals' minds and bodies are constituted, but out of God's immanence. This argument unfolds like the one he used in reinscribing Newtonian physics with the divine spirit and will. So we are constitutionally constructed for sympathy, by the efficacious grace of God, and this grace is symbolically figured by the poet-prophet in such terms as "voice" or "sound":

> For SOUND is propagated in the spirit and in all directions. . . .
> For a man speaks HIMSELF from the crown of his head to the sole of his feet. (B226-28)
>
> * * *
>
> For the VOICE is from the body and the spirit—and is a body and a spirit. (B239)

Voice and sound, both of which begin with the Lord, are the means—or as Burke puts it, the agency—for connecting humankind to the heavens, body to the spirit. When the poet speaks, he speaks himself completely from top to bottom, from body and spirit. Smart goes on to say that "ECHO is the soul of the voice" (B235) and that "a good voice hath its Echo with it and it is attainable by much supplication" (B237): it is prayer—words addressed to and about God—that brings us into relation to our spirituality, that establishes a sympathetic connection to the Divine, that makes us see that our bodies and our spirits are not of necessity divided, for both are holy.

Smart conceives of language itself as divine and exalting:

> For all good words are from GOD, and all others are cant. . . .
> For I am enabled by my ascent and the Lord haith [sic] raised me above my peers. (B85- 86).

Moreover, he carries this idea down to the smallest unit of the word, the letter, in two sequences (B513-61) where he invests the alphabet itself with meaning, often spiritual in nature: thus, "A is the beginning of learning and the door of heaven" (B513), "E is eternity" (B517), and "R is rain, or thus reign, or thus rein" (B554), this last example especially reflecting a notion of language that embodies a symbolic function for things in nature ("rain"), for ideas of the sociopolitical realm ("reign," as in justice and governance) and for moral ideas ("rein" as in spiritual control).[35] Smart also offers a series on the Hebrew *lamed,* which "*signifies GOD by himself is on the fibre of some leaf in every Tree*" and exists everywhere throughout nature (B477-91). And finally, he conducts a series of lines "on flowers," which refer both to the natural thing and to metaphors and other "*flowers of language*" (B497-510): "*flowers,*" he observes, "*are the poetry of Christ,*" whose "*right names . . . are yet in heaven. God make gard'ners better nomenclators*" (B506, 509; see also Chapter 12). The prophet, who has the God-granted power to name, uses the agency of his inspired verse to make us "better nomenclators." His naming itself is filled with the spirit of God and the force of creation.

Smart's rhetorical strategies illuminate the nature of language and what it accomplishes as symbolic action, especially when it has to do with theology, or "words about God." As Burke contends, language itself is profoundly about transcendence: our words for things in nature soon become words about things in conceptual realms having to do with human affairs or the affairs of God. Thus, Burke gives us the example of "spirit" in "its natural meaning, as 'breath,'" which moves "analogically . . . to connotations that flowered in its usage as term for the supernatural.[36] Language takes us from one realm to the next, allowing us to enact symbolic movements from naturalistic to transcendent experience; language itself represents what Burke sees as a technical or formal transcendence, which can be deployed—as Smart does—to enact another sort of transcendence in his role as the poet-prophet. For Smart, the prophetic *Logos* dramatistically enacts what is implicit or potential in our very natures as "symbol-using animals." His *Jubilate* makes visible, or incarnates, the Divine *Logos* through the rhetoric of prophecy and acquaints us with redemption as "entelechy," a transformative power always residing within us.

NOTES

1. Edward J. Katz, "Transcendent Dialogic: Madness, Prophecy, and the Sublime in Christopher Smart," in *Compendious Conversations: The Method of Dialogue in the Early Enlightenment,* ed. Kevin L. Cope (Frankfurt am Main: Peter Lang), 151-64.

2. Kenneth Burke, "A Dramatistic View of the Origins of Language," *Quarterly Journal of Speech* 38 (October, 1952), 246.

3. William H. Rueckert, *Kenneth Burke and the Drama of Human Relations* (Berkeley: University of California Press, 1982), 228. For a discussion of dramatism and the subject, see also Robert Wess, *Kenneth Burke: Rhetoric, Subjectivity, Postmodernism* (Cambridge: Cambridge University Press, 1996), especially chapter 6, "*A Grammar of Motives:* The Rhetorical Constitution of the Subject," 136-85. Wess reminds us of Burke's comparison of dramatism and logology to ontology and epistemology, which casts logology as the "theoretical center" to the method of dramatism (234). In "The Rhetoric of Allegory: Burke and Augustine," David Damrosch concurs with Wess, observing that "Burke finds a natural grounding for his dramatism in religious experience: the view of reading a text as performance can be fruitfully assimilated to the religious view of God's language as performative" (*The Legacy of Kenneth Burke,* eds. Herbert W. Simons and Trevor Melia [Madison: University of Wisconsin Press, 1989], 225).

4. Kenneth Burke, *The Rhetoric of Religion: Studies in Logology* (Berkeley: University of California Press, 1970), vi.

5. Ibid., 246.

6. William Rueckert, "Some of the Many Kenneth Burkes," in *Representing Kenneth Burke: Selected Papers from the English Institute,* eds. Hayden White and Margaret Brose, new series, no. 6 (Baltimore, MD: Johns Hopkins University Press, 1982), 15-16.

7. Pierre Bourdieu, *Language and Symbolic Power,* ed. John B. Thompson, trans. Gino Raymond and Matthew Adamson (Cambridge, MA: Harvard University Press, 1991), 239.

8. Kenneth Burke, Rhetoric of Religion, 38-39.

9. Ibid., 40.

10. Ibid., 41.

11. Herbert Marks, "The Twelve Apostles," *The Literary Guide to the Bible,* eds. Robert Alter and Frank Kermode (Cambridge, MA.: Harvard University Press, 1987), 223-24.

12. See Kenneth Burke, "Terministic Screens," *Language as Symbolic Action: Essays on Life, Literature, and Method* (Berkeley: University of California Press, 1966), 45: "The dramatistic view of language, in terms of 'symbolic action,' is exercised about the necessarily *suasive* nature of even the most the most unemotional scientific nomenclatures. . . . Even if any given terminology is a *reflection* of reality, by its very nature as a terminology it must be a *selection* of reality; and to this extent it must function also as a *deflection* of reality." The poet-prophet's *purpose as agent,* in Burke's sense of these words, is to move humankind to engage the symbolic action of prophetic revelation, to come to understand this prophetic "selection of reality." Burke works out his five key terms of dramatism—act, scene, agent, agency, purpose—in *The Grammar of Motives* (Englewood Cliffs, NJ: Prentice-Hall, 1952). See also, Rueckert, "Some of the Many Kenneth Burkes," 9-13. For a useful discussion of prophetic rhetoric, free agency, and persuasion, see Meir Sternberg, *The Poetics of Biblical Narrative: Ideological Literature and the Drama of Reading* (Bloomington: Indiana University Press, 1985), 157-58.

13. Robert Alter, *The Art of Biblical Poetry* (N.Y.: Basic Books, 1985): 140. Prophets, however, do address God with the force of persuasive rhetoric: see, for example, Daniel 10:14-19, in which the prophet persuades God that the plight of Jerusalem and the Israelites in captivity has brought others around them to hold God in lower esteem; in Daniel 10:20-27, God sends Gabriel to bring the prophet a vision of Jerusalem restored to future glory.

14. See Geoffrey H. Hartman, "Christopher Smart's 'Magnificat': Towards a Theory of Representation," in *The Fate of Reading* (Chicago, IL: University of Chicago Press, 1975), 75. Hartman notes that "Representation implies that the subject cannot be adequately 'present' in his own person or substance, so that advocacy is called for." This formulation of the prophet's vocative utterance is very useful, for it clarifies that it is the prophet who presents to us power of God, which we cannot yet see; it is prophetic "representation" that advocates for, or calls forward, the presence of God.

15. Alter, *Art of Biblical Poetry,* 140. See also John Barton, "History and Rhetoric in the Prophets," *The Bible as Rhetoric: Studies in Biblical Persuasion and Credibility,* ed. Martin Warner (London: Routledge, 1990), 53: "the classical prophets did not receive their message of coming judgement as a revelation, but arrived at it as the conclusion to a moral analysis of the contemporary social and political scene. Far from being visionaries filled with a non-rational foreboding, they were clear-sighted commentators on the society of their day."

16. Alter, *Biblical Poetry,* 140-41.

17. Karina Williamson, introduction, in *PW,* I: xxv. For Peter's baptism of Cornelius and the vision instructing him that no man should be turned away as unclean, see Acts 10.

18. Williamson, introduction, in *PW,* I: xxvii. See also Arthur Sherbo, "Christopher Smart, Reader of Obituaries," *Modern Language Notes* 71 (1956): 177-82.

19. See Paul Ricoeur, *Time and Narrative,* trans. Kathleen McLaughlin and David Pellauer, 2 vols. (Chicago, IL: University of Chicago Press, 1985), vol. 2, 15. Ricoeur conveys a similar conception of the transhistorical in his idea of traditionality: "Traditionality is that irreducible phenomenon that allows criticism to stand between the contingency of a mere history of genres, or types, or works arising from the narrative function, and an eventual logic of possible narratives that would escape history. The order that can be extricated from this self-structuring of tradition is neither historical nor ahistorical but rather 'transhistorical'.... Even if this order includes breaks, or sudden changes of paradigms, these breaks are not themselves simply forgotten. . . .They too are part of the phenomenon of tradition and its cumulative style." Ricoeur's formulation of traditionality and the trans-historical captures the cumulative or associative dynamics of the *Jubilate* and of prophetic discourse in general: the ability of the prophet's rhetoric to critique both his time and ours is what enables him, in Bourdieu's terms, to authorize or legitimate his vision of the world. For a discussion of the transhistoricity of Burke's dramatism, see Wess, *Kenneth Burke,* 131-33.

20. For a discussion of oracular vision in scriptural prophecy, see Alter, *Biblical Poetry,* 137-39.

21. Hawes, 20.

22. Ibid., 131. Hawes argues that "though Smart did not intend to stray from the Church of England, he nevertheless belonged to a social and doxological borderland." See esp. pp. 129-33, for a treatment of Smart's rhetoric and the ideas advanced in mid-century Methodism. Hawes's account clarifies Smart's self-conception as not so much a revolutionary, but as an agent who desires to transform the existing orthodoxy.

23. See Williamson's note to B124 and her reference to Alexander Cruden's observation that, "if the Prisoners in this Madhouse refuse to take what is ordered them, there is a terrible Instrument put into their mouths to hold down their tongues, and to force the physick down their throats." Cruden's account is found in *The London Citizen Exceedingly Injured* (London, 1739), 7. For a discussion of asylum conditions in the mid- to

late-eighteenth century, see Roy Porter, *A Social History of Madness: The World Through the Eyes of the Insane* (N.Y.: Weidenfeld and Nicolson, 1987), 16-21, 167-88. Porter observes that medical models for treating madness were "organic," designed to cure the mind by addressing the infirmities of the body: treatments included drug therapies and mechanical approaches, such as electric shocks, restraints, solitary confinement, and forced tranquilization. Segregation in the asylum protected society from the insane, but allowed the problems of the afflicted to be more effectively addressed. The aim of treatment, Porter explains, is to render the insane normal, rational. For a discussion of the division of psychiatry into somatic and psychic (or moral) schools, see H. C. Erik Midelfort, "Madness and Civilization in Early Modern Europe: A Reappraisal of Michel Foucault," *After the Reformation: Essays in Honor of J. H. Hexter,* ed. Barbara C. Malament (Philadelphia: University of Pennsylvania Press, 1980), 256-58.

24. For treatment of the "sincerity topos," see Hawes, 222-25.

25. For his refutation of innate ideas, see John Locke, *Essay Concerning Human Understanding,* ed. Peter H. Nidditch (Oxford: Oxford University Press, 1975), I.i, 43-103.

26. Alter, *Biblical Poetry,* 144.

27. For a more detailed discussion of Smart's "jeopardy" theme, see Hawes, 155-78; and Tom Keymer, "Presenting Jeopardy: Language, Authority, and the Voice of Smart in *Jubilate Agno,*" in *Presenting Poetry: Composition, Publication, Reception: Essays in Honour of Ian Jack,* eds. Howard Erskine-Hill and Richard A. McCabe (Cambridge: Cambridge University Press, 1995), 97-116.

28. Burke, *Language as Symbolic Action,* 186.

29. See Hawes, 158. Hawes notes that Smart's is "an enthusiasm that challenges, above all, the eighteenth-century privatization of 'madness.'" In this sense, Smart's project, interestingly, is to deploy enthusiasm, a discourse of radical individualism, to get beyond or bridge the alienating gap between what Hawes identifies as the private and public spheres of experience for the Enlightenment individual. See also Chapter 10.

30. For a discussion of prophetic sympathy, an openness to the presence of God and humankind in their respective suffering, see Abraham J. Heschel, *The Prophets* (N.Y.: Jewish Publication Society, 1962), 307-23 and especially his examination of the "dialogical structure" of religious sympathy, 309-10.

31. Burke, *Language as Symbolic Action,* 187.

32. Ibid., 189-90.

33. See Christopher Smart, preface to *The Works of Horace, Translated into Verse, PW,* v, 6-7.
34. See, for example, Locke, *Essay,* IX 11-1v, 143-44.
35. See Burke, *Rhetoric of Religion,* 14-15, for discussion of the "four realms to which words may refer."
36. Ibid., 8.

CHAPTER 3

Syntax and Paradigm in Smart's
Hymns for the Amusement of Children

MARK BOOTH

THE POEMS THAT CHRISTOPHER SMART published at the very end of his life as "hymns for the amusement of children" are not hymns, in the singing sense (Marcus Walsh and Karina Williamson, the Oxford editors, argue the same negative with respect to his *Hymns and Spiritual Songs* for adults published six years earlier).[1] They may not at first seem calculated for anyone's amusement—though Isaac Watts had used the word too in his prefatory defense of his own *Divine Songs for Children,* as did Smart in the titles of two less serious compilations. There is no question that there is writing to, for, and about children in this poetry, but there is a puzzle in this term of the title too, because the verse is surprisingly challenging. Walsh and Williamson write, "Even at the surface level the hymns are not always simple. Smart sometimes forgets to 'sink' his language to a child's level, and his clipped, allusive manner can itself make for local difficulties."[2]

They go on to agree with Donald Davie that there is a lofty "*naivete,* in the best sense" in Smart's religious verse—hence here—and by implication there is then a certain propriety in the aim to address children. That Smart had acquired a pure and defiantly unworldly spiritual vision, as accessible to children as to adults, is a reasonable claim; the fact remains that, by comparison for example with Watts's *Songs*, Smart's verses are sometimes difficult to untangle into prose paraphrase—not impossible, but not immediately easy. We could conjecture that Smart had been alienated from his own children too long to have a good idea of what we would call today "developmental appropriateness" of reading difficulty. On the other hand, we might remember that he had been gracefully adept throughout his career in adopting many tones for many occasions in his verse, and that he had been immersed for a good while in the projects of his father-in-law John Newbery, the first great entrepreneur of children's literature.

I wish to pose the question of the significance of these poems being sometimes hard to read. One begins, "O Sweet—attentive to the pray'r, / Ye forward hope and stave despair. . . ." If we have seen that the title is "Mercy," we have something to go on, but some alert adults may nevertheless hesitate before deciding just what parts of speech one, two, or three words in the second line are. Another says, "If I of honesty suspend / My judgment, making doubt, / I have a good domestic friend, / That soon shall point it out."

When we have read the first two lines, do we know whether a good or a bad thing has been postulated? "'Tis in the spirit that attire, / Th' investiture of saints in heav'n. / Those robes of intellectual fire, / Which to the great elect are given." How much does it help to know this is the beginning of "Elegance"? "Honour" begins, "In Man it is the truth affirm'd, / Mean craft and guile withstood, / And variously by various term'd, / Is both by grace and blood"—"is both by" surely takes a moment for most readers to pin down. None of these are deep obscurities, but as passages of children's verse they are sharply different from the verse of Smart's main predecessor in the genre, Isaac Watts: "Let dogs delight to bark and bite, / For God hath made them so. . . . But, children, you should never let / Such angry passions rise. . . ."[3]

Professional close readers of literature have affirmed for much of this century that literature is full of ambiguities, or more boldly that discourse itself has inevitable discontinuities and contradictions. It has become clear that ingenuity can show complexity everywhere, and so nothing is established merely by demonstrating ambiguities in these poems. The question raised here is why, in this carefully polished writing, where many references, manipulations of point of view, rigorously disciplined singsong meter and rhyme, and forceful monosyllabic diction all testify to a considered project of writing for children, are the lines sometimes relatively hard to read for their paraphrasable sense?

The question can be usefully pursued in terms familiar to theoretical linguistics, the terms that analyze language into the dimensions of *syntagmatic* and *paradigmatic*.[4] Syntax carries a thread of narrative or argumentation forward, and constitutes the "horizontal" links from one word to another to build sequential signification. Words are chosen, in theory, from among alternatives, to fit into that syntagmatic chain. In obvious practical terms they are chosen from among near-synonyms, but in a wider sense they are chosen from an indefinite array of signifiers related by similarity, opposition, inflectional variation, and so on, verging out to the most tenuous associations. All these terms not chosen can be pictured as floating outside the signifying chain of language in dimensions of paradigm (for example all the words related to a given word by variations in a grammatical paradigm) or of association, hence paradigmatic or associative. Roman Jakobson remarked that "the poetic function projects the principle of equivalence from the axis of selection onto the axis of combination."[5] The implication is that the other-than-syntactic connections that words have to one another in poetry fall onto, and can complicate and even displace, the sense-making logic of poetic syntax.

These analytic terms offer, I believe, insight into the question of how Smart's last poems resist casual reading. The Oxford editors help scholarly readers make their ways through these poems by extensive documentation of allusions to the Bible, the Apocrypha, the feast days of the Anglican Church, and the Book of Common Prayer. Allusion itself belongs to the associative dimension of language, evoking unspoken discourse, even specific absent words: "The Father of the Faithful [='Abraham'] said . . ." (Hymn 1, first line). So do all the devices of versification that emphasize nonsemantic relations among words: the relationship of rhyme in general (and these short lines are very rhyme-intensive) and the relationship of alliteration (a favorite device of Smart's that is luxuriant in these poems). When such words call back and forth to each other in two-dimensional patterns that can be drawn on the page, they pull aside from the linear. The preference for short words is also a principle of choice that values an arbitrary quality of a word: the diction of these poems is remarkably monosyllabic, giving the verses a sound and look of language for children that is sometimes belied by the difficulty of connecting these short words into an unobstructed chain of thought.

An enigmatic remark of Smart's in *Jubilate Agno*, echoed later in his preface to the verse translation of Horace, claims for himself a special gift with words: *"For my talent is to give an impression upon words by punching, that when a reader casts his eye upon 'em, he takes up the image of the mould wch I have made"* (B404).[6] Whatever exactly he meant, he was clearly not referring to how he fitted words together in syntax to say something, where the less memorable and vivid the words are, the less distraction there is, and the more efficient the communication will be. The metaphor of "punching" is of something hitting words in the line on the page from another dimension, outside the line of syntax, stamping them so that those words are "taken up" out of that line into the eye and mind. The idea of taking up the "mould" or form of words is something other than following the unimpeded flow of what the words say. Smart's avowed craft concerns itself with diction that calls attention to itself.

When words themselves are made remarkable and memorable ("foregrounding the utterance," in the influential formulation of Jan Mukarovsky[7]), reading is made slower and harder, or at least more complicated, and differently rewarding. In the ways Smart chose and arrayed his words in *Hymns for the Amusement of Children* various forces converge to disrupt a simple reading of the sense that most readers then and now must have expected children's poetry to have. Tracing what happens to syntax in these poems reveals how it is intersected by those distinctive forces. It suggests the practical effects of Smart's word-choice and consequently illuminates this particular poetic project.

A good example of some of the workings of these texts is the fourteenth hymn, called "Loveliness":

> GOOD-nature is thy sterling name,
>   Yet loveliness is English too;
> Sweet disposition, whose bright aim,
>   Is to the mark of Jesus true.
>
> I've seen thee in an homely face,
>   Excel by pulchritude of mind;
> To ill-form'd features give a grace,
>   Serene, benevolent and kind.
>
> 'Tis when the spirit is so great,
>   That it the body still controuls,
> As godly inclinations meet,
>   In sweet society of souls.
>
> It is that condescending air,
>   Where perfect willingness is plain,
> To smile assent, to join in pray'r,
>   And urg'd a mile to go it twain.
>
> To grant at once the boon preferr'd,
>   By contrite foe, or needy friend;
> To be obliging is the word,
>   And God's good blessing is the end.

This is an apostrophe, a hymn to a virtue. Since it begins by hesitating over the name of the virtue, and ends by offering "to be obliging" as yet another "word" (or phrase; or commandment?) for the virtue, it has a slightly riddling quality. All of the hymns, in fact, have a bit of that quality, reinforced by the typography into which their titles nestle. Each hymn is topped by a woodcut that dominates the page, occupying about a third of the letterpress space under the running head "HYMNS for CHILDREN." In larger caps under the picture is "H Y M N XIV." Below that in smaller caps is the title ("L O V E L I N E S S") and then an intervening capital roman number "I" before the first verse. The title, then, is subordinated under a more prominent hymn numbering, in a mediating position that captions the woodcut and announces the poem. Much of this typography is conventional of the day, but it builds up the riddling quality. Smart for the most part does not name his topics in the apostrophes or propositions that begin the poems. Sometimes title words appear unobtrusively a few lines into the text. In "Hope," "hope" appears as object of a preposition in the eighth of sixteen lines, not obviously the theme of the story told. "Charity" appears in the sixteenth of twenty-eight lines, while apostrophized in quite a riddling way in a first stanza.

> O Queen of virtues, whose sweet pow'r
> Does o'er the first perfections tow'r. . . .

For each hymn, the topic is available in plain sight but floats outside the signifying syntax or takes a casual place within it.

The titles can function for the reader as something to go back to, to get one's bearings for working out the sense, but—and this is not uncommon in lyric poetry of any age—they do not much intervene into the experience of reading the lyric itself. One can picture, as the poet or the purchasing family member might also have pictured, a child standing with hands clasped behind back and announcing the title before reciting text: "Charity." Pause. Recitation. The separation is as definitive as the connection. The separation can serve the present argument as the first instance of how these poems resist a quick survey-comprehension of their syntactic logic.

The first stanza of XIV plays with multiple uncertainties. It is not certain when we read the first line, "Good-nature is thy sterling name," that the line is an apostrophe, since some of these poems address the child reader in the second person. "Sterling" is a striking word to describe a name, and evidently an instance of the punching/stamping effect that Smart claimed to practice, and in fact is a variation on the metaphor he used for that process, of a word stamped with the true distinctive impress of coinage, a word legitimately coined. (Johnson's dictionary says "1. An epithet by which genuine English money is discriminated. 2. Genuine; having passed the test.") The sentence is about the word in it, rather than the quality named and apostrophized, and it makes a concessive gesture as if we were in the middle of a debate over what name to give to the topic, a curiously direct case of the axis of selection becoming the object of our explicit attention, continued in the second line where an alternative term comes forward, which turns out to be the title.

This opening argument is ambiguous: it makes equal sense two ways, that loveliness the quality is (culturally) English, and that "loveliness" the word is (lexically) English. Various ambiguities are of course even more rife in poetry than they are in common language use, but this particular ambiguity is quite characteristic of the specific textual project of the *Hymns*. The forward motion of reading, tracking the syntax, is interrupted by a briefly puzzling choice. It can be confidently decided: we are reading about names, so the application to names is the correct one to choose. The moment of choosing interrupts forward progress, the reader is challenged with the puzzle, solves it (with some satisfaction), and proceeds again. A game is played, which the writer could have avoided by putting quotation marks around the word or in some other conventional way foregrounding its word-ness. Here the crossing of the syntagmatic by an occasion of choice is left for the reader to enact: a signifier is *not* foregrounded when the reader would need it to be if progress were to be uninterrupted. Perhaps, of course, the reader may blithely notice only the correct alternative and not be derailed, but to the English youngster a title to loveliness might well be attractive; in fact, as noted earlier, since some of these poems address the reader in the second person, that reader may have already taken the opening lines to have praised him or her for meriting the name of good-nature.

These aspects of the stanza are not forbiddingly difficult. Smart's *Hymns for Children* has been compared more than once to William Blake's *Songs of Innocence and Experience*, but the lines cited here are not like such lines as "O Rose thou art sick. / The invisible worm / That flies in the night / In the howling storm / Has found out thy bed. . . ." The first and the other stanzas of "Loveliness" say vividly, with elements of puzzle and distraction, perfectly comprehensible and expectable things. The uncertainties embodied in the poem reflect what the Oxford editors call the "clipped and allusive manner" that Smart had also been cultivating in other writing, where "clipped" suggests a concision that gains striking energy at the expense of explanatory clarity.

We have said that what is allusive is associative (or paradigmatic). Perhaps surprisingly, so is what is "clipped." If lines say things with striking brevity in words that neatly fit a rhythm and a rhyme pattern, the whole show is a display of word choice. The ancient magic of poetry is that *we cannot talk like that*. Ordinary speakers are not able to choose words quickly enough, nor to look forward and backward at the requirements of pattern quickly enough, to produce verse like this spontaneously. The formulaic bard might have, although he would work for the most part in longer lines that were not clipped. The rap-master draws on the power of seeming to do so. The magic and power flow from the dimension of choice, not only as a command of it by the artist demonstrates the power of the maker, but as the reader participates in a short course of halting, turning, referring, and echoing language. *Re*ference carries us back or calls us to the side as syntax carries us forward. *Recognition of rightness in patterned language pulls us up to notice the pattern.*

To return to the quality in the *Hymns* of being puzzling: as such, these occasions of ambiguity, these puzzles, come into an arena of playfulness; and as play of ideas they show kinship with the prominent sound-play that is perhaps the most striking aspect of the poetic language deployed in these verses. The third stanza, for example, has a striking sound pattern of five voiced and six prominent unvoiced sibilant phonemes, culminating in "sweet society of souls." The last stanza has a lovely balanced play of *b* and hard and soft *g* sounds at the end: "To be obliging is the word / And God's good blessing is the end." These sound effects that Smart relished in most of his late poetry do subtly what is also done by lexical ambiguities, creating slightly skewed parallels (the simile in stanza three), and such small tricks as making "the end" the end of the poem. These sound effects capture the plain sense in charged words and forms. The language plays, makes the reader play with it, and in so doing distracts the reader from the signified "content." We will now consider whether that playfulness itself can actually itself serve a didactic purpose.

Here is a second example of the workings of these texts:

ELEGANCE
'Tis in the spirit that attire
Th' investiture of saints in heav'n
Those robes of intellectual fire,
Which to the great elect are giv'n.

"Bring out to my returning son,
The robes for elegance the best;"
Thus in the height it shall be done,
And thus the penitent be blest.

'Tis in the body, that sweet mien,
Ingenuous Christians all possess,
Grace, easy motions, smiles serene,
Clean hands and seemliness of dress.

Whoever has thy charming pow'rs,
Is amiable as Kidron's * swan,
Like holy Esdras feeds on flow'rs,
And lives on honey like St. John.
　　* David

This poem begins by offering the first of two definitions of its title, again calling attention to the word as word. Neither definition is obvious, and in general the poem mystifies its subject while celebrating it.[8] The title-topic is the reference of a low-profile pronoun, twice: "'Tis" is particularly a teaser here because as an opener of sentence and poem it might well be taken to begin an existential claim of the form, "'Tis in the spirit that we live and move. . . ." in which the "It" in "'Tis" would have no referent at all. In fact, the "It" in Smart's "'Tis" has a referent, but determining that it does awaits the reader's decisions that "attire" is a noun, that "attire" is not going to be the subject of a further predicate ("is unnecessary"?), that "that" consequently is an emphatic indicative rather than a conjunction, that "in the spirit" is not the emphatic locating of something but the first half of a contrasting pair of senses of something (the absent referent of the pronoun) whose function is not confirmed until "in the body" appears seven lines later. The specific puzzle to be solved in this case, even if the reader has just read the title, is the sentence itself.

The sentence is contorted and obscure, while solvable. It uses the indicative "that"—"you see, *that* one"—to point to something we have little, or the wrong, picture of, namely the clothes worn in heaven, and this statement requires a further appositive line to explain it in turn—"Those robes of intellectual fire"—which is rather hard to visualize and harder still to see as epitomizing elegance. "Attire" is explained by "investiture," a more obscure word, twice as long, which has a competing, irrelevant sense that might characterize the *welcoming* of saints *into* heaven.

That these verses actively tease the reader by obstructing quick processing is further shown by the opening of the second stanza with its abrupt shift to words of an unnamed speaker, quickly inferable to be the father of the prodigal son who is then quickly analogized back to God the father. In that stanza "elegance" makes its only appearance in the poem, foisted into a biblical paraphrase, but only to name a quality of earthly robes, not a quality obviously relevant to the scene evoked in the previous stanza. In that stanza, which this one appears to explain, "elegance" *is* the attire.

The last stanza switches to apostrophe and says rhapsodic things: who has it, feeds on flowers, lives on honey. By this time the name and ordinary idea of elegance are again submerged. Whatever the young biblical scholar remembers of Esdras, his or her picture of John the Baptist is surely different from the usual picture of elegance. Brooding over these verses, playing with them, that young person might uncover the idea that John was being extremely choosy in his food, living by a discipline of the sparest diet. A stretching of the idea of elegance, with its root of "choice," is possible. The estranging strategy in this poem, which uses the actual word only for the literal and mundane best clothes of the earthly father's wardrobe, works by floating the word away from its rhapsodic celebration in the first two and last stanzas, and leaving the reader to fetch it back and apply it.

The last stanza returns to being mildly challenging with exotic references to Kidron and Esdras, and in it the exhortation is sweetened with promise. Smart's recourse to a footnote (there is another below Hymn XXI to point out that the author is paraphrasing Virgil) shows plainly that the value of the exotic substituted term is greater than the cost of distraction, that the exotic word is more valuable for its impact than it is a liability for its incomprehensibility. The substitution for "David" graphically represents the dimension of association or paradigm, making the latent, unchosen term appear visibly outside the syntax from which it was displaced.

The interruption represented by the footnote also dramatizes a curious fact about selectivity of diction in general: paradoxically, whenever a word is conspicuously well-chosen by whatever criterion, that is, whenever it is conspicuously *chosen*, it is to some extent a distraction and an interruption. Every coloring of diction interferes with the (apparent) transparency of words to the thoughts they signify. A word so far-fetched as to need the footnote merely requires of the reader a physical looking-down that enacts with the eyes the pull of the associative axis. Any of these hymns, and any such poetry, is actively promoting hesitation, attention to the signifiers with their euphony, exoticism, loftiness, or whatever associated quality gives a reader satisfactions separate from the literal sense conveyed.

Hymn XV, "Taste," apparently an adult-to-child discourse throughout, begins with a meditation on the Bible that seems the author's own. Here are the first two stanzas:

> O Guide my judgment and my taste,
> Sweet SPIRIT, author of the book
> Of wonders, told in language chaste,
> And plainness not to be mistook.

> O let me muse, and yet at sight
> The page admire, the page believe;
> "Let there be light, and there was light,
> "Let there be Paradise and Eve."

Whether or not this prayer characterized for Smart his own book in which it appears, it seems quite unlikely that he was practicing his craft in simple contradiction of it. As to chastity and plainness of language, the second stanza of this statement is entirely monosyllabic except for "admire," "believe," and "Paradise," and as such is not far from typical of the rest of the book. Even his most puzzling locutions, where "plainness not to be mistook" is not offered at first reading, are more characterized by blunt than by elaborate language.

Equally revealing with the praise of plain language, however, and in fact a comment upon it, is the sketch of a reading process: "O let me *muse*, and yet . . . admire, . . . believe." Johnson defines "muse" as "to ponder; to think close; to study in silence"; "to be absent of mind"; "to wonder; to be amazed." As these terms characterize responses to a reading, they deny and oppose what much reading is, the reading that tracks a methodical explanation or a concrete narrative. They describe, not a rapid and continuous progress through discourse, but an interrupted progress, and as such they agree with the effects of Smart's *Hymns for the Amusement of Children* traced here.

"Muse" is the root of "amusement." Johnson gives for "amusement" "that which amuses; entertainment"; for "amuse," he is cautious: "to entertain with tranquillity; to fill the mind with thoughts that engage the mind, without distracting it. To *divert* implies something more lively; and to *please*, something more important. It is therefore frequently taken in a sense bordering on contempt." Not having actually passed the border of contempt, we might say "patronization," or what Smart used quite positively to characterize "loveliness" in XIV, "a condescending air." Hymns for the amusement of adults would be inappropriate. Hymns for the serious edification of children were what Charles Wesley had recently written, but Smart was of a different mind, as Watts had been in 1715 in his *Divine Songs for Children* where he observed that "There is something so amusing and entertaining in rhymes and metre, that will incline children to make this part of their business a diversion."[9]

Further, Watts's preface to his children's hymns defends them with a hope of instructional efficacy in terms that can illuminate Smart's practice, setting a program that Smart takes much further than Watts had in his spare and forthright verses:

> What is learned in verse is longer retained in memory, and sooner recollected. The like sounds, and the like number of syllables, exceedingly assist the remembrance. And it may often happen that the end of a song running in the mind may be an effectual means to keep off some temptations, or to incline to some duty, when a word of scripture is not upon their thoughts.

This will be a constant furniture for the minds of children, that they may have something to think upon when alone, and sing over to themselves. This may sometimes give their thoughts a divine turn, and raise a young meditation. (316)

Smart's verse is much denser with the devices that lodge verse in memory and make it run in the mind. Its patterning of sounds is much fuller (though some can be found in Watts), offering more of the deep-seated pleasure of vocal or subvocal play with sounds that is first seen in infants. Its riddling and puzzling moves demand the musings of "young meditation" and reward them with clear and usually cheerful doctrines that fold out upon examination. Smart may sometimes miscalculate difficulties, or drift into private versions or idiosyncratic emphases of conventional lessons, but a reasonable expectation is that the young reader will be engaged by the challenge as well as be charmed by the play of the signifiers. What makes the lines a challenge to read is what makes them memorable when read.

The program evinced is maximal musing consistent with continued (not uninterrupted) reading. The resistance posed to linear reading is insistent, while at the same time the rhythms of the poetry carry a reader forward. Having speculated so confidently on the experience of the appropriate reader of these poems, we might venture to schematize a sequence of that reading experience: first, a determined reading right through while not clearly getting the didactic point, though not missing the general air of high-minded affirmation; second, going back to try to get it straight, because it is a friendly challenge that doesn't threaten to be impossible, or unpleasant, holding something back out of reach; third, with rereading, getting a more satisfying sense, but also an increasing awareness of the musical sounds, which begin to hook into memory, bit by bit; and finally, having the lesson return when the catchy poem runs in the mind, not only because the lesson is the sense, but because it was satisfying to puzzle out. Seeing the answer to the puzzle is a mutually reinforcing satisfaction with the reading, recall, or recitation of the pleasingly formed verses themselves.

To return briefly to the analysis of these texts by the scheme of axes of discourse: like other poetry these *Hymns* artfully resist the dismissive prose-reading that is invited by writing where the syntagmatic dominates. As a special kind of poetry for children, they seem to offer what can be called pure and applied effects of their emphasis of the paradigmatic. Applied effects, we might say, are those that put the poetry to the uses described by Watts: the versified content hangs in the mind, and if consulted may do the child good. There are lessons tendered and received, delivered into the mind by the catchiness of versification and by the special aura around the chosen, strikingly and distractingly right words.

The "pure" kind of paradigmatic effect is that which a strictly doctrinal evaluation would consider the empty effect: elevation, escape from the mundane and temporal, exhilaration, joy. It is what the "Song to David" is famous for, a kind of rapture, in which doctrine appears to be present but is hard to get into focus in the midst of celebratory energy and marvels of language. Despite their earnestness, the *Hymns for Children* show glimpses of such elevation. A concluding example of a hymn, "Gratitude," may illustrate both sides of the distinction, with rapture to some extent intercepted by doctrine:

> I upon the first creation
> Clap'd my wings with loud applause
> Cherub of the highest station,
> Praising, blessing, without pause.
>
> I in Eden's bloomy bowers
> Was the heav'nly gard'ner's pride,
> Sweet of sweets, and flow'r of flowers
> With the scented tinctures dy'd,
>
> Hear, ye little children, hear me,
> I am God's delightful voice;
> They who sweetly still revere me,
> Still shall make the wisest choice.
>
> Hear me not like Adam trembling,
> When I walk'd in Eden's grove;
> And the host of heav'n assembling,
> From the spot the traitor drove.
>
> Hear me rather as the lover
> Of mankind, restor'd and free,
> By the word ye shall recover
> More than that ye lost by Me.
>
> I'm the Phoenix of the singers
> That in upper Eden dwell;
> Hearing me Euphrates lingers,
> As my wond'rous tale I tell.

'Tis the story of the Graces,
Mercies without end or sum;
And the sketches and the traces
Of ten thousand more to come.

List, my children, list within you,
Dread not ye the tempter's rod;
Christ our gratitude shall win you,
Wean'd from earth, and led to God.

This ecstatic chant has the trochaic ("running") meter and much of the mood achieved in Friedrich von Schiller's "An die Freude" set at the end of Ludwig van Beethoven's ninth symphony, or Henry Van Dyke's "Joyful, Joyful, We Adore Thee" set to the same tune. Like them it offers a collage of brief and indistinct visions. Perhaps stanzas four and five allow the weight of doctrine to drop them back to earth, but as seven says, "sketches and traces" make up the "wondrous story" so far as it is told in all the other stanzas.

The rapid forward movement might suggest that the syntagmatic forward dimension dominates in this poem, but narrative (through the whole history of creation) is only an excuse here for incantatory effects of "praising, blessing, without pause," that is, without articulation, where the connected narrative and doctrinal sense is overpowered by the effects of rhythmic pattern. Words wear the aspect of their insistent rightness to pattern rather than to communicated sense. In "Sweet of sweets, and flow'r of flowers," repetition dilutes sense; the second word in each doublet collapses back to the first rather than carrying forward the implications of one term to the next. In practical terms, it is hard to remember that "gratitude" is the object of the celebration, and the subject of sentences. Gratitude is a cherub, the voice of God, and at end apparently Christ. These associations apparently made doctrinal sense to Smart, but in the poem they function as striking substitutive terms in something more like a pageant than a story.

This poem achieves, I think, a significant degree of the exaltation function. Without attempting to explain away the experience that such art offers, that experience can be connected to the kind of language that enables it. Emile Benveniste, a theoretician of linguistics, writes, "It is in and through language that man constitutes himself as a *subject*, because language alone establishes the concept of "ego" in reality . . . the basis of subjectivity is in the exercise of language."[10] Students of linguistics have gone further to argue in detail that different meters of poetry offer differing subject positions to the same readers.

Pentameter allows the syntax "a more powerful voice"; compared to other metres it is a *syntagmatic form.* And since coherence in the subject is an effect of meaning intended along the syntagmatic chain, iambic pentameter in verse will support and promote coherence in the subject.

In [four-stress] accentual metre the stress of the intonation and the abstract pattern coincide and reinforce each other . . . [which] calls for an emphatic, heavily stressed performance, one typically recited or chanted. . . . In chanting, rhythmic repetitions take complete priority over natural intonation, subsuming it, and this is the metrical "space" for a collective voice.[11]

The claim has a provocative convergence with the case at hand. If highly interrupted, highly associative language use in such (tetrameter) poetry as "Gratitude" seems to have power to elevate readers out of time and place, to offer a sense of escape from the ordinary and of access to the self-transcendence of community or communion, that language is orthogonal to the language used in propositional, syntagmatic ways, the language of individual voice, rational thought, and practical business—and even of certain styles of poetry—in which sense of selfhood is strong. The effects that have been analyzed here in the *Hymns* negatively as distraction from the syntagmatic can also be defined as offering positive access to a different frame of mind.

NOTES

1. *PW,* ii: 23.
2. Ibid., 313. For a contrasting view with respect to another work that Smart calculated for a young audience, see Chapter 4.
3. XVI, "Against Quarrelling and Fighting," *Divine Songs for Children,* in *The Poetical Works of Isaac Watts and Henry Kirke White, with a Memoir of Each, Two Volumes in One* (Boston, MA: Houghton, Mifflin, 1881), I: 336.
4. The conceptions derive from Ferdinand de Saussure, in lectures published as *Course in General Linguistics,* eds. Charles Bally and Albert Sechehaye, with Albert Reidlinger, trans. Wade Baskin (New York: Philosophical Library, 1959), ch.5, "Syntagmatic and Associative Relations," 122-27, and have been elaborated by Roman Jakobson, Emile Benveniste, Jacques Lacan, and others. For a lucid discussion see Antony Easthope, *Poetry as Discourse* (London: Methuen, 1983), 34ff.
5. Roman Jakobson, "Linguistics and Poetics," reprinted in Richard and Fernande De George, eds., *The Structuralists: From Marx to Levi-Strauss* (Garden City, NY: Doubleday, 1972), 95.
6. In praise of Horace, Smart celebrates "the beauty, force and vehemence of *Impression* . . . a talent . . . by which a Genius is impowered to throw an emphasis upon a word or sentence . . ." (*PW,* v: 6). Smart comments that it can sometimes be translated, even into prose, which blurs the focus on diction *per se,* although he makes that point especially to include "scripture," and hence to assimilate the power to divine inspiration.
7. Jan Mukarovsky, "Standard Language and Poetic Language," 1948, trans. Paul Garvin, excerpted in Hazard Adams, *Critical Theory Since Plato,* rev. ed. (Fort Worth, TX: Harcourt Brace Jovanovich, 1992), 976-82. "The function of poetic language consists in the maximum of foregrounding of the utterance" (977).
8. Moira Dearnley strangely says, "'Elegance,' in the *Hymns* . . . is about elegant clothes. . . ." See *The Poetry of Christopher Smart* (London: Routledge and Kegan Paul, 1968), 46.
9. Isaac Watts, "Preface, to all that are concerned in the education of children," *Poetical Works,* 316.
10. Emile Benveniste, *Problems in General Linguistics,* trans. Mary Elizabeth Meek (Coral Gables, FL: University of Miami, 1971), 224, 226.
11. Easthope, *Poetry as Discourse,* 71, 73.

Chapter 4

Smart's Enlightened Parables and the Problem of Genre

Todd C. Parker

And also I heard the voice of the Lord, saying, Whom shall I send, and who will go for us? Then said I, Here am I; send me. And he said, Go, and tell this people, Hear ye indeed, but understand not; and see ye indeed, but perceive not. Make the heart of this people fat, and make their ears heavy, and shut their eyes; lest they see with their eyes, and hear with their ears, and understand with their heart, and convert, and be healed.

—Isaiah 6:8-10

And he said unto them, Unto you it is given to know the mystery of the kingdom of God: but unto them that are without, all these things are done in parables: That seeing they may see, and not perceive; and hearing they may hear, and not understand; lest at any time they should be converted and their sins should be forgiven them. And he said unto them, Know ye not this parable? and how then will ye know all parables?

—Mark 4:11-13

At that time Jesus answered and said, I thank thee, O Father, Lord of heaven and earth, because thou hast hid these things from the wise and prudent, and hast revealed them unto babes.

—Matthew 11:25

Jesus' parables can be hard nuts to crack. Indeed, what most often characterizes the twelve apostles is their inability to comprehend the parabolic lessons Jesus relates. Such incomprehension is not, however, entirely their fault. The parables exist as a kind of doubled discourse that partly conveys, and partly conceals its meaning, so that the audience "may see, and not perceive; and hearing they may hear, and not understand," as the Gospel of Mark suggests. To the unblessed auditor, a parable is an oddity, an irrelevance narrating some bit of everyday trivia. To the appropriate listener, though, the parable gives a glimpse of the true relation between God and humanity. But if we take Jesus' words as a statement on genre, a "parable" requires that the relationship between moral content and audience remains at best mediated and at worst occluded. In other words, the parable's transcendent meaning is lost unless a competent translator decodes the divine and relates it to its mundane context. Parables use the partial perspective of this world to encompass a more holistic vision of the divine world. It is appropriate, as John Drury notes, that Jesus purveys such parabolic wisdom: "Jesus alone tells [parables] because he is the whole subject of the story, and because in him the two worlds meet."[1]

It is tantalizing to imagine what Christopher Smart thought of this generic question when he published *The Parables of Our Lord and Saviour Jesus Christ* in the spring of 1768.[2] The *Parables* represent part of Smart's ongoing evangelization of London's reading public, and, as Karina Williamson observes in her introduction to the text of the *Parables,* Smart considerably expands the idea of a parable: instead of limiting himself to Jesus' own examples, Smart "seems to have extended the term to cover what may be called 'parabolic discourse' of any kind, in which Christian doctrine is conveyed through, or with the aid of, similes, metaphors, proverbs, and other indirect forms of expression."[3] Williamson also argues that "the knowledge required for salvation . . . demands no intellectual superiority; on the contrary, it may be more readily acquired by those who trust to the intuitive wisdom that comes through faith."[4] But even the parabolic material Smart includes from other than Gospel sources amplifies what Smart sees as the unifying themes of Jesus' parables. It is to Jesus, his identity, and his function as savior that all of Smart's parabolic paraphrases refer for their full significance. Jesus' parables represent, for Smart, the essence of the Gospel spirit and the point where individual faith and public evangelism coincide. Granted the generic reticence of parables to give up their meaning easily, we should ask how Smart realizes his evangelical project by first identifying parabolic content and by second versifying that content for a popular audience. Why does Smart supplement Jesus' parables with his own periphrastic addenda? What does it mean, theologically and rhetorically, to adapt a genre privileged by the Christ himself? Is it a simple matter of "fit audience though few," or does Smart accomplish something more profound?

In this chapter, I will argue that Smart's parables do more than modulate their subject from prose to poetry. Hardly a doctrinaire exponent of Scripture anyway, Smart plays much more freely with parabolic form than our conventional understanding of the genre can allow. In effect, Smart's parables revise the standard of competence that traditionally applies to "reader" and to "listener." If the traditional parable must, as representative of its genre, exclude certain individuals from full comprehension, and thus from full salvation, Smart's parables amplify their own content in accord with Smart's conception of the enlightened, humanistic reader his verses call into being. Smart's verses "reverse," as it were, the distinction between the knowing and the ignorant, so that "ignorance" is no longer built into the reading process. Such a reversal in its turn presupposes—and, in the form of Smart's texts, calls into being as part of the act of reading—an audience universally worth saving, one whose principal characteristic is its equality before God.[5] The parables thus become a way for Smart to claim the authority of the Gospels and to place himself in the Christlike position of editor while at the same time extending the parables' salvific potential to a much wider audience. This project is, I contend, a risky one—by versifying Gospel text, Smart runs the risk of mis-editing or -translating the privileged genre Christ uses to express his true identity. But by hypothesizing an ideal, and an ideally childlike, reader, Smart reconfigures the traditional dimensions of the parable: when read by Smart's enlightened child, the parable ceases to occlude the divine and becomes itself a transparent salvific medium.

What, though, is a parable? How might we define a parable's generic contours? Frank Kermode answers that "a parable is, first, a similitude": "'With what can we compare the kingdom of God, or what parable shall we use for it?' (Mark 4:30): here the word for parable—*parabolē*—could as well be translated 'comparison,' and it sometimes is. It means a placing of one thing beside another; in classical Greek it means 'comparison' or 'illustration' or 'analogy.' But in the Greek Bible it is equivalent to Hebrew *mashal*, which means 'riddle' or 'dark saying,' but I gather it can extend its range to include 'exemplary tale.' Sometimes the Greek word is also used to translate *hidah*, meaning 'riddle.'"[6] Here, Kermode captures the essential tension of the genre: by simultaneously producing meaning as a "comparison" or "illustration" and veiling that meaning as a "dark saying," the parable folds over upon itself, almost like a Möbius strip. Precisely because they exhibit "all the marks of narrativity," parables "insofar as they *are* stories . . . are not to be taken at face value, and bear various indications to make this condition plain to the interpreter; so the other scale [by which parables may be identified] is a measure of their darkness."[7] For most contemporary readers, a parable is a short (sometimes very short) story with a doubled meaning. While biblical hermeneutics—as Kermode points out—as a general rule gathers under the rubric of "parable" a wide range of literature including *mashal* (also translatable as "proverbs"), riddles, aphorisms, stories, and other forms of metaphorical discourse, the parables of Jesus tend to use metaphor and allegory to serve some inductive purpose. "Parable" as a critical term consequently conveys, as John Dominic Crossan puts it, "the sense of figurative stories whose plot is not just the inevitable unfolding of the opening sentence."[8] In another context, Crossan argues that, "The term *parable,* then, should be used technically and specifically, from ancient to contemporary example, for *paradoxes formed into story by effecting single or double reversals of the audience's most profound expectations."* The structure of parable is a deliberate but comic reversal of the expected story.[9] The parable's figural nature, its doubleness, is what makes it appropriate to the discourse of the Gospels, since the purpose of Jesus' parables is as much to establish his theological identity in this world as it is to point to the world of the divine: "A parable," as Crossan puts it, "tells a story which, on its surface level, is absolutely possible or even factual within the normalcy of life." It is "a metaphor of normalcy which intends to create participation in its referent. It talks of A so that one can participate in B, or, more accurately, it talks of x so that one can participate in X and so understand the validity of x itself. Its structural pattern is X-in-x, and the hyphens are not dispensable."[10]

The audience's most profound expectation upon encountering a parable is that the parable will read conventionally; it is only by understanding the figural nature of the parabolic content that "X" appears in shadowy outline behind the conventional readability of "x." Thus, the reversal Crossan describes is one that necessarily identifies the parable as genre with the critical act of interpretation. That is, the parable only emerges if one can recognize that such a reversal from "x" to "X" is the meaning of the story. Like satire, the parable only exists as such if one "gets it," and the shock of "getting it"— particularly in a New Testament context—is to realize that straightforward, realistic, even historical narratives cannot sufficiently interpret their own content because "historicity" itself is only a partial perspective. In other words, history in the parabolic discourse of the Gospels is only a part of its own larger meaning.

Little criticism on Smart's *Parables* exists, and what has been written is fairly unflattering. Arthur Sherbo sums up the *Parables* stylistically when he describes them as "a mechanical versification in octosyllabic couplets" (Sherbo, 246), and his assessment is kind compared to reviews of the time. The *Monthly Review* dismissed Smart with the stinging line: "This version of the parables is, with great propriety, dedicated to Master *Bonnell George Thornton:* a child of three years old," while the *Critical Review* observed that, "We do not remember to have met with any poet whose compositions are more unequal than those of Mr. Smart. Some of his pieces are distinguished by undoubted marks of genius, agreeable imagery, and a fine poetical enthusiasm. Others are hardly superior to the productions of Sternhold or Quarles. The work before us is of the lower class, containing about seventy parables and some other passages of the New Testament, in plain, familiar verse, adapted to the capacities of children; to whom it may certainly be of use, as it will serve to give them an idea of our Saviour's discourses and furnish them with pious instructions; but it is not calculated to please their imaginations, or improve their taste in poetry. . . ."[11]

Sherbo concludes that "had the periodicals been silent . . . they would have performed Smart a service, but he had angered the reviewers and they had not yet forgotten or relented" (Sherbo, 249). As Betty Rizzo and Robert Mahony note, "the reviewers seized upon Smart's approach to children as another symptom of his degeneration" (*Letters,* 116); Ralph Griffith's *Monthly Review* derided the *Parables* as "*Familiar* verse, indeed, as the title page justly intimates" (Sherbo, 249), and quoted parable XXI as its example:

> Or thus,—What woman, that retains
> Ten silver pieces, all her gains,
> And loses one, does not explore,
> With candle light, and sweep the floor,
> And use all diligence, to find
> The Coin on which she sets her mind;
> And, when she finds it, does not call
> Her friends and neighbours, one and all,
> 'Your gratulations here be paid,
> 'I've found the piece that I mislaid!'
> Likewise there's joy, you may rely,
> Before th' angelic host on high,
> If one poor sinner meekly prays,
> Repenting all his evil ways. (*PW*, ii: 238, ll. 1-14)

Even when we account for the relatively recent recognition of Smart's status as a major eighteenth-century poet, the critical silence surrounding the *Parables* seems to confirm that these are minor works from a poet past his creative prime. Yet such a judgment is strongly belied, as Clement Hawes puts it when writing of *Jubilate Agno,* by "Smart's superb education, by his years of work as a sophisticated neoclassical poet and translator, by his innumerable ties to the artistic traditions of high culture" (Hawes, 132). Why should the *Parables* in particular stand for Smart at his worst, even after factoring in the stylistic accommodations they make as a species of children's literature? Why did the *Parables* receive such uniformly rotten reviews, and why have they been so lukewarmly welcomed as part of Smart's oeuvre?[12] It is, perhaps, too easy to explain the badness of the *Parables* as the natural sign of Smart's dissolution as a poet or as the degradation of his creative faculty by years of enthusiasm and madness. What we read, and what the critics of the *Monthly* and *Critical Reviews* condemn as an impoverished compositional style, is, I argue, Smart's daring reappropriation of the power and authority of Scripture. The "badness" of the *Parables*—their clunky octosyllabic couplets, trite phrasings, and simplistic rhyme schemes—marks their very radical nature as permutations of the parable genre. Their "badness," that is, is their easy accessibility, their childlike appropriateness.[13]

Parable XXI, cited above, is one of a particularly Lucan series of parables that involves short, realistic narratives from which Smart draws his moral similitude. Its simple true rhymes and octosyllabic, almost hudibrastic, couplet pattern deliberately distance Smart's paraphrase from the elegant formality of Pope's heroic couplet or the drama of Miltonic blank verse, while its common diction and close fidelity to Luke's Gospel indicate that this poem is intentionally accessible, even to those unfamiliar with or wary of more aesthetically sophisticated forms. In his reading of the Lucan cycle from which this parable comes, John Drury comments, "So through the series of parables, *lost sheep—lost coin—prodigal son—unjust steward,* there is a progressive decline of the allegorical references which had once . . . been constitutive of the parable, and a congruently progressive rise of the purely human and realistic narrative."[14] Smart's stylistic decisions are thus theological and political as well. Insofar as the style of the *Parables* helps the reader to "imitate" the "Innocence and Simplicity" of children and to accept the redemptive potential of Smart's public discourse of salvation, the plain language in which Smart casts the parables constitutes a reordering of mid–eighteenth-century English poetry as a public space of faith.[15] The "familiarity" the *Monthly Review* decries is, in reality, part of Smart's program of religious reform: it recasts public notions of acceptable poetry and invades what we might call the "decorous space" of the polite reader with "innocent," childlike verses. And since, in Addisonian terms, the sophisticated reader is the exact opposite of the child, it seems little wonder that the reviewers react with hostility to Smart's project—reading like a child means renouncing the status and aesthetic merit that to no small extent defines the privileged classes.[16] That which sophisticated readers understand as poor style and degraded technique is, for Smart, the revitalization of an evangelical medium.

The dilemma Smart faces when paraphrasing the parables is how to negotiate this stylistic divide between form and content for all of his readers, not just the privileged few. If we look at a typical parable, we notice that in addition to versifying Scripture, Smart often appends a critical summation of the parable's content. In parable XXII, for example, Smart reworks the account of the householder in Matthew 13:51-2:

> They say unto him, "Lord, we do."
> Then did he his discourse renew—
> "On this account each learned scribe,
> "That can Christ's heav'nly truths imbibe,
> "Hence shall his ghostly charge subsist,
> "And act the good oeconomist,
> "While new and old, from all his store,
> "He gives each guest, that haunts his door."
> *The Lord would here his converts teach*
> *How his good saints should read and preach,*
> *By copying all his faith and force,*
> *As he sets off his plain discourse;*
> *Brings forth new truths, the old he cites,*
> *Puts diff'rent things in various light;*
> *Disposes all things for the best,*
> *And treats his hearers as his guests.* (*PW*, ii: 239, ll. 1-18)

Smart designs the poem's structure to reflect its accessibility to children—the repeated use of alliteration in the phrases "comprehend them clear," "Then did he his discourse renew," "He gives each guest, that haunts his door," "By copying all his faith and force"; the assonance of "call'd the throng," "read and preach," and "new truths"—such features suggest both that the poem's sound and its sense harmonize with and reinforce each other, as would be appropriate to Christ's utterance, and also that the poem serves as a mnemonic for children trying to learn the parables by heart. But of equal importance is the way Smart's supplement to the parabolic material repeats and amplifies the parabolic narrative. The supplement is explicitly didactic. Anyone who misses the parable's meaning can turn to the supplement for enlightenment: "The Lord would here his converts teach / How his good saints should read and preach." Unlike its biblical referent, which never articulates a clear relationship between narrative and moral, Smart's text confidently links narrative to an exemplary code of conduct, and it does so in a language identical to that of the paraphrase. Parity of diction, phrasing, and poetic structure indicate that the parable and its supplement exist on equal terms: indeed, Smart seems to be making the stylistic suggestion that the meaning of paraphrase and supplement are interchangeable.[17] Like the "good oeconomist," Smart's paraphrase gives equally of "new and old" without distinguishing hierarchically between the scriptural source and Smart's own addition. "Enlightenment" is thus something Smart dispenses from his superior position as editor/paraphraser; it is no longer something available only to a minority of the audience. What Smart purveys as the meaning of the parable is more than an ethics of charity; it is an economy of the word in which the parable itself becomes a gift from Christ to each of his "hearers." The true Christian economy as Smart defines it, then, is not one regulated by exchange for profit. It is instead a heavenly economy of the gift, which Christ, through Smart's poem, offers to all.

The plain language and parity of poetic expression we find in parable XXII suggest that, unlike Smart's other works, the *Parables* mark a critically significant departure from Smart's usual poetic practices. We have only to compare the *Parables* to the richly allusive biblical poetics of *Jubilate Agno* or to the complex numerological relations that typify "A Song to David" to see how far Smart ranges in the *Parables* from the poetic techniques that have made him (in)famous. Indeed, Smart is acutely aware of his poetry's figural potential, as he makes clear when he discusses his notion of poetic "impression": "*Impression* then, is a talent or gift of Almighty God, by which a Genius is impowered to throw an emphasis upon a word or sentence in such wise, that it cannot escape any reader of sheer good sense, and true critical sagacity. This power will sometimes keep up thro' the *medium* of a prose translation; especially in scripture, for in justice to truth and everlasting preeminence, we must confess this virtue to be far more powerful and abundant in the sacred writings" (*PW,* v: 6-7). Smart identifies "impression" as the rhetorical characteristic of genius and argues that such a gift originates as an expression of God's will. Smart also seems to claim implicitly that poetry is a more natural medium for impression than prose, since the only prose in which one finds the principle of impression "powerfully and abundantly" at work is in Scripture. As various critics have noted, Smart also theorizes "impression" in *Jubilate Agno,* but here the term supposes a different effect on the reader:

> For my talent is to give an impression upon words by punching, that when the reader casts his eye upon 'em, he takes up the image from the mould which I have made (B404).

Smart clearly suggests in the preface to his verse translation of Horace that "impression" marks a text as somehow eccentric, somehow beyond the "prosaic." The "emphasis" impression "throws" "upon a word or sentence in such wise, that it cannot escape a reader of sheer good sense" is also, in its own way, an exclusive rhetorical principle, since those "impressed" by Smart's genius possess "sheer good sense, and true critical sagacity." As such, these readers represent a privileged audience, and it is precisely such privileging of and differentiation between groups that Smart's *Parables* are designed to avoid. "Impression" as an aesthetic criterion creates a vertical hierarchy of readers and, by doing so, leaves aesthetically less sophisticated readers with an imperfect understanding of a particular text's full rhetorical significance—a significance analogous to that of a parable.

We should notice, though, that while impression works as a principle of rhetorical differentiation in both the preface to Horace and *Jubilate Agno,* it is only in the preface that it also serves as a principle of *aesthetic* differentiation. The lines from *Jubilate Agno* argue that the writer's genius, expressed rhetorically as the phenomenon of "punching," has the same effect on each reader who encounters the text. Smart's remarks on impression thus pull two ways—one toward an aesthetic of reception that instates a hierarchy among Smart's readership, and the other toward an aesthetic of genius that enfolds the text rhetorically into the reader's experience. The passage from *Jubilate Agno* subtly insures the kind of readerly participation Smart will take such pains to enact through the poetics of his *Parables.* What strikes me about the *Parables* is how little they appear to exhibit "impression" as an aesthetically exclusive practice. Smart seems deliberately to have designed poems that avoid the sort of linguistic excess that characterizes his other works. By doing so, Smart's *Parables* exhibit a rhetoric typified by Smart's tendency to reiterate parables in plain words and conventional metaphors.[18]

Paradoxically, by reiterating the parabolic content, Smart's supplement to parable XXII annihilates the parable itself, since the occlusions that distinguish parabolic material disappear in the ambient light Smart's additional lines provide. Perhaps more profoundly, a "parable" cannot exist without some notion of occluded meaning, so whatever the meaning Smart conveys in his supplements, the supplements themselves implicitly challenge the parable's generic structure. In Matthew 21, for instance, Jesus rebukes the chief priests and elders of Jerusalem with the parable of the father with two sons:

> But what think ye? A *certain* man had two sons; and he came to the first, and said, Son, go work today in my vineyard. He answered and said, I will not: but afterward he repented, and went. And he came to the second and said likewise. And he answered and said, I *go*, sir: and went not. Whether of them twain did the will of *his* father? They say unto him, The first.

Jesus saith unto them, Verily I say unto you, That the publicans and the harlots go into the kingdom of God before you. For John came unto you in the way of righteousness, and ye believed him not: but the publicans and the harlots believed him: and ye, when ye had seen *it,* repented not afterward, that ye might believe him. (Matthew 21:28-32)

Smart paraphrases the parable thus:

> A Certain man, whose sons were twain,
> Who had a vineyard to maintain,
> Address'd the first "My son, away,
> "To work, and prune my vines to-day."
> He said, I will not go, but went
> When wrought by conscience to repent.
> The second had the like command,
> And said, "I go, sir, out of hand,"
> But did not stir—which of these two
> Had grace the father's will to do?
> They answer, Lord, the first—if so,
> The Lord reply'd, for certain know,
> As touching Christ's eternal meed,
> Harlots and publicans precede
> You, elders—for when John express
> Came in the way of righteousness,
> Him whom nor priest nor scribe believ'd,
> Harlots and publicans receiv'd.
> And when his ways and works were known,
> Yet would ye not amend your own;
> Nor did your froward hearts dispose,
> Nor unto faith repentance chose. (*PW*, ii: 223, ll. 1-22)

In terms of content, the greatest difference between parable XI and the King James Version is that Smart's priests and elders openly acknowledge Jesus as "Lord," a circumstance significantly different from Scripture. Particularly in Matthew, knowledge of Jesus' status remains, like the meaning of the parables, available only to the chosen few. Indeed, the mise-en-scène of this parable is a dramatic confrontation in the temple over the question of Jesus' identity and the right by which he heals and preaches: "And when he was come into the temple, the chief priests and the elders of the people came unto him as he was teaching, and said, By what authority doest thou these things?

And who gave thee this authority?" (Matthew 21: 23). Jesus responds by offering a quid pro quo: he will answer the elders' question if they will tell him whether John was baptized by the will of heaven or by the will of men. Torn between admitting John's divine mission (and thereby earning a reproach for ignoring John's message) or repudiating it (and earning the wrath of the people) the elders admit the quandary in which Jesus has placed them: "And they answered Jesus and said, We cannot tell" (Matthew 21:27). It is to this apparent inability to speak the truth that Jesus addresses his parable.

Not content, though, with paraphrasing Jesus' story, Smart supplements the parable with his own versified interpretation of the scene:

> *Christ in the parable decries*
> *A mere professor's life of lies,*
> *Who's bold to preach and reprimand*
> *In words magnificent and grand,*
> *The pompous self-applauding saint,*
> *All inward filth and outward paint;*
> *But conscious meekness, which appears*
> *To give the glory voice and tears,*
> *At once uncloaking all offence*
> *By duty and by diffidence,*
> *Not only brings the pardon down*
> *But gains th' incorruptible crown.* (23-34)

Since this moral comes after the parable, it seems logical to read it as an amplification of parabolic meaning, an elucidation, as it were, of the parabolic content for any reader who still does not get the point. By describing Christ as he who "decries / A mere professor's life of lies," Smart seems merely to rephrase the gist of Matthew 21:27. The elders are those "professors" who live in fear of the truth Christ brings: the "pompous self-applauding saint" who is "bold to preach and reprimand" must wait until society's outcasts, the "harlots and publicans," rightfully take their place in heaven. But unlike the elders in the biblical account, Smart's elders are aware of Jesus' extraordinary nature as "Lord," and Smart does not hesitate to announce Jesus as the "Christ," or "anointed one" of Hebrew history. In Matthew's Gospel, comprehending Jesus' identity as "the Christ, the Son of the living God" (Matthew 16:15) is enough to establish Peter as the foundation of the church. What distinguishes the Matthean parable from, say, its Lucan counterpart is the eschatological nature of the parabolic content. Matthew's parables tend to focus on last things and the apocalyptic relationship between God and humankind, as Jesus makes clear in his allegory of the vineyard. For Smart thus to name Jesus as "Lord" and "Christ" is significantly to rewrite the terms of the parabolic event, since the ultimate truth of the parable—the one the elders fail signally to get—is the truth of Jesus' nature. In this case, the parabolic character of the story is not its hidden moral, since even the elders understand the difference between the two sons. Instead, Smart's paraphrase substitutes Jesus himself for the parabolic content: Jesus' true identity as lord functions as the veiled content of the story that must be elucidated. It is Jesus' underlying authority to relate this story that Smart unveils. By describing Christ's actions in declarative terms ("Christ in the parables decries / a mere professor's life of lies"), Smart correlates the act of telling a parable and the authority to interpret that parable with Christ himself. In effect, Smart uses the parable's verse supplement to focus on Jesus and his unique position in the Gospels. Smart then opens the parable to his reader by interposing a third term, the figure of "conscious meekness," which by giving the "glory" "voice and tears" embodies and humanizes the parabolic moral just as the parable itself has "embodied" Christ's nature for the reader. The "conscious meekness" that "gives the glory voice and tears," in other words, is itself a trope for Christ's dual identity, but it is a trope that also exemplifies the conduct we should follow once we understand the trope qua trope. Smart thus uses his supplement as a bridge between Christ's alterity—his "glory" as God—and his redemptive role as he who *brings the pardon down*" and "*gains th' incorruptible crown.*" If we thus ask whether or not Smart's supplement expounds the "right" meaning of the parable, we miss the transgressive character of the supplements themselves: what is important is that the supplement enacts a stable and reliable interpretation of the parable, which in this case unifies narrative and theology. The supplement interprets the parable for Smart's audience; it is this act of interpretation that subverts the parable's generic reticence and asserts Christ's identity and his relationship to the world of history for an ideally "common" reader.

In her analysis of "A Song to David," Harriet Guest reflects on the difficulty most readers had (and continue to have) with Smart's religious writings: "In Smart's poetry the language of type and emblem may seem to demand a knowledge of scripture which requires an extraordinarily diligent attention on behalf of the Christian, but that language can also be seen as the key to an attempt to reclaim, for poetry and thus for the congregation, an access to the Bible, and in particular to the Old Testament, which was increasingly denied, or granted only to the scholar, as a result of the development of kinds of biblical criticism which did not remove the Bible from controversy because they clarified its obscurer passages, but because they appropriated them only to the enquiries of the learned" (Guest, 260). Given the complexity of Smart's poetical language in general, the *Parables* represent an important departure for Smart. Guest correctly identifies the effort most of Smart's contemporary readers would have had to invest in his more famous works simply to make those texts comprehensible. But with the *Parables,* Smart evolves a new poetics designed specifically to circumvent the generic constraints of parabolic literature. Parables only make sense once they can be set in a larger narrative context: who tells a parable, to whom the parable is told, and the circumstances of the narration all play a part in establishing the parable per se, but since parables are also compact stories with discrete narrative shapes, they seem particularly to invite a decontextualized reading that can reduce the parable to mere story. "The very character of parables is to blame. They are compact and attractive units which, as such, seem to invite detachment from their narrative settings."[19] Smart's verse translations recontextualize the parables in a narrative environment that Smart himself determines.

The sum of Smart's poetic choices for the *Parables* registers, then, as a way to renegotiate parabolic literature and to re-present that literature so as to make the act of reading transparent. The transition from complexity to clarity requires, in concrete terms, a poetic style that approaches as nearly as possible the cadences and inflections of eighteenth-century middle-class prose. More important, Smart's parabolic poetics asserts an equality between Christ's utterances and Smart's reiteration of those utterances, since—as we have seen—the supplements Smart makes integral to his paraphrases refocus the reader's attention as Smart wishes and not according to some infallible quality of the biblical material itself. Smart's parables thus work deconstructively, in that they repeat with a difference the content they purport to convey. But Smart subverts the parable form only to realize what he sees as its true function: the parables distill Christ's dual identity as man and God and offer the reader access to that identity. The parables remain deeply embedded in their Gospel matrix, but they also open that matrix to Smart's revisionary understanding of Jesus and of his salvific role. That, finally, is most indicative of Smart's commitment to the *Parables.* Smart's love for his childlike audience, his faith that "faith" can render the act of reading transparent, his determination to accommodate his poetic genius to the lowest common denominator, and his deep conviction that by puzzling out the parables for his audience he can liberate that audience from its blinkered understanding and open the way for Jesus to work his intentions through Smart's language—all of these factors mark the centrality of the *Parables* to Smart's evangelical vision.

NOTES

1. John Drury, "Luke," in *The Literary Guide to the Bible*, eds. Robert Alter and Frank Kermode (Cambridge, MA: Harvard University Press, 1987), 432.
2. For the publication date of the *Parables*, see Sherbo, 246.
3. Karina Williamson, "Introduction," in *PW*, ii: 203.
4. Ibid.
5. Harriet Guest proposes a similar function for *Jubilate Agno* when she describes the poem's ideal audience as one "that is conjured or exhorted into immanent being in the prophetic future the poem gestures towards." See Guest, 242.
6. Frank Kermode, "Hoti's Business: Why Are Narratives Obscure?" in *The Genesis of Secrecy: On the Interpretation of Narrative* (Cambridge, MA: Harvard University Press, 1979), 23.
7. Kermode, "Hoti's Business," 24.
8. John Dominic Crossan, "Parables," in *Harper's Bible Dictionary*, ed. Paul J. Achtemeier (San Francisco, CA: Harper Collins Publishers, 1985), 747-48.
9. John Dominic Crossan, "Parable, Allegory, and Paradox," in *Semiology and Parables: An Exploration of the Possibilities Offered by Structuralism for Exegesis*, ed. Daniel Patte (Pittsburgh: The Pickwick Press, 1976), 253.
10. John Dominic Crossan, *In Parables: The Challenge of the Historical Jesus* (N.Y.: Harper and Row, 1973), 15-16.
11. Reprinted in the "Introduction" to *PW*, ii: 201.
12. It seems only fair to note that Christopher Devlin considered the *Parables* "a most meritorious work, straightforward and thoughtful." Devlin's praise though, is more for the *Parables'* pedagogical value to children than it is for their artistic merit: "There is no sanctimoniousness in them and they are completely sincere." See *Devlin*, 176, 186.
13. For a contrasting perspective on Smart's devotional children's literature, compare Mark Booth's interesting and well-argued chapter in this volume.
14. Drury, *The Parables in the Gospels: History and Allegory* (New York: The Crossroad Publishing Company, 1985), 147-48.
15. In letter XXVIII, Smart begins his dedication of the *Parables* to Bonnell George Thornton by writing, "THERE are sundry Instances of our Blessed SAVIOUR'S Fondness for Children, as a Man; and he has assured us, we can have no Part in Him without imitating their Innocence and Simplicity." See *Letters*, 116-117.

16. Addison contrasts adult and childish states in *Spectator* 409 when he describes the acquisition of fine taste in literature in terms of a developmental and genetic narrative: "But notwithstanding this Faculty must in some measure be born with us, there are several Methods for Cultivating and Improving it, and without which it will be very uncertain, and of little use to the Person that possesses it. The most natural Method for this Purpose is to be conversant among the Writings of Polite Authors." Since aesthetic appreciation is finally the result of cultivation and training, and the purpose for consuming literature, to read like a child in an Addisonian sense would be a contradiction in terms. See *The Spectator*, 5 vols., ed. Donald F. Bond (Oxford: Clarendon Press, 1965), III: 529.

17. Smart's supplements consistently appear in italics, but rather than reinstituting a hierarchical relationship between paraphrase and supplement, this feature suggests that such typography reinforces Smart's own editorial position as above either paraphrase or supplement.

18. Donald Davie makes a related argument when he remarks that poetry "can be written in unmetaphorical language." Davie contends that English poetry at its best often utilizes the syntactic patterns of prose to "purify" and "strengthen" poetic language; such poetry thus conveys meaning "in conversational and unmetaphorical language, chiefly by apt handling of syntax." Davie's notion of "prosaic strength" entails a syntactic arrangement of words dependent less on the figural equation of unlike terms and more on the poet's ability to position a word "artfully with and against the others," so that each word "takes on new life, defined freshly and closely." Instead of the usual opposition between poetry and prose, Davie juxtaposes prose and metaphor, thus making prosaic language yet another poetic strategy. Smart's parables employ plain and conventional language in a similar fashion: the poetry of the parables is predicated upon a "literal" use of language, language deployed by the author and understood by the reader as working without the intention of additional or hidden significance. This is not to repudiate the metaphorical nature of language; it is instead to define a poetics of metaphorical economy in which conventional metaphorical associations—associations that Smart's critics would identify with lofty aesthetic configurations of "imagination" and "taste"—give way to the cadences and patterns of a print-based popular discourse. See Donald Davie, *Purity of Diction in English Verse* (London: Chatto and Windus, 1952), 62, 65.

19. Drury, *The Parables in the Gospels*, 1.

CHAPTER 5

Taxonomy and Confession in Christopher Smart and Jean-Jacques Rousseau

ERIC MILLER

My eyes, wide open, had the run
Of some ten weeds to fix upon;
Among those few, out of the sun,
The woodspurge flowered, three cups in one.

From perfect grief there need not be
Wisdom or even memory:
One thing then learnt remains to me—
The woodspurge has a cup of three.
—Dante Gabriel Rossetti, "The Woodspurge"

According to Michel Foucault, the scientific epoch consummated with the work of the taxonomist Carolus Linnaeus saw a decisive change in the European conception of natural history. Until the late seventeenth century, natural historians did not respect the "division, so evident to us, between what we see, what others have observed . . . and what others imagine or naively believe; the great tripartition . . . into *Observation, Document,* and *Fable,* did not exist."[1] With manuals such as *Philosophia botanica* (1751), Linnaeus instituted the usages of a new order: the true natural historian should now address himself, in descending sequence, to "name, theory, kind, species, attributes, use, and . . . *Litteraria.*" The informed nomenclator ought unequivocally to relegate into the last of these categories "all the language deposited upon things by time."[2]

If Foucault's analysis of this revolution in natural history is correct, then Christopher Smart's *Jubilate Agno* and Jean-Jacques Rousseau's *Les Rêveries du Promeneur solitaire* register both the success and the limits of that evacuation of figurative meaning which Linnaeus and his colleagues hoped, perhaps, to secure. Smart fuses the allegorical and heraldic lore of Bible, bestiary, and emblem-book with contemporary natural history, but—significantly—

attaches his mass of inherited *Litteraria* to autobiographical initiatives. A vatic Noah, Smart contrives to perpetuate the whole zoo of legend by packing it into the ark of his intensely confessional, though prophetic, poem. Smart's own experience coordinates, at the same time that it justifies, the accumulations of tradition and the reforms of the present day. The poet invents a hybrid genre, at once versified journal and liturgy. *Jubilate Agno* links the archaic sphere of myth with the new orthodoxy of field and laboratory description by the device of punning—a kind of philological-typological reasoning. Smart understands the conventions of the bestiary and of modern natural history alike; he applies scientific formalities to legendary beasts, and venerable symbolic usages to recently reported discoveries.

Rousseau contrastingly turns to Linnaeus's majestic *Systema naturae* as a counterweight against—an active contestation of—the systematic conspiracy by which he felt oppressed. The Linnaean method supplied Rousseau with a guarantee of veridicality. The "Solitary Walker" uses this guarantee to endorse the truth-value of his polemical excursions. Rousseau anticipates the largely North American genre, a hybrid of taxonomic science with autobiography, that Peter Fritzell calls "nature writing."[3] Responding to the emptying out of ancestral content that Foucault recognizes, Smart and Rousseau divergently recruit natural history to sponsor the arguments of their all-too-human histories.

Adducing the identities of *naturalia,* each labors under threatening circumstances (Mr. Potter's madhouse in one case, ostracism and senescent decrepitude in the other) to assert a persuasive identity, to announce a vocation, to advance apologetics. Smart recovers pre-Linnaean protocols and reconciles them with the innovations of the period; Rousseau requisitions in his own behalf the vaunted empirical accuracy of Foucault's new natural historian. Smart fills the chasm between science and religion, and Rousseau the space formerly engrossed by traditional imagery, with autobiography. Both mirror the ascendancy of the bildungsroman, which offered fictitious accounts of identity-formation after the disabling of old models, chiefly scriptural, for this task. Smart and Rousseau, however, never relinquish the first-person singular and the identity conferred by their proper names.

The accuracy of Foucault's conjectures must be proven before further discussion of Smart and Rousseau can proceed. The test case ought to be Foucault's supreme example, Linnaeus himself. Does the taxonomist himself consistently demote *Litteraria* to a nominal place? The adjective "nominal" has unusual pertinence, because the very names propounded by the nomenclator partially reconstitute the fabulous—a category Foucault claims that

Linnaeus banished. Linnaeus retained Latin as the universal language of science. His binomials thus could not but reflect a tradition as long as, and often interpenetrating with, that of the *Litteraria* he is alleged to have subordinated and curtailed. Lisbet Koerner has argued that Linnaeus pioneered the employment of science as both "legitimation and technique of state governance"[4]; Latin is the tongue of the West's foundational empire-state, Rome.

In a real sense, then, *Litteraria* shared first place in the Linnaean hierarchy of importance with *Nomina.* John L. Heller has vindicated Linnaeus's mythographic erudition in the choice of names for *naturalia.*[5] Heller establishes the locus classicus of this feature of Linnaean naming: the genus PAPILIO, "Butterflies." Among other illustrious companies, Linnaeus enrolled all the Trojan knights as alter egos of the genus PAPILIO. The winged "EQUITES *Trojani*" include Priamus, Hector, and Paris. To identify a butterfly thus often amounted to the compulsive recollection of Homer (and of Virgil after him); indeed, it entailed inevitable evocation of the whole *Nachleben,* or afterlife, of antiquity.

In defense of Foucault, however, the arbitrariness of Linnaeus's nomenclatural procedure ought to be urged. To Linnaeus, the shared gaudiness of butterflies and of Troy's *jeunesse dorée* might have legitimated an association as logically defensible as it was witty. But this association lacks any imprimatur of folklore, scholarship, or theology. No aetiology clarifies why one butterfly goes by Priam's, and another by Hector's name. The literary resonance has a merely mnemonic motive. Epic is elegantly made to subserve the art of memory; *naturalia* receive titles at Linnaeus's fiat.

Contrary to Foucault, Linnaeus does not always refrain from moralizing his field-guide entries. The taxonomist preserves some prerogatives of the bestiary. Anyone who consults the *Systema naturae* in search of enlightenment as to his or her species identity confronts at once the wisdom of Delphi: *HOMO nosce Te ipsum,* "Man know thyself." Footnotes—some extensive—quote Solon, Seneca, and Augustine on the unique characteristics and responsibilities of humanity.[6]

Yet the bibliographical fact that these recrudescences of *Litteraria* appear predominantly in footnotes testifies to their subordination in the Linnaean system of nature. Philosophy densely pads the *Systema naturae*'s entry for Homo sapiens; it becomes vestigial in association with other species. Linnaeus does not debar morally and aesthetically inflected description from his account of the birds (*pulcherrimae,* "most beautiful" [78]) or from his sketch of the horse (*animal generosum, superbum, fortissimum,* "a noble, proud, supremely courageous beast" [73]). But these judgments amount to a few adjectives. Notwithstanding the frequent presence of evaluative epithets, the *Systema naturae* represents the achievement of a new, profoundly laconic idiom for natural history—the virtual exorcism of *Litteraria.*

Foucault's contentions find strong support in Linnaeus's animadversions upon redundancy. *Philosophia Botanica* makes it axiomatic that all pleonasm be excluded from botany—a principle opposite to that which animates Smart's rich *Jubilate Agno. Jubilate Agno* celebrates pleonasm, redoubles it by analogy upon analogy. In the section devoted to *Nomina,* "Names," Linnaeus insists: *Nomina si nescis, perit & cognitio rerum,* "If you do not know the names, the understanding of things also perishes"; *Unicum ubi genus, unicum erit nomen,* "Where the genus is unique, there the name will be unique."[7] Under *Differentiae* ("Distinctions"), Linnaeus even advances the extreme claim that *res* and *verbum* can achieve perfect congruency: *Nomen specificum primo intuito plantam suam manifestabit, cum differentiam ipsi plantae inscriptam contineat,* "The species-name will demonstrate its plant at first glance, since it contains the difference *inscribed in the very plant*" (203). This faith in an innate alphabet has corollaries in Smart (see B477 and following); but unlike the exuberant poet, Linnaeus considers that decipherment of such signs must conduce to finer and finer trials of linguistic compunction on the part of the natural historian, to the exclusion of ambiguity. In keeping with Foucault's general argument, Linnaeus attempts to quell the fecundity of proliferating signifiers, starting with synonyms.

As though in conscious defiance of Linnaean laconicism and Foucauldian theory, Smart opens *Jubilate Agno* with programmatic advocacy of pluralism, using a psalmist's two moods of command, the imperative and the jussive (A1-3):

> Rejoice in God, O ye Tongues; give the glory to the Lord, and the Lamb.
> Nations, and languages, and every Creature, in which is the breath of Life.
> Let man and beast appear before him, and magnify his name together.

This exordium permits a number of protocols to be inferred. The vocative is a favored case, praise a preferred end. Maximal multiplicity (of tongues and themes to which the tongues address themselves) will obtain not just men and beasts, but names ought to be fruitful, and multiply. Even God has an alias among *naturalia* (the Lamb). "Man" and "beast," as fellow creatures, collaborate in a panegyrical project. To begin to study the practical roles, in *Jubilate Agno,* of man and beast, and the place of personal confession in uniting these domains, no better approach can be made than through that exemplary "man," the liturgist Christopher Smart, and his famous "beast," the cat Jeoffry. Smart's loving natural history of Jeoffry sponsors the procedures of his own autobiographical enterprise—"autobiography" being nothing other than one *naturale* (*-bio-*) inscribing (*-graphy*) its life (*auto-*).

The natural history of Jeoffry begins after a demonstration that the power of an animal governs every language. Because the first person plural "-mus" appears in Latin verbs, therefore the mouse rules Latin (B636-638). The "cat" predominates in Greek, being a frequent prefix (B626-636). Honored in the national figure of John Bull, the adjectival "-ble" supports Smart's punning assertion that this "strong" beast presides over English (B647). Taxonomic distribution of languages under emblematic *naturalia,* rhetorically distinguished by the causal "for," abruptly inaugurates an itemized description of a specific cat, Jeoffry.

Designated by a personal name, Jeoffry breaks free of one kind of symbolic status, that of the generic cat charged with managing the characteristic constituent of Greek. Jeoffry promptly assumes other symbolic offices. Like a human being, he has, with his unique name, a particular identity; in that identity, "he is the servant of the Living God duly and daily serving him" (B696). The cat's continuous, exemplary service provides the rationale for exhaustive enumeration of his behaviors. Just as Augustine confessionally recorded his life as an instance—at once singular and representative—of all human experience, not omitting to testify even to his infant petulance, so Smart licenses an intimate field-guide entry about Jeoffry by emphasizing the worship of God inherent in every one of the cat's actions. Jeoffry magnifies the glory of the Lord in the most trivial of his daily behaviors: *"For Eighthly he rubs himself against a post"* (B710). Smart feels no need here to aggrandize the feline delight in friction; like Keats's poet, Jeoffry lives a life of allegory. Smart observes the cat with the intentness of an ethologist. Jeoffry's contribution to the unbroken ceremony of holy service justifies every fact.

Smart's excursus on his pet starts with the famous assertion, *"I will consider my cat Jeoffry"* (B695). Smart grants the cat powers of consideration in his own right: *"For having consider'd God and himself he will consider his neighbour"* (B713). Jeoffry exists in a social milieu, among fellow cats (they enjoy his kisses), among prey species (he grants them a fighting chance), among men and women of differing moral valencies (*"he is hated by the hypocrite and miser"* [B751]). Moreover, Jeoffry offers himself pedagogically for other people's edification: *"he is an instrument for the children to learn benevolence upon"* (B727).

If every aspect of Jeoffry's deportment signifies the ministry of God, then the cat is, in the root sense, a liturgist—for the Greeks, a "public servant." Even the cat's acts of elimination magnify God publicly, inasmuch as they are observable, amenable of public record, and without exception classifiable as perfect rites of piety. Christ represents the word made flesh; not blasphemously, but with the ecumenicism of a pious naturalist, Smart extends this privileged incarnation of the divine word to an individual of the genus *Felis.* On this analogy, the author of *Jubilate Agno,* otherwise known as *"the Lord's News-Writer,"* *"the scribe-evangelist"* (B327), and *"the Reviver of ADORATION amongst ENGLISH-MEN"* (B332), may treat the individual traits of his person, the circle of his personal acquaintances, and the repertoire of his epiphanies on a par with science and politics.

Thus, the proposal of a color theory to supplement or replace Isaac Newton's probably musters in its defense nothing other than a reminiscence of the bloom on Ann Vane's cheek (C662-667):

> NOW *that color is spiritual appears inasmuch as the blessing of God upon all things descends in color.*
> *For the blessing of health upon the human face is in color.*
> *For the blessing of God upon purity is in the Virgin's blushes.*
> *For the blessing of God in color is on him that keeps his virgin.*
> *For I saw a blush in Staindrop Church, which was of God's own colouring.*
> *For it was the benevolence of a virgin shewn to me before the whole congregation.*

A memoiristic moment of panegyric subserves a taxonomy of color, a spectrum. The red of the blush signifies not only the proof of a chromatic hypothesis, but also the presence of piety. Smart's autobiographical recollection, introduced as evidence for a theory, flatters a woman who played an important role in Smart's youth (she was the daughter of his father's employer). A topographical pun renders Staindrop Church a decorous site for Smart's demonstration, from his own experience, of the spirituality of a blush staining a virginal cheek.

Like Jeoffry the cat, then, Smart constitutes a living, comprehensive example. Smart's every memory, whether personal or drawn from the fund of others' writings, has an equally valid place in the protraction of the mighty *Jubilate Agno.* In other words, Smart confounds observation, document, and fable in the manner that Foucault claims Linnaean natural historians strove to proscribe. Smart demonstrates in passing the impossibility of separating observation from self-observation (the anecdote of Ann Vane's blush betrays his equivocal attentiveness, in church, to the vagaries of this woman's person). But everything public is private, and vice versa, insofar as it impinges on the life of a prophet. Confession logically comprehends the whole system of nature, including one fleeting erubescence.

In the case of this blush, Smart narrates an epiphany of sorts in the course of an exposition on color theory. By what other techniques does Smart merge taxonomical natural history with confession in *Jubilate Agno?* Throughout the poem, of course, Smart's religious conviction and prophetic calling create the necessary condition for confession in the orthodox sense. Harriet Guest has elucidated the probable relationship between the "Let" and "For" clauses that characterize much of Fragment B of *Jubilate Agno;* she suggests that "we read the 'For' verses as a private and personal commentary on the 'public' 'Let' verses" (142). The jussive clauses stand in a high degree of independence from the causal ones, which offer, in general, with many eccentricities and obliquities, a commentary illustrative of the "tensions between private conscience and public faith," the latter being manifest in the "Let" verses (144).

Guest turns to William Law's *A Serious Call to a Devout and Holy Life* (1728) to suggest a provenance for Smart's method. Law writes: "Let, therefore, praise and thanksgiving, and oblation of yourself unto God, be always the fixed and certain object of your first prayers . . . then take the liberty of adding such other devotions, as the accidental difference of your state, or the accidental difference of your heart, shall then make most needful and expedient for you" (quoted in Guest, 145). Smart's program of inclusive praise licenses the laudatory *Systema naturae* of *Jubilate Agno.* William Law's prescription of liberty to subjoin to the sphere of the canonical the intimacies of accidental difference excuses, even encourages, Smart's coordination of personal confession with global zoology. The passage in *Jubilate Agno* concerned with what Smart terms his "inheritance" displays the mechanism of assimilation and confession clearly.

Arthur Sherbo conjectures that Smart forfeited control over his capital or "inheritance" as a legal consequence of the writ *de Lunatico Inquirendo* taken out against him at the time of his confinement to Mr. Potter's madhouse (123). Disturbed by this expropriation of his own estate, Smart uses the symbolic thesaurus of natural history to publicize his ambivalent interpretation of the fate that has befallen him (B45-52):

> Let Areli rejoice with the Criel, who is a dwarf that towereth above others.
> *For I am a little fellow, which is intitled to the great mess by the benevolence of God my father.*
> Let Phuvah rejoice with Platycerotes, whose weapons of defense keep them innocent.

For I this day made over my inheritance to my mother in consideration of her infirmities.

Let Shimron rejoice with the Kite, who is of more value than many sparrows.

For I this day made over my inheritance to my mother in consideration of her age.

Let Sered rejoice with the Wittal—a silly bird is wise unto his own preservation.

For I this day made over my inheritance to my mother in consideration of her poverty.

Let Elon rejoice with Attelabus, who is the Locust without wings.

For I bless the thirteenth of August, in which I had the grace to obey the voice of Christ in my conscience.

Let Jahleel rejoice with the Woodcock, who liveth upon suction and is pure from his diet.

For I bless the thirteenth of August, in which I was willing to run all hazards for the sake of the Lord.

Let Shuni rejoice with the Gull, who is happy in not being good for food.

For I bless the thirteenth of August, in which I was willing to be called a fool for the sake of Christ.

Let Ezbon rejoice with Musimon, who is from the ram and she-goat.

For I lent my flocks and my herds and my lands at once unto the Lord.

Personnel whose proper names appear in Genesis and Numbers are bidden to exult with a parallel diversity of *naturalia*. Verse B45 aligns a figure enrolled in the populous Bible with the Criel, or Lesser White Heron. The word *Criel* identifies a bird of upright posture, which by reason of its long legs empirically "towers," despite its relative shortness, above those many birds not belonging to the vertical class of herons.

This paradox—a diminutive creature that nevertheless excels the majority of its kind in height—plainly inspires or supports the personal admission and boast of the conjoined causal clause: "*For I am a little fellow, which is intitled to the great mess by the benevolence of God my father.*" To "intitle" is to grant a designation to a person or thing; the great nomenclator Smart has received his entitlement from God. This privilege in spite of confessed low stature (a physical detail that permits the reader to visualize the writer) forms an analogy with the Criel's case, the dwarfish bird that is yet, in conditional respects, gigantic.

If Smart alleges the paternity of God in B45, his mother is of markedly less exalted rank in B46. Phuvah, another Old Testament personage, rejoices with Platycerotes, a Plinian beast denominating "the one who has spreading horns," a stag. Smart describes the armament of the animal as defensive, employed exclusively in the maintenance of innocence; but any mention of horns, with Smart, inevitably brings with it, as a leitmotiv, hostility against female insubordination—a misogynistic strain that reaches its nadir in the fantastic prophecy of Fragment C, wherein Smart presages the imminent restoration of the masculine horn, a secondary sexual characteristic forfeited since the time of David, and once "instrumental in subjecting the woman" (C140; see also Chapter 8).

With the confessional precision of a diarist, Smart remarks in B46 that the very day on which he composes his words he has "made over my inheritance to my mother in consideration of her infirmities." This version of the consequences of the writ *de Lunatico Inquirendo* inverts the roles of Smart and his mother. His weakness becomes strength. Not Smart, but his mother suffers "infirmities." The forfeiture of his property becomes an act of volition, of "consideration" for his mother. The Platycerotes, a magnanimous beast who uses his formidable endowment of horns only for blameless purposes, stands incongruously juxtaposed to the figure of a woman who, we know, had to commit her son because his conduct suggested his impotence to regulate his own affairs.

The next verse (B47) introduces the Kite. Like the Criel, this species stands at once on its own, empirically, and absorbed into the argumentative confession Smart pursues. A Kite is "of more value than many sparrows" perhaps because it literally consumes them: by eating numerous representatives of its favored prey, it assimilates their aggregate worth. This attribution of cumulative merit has a sinister edge, because it accrues through predation—and the named bird furnished a synonym, as Karina Williamson observes (notes, B46-52), for a cheat. The succeeding causal clause anxiously reiterates Smart's "consideration" for his mother, this time professing her age as a reason for yielding his "inheritance" to her. Smart manipulates a double narrative: the natural history hints at his captors' duplicity; the manifest personal confession insists, with a kind of domineering pathos, on the continuance of the poet's virile autonomy. The Kite is simultaneously a real raptor, an emblematic swindler, and a figure for everyone who is defrauding Smart—especially the mother of whom he anaphorically claims to be considerate. Smart contrives to accuse and to exculpate within the binary structure he has invented. *Jubilate Agno* provides the vehicle of a magnificent ambivalence.

As Williamson remarks (20), B48 features a portmanteau word—half Witwall (or woodpecker), half Wittol (or halfwit). Smart assesses his own situation as being "silly . . . unto his own preservation," a subtle understanding of the terms of his incarceration. Meanwhile, the "For" verse continues to assert the countertheme of proud sovereignty: the personal pronoun advertises its power to choose and delegate, and its magnanimity in the face of Smart's mother's "poverty."

The choice of *naturalia* for B49 obliquely refers, like the Criel, to Smart's stature: according to Pliny, Attelabus is the most diminutive of locusts. Smart mythologizes his life, person, and plight by means of this insect. Its incapacity to fly, and the state of reduction that it expresses, inflects oddly the diaristically annotated declaration of the causal clause: *"I bless the thirteenth of August, in which I had the grace to obey the voice of Christ in my conscience."* This benediction publicizes Smart's psychomachia over the matter of his inheritance; the heron, the woodpecker, and the locust are heraldic conscripts of that struggle.

The next animal recruited is the Woodcock, a legendary dupe Smart celebrates, at least on the surface, for its purity (B50). Woodcock are caught with "springes," or snares, set on their customary paths. Perhaps this association motivates Smart's remark that he would "run all hazards for the sake of the Lord." The Woodcock expresses Smart's hope that his humiliation in Mr. Potter's madhouse entails a compensatory sacred integrity.

With the introduction of the Gull, a type of credulity, Smart puns on his willingness *"to be called a fool for the sake of Christ"* (B51). After all, the capacity to believe is the foundation of faith just as it is the basis of gullibility. This verse lifts Smart's situational ignominy into a religious context, a context of redemption—the last shall be first. The Gull's exemption from "being good for food" implicitly releases it from the hierarchy of sanguinary appetite that dominates other parts of Fragment B. At once pastoral and monstrous (with its vision of copulating rams and she-goats), verse B52 permits Smart to allegorize his involuntary munificence as an act of pious largesse. *"I lent my flocks and my herds and my lands at once unto the Lord,"* he writes, implying reciprocity and eliding into the ultimate figure of God, a celestial borrower, the proximate recipient of his renounced goods—his mother.

The multiple perspectives permitted by Smart's method of dynamic collage (of the Old Testament, ancient and modern zoology, autobiography) are perhaps acknowledged in the causal clause of B53: *"For nature is more various than observation tho' observers be innumerable."* *Jubilate Agno* conserves the twists and turns of rationalization. Even to the present day they live in polysemous suspension, in philological equivocality, forever unresolved.

Verse B54 celebrates the union of "the bird of prey and the man of prayer." Surely this *monstrum biforme* presides over much of *Jubilate Agno*. The raptor embodies the accusatory aggression, the meditated revenges, the grandiose self-righteousness of someone who feels unfairly relegated to a madhouse. Yet the man of prayer inventively extols natural and supernatural worlds; remembers men and women who helped him in the past (conscribing, for example, many of his one-time subscribers to his encyclopedic blessing); and eulogizes within a cosmopolitan—cosmic—context his native Britain embattled in the Seven Years' War. *Jubilate Agno* manages, in the terms offered by Dante Gabriel Rossetti's "The Woodspurge," to perpetuate both the record of "perfect grief" and of the *naturalia* Linnaean science put on its imperiously concise register.

Combining belatedness and prolepsis, Smart parallels Linnaeus. According to Koerner, Linnaean science has "premodern" content (145). Yet Linnaeus's effort to inaugurate a scientific-managerial state anticipates the modern norm. Just so, Smart's *Litteraria* fasten him to the past with the same force with which his ambivalent autobiographical drive renders him unmistakably modern—comparable to Jean-Jacques Rousseau.

In *Les Rêveries du Promeneur solitaire,* Rousseau reflects autobiographically on the 1760s—on events contemporary with Christopher Smart's sojourn at Mr. Potter's madhouse. Five years before beginning these apologetic memoirs, on September 21, 1771, Rousseau wrote to Linnaeus: "Alone with nature and with you, I spend delicious hours in my rural walks, and I derive more profit from your *Philosophia botanica* than from all ethical treatises."[8]

Praising Linnaeus, Rousseau compares *Philosophia Botanica* favorably with every conceivable moral tract. Lindroth paraphrases the intended sense of Linnaeus's title *Philosophia Botanica* as "the theoretical basis for [a] reformation of botany."[9] Linnaeus's own prefatory *Lectori Botanico* ("To the botanist reader") lays out his aim of explicating a technical lexicon and describing the organs of plants. The "philosophy" of Linnaeus's manual has, therefore, scientific (Aristotelian) rather than obviously moral (Boethian) force. Rousseau's implicit collation of different genres—the botanical guide, the manual for moral direction—may seem mystifying, especially because he acknowledges his rudimentary grasp of the science for which he claims so much: "Accept with kindness, Sir, the homage of an exceedingly ignorant but extremely ardent disciple of your disciples, who owes in large measure to the contemplation of your writings the calm he enjoys even in the midst of persecution all the crueller because it is the more covert and because it conceals beneath the mask of goodwill and of friendship a greater detestation than hell ever before incited." It is to the Linnaean system that Rousseau attributes his precarious attainment of philosophic tranquillity in the midst of a conspiracy as all-engrossing in its own sphere as Linnaeus's *Systema naturae.* A reading of *Les Rêveries du Promeneur solitaire* reveals not so much the evidence of achieved equanimity as the ways in which Linnaean rhetoric—so devoid of resonance, according to Foucault—could be made to authenticate Rousseau's tendentious autobiography.

The *Rêveries* start by claiming unconditional isolation: "Look at me then, alone on earth. . . . The most affable and the most loving of human beings has been proscribed by a universal agreement."[10] Rousseau's letter to Linnaeus used similar language, notably the crucial adjective "alone"; but in that letter Rousseau formed even in his solitude one of a trinity, his other associates being the botanical philosopher Linnaeus and a characteristically personified nature. This triune companionship, despite the assertion of the opening sentence, continues throughout the *Rêveries*.

Early in the first promenade, Rousseau compares his 15 years of ostracism to "a dream." Nightmare is a better designation: "Torn I know not how from the order of things, I saw that I was thrown into an incomprehensible chaos where I perceived nothing at all; and the more I consider my present circumstances, the less I can understand where I am" (36). The phrase "the order of things" at once strikes the eye of anyone familiar with the works of Michel Foucault. The same phrase furnished the English edition of Foucault's *Les mots et les choses,* an "archaeology of the human sciences," with a title. The publisher's note indicates that *L'ordre des choses* was "Foucault's original [titular] preference."[11] For Rousseau, in his time, to invoke the order of things was to call to mind at once, and ambiguously, the hierarchies of human society and the structures of taxonomical natural history.

When Rousseau says that he is torn from the order of things, he expresses his disorientation in spatial terms. He has difficulty in discerning where he now is. To locate oneself, one requires place-names. In this context, Linnaeus's frequent adjuration, "If you do not know names, knowledge of things also perishes," acquires special force.[12] Rousseau claims to inhabit chaos. This spatialization of his bewilderment mirrors and complements the use of the generic marker "promenade" in the chapter divisions of the *Rêveries*. Sometimes, "promenade" describes an argumentative excursion licensed to a degree of errancy or exorbitancy; sometimes, it denotes the recounting of actual botanizing walks.

Rousseau announces the peculiar relationship his book will have with models of systematic thought. He claims that his (figuratively botanical) "leaves" will be "formless" (41). A lack of consecutiveness is promised: "I will say what I've thought entirely as it came to me and with as little connection as the thoughts of the night share with those of the day after" (41). Rousseau eschews "order and method," two Linnaean imperatives (42). He does not intend to "reduce" his findings to a "system" (42). Yet his conviction of a conspiracy centered on him, and his reliance on Linnaean taxonomy, indicate that these systems—persecutory cabal and field-guide classification—have reciprocal roles to play in the *Rêveries.* Claiming that the very intensity of his ostracism heightens his bliss, Rousseau poses the important question, "How keep a faithful record?" (45). Enlisting botany in the service of a rhetoric of verifiability and identity, Rousseau's *Rêveries* read as a perfect specimen of "nature writing" according to Peter Fritzell's definition. Fritzell characterizes the genre by its oscillating reliance on a first-person narrator and on the ostensible impersonality of systematic science. The *Rêveries,* however, modify or undermine Fritzell's theory of geopolitical motivation for the development of the genre. For Fritzell, nature writing "is fundamentally an American phenomenon," generated out of an "attempt to . . . blend the traditions and forms of Aristotle's *Historia Animalium* on the one hand, and Saint Augustine's *Confessions,* on the other" (3).

Fritzell overlooks the *Rêveries* as Rousseau's venture in conflating confession and taxonomy. The acme of Linnaean science coincided with the establishment of the United States. Foucault's theory of a revolution in natural history may therefore explain the simultaneous emergence of prototypical "nature writing" in the European Rousseau and among the rebellious Americans who were his contemporaries; Fritzell notes that "nature writing" takes for its province doubts about "spiritual identity, on the one hand, and driving dedications, on the other hand, to compose . . . scientific accounts . . . of one's nonhuman surroundings" (5).

Percy Bysshe Shelley's "The Triumph of Life" offers a useful image of nature writing, as Fritzell defines and Rousseau practices it. In Shelley's poem, the vegetable world assimilates Rousseau, who resembles "an old root"; for hair he has grass, for eyes hollows in wood (182-88). This apparition divulges its identity (200-4):

> "I feared, loved, hated, suffered, did and died,
> And if the spark with which Heaven lit my spirit
> Had been with purer nutriment supplied,
>
> "Corruption would not now thus much inherit
> Of what was once Rousseau."

Shelley's Rousseau secures his identity among *naturalia*—*where* he is becomes *who* he is. For Shelley, identifying with the *ordo rerum* so successfully constituted at best an ambivalent success, culminating in torments like those with which Dante afflicted his infernal personages. Rousseau speaks in the *Septième promenade* of nourishing himself exclusively on grass: "Behold me then at grass for my entire sustenance, with botany for my entire occupation" (119). Shelley literalizes Rousseau's comic trope, and condemns the diet as inadequate.

If Smart personally undertook to revivify in its numinous splendor the whole realm of *Litteraria,* then Rousseau, like the New World colonists, seized on the vaunted neutrality of the new taxonomy precisely because it promised an indisputable transparency. Plausible allegations of identity depended on the capacity to identify *naturalia.* Smart's adaptations of *naturalia* to his autobiographical concerns are often more explicit than Rousseau's. The *Rêveries* illustrate that Rousseau personalizes Linnaean natural history as ingeniously as the poet of *Jubilate Agno.* Whereas Smart packs his *naturalia* into the Ark of Salvation (his prophetic verse), Rousseau concentrates them into his own, autobiographical *arca* (the term by which Linnaeus designates a herbarium).

Rousseau's narrative of his accident at Ménilmontant on Thursday October 24, 1776, offers a spectacular example of the interplay between personal identity and the capacity to make identifications among *naturalia.* The completeness of the date Rousseau supplies already points to a heightened empiricism. Rousseau begins by reporting the fruits of a botanizing expedition undertaken in the outskirts of Paris—capital of literary France and of Rousseau's persecution. Liberty and precision are the imperatives of a naturalist's promenade. Rousseau pauses in his waywardness painstakingly to identify vegetation according to Linnaeus (46). He traverses the landscape and documents the trajectory of this errancy by determining the Latin binomials of species that typify—or variegate—that landscape (each furnishing a synecdoche for the environment, its biotic potentials).

To contrast his imminent loss of consciousness with the uttermost natural-historical circumstantiality, Rousseau documents the conscientious results of his *herborisation* (46): "I glimpsed two [plants] that I had very rarely seen in the Paris area . . . *Picris hieracioides* . . . and . . . *Buplevrum falcatum.* . . . This discovery . . . diverted me a long time and it concluded with that of a plant still rarer . . . the *Cerastium aquaticum* that, despite the accident which befell me on the same day, I found in a book which I had on me and placed in my herbarium." These specimens have something in common with the flower Coleridge once imagined, that a dreamer might pluck and carry into waking reality.[13] A Great Dane summarily knocks Rousseau unconscious. If, waking, he then undergoes a manner of rebirth experience, nevertheless the Linnaean system offers an armature, an explicatory scheme whose neutrality stretches a filament, an Ariadne's thread of continuity to link Rousseau's past and future across this oblivious hiatus. Linnaeus proposed his method as such an Ariadnean thread: "KNOWLEDGE of *Nature* relies on the learning of a methodical and systematic nomenclature of natural things as if on Ariadne's thread, following which one can negotiate the twists and turns of Nature in unexampled certainty" (8).

The herbarium invoked at the end of Rousseau's paragraph is a repository for the "institutionally sanctioned" *naturalia* of which Fritzell insisted his American colonists stood in psychic need (142). For Rousseau as for the nature-writing Americans, such *naturalia* serve as instruments by which exiles, whether internal or émigré, could maintain a kind of liaison with their original society. The herbarium furnishes a material reply to Rousseau's question, "How keep a faithful record?" Such a record's fidelity derives in part from its institutional legibility.

This herbarium harbors desiccated vegetable scraps. By their very exiguousness, however, they suggest the immensity of that space that Foucault claims Linnaeus opened up in natural history by suppressing all ancient accretions. Like the loci or sites of an *ars memoriae,* the herbarium conserves an archive of objective mnemotechnic icons. Symptomatically choosing one narcissistic and one scientific image, Rousseau compares the repository of his specimens at once to a diary and to a scientific instrument: "This herbarium is for me a diary . . . and it produces the effect of an optical device" (136).

The Great Dane collides with Rousseau opposite the aptly named Jolly Gardener Tavern. Rousseau subsequently discovers the *Cerastium aquaticum* pressed in the leaves of a book. The pun on "page" and "leaf" reconciles, with a philological obliquity like Smart's, the spheres of literature and nature; the act of pressing the living plant suggests the act of keeping written records. The compression of natural fact against autobiographical argument merges these distinct domains.

After noting the collection and identities of his fateful specimens, Rousseau moves from the literal promenade to the reverie, which makes figurative use of natural (collected) particulars: "After having scrutinized in detail many other plants that I saw still in flower . . . I gradually left behind these minute observations to deliver myself to the impression not less agreeable but more poignant which the whole ensemble made on me" (46).

Foucault remarks that, with the advent of Linnaeus, "all the language deposited upon things by time is pushed back into the very last category" (130). This demotion of the fabular and anecdotal permits the infusion of those demystified particulars encountered in the Enlightenment fieldguide with personal—confessional—elements. Passage from the specific (*Cerastium aquaticum*) to the universal cannot escape the gravitational pull of Rousseau's self-concern: "There originated out of this view a mix of impressions, sweet and sad, too like my age and my fate for me not to make the application" (46). Foucault claims that Linnaeus intended to prune away the mythical excrescences from each species. Rousseau supplies his own substance to compensate this connotative loss. Seeing autumn around him, he applies the lesson of the season to himself: his spirit is likewise "adorned still with a few flowers" (46).

For Rousseau, Linnaean botany can be perceived working in two complementary ways. On the one hand, *naturalia* are turned to as a kind of alibi. *Cerastium aquaticum* functions as a witness, a fragment of objective truth, material corroboration to Rousseau's rebirth in the trauma of his accident. Rousseau emphasizes his real sense of having been born again. Yet the reader knows that the man has in his pocket identifiable markers of a preexistent system that rationalizes every apparently random efflorescence of the soil. Linnaeus cannot vouch for the accuracy of Rousseau's recollections; but Rousseau juxtaposes the discourse of botany with the justifications of his memoir so that the precisions of science imply the equivalent credibility of his narrative. *Cerastium aquaticum* lies compressed against his book, virtually of one substance with it. In *Jubilate Agno,* Smart likewise contrived a binary structure (of zoological praise and its autobiographical application).

Rousseau also depicts his rebirth as cosmic self-diffusion: "It seemed to me that I filled all the objects that I saw with my light existence" (48). This ubiquity throughout the visible corresponds to the condition of mind in which the entire vegetable world of October is conscripted—as a *paysage* personally *moralisé*—to mirror Rousseau's unique age and estate. Botany operates metonymically in the service of "objective" truth (*Cerastium aquaticum*) and "subjective" truth (the panoramic confirmation of Rousseau's decrepitude). Like Rousseau's justificatory exercise, the *Rêveries* themselves, the botany of the second promenade provides a legitimating sphere in which opposed forms of truth may coincide. This paradoxical conjunction resembles Rousseau's own role in his *Confessions,* in that the autobiography was offered as exemplary. To be exemplary is at one and the same time to stand for every possible instance and to be, notwithstanding, extraordinary—literally *extra ordinem,* outside the very system of which the example is somehow representative.

In the first promenade, Rousseau claims to have been torn out of the order of things. A literal consequence of his collision with the Great Dane in the second promenade is complete disorientation: "Someone asked me where I lived; it was impossible for me to say. I asked where I was; he said to me, '*At Haute-*

Borne'; it was as though he had said, '*On Mount Atlas*'" (49). The choice of Mount Atlas to express the degree of his amnesiac bewilderment reinforces the sense that Rousseau finds himself, after reviving, burdened with the whole mass of a world, a total system of nature, even then in process of reconstitution. Like Atlas, he carries on his shoulders the weight of the globe.

The stranger who asks where he lives guides Rousseau from Atlantean universals to particulars, reversing the current characteristic of reverie: "I had to ask successively the country, the city and the quarter in which I found myself. Even that didn't suffice for recognition; it required the whole trajectory right up to the boulevard for me to recall my residence and my name" (49). The man who could assign the *nomen proprium* to that rarity, *Cerastium aquaticum,* only painfully recovers his own proper name. He identifies himself, his place in the order of things as though through the use of a botanical key, moving from general toward limitary characteristics, the grid of geography contracting orbit by orbit to conclude with an act of self-identification. For his part, Smart discovers traces of himself dispersed throughout the entire *Systema naturae,* discernible through various kinds of analogy. Thus that towering dwarf, the Criel, suggests the Smart who believes, at least intermittently, that he has founded, despite his diminutive stature and reduced circumstances, a new liturgy for the edification of posterity.

After the accident at Ménilmontant, Rousseau recovers his sense of continuous identity in part by discovering the *Cerastium aquaticum* in his pocket. This fragment stands synecdochally for the whole of Linnaeus's *Systema naturae*—the warrant of an unimpeachably existent world. Concluding his Ménilmontant chapter, Rousseau defends his conviction that a gigantic conspiracy has him for its focus by advancing a claim intended to reflect the same empirical outlook (54): "The accumulation of so many chance events, the promotion of all my cruellest enemies as though fortune seconded them . . . all of them converging in the common conspiracy—this universal accord is too extraordinary to be purely fortuitous. . . . [A] concord so striking . . . leaves me no doubt that its full success is written in the ordinances of eternity." Rousseau insists here that he identified not chance but design as the agent of his persecution only after evidence for concerted—indeed unanimous—malice overwhelmed him. Like a good botanist, he tarries with the phenomenon until such time as a conclusion is warranted. Two tokens of that incontrovertible conclusion are the adjectives "universal" and "extraordinary." The first designates a scope only to be equaled, and perhaps neutralized, by the grandeur of the Linnaean *Systema naturae.* The second epithet echoes Rousseau's sense of alienation and exceptionality, bearing the etymological implication of *quod est extra ordinem*—except that now the dominant order itself merits this outlaw status. Indeed, Rousseau leaps from the domain of nature—human nature—to that of providence, becoming a theodicean of sorts: the success of the conspiracy is written "in the ordinances of eternity." Here he aspires to the plane of Smart, "the Lord's News-writer."

Rousseau repudiates ethical manuals because their authorship and readership coincide inescapably with the roster of the universal plot. The conspirators, characterized by Rousseau in his letter to Linnaeus as "hidden" and masked, use such manuals cynically. Even the moral philosophers to whom his persecutors resort for counsel display immunity to their own insights, depriving such insights of legitimacy: "their philosophy is . . . alien to them" (58). The invocation of philosophy recalls *Philosophia botanica,* Rousseau's favorite among Linnaeus's works.

Rousseau despises the non-botanical philosophers for their ambition: they "only wanted to put together a book, no matter what kind. . . . When theirs had been . . . published, its contents didn't interest them any more . . . unless . . . to defend it . . . but otherwise without care for its appropriate usage, without a qualm about the truth or falsity of its contents . . . provided that it wasn't refuted" (58).

Linnaeus's *Philosophia botanica* circumvents such criticisms. The book contains clear directives as to proper usage, especially in the domain of nomenclature; embodies in its successive editions the continuing interest of its author; and, assuming scrupulous adherence to appropriate protocol, invites anyone to refine and augment the findings of botanical science. Propagating laws, the book notwithstanding solicits revision and expansion. In the *Rêveries,* Rousseau states his ambition to discover for himself "a fixed rule of conduct for the remainder of my days" (63). The prescriptive quality of Linnaeus's work answers, in its exaltation of orthodoxy, to such a desire. A field guide is just that—a sure conductor through the perplexities of a field.

To secure similar ends, *Jubilate Agno* works in almost precisely the opposite way. The bewilderment of Christopher Smart, inmate of Mr. Potter's asylum, seeks resolution by forging mighty analogies from natural and supernatural history. Scripture, science, and the latest bulletins from the Seven Years' War do not merely underwrite, they are made linguistically to resonate with the preoccupations of the poet. Smart renders every specimen of *naturalia* an emblem, philology proving itself to be prophetically absorptive; contrastingly, Rousseau labors to make his interpretation of things as objectively irrefutable as botanical philosophy, as if apologetics amounted to a genre of field notes.

At one fascinating juncture, Rousseau performs a substitution that proves his almost religious reliance on the neutrality of Linnaean science. In the

Cinquième promenade, devoted to an account of Rousseau's sojourn on the Ile de Saint-Pierre, the would-be compiler of a *Flora petrinsularis* ("A Botanical Inventory of the Ile de Saint-Pierre") rejoices in Linnaeus's point-for-point veridicality.[14] The detail that Rousseau selects for special emphasis is "the horns of the self-heal." Rousseau likens his enthusiasm for the minute structures of the self-heal to La Fontaine's irrepressible appreciation of a biblical prophet: "I went around asking if people had observed the horns of the self-heal as La Fontaine used to ask if people had read Habakkuk" (97). This allusion identifies Linnaean taxonomic practice with theodicy. Habakkuk memorably phrases the terms of a problem that obsessed both the incarcerated Smart and the ostracized Rousseau: "The law is slacked and justice never goes forth. For the wicked surround the righteous, so justice goes perverted" (Hab 1:2). The Ile de Saint-Pierre, insular by definition, offered asylum from encompassing hostility: Rousseau withdrew to this refuge after his lodging at Môtiers was pelted with stones. Habakkuk proposes, as an answer to the conundrum injustice presents, the operation of a kind of Nemesis: "If it seem slow, wait for it; it will surely come" (Hab 2:3).

An instrument of impeccable accuracy, Linnaeus's *Systema naturae* bears comparison, in Rousseau, with one of the West's fundamental ethical treatises. Rousseau distinguishes between the powers of Linnaeus and of Habakkuk, recognizing the former as an adequate substitute for the latter. Unlike Smart, he accepts the supremacy of Linnaeus, the supersession of Habakkuk.

Rousseau's herbarium—safeguarding scientific collection *and* autobiographical recollection—allows him to exceed the terms of Rossetti's "The Woodspurge." The speaker of that poem remembers from the trauma of "perfect grief" only the plant's "cup of three," a diagnostic character such as Linnaeus systematized. From his past, Rousseau wrests more than the indelible cognizance of a flower's anatomical structure. Botanical specimens actually enfranchise the reverist's and polemicist's memory.

As for Smart, he takes woodspurge or an equivalent and, not neglecting its proper name or its empirical qualities, renders it a providentially versatile advocate for his case. Foucault correctly identifies the Linnaean drive to subordinate *Litteraria.* But human (no less than nonhuman) nature abhors a vacuum. Christopher Smart and Jean-Jacques Rousseau testify to nature's ineradicable, eloquent, and equivocal plenty.

NOTES

1. See Michel Foucault, *The Order of Things: An Archaeology of the Human Sciences* (New York: Pantheon, 1970), 129.

2. Ibid., 130.

3. See Peter Fritzell, *Nature Writing and America* (Ames: Iowa State University Press, 1990).

4. See Lisbet Koerner, "Linnaeus' Floral Transplants," *Representations* 47 (1994): 144-69, esp. page 145.

5. See John L. Heller, "Classical Mythology in the *Systema Naturae* of Linnaeus," *Transactions and Proceedings of the American Philological Association* 76 (1945): 333-57; also "Classical Poetry in the *Systema Naturae* of Linnaeus," *TAPA* 102 (1971): 183-216.

6. I refer to Caroli Linnaei, *Systema Naturae,* ed. Jo. Frid. Gmelin, vol. 1 (Stockholm: Laurentius Salvius, 1758), 20-24.

7. I refer to Caroli Linnaei, *Philosophia botanica* (Stockholm: Godofr Kiesewetter, 1751), 158.

8. I have translated from R.A. Leigh, ed., *Correspondance complète de Jean-Jacques Rousseau,* vol. 38 (Oxford: The Voltaire Foundation, 1981), 267.

9. Sten Lindroth, "The Two Faces of Linnaeus," in *Linnaeus, the Man and His Work,* eds. Tore Frängsmyr et al. (Berkeley, CA: University of California Press, 1983), 28.

10. Jean-Jacques Rousseau, *Les Rêveries du Promeneur solitaire,* ed. S. de Sacy (—: Editions Gallimard, 1972): 35. My translation throughout.

11. *The Order of Things,* viii.

12. See, for example, *Philosophia botanica,* part VII, no. 210, 158.

13. *Picris hieracioides* is Bitter Lettuce. It blooms all year round. The bitterness and the persistent power of flowering are suggestive. *Buplevrum falcatum* is Hare's-ear. *Cerastium aquaticum* may be Parsnip.

14. Rousseau planned to divide the whole Ile de Saint-Pierre into quadrants for botanical inventory. This inventory may supply a figure for the impossible project of a total autobiography.

PART II

AUTHORSHIP IN TRANSITION

CHAPTER 6

Christopher Smart's Poetics

BETTY RIZZO

"Where ask is have, where seek is find, / Where knock is open wide" (*Song to David,* Stanza LXXVII, *PW,* ii: 145) are startling and stunning lines that obviously exemplify their author's commitment to two rhetorical strategies, *brevitas* or compact concision and *energia* or vigor of attack. That is, his commitment to these strategies in order to convey a strong *impression* has induced him thus to distill and concentrate his original—"And I say unto you, Ask, and it shall be given you: seek, and ye shall find: knock and it shall be opened unto you" (Luke 11:9)—a text, one might have thought, already as concisely strong as possible. Only syntactical violence could produce Smart's further reduction and concentration, a distillation aimed at producing strong impression (see Chapter 12 for the impact of this passage on Theodore Roethke and other twentieth-century poets). Less obviously, the lines exemplify his commitment to two more aesthetic principles, imitation and/or emulation, to be discussed below, and comprehension or complete inclusiveness. Together these four principles—imitation/emulation, *brevitas, energia,* comprehension—define his aesthetics, though to them should be added one more: what Smart defined as "peculiarity of expression," or novel and arresting diction. This diction and the other four principles were enlisted to aid *impression,* his aesthetic objective, the key to his self-fashioning as an author.

In the production of his work, Smart relied heavily on contemporary theory, and certainly he modified his aesthetics as his life situation changed and as new critical treatises appeared. He began his poetical career very early and, as was proper, did a great deal of apprentice translation work: a form of the vocationally prescribed course of imitation. Richard Hurd's essay *On Poetical Imitation* (1751) discusses imitation, brevity, comprehension, *energia,* and impression, and very possibly inspired Smart's own application of these principles. In a passage that would seem to have been important to Smart, Hurd considers the choice of brevity, vigor, and comprehension as a consequence of character: "Thus a short and compact, and a diffused and flowing expression are the proper consequences of certain corresponding characters of the human genius. One has a vigorous comprehensive conception, and therefore collects his sense into few words. Another, whose imagination is more languid, contemplates his objects leisurely, and so displays their beauties in a greater compass of words."[1] Smart opted not for the languid imagination but for the vigorous comprehensive conception that necessitated concision.

Hurd also returns to the concept of impression again and again. "To give life and colour to the selected circumstances, and imprint it on the imagination with distinctness and vivacity, this is the proper office of true genius" (ii: 128), a statement echoed by Smart in his well-known claim in *Jubilate Agno:*

> *For my talent is to give an impression upon words by punching, that when*
> *the reader casts his eye upon 'em, he takes up the image from the*
> *mould wch I have made* (B404).

Here is Hurd again: "The superiority of Homer and Shakespear to other poets doth not lie in their discovery of new *sentiments or images,* but in the forceable manner, in which their sublime genius taught them to convey and impress *old ones"* (ii: 159-60). As in the case of Homer and Shakespeare, impression also necessitates the careful choice of words. Smart's preface to Horace praises his "unrivalled peculiarity of expression," another technique for which he always strove.

In 1753, Bishop Robert Lowth published his *De Sacra Poesi Hebraeorum* in which he located the origin of poetry in religion and noted that the first office of poetry was to praise the Creator and display His mysteries.[2] While emphasizing the sublimity of sacred poetry, Lowth also consistently valorizes brevity: for instance, both the sententious and the truly poetical styles of poetry are brief and metrical (I: 99); the language is elliptical (i: 314); the sublime style too is "sparing in words, concise, and energetic" (ii: 250).

From early to late days, Smart was observing the rules of *brevitas,* though Lowth on sublimity was enormously influential in term of the religious poetry. Both *brevitas*—strong concision of expression—and *energia*—vigor of style and acuteness of attack (sometimes distinguished from *enargia* or vividness, distinctness, certainly also an objective)[3]—were always for Smart critically important rhetorical and poetical strategies. A facetious quatrain from the *Midwife* (1751), translated from Phaedrus, is entitled "On the Merit of Brevity":

> If you think that my works are too puft up with levity,
> Yet at least approbation is due to my brevity,

> The praises of which should be now more egregious,
> As our bards at this time are confoundedly tedious (iv: 388) .[4]

And in 1767, he translated lines from Horace's *Ars Poetica*

> Whate'er you teach be brief and plain,
> That they conceive you and retain.[5]

Brevitas, or *brachylogia,* is a classical rhetorical figure. Lanham groups it with a number of poetical tropes naturalized in the eighteenth century: types of zeugma, oxymoron, epiphonema. Under brachylogia he groups such tropes as asyndeton, or the omission of conjunctions between words, and ellipsis (18-20, 39-40).

Impression, the effect of his other strategies, was Smart's vaunted talent. Contemporary Lockean theory recited that one's sensory equipment produced impressions on the mind that in combination with each other then produced ideas. One's impressions naturally were stronger or weaker according to the strength of one's sensory and mental equipment. But the impression made by an *imitation* of a natural phenomenon (as in poetry) must always be weaker than the original impression of the phenomenon itself. Smart, as a theorist of poetics, was designing a strategy to overcome as far as possible this loss of force. The concision of brevity, the force of *energia,* the arresting peculiarity of diction, he postulated, enabled him to produce words that acted much like the punch that produced type: they could project and deeply impress an image.

Impression was apparently not entirely a new (Lockean) concept. Quintilian had noted the connection between *brachylogia* and force of impression. Praising asyndeton he says *"nam et singula inculcantur et quasi plura fiunt,"* translated in 1921 as "It at once impresses the details on the mind and makes them seem more numerous than they really are." It is useful, he says "when we are speaking with special vigour." It is a figure that makes "our utterances more vigorous and emphatic and produce[s] an impression of vehemence [vim] such as might spring from repeated outbursts of emotion."[6]

Smart, of course, used all the compressing figures, including asyndeton:

> All hearts at once devising bad,
> Hands, mouths, against their Maker mad,
> With Satan at the head.[7]

Cicero, providing a list of useful rhetorical devices, also identifies concision as one strategy for making what is translated in 1960 as "a great

impression" (*nam et commoratio una in re permultum movet*): "For a great im-
pression is made by dwelling on a single point . . . and explanation is often coun-
tered by a rapid review, and by a suggestion that causes more to be understood
than what one actually says, and by conciseness achieved with due regard to
clearness."[8] Concision, the concentration of meaning into as few words as pos-
sible, was defined in the *Ad Herennium* as "the expressing of an idea by the very
minimum of essential words."[9] Concision naturally facilitates strong impres-
sion; concentration of meaning into a few inspired words provides a stronger
and better effect and therefore a more vivid image. As Smart wrote in the pref-
ace to the verse *Horace*, "Impression . . . is a talent or gift of Almighty God, by
which a Genius is impowered to throw an emphasis upon a word or sentence in
such wise, that it cannot escape any reader of sheer good sense, and true critical
sagacity" (*PW*, v: 6)—another oblique valorization of peculiarity of expression.

Hurd discerned the force in the brief and the compact: "A severe and melan-
cholic spirit inspires a forcible but involved expression" (204). Smart wrote
lines in 1756 that celebrate the force or energy of the English language and that
imitate John Milton and Alexander Pope and at the same time demonstrate gen-
erous emulation—for at thirty-four he had outgrown imitation.[10] The 58 lines
of Milton's "At a Vacation Exercise in the College," which in sublime style re-
quest his words to penetrate realms and times unknown, begin

> Hail native Language, that by sinews weak
> Didst move my first endeavoring tongue to speak.[11]

Smart's own 14-line verses apostrophize Energeia.

> Hail, Energeia! hail, my native tongue,
> Concisely full, and musically strong!
> Thou, with the pencil, hold'st a glorious strife,
> And paints the passions greater than the life:
> In thunders now tremendously array'd,
> Now soft as murmurs of the melting maid:
> Now piercing loud, and as the clarion clear,
> And now resounding rough to rouse the ear:
> Now quick as light'ning in its rapid flow,
> Now in its stately march magnificently slow. . . (*PW*, iv: 312).

Thus, imitation/emulation of preceding great poets, this brevity and energy,
comprehension or fullness, all conducing to effective impression, were from
the beginning the principles of Smart's poetics.

Pope was Smart's first important model. In fact Smart modeled his career on Pope's (and accordingly on Virgil's), proceeding in the same progression from pastoral and georgic, translation and imitation, to epistles, didactic poems, and epic (or mock-epic). Smart called on Pope and was subsequently painted with a letter from Pope under the hand in which he holds a pen: visually, Smart's pen thus rests upon Pope. And one attribute of Pope's verse always noted by his critics is concision, compactness, or brevity. Pope, "whenever he judged it expedient, could compress more meaning into fewer words than almost any other in our language," writes Lady Mary Wortley Montagu's granddaughter Lady Louisa Stuart. Geoffrey Tillotson notes his poems' "tightly packed constituents," his syntax as compressed as possible, his meaning "left to grow at leisure out of its confined context," expressed "as much through points of syntax as through vocabulary." Maynard Mack identifies as compressing devices Pope's use of allusion, puns, obvious metaphors, closed couplets, and zeugma.[12] But whereas Pope's syntax was compressed, Smart's was often crunched.

A possibly compelling incentive toward comprehension and vigor in compactness may have been the dwarfish stature of both Pope and Smart. Pope's deformed body was often enough read by his enemies as the index to both his soul and his verse;[13] a brilliant comprehensive brevity represented a riposte. Ronald Paulson notes the relevance of Pope's littleness to his verse, describes his papers on the "Club of Little Men" in the Guardian of June 1713, and quotes from his translation of Ovid's *Sappho to Phaeon:* "Tho' short my Stature, yet my Name extends / To Heaven it self, and Earth's remotest ends."[14] Pope's comic description of himself in the *Guardian* as Dick Distick, of whom a spider was no ill emblem, who had been "taken at a Distance for a small Windmill," was probably the model for Smart's apparent comic self-portrait in *The Student* as Chimaericus Cantabrigiensis: his stature so low that a dwarf on show is jealous; his eyes crossed, his legs bandy.[15] The exaggeration in the context of Pope's own jest is a claim or boast, a form of generous emulation, as we shall see. That Pope's and Smart's subscription to an aesthetic of concise strength may have been supported, may even have originated, in their littleness is not impossible. Pope also emblematically created a charming and seemingly ample garden from a tiny unpromising plot of ground, analogous to the poetry that issued from his unpromising person. Smart followed in his "The Author apologizes to a Lady, for his being a little man." He describes equally his compressed person, the compressed force of his sexuality, the compressed force of his verses.

> Say, is it carnage makes the man?
> Is to be monstrous really to be great?
> Say is it wise or just to scan
> Your lover's worth by quantity or weight? . . .
> The less the body to the view,
> The soul (like springs in closer durance pent)
> Is all exertion, ever new,
> Unceasing, unextinguished, and unspent;
> Still pouring forth executive desire—
> As bright, as brisk, and lasting, as the vestal fire (*PW*, iv: 170).

The fact that Smart was also, as John Hill wrote in 1752, "the boldest borrower we shall meet with among the men of real genius,"[16] emphasizes another of his poetic principles, imitation, which did not cease with his apprentice work. Imitation had been most recently theorized by Hurd in *On Poetical Imitation,* where he summed up current (and Popean) ideology that all art is imitation, that one might as well copy Homer as nature, but that a good modern poet might also contend with his original and strive to surpass it. Such a poet, "in aiming to be like, contends also to be equal to his original" (ii: 232). Smart had already been applying these tenets, which in important part derived from Longinus's description of the noble struggle with preceding authors for the crown of glory, suggesting that imitation at its best is far from servile, can represent a contest for supremacy with the master. The phrase "generous emulation," adapted from Longinus to describe this contest, had been used as early as 1702.[17] Edward Young in his *Conjectures on Original Composition* (1759) continued to justify emulation: "Imitation is inferiority confessed; emulation is superiority contested, or denied; imitation is servile, emulation generous; that fetters, this fires; that may give a name; this, a name immortal."[18] From at least the late 1740s, Smart was no longer imitating, but competitively emulating.

It is not surprising, then, that his adherence to the principles of brevity and imitation produced both brevity, or compactness, of expression and a brevity and compactness of form. Whereas the first appeared consistently in his work, the second—a pronounced shortening of the imitated form— decreased as Smart increasingly proclaimed his own mastery of his craft.

This compactness of expression was a result of a conviction that concision must create superior impression. Examples are found everywhere in Smart's work. Some, like the lines with which this chapter opens, are strikingly effective. Others create something like a knot or knur in the line: it is brevity "without due regard to clearness," as Cicero warned. An early exam-

ple occurs in the *Hilliad* where Hill is described as "th' insolvent tenant of in-
cumber'd space" (*PW,* iv: 251). A note explains that Hill is an insolvent ten-
ant of earth because "he is employed in pursuit of insects in
Kensington-gardens, and . . . this is all the gratitude he pays for the being con-
ferred upon him" (*PW,* iv: 251). "The Famous General Epitaph from Demos-
thenes" (1763) ends bafflingly: "And Earth's kind bosom hides them in the
field / Of battle, so the WILL SUPREME ordains; / To conquer chance and error's
not reveal'd, / For mortals sure mortality remains" (*PW,* iv: 355). When he
crunched syntax, Smart was in "generous strife" for eminence.

A crunching of imitated form, on the other hand, might sometimes reflect
modesty, and sometimes haste and lack of application. Smart's early con-
tention with John Milton resulted in a number of Miltonic imitations in ad-
dition to "Hail Energeia!" The Latin translation of *L'allegro* (published in
Poems on Several Occasions in 1752) was in a sense, like many of Smart's
translations, generous emulation; Milton's 152 lines required 155 lines by
Smart. When in the summer of 1747 Smart was engaged in writing a masque
(a necessary inclusion for the *Poems,* given his implicit claim) he requested
"Dalton's alteration of *Comus*" from Robert Dodsley.[19] Smart's "Midas, a
Masque" is, however, 152 lines; "Comus" is 1023. Smart's theme is actually
a Popean as well as a personal plaint: Colley Cibber was poet laureate and
that year Henry Jones, the bricklayer poet, was being considered as a re-
placement. Smart, unlike Pope, would have been eligible for the laureate-
ship, for which, with his volume of poems, he was probably advancing
himself. No wonder Midas deserves his ass's ears for preferring Pan's art to
Apollo's. The brevity of the Miltonic imitations is probably, but not certainly,
due more to modesty than to sloth. Smart considered *L'allegro* and *Il
Penseroso* the finest lyric poems in any language (*PW,* iv: 94). Smart's allu-
sive companion pieces "On Good-Nature" and "Against Ill-Nature" (*Poems,*
1752) are far shorter: 40 and 60 lines compared to 152 and 176.

If Smart quailed before Milton, he could more directly challenge Pope.
He chose a satire of Horace (the third satire of the first book) not adapted by
Pope in his *Horatian Canons of Friendship* and produced a respectable 217
lines, a length that is consonant with the lengths of Pope's Horatian imita-
tions. And it is probably significant that the *Hilliad,* an imitation of the *Dun-
ciad* in one book, is 259 lines long, compared to the 260 lines of the first book
of the *Dunciad Variorum.* But in his less ambitious works, Smart could deci-
sively abbreviate an imitated form.

A stunning example of *brevitas* of form combined with *energia* of attack
is Smart's 68-line *Epithalamium,* which closely follows in form Edmund
Spenser's 433-line ode. Spenser opens with an invocation to the muses to

bring nymphs to strew flowers; Smart opens with an invocation to the muses and to Flora to bring flowers for a bridal couch. Spenser's bride appears: "Lo where she comes along with portly pace" (1. 148) as does Smart's: "But see the bride—-she comes with silent pace" (1. 24). Spenser describes his bride at length; Smart invokes *occupatio:* Phoebus himself is unable to describe her charms. Spenser's bridegroom is impatient: "Ah when will this long weary day have end, / And lende me leave to come unto my love?" (11. 278-79). Smart condenses: "Now see the bridegroom rise, / Oh! how impatient are his joys!" (11. 46-47) Spenser ends with a gift of his verse to his bride as an endless monument. Smart ends with a prayer for a happy marriage and eventual Christian salvation, a more modest conclusion.

Modesty may have been prescribed; while Spenser's verses are addressed to his own bride, Smart's are probably to his former love Anne Vane, who married Charles Hope Weir in 1746, and he could now scarcely have luxuriated in anticipation himself. His withdrawal to a Christian vision of the couple's future in four neoclassical couplets, which serve to bring the sublime ambitions of the ode to earth, is therefore reasonable.

But the diction of this early verse is not condensed. Smart twice attempts striking usages—the bride is an *egregious* nymph, the bridegroom "leaps, he springs, he flies into her arms, / With joy intense, / Feeds ev'ry sense, / And *sultanates* o'er all her charms."[20] These words were crafted to make strong impressions. But there are no knurs in the verses. Smart does express a desire for both comprehension and concision. He wants every word of his poem to be exactly effective, but admits defeat:

> Oh! had I Virgil's comprehensive strain,
> Or sung like Pope, without a word in vain,
> Then should I hope my numbers might contain,
> Egregious nymph, thy boundless happiness (11. 54-57).

It is probably Smart's prejudice against an enervating softness and smoothness in verse that causes him, in quest of *energia,* to use a nervous vocabulary full of words beginning and ending with plosives and fricatives, words that take time to enunciate. "What the prophetic Muse foretold is true," "Yes, contumelious fair, you scorn," and "Whate'er distinguished patriots rise" are first lines that offer resistance to the lips. His Latin translation of Pope's *Essay on Criticism,* his virtuoso turn in "Hail, Energeia," demonstrate his mastery of sound chosen for effect. That he could write limpid poetry he demonstrated more than once. Consider the lines in "Idleness": "Bring, Muse, bring numbers soft and slow / Elaborately void of sense, / And sweetly thoughtless let them flow" (*PW,* iv: 89). But he had no wish to write limpid poetry. His diction was carefully selected; it might deliberately retard the reading of his lines, but was also chosen to be as spare as possible.

On the other hand, when Smart really forwards a claim to greatness, he can outdo his original in length as he strives to do in genius. His *Ode for Musick on St. Cecilia's Day* (192 lines), in which his generous emulation is abundantly apparent, is longer than Pope's *Ode for Musick on St. Cecilia's Day* (134 lines), John Dryden's *Song for St. Cecilia's Day* (63 lines), and Dryden's *Alexander's Feast* (141 lines). Everything about Smart's presentation of his *Ode for Musick* smacked of challenge. He was twenty-four in 1746 when he reissued his Latin translation of Pope's ode (first published in 1743) with his own. In his preface he remarks that he has been warned that writing his own ode is presumptuous, but "he does not pretend to equal the very worst part of the two celebrated performances . . . which acknowledgment . . . will . . . acquit him of presumption." But from this disclaimer he immediately proceeds to point out the blemishes in the work of his two great predecessors, blemishes for which we are to note his own felicitous amendments. The earlier odes suffer from an exact unity of design, an impropriety in the Pindaric, "which should consist in the vehemence of sudden and unlook'd-for transitions." He notes low stanzas in the odes that "would make no inconsiderable figure in a Ballad." He objects—a charge often leveled at Pope—to the epigrammatical turn of Pope's conclusion. Speaking of a contemporary verdict in favor of Dryden's ode, he registers an objection to the "prevailing but absurd custom . . . of preferring Authors to the Bays by seniority," almost certainly a hint in favor of himself, and probably again with the laureateship in view. It might be argued that toward this end he had shaped his entire corpus.

Though Smart takes hints from both odes, he is more indebted to *Alexander's Feast,* from which he adapts the choruses. Like the two odes, his poem is divided into eight sections (*Alexander's Feast* has seven). Both Hurd and Lowth identify religion as the primary wellspring of poetry, and Smart's first section is structured on Pope's but is an invocation not to the muses but to the angels, asking them to praise Cecilia. He would have considered this innovation original, striking, and corrective. His second section invites mankind to join the angelic praise he has orchestrated:

> And you, ye sons of Harmony below,
>   How little less than angels, when ye sing!
> With emulation's kindling warmth shall glow. . . .

Smart too is emulating angelic voices.

Dryden in *Alexander's Feast* invokes the music of Timotheus to show his superior power over Alexander, greatest of kings. Pope's ode invokes Orpheus to illustrate the power of poetry even over death. Smart, again corrective, substitutes an English example: Waller, sick with love at Penshurst, plays strains that, traveling down the Medway to the sea, calm it as it "listens into sense"; Arion too subdues the ocean. Purcell is invoked to praise Cecilia. Thus the contender has produced new scenes, new episodes, and a more Christian and British context: both religion and patriotism are developments of his early as well as his later corpus. His ending is intentionally sublime in the romance-six stanza of *Song to David* and returns to the angels.

> When *Death* shall blot out every name,
> And *Time* shall break the trump of Fame,
> Angels may listen to thy lute:
> Thy pow'r shall last, thy bays shall bloom,
> When tongues shall cease, and worlds consume,
> And all the tuneful spheres be mute.

The form is not condensed, as none of Smart's major efforts are condensed.

But in this ambitious poem, the language is, and peculiarity of expression abounds, which offers an insight into the poetic precepts most precious to Smart. For instance:

> Rolling floods in sweet suspence
> Are held, and listen into sense (11. 43-44).

On stalactites:

> . . . each roof-suspended drop,
> That lightly lingers on the top,
> And hesitates into a gem (11. 85-87).

On the leaping dolphin, the sun glinting from his back:

> Ten thousand variegated dies
> In copious streams of lustre rise,
> Rise o'er the level main and signify his way—(11.105-07).

Purcell's music is not Italianate, "where sense and music are at strife," but instead (like the poet's own verse)

His vigorous notes with meaning teem,
With fire, with force explain the theme,
And sing the subject into life (11. 166-69).

In a crucial year for Smart, 1756, the year that with the onset of his mental illness divides his early from his later poetry, he may arguably have been profoundly disturbed by Joseph Warton's *Essay on the Writings and Genius of Pope,* in which Warton relegated Pope to the second class of poets, Shakespeare, Spenser, and Milton to the first. That book and Lowth's, with its analysis of the sublime, contributed to a change of poetic direction. And certainly in 1759 Smart read Edward Young's *Conjectures on Original Composition,*[21] which defended an emulative dependence on earlier models, but also accused Pope of servile imitation and contended that learning was a drawback to genius. But by that time Smart was deep into *Jubilate Agno* and appears to have achieved a maturity and a confidence in his work that no longer admitted brevity of form. *Jubilate Agno* went on, open-ended, and was to do so until the poet had exhausted creation, including his acquaintance and his personal experience. The *Song to David* was a long masterwork. The parables, hymns, and Horatian translations were comprehensive and thorough in a manner that Smart may not even have been capable of in his first career. Comprehension, in fact, moves into an increasingly important position as Smart daringly emulates the prime Creator in an attempt to comprehend all creation. It becomes the Creator's work that Smart emulates. The brevity and strength of diction and the *energia,* or energetic attack intended to assist impression, remain, however, everywhere apparent. It is the objects of impression that have changed.

Jubilate Agno, though written at the start with clarity and *energia,* soon adopts Smart's characteristic tightened and compacted brevity. Combined with an astonishing reach for comprehensibility—the inclusion of everything in the universe—this produces a density of meaning that still defies explicators. He achieves many layers of meaning that include an apparent desire to incorporate all knowledge in addition to a consistent combined biblical and personal reference. Occasionally there is an insight into his experience at the time. This is a private poem and Smart was thus able to admit the baffling personal references that may never be understood. He was permitted, while in his private madhouse, to garden. In a catalogue of colors he declares *"For black blooms and it is PURPLE"* (B658). Here he expresses the disappointment of the gardener who has planted a new Dutch bulb purporting to produce a black tulip. The expression is brief but it is also obscure. However, the poet is not mad; he is incorporating material necessary for full comprehensiveness of both subject and object—the rest of creation—but material not admissible into a public poem. He is using the strategies of both *brevitas* and *energia,* and he is practicing impression. Smart's poetics, then, were a synthesis of classical rhetorical strategies and modern critical notions culminating in a resort to Enlightenment physiology.

In *A Song to David,* of course, no such private revelations are included. But the same strategy of seeking comprehension through brevity, of aiding impression through peculiarity of diction, is everywhere apparent. Any stanza might provide illustration. But consider

> Beauteous the fleet before the gale;
> Beauteous the multitudes in mail,
> Rank'd arms and crested heads:
> Beauteous the garden's umbrage mild,
> Walk, water, meditated wild,
> And all the bloomy beds (Stanza LXXVIII).

The first of three stanzas cataloguing the multitudinous beauties of creation, it at once establishes the principle of comprehension with its startling juxtaposition of fleets and armies to a garden with its shades, walks, lake wilderness, and flowerbeds. The attack is vigorous, the repetitive syntax like hammer blows. Economically delineated objects convey diversity; harmony of numbers and alliteration convey unity. Carefully chosen diction, including one peculiarity (*meditated wild:* a cultivated, mediated wilderness), aims, like everything else, at impression. In the next stanza, David on his knees comprehends in his prayer all creation, "man, beast, mute."

It might be suggested here that all of Smart's poetic principles are operating more effectively than ever. Emulation here, however, is less of the form of preceding poets—even the poets of the Old Testament—than of the Creator's own originality, comprehensiveness, vigor, concision, peculiarity of expression, and mark, or impression, upon his creation.

NOTES

1. Richard Hurd, "On Poetical Imitation," *The Works of Richard Hurd, D.D.,* 8 vols. (London: T. Cadell and W. Davies, 1811), ii: 204. Subsequent references to this work will be by page numbers in the text.

2. Robert Lowth, *Lectures on the Sacred Poetry of the Hebrews,* trans. G. Gregory, 2 vols. (London: J. Johnson, 1787), i:47. Subsequent references will be to this edition in the text.

3. See, for instance, Richard A. Lanham, *A Handlist of Rhetorical Terms* (Berkeley and Los Angeles: University of California Press, 1969), 20, 40, 120.

4. Williamson notes that the lines are a translation of the last three lines of Phaedrus's *Scurra et Rusticus* (book 5, fable 5 in old editions; in modern editions they form the conclusion of an epilogue to book 4.) The choice of the word *egregious* is an example, as discussed in the body of this chapter, of Smart's "peculiarity of diction."

5. Lines 620-21, published in 1767. See *PW,* v: 354-77. In a list of a poet's errors; see lines 46-47; however, note, "I wou'd be brief with all my might, / And so become as dark as night." This was a conventional warning about the overapplication of *brevitas.*

6. Loeb Classical Library, *The Institute Oratoria of Quintilian with an English Translation by H.E. Butler, M.A.,* 4 vols. (London: William Heinemann, 1921), 475-77. It is of course the translation that introduces the term *impression.* I am indebted to Dr. Frederick Golden for classical references to *brevitas.*

7. "Hymn X," in *PW,* ii: 48.

8. Loeb Classical Library, *Cicero, De Oratore,* trans. H. Rackham, M.A. (Cambridge, MA: Harvard University Press, 1960), 161-63.

9. Loeb Classical Library, [Cicero] *Ad C. Herennium,* trans. Harry Caplan (Cambridge, MA: Harvard University Press, 1977), 403. Caplan, vii-viii, notes that the treatise from Jerome's time onward for a thousand years was thought to be Cicero's and was greatly prestigious.

10. For generous emulation, see the body of this argument, as well as note 17. Smart's lines announce a "glorious strife" (or generous emulation) with painters and imitate Milton without a glorious strife for preeminence, but offer a competitive imitation of Pope's *Essay on Criticism* (see *The Poems of Alexander Pope,* ed. John Butt [New Haven: Yale University Press, 1963], 155, lines 366-73); note the final hexameter line in Smart.

11. Karina Williamson notes the Milton original in *PW,* iv: 458.

12. Lady Louisa Stuart, "Biographical Anecdotes of Lady M.W. Montagu,"

Lady Mary Wortley Montagu: Essays and Poems and Simplicity, *a Comedy,* ed. Robert Halsband and Isobel Grundy (Oxford: Clarendon Press, 1993), 49; Geoffrey Tillotson, *On the Poetry of Pope,* 2nd ed. (Oxford: Clarendon Press, 1950), 129, 150-51; Maynard Mack, "'Wit and Poetry and Pope': Some Observations on his Imagery," *Pope and his Contemporaries: Essays Presented to George Sherburn,* eds. James L. Clifford and Louis A. Landa (Oxford: Clarendon Press, 1949), 23-32, 40.

13. See J. V. Guerinot, *Pamphlet Attacks on Alexander Pope, 1711-1744* (N.Y.: New York University Press, 1969), passim, but particularly pages 225-26, where Lady Mary Wortley Montagu is quoted: "It was the Equity of righteous Heav'n, / That such a Soul to such a Form was giv'n. . . . / But as thou hate'st, be hated by Mankind, / And with the Emblem of thy crooked Mind, / Mark'd on thy Back, like Cain, by God's own Hand, / Wander like him, accursed through the Land." On the subject of representations of Pope, see also Helen Deutsch, *Resemblance and Disgrace: Alexander Pope and the Deformation of Culture* (Cambridge, MA: Harvard University Press, 1996).

14. Ronald Paulson, *Breaking and Remaking: Aesthetic Practice in England, 1700-1820* (New Brunswick and London: Rutgers University Press, 1989), 62.

15. "A New System of Castle-Building, Chap. I," *The Student,* 1:vii (July 30, 1750): 249. The essay series was by Smart.

16. John Hill, in a review of Smart's *Poems on Several Occasions* (1752), *Monthly Review* (August 1752): 131-43.

17. Longinus considered imitation not as plagiarism but as a struggle for the crown of glory, one of the sources of the sublime. Edward Bysshe in his preface to *The Art of English Poetry,* 2 vols. (London, 1702) expressed this concept as "generous emulation." The word *generous* is used here in its meaning of high-minded or noble.

18. Edward Young, *Conjectures on Original Composition,* ed. Edith J. Morley (London: Longmans, Green & Co., 1918), 63-64, quoted by Elizabeth Nitchie in "Longinus and the Theory of Poetic Imitation in Seventeenth and Eighteenth Century England," *Studies in Philology,* xxxii:4 (Oct. 1935): 582.

19. *Letters,* 25, 26 n. 3.

20. Johnson's Dictionary gives "eminently bad" as the usual meaning of egregious, but first quotes Thomas More to support a definition of "Eminent; remarkable; extraordinary." As neither Johnson nor the Oxford English Dictionary lists *sultanate* as a verb, the usage is probably Smart's own invention.

21. In *Jubilate Agno* Smart prays for "Dr. Young" and then controverts a statement from *Conjectures* a few lines later (B560, 571, and note [*PW,* i: 79]).

CHAPTER 7

"Neutral Nonsense, neither false nor true": Christopher Smart and the Paper War(s) of 1752-53

LANCE BERTELSEN

IN THE LONDON DAILY ADVERTISER of January 9, 1752, John Hill accused Henry Fielding of proposing that they fake a paper war, "giving Blows that would not hurt, and sharing the Advantage in Silence."[1] In the event, this proposal helped provoke a real paper war in which Hill and Fielding were the central antagonists, around whom ranged a group of professional writers including Christopher Smart, Bonnell Thornton, William Kenrick, Arthur Murphy, and Tobias Smollett, among others. This war has been recounted many times in historical terms, but less often approached as an interesting cultural phenomenon in its own right, one that can tell us something not only about the way that eighteenth-century commercial literary production worked, but about how those involved in the process perceived it to work.[2] Among the myriad disputants some alliances and antagonisms appear to have been real, but others fall squarely within the category of "giving Blows that would not hurt" in order to profit from "the Advantage in Silence." My purpose in this chapter is to attempt to separate out the various strands of this year-long publishing phenomenon with particular attention to the role played by Christopher Smart, as a participant and a character, in the real and metaphorical worlds of the paper wars of 1752-53.

As a secondary participant in (and potential beneficiary of) the publishing flurry generated by the dispute, Smart was well positioned to bring his own particularly relativized (and monetarily distressed) point of view to a cultural site rich in pseudonyms, literary cross-dressing, transgressive performance, formal experimentation, and economic possibility. As Mrs. Mary Midnight, Smart was deeply implicated in the metaphorical world of the war, appearing in character along with "Sir Alexander Drawcansir" (Fielding), "Madam Roxana Termagant" (Thornton), and "The Inspector" (Hill) in a variety of publications—all of which provide interesting clues to Smart's relations with the writers behind those pseudonyms. As a contributor to the war, Smart authored *The Hilliad,* a mock-epic poem with machinery by Arthur Murphy and, if Betty Rizzo is correct, Fielding himself. Yet because Smart was cast by other writers in both pro-Fielding and anti-Fielding roles, he seems a protean character—one whose individual transformations may serve as something of a metaphor for the crisscrossing loyalties and motivations of such literary battles. It is important to remember that even before the war Smart was particularly susceptible to the blandishments of multiple personae, divided loyalties, and contradictory (not to say hypocritical) motivations that characterize most Grub Street production. A close reading of Smart's activity in the war, then, taking into special account his association with Fielding, Thornton, and Kenrick, may help to illuminate the schizophrenia, relativism, and fraternal literary relations that complicate the well-publicized alliances and animosities of the war's public dimension.

I

Prior to the beginning of the war, Smart had had both positive and negative exchanges with John Hill, while his view of Henry Fielding was certainly favorable—but with cheeky undertones. In *The Midwife* of February 16, 1751, for example, Mary Midnight praised Fielding's Universal Register Office—a sort of employment bureau and all-purpose commercial brokering agency[3]—but only within the distancing fiction of a "sedulous Application to the useful Science of Astrology." Bragging that her gift allowed her to see "whenever a lucky Coincidence of propitious Symptoms attends the Birth of anything," Midnight "foresaw from the favourable Appearances, which attended the Birth of an Office some time since erected opposite Cecil-street in the Strand, under the Title of the "UNIVERSAL REGISTER OFFICE" that such an institution would prosper. Indeed, Midnight found the register office, "by the general Approbation of the Publick and Countenance of the People of Fashion, to have already in great Measure answer'd, and to be every Day more and more likely to answer its extensive Design, and the Purpose of Publick Good."[4] Smart did not repeat the praise, but later he did explore the institution's satirical possibilities. In *The Midwife* of June 29, 1751, Mary Midnight advertised her own plans to open ("at the Sign of the Mop Handle in Shoe-Lane") a similar shop:

An Office for the IGNORANT
OR,

A Warehouse of Intelligence
Where Physicians may learn the true Practice of Physic, Divines the true
Practice of Piety, and Lawyers the true Practice of Law. In a Word,
Fumblers of all Faculties will be corroborated without Loss of Time.
(2:130)

And later still, after the opening of *The Old Woman's Oratory,* Mary Midnight proposed from her "Rostrum" that a "Thought-Warehouse or Opinion-Office, be erected in the most conspicuous and commodious Part of this City" (3:74-75). Although lighthearted, such references indicate that Smart was not averse to laughing at Fielding, or at least to using the register office as a model for humorous parody. Indeed there is a certain affinity between the borderline preposterousness of Fielding's "universalizing" impulses in the Register Office, in which "The Curious will be supplied with every thing which it is in the Power of Art to produce" (my emphasis), and the motto to Smart's eclectic *Midwife,* which advertised itself as "Containing all the WIT and all the HUMOUR, and all the LEARNING, and all the JUDGEMENT, that has ever been, or ever will be inserted in all the other Magazines."[5] The congruence of these two examples of aggrandizing rhetoric and advertisement—Fielding's serious, Smart's comic—throws into relief the ambiguous ambitions of Fielding's project. For as Smart would surely have recognized, there was something in the choice of the term "Universal" itself to designate the scope of Fielding's office that recalled both the Duncean lunacy of totalizing projects and the brilliance of Augustan parodic entertainments based upon them. It seems almost fitting, then, that Fielding's puffing of himself and the Universal Register Office would become the cause of the first major campaign in the wars of 1752-53—one in which Smart's Mary Midnight would become a central symbolic figure.

As 1751 drew to a close, the confusing mobilization preceding the outbreak of the paper war proceeded on two distinct fronts, both of which were very familiar to Smart. On the eastern front (in Bow Street), Fielding was about to make his ill-fated proposition of December 28 to John Hill—apothecary, journalist, author of the "Inspector" essays in the *London Daily Advertiser,* and a writer whom Smart had already satirized in 1751[6]—thereby providing Hill ammunition for his accusation in the "Inspector" of January 9, 1752 that Fielding had tried to "fix" the war. On the western front (at the Universal Register Office in the Strand), the Fielding brothers had already launched an attack on a former employee, Philip D'Halluin, who had set up the rival Public Register Office in King Street, Covent Garden. The attack appeared in the form of a letter of November 4, 1751 (presumably by John

Fielding) to the *London Daily Advertiser* where John Hill had previously run
puffing letters about the Universal Register Office in his "Inspector" column.
Thus, just prior to the outbreak of hostilities, Hill, an enemy of Smart's, was
aiding John Fielding in the attack against D'Halluin—an attack D'Halluin
would soon answer by hiring Bonnell Thornton, one of Smart's closest friends
and literary colleagues, to lambaste both the Fieldings and Hill—while Henry
Fielding, perhaps encouraged by his brother's relations with Hill, was con-
templating new ways to advertise and aggrandize the Universal Register Of-
fice, one of which seems to have been to propose a mock paper war with Hill
to kick off Fielding's new periodical, *The Covent-Garden Journal.*[7]

In this contentious spirit, the first issue of *The Covent-Garden Journal*
(January 4, 1752) attacked not only Hill (as planned?) but all of Grub Street,
and was immediately seized upon by all of Grub Street as a publishing op-
portunity. Hill played along for one column and then "exposed" Fielding on
January 9, Smollett counterattacked with Habakkuk Hilding on January 15,
and D'Halluin brought Thornton into action as the author of a continuing as-
sault on Fielding (and, as the title implies, others) in *Have At You All: or, The
Drury Lane Journal,* first published from the Public Register Office on Jan-
uary 16, 1752.[8]

The Thornton connection was crucial to Smart's metaphorical impor-
tance in the war. Thornton and Smart knew each other well, having served as
sequential editors of Newbery's *The Student,* and Thornton was clearly en-
amored of Smart's Mary Midnight persona in *The Midwife.* In the first issue
of *The Drury-Lane Journal,* Thornton as "Roxana Termagant" closely asso-
ciated his work and Smart's by loudly disclaiming the rumor that "from the
similitude of our manner, I am the very, identical, one and the same person
with the famous, the celebrated, the remarkable, the notified Mrs. Mary Mid-
night."[9] *The Drury-Lane Journal's* persona, style, and tone were, in fact, re-
markably close to *The Midwife's,* and Thornton continued to emphasize the
connection in the next issue when he had Roxana remark that her "sharp-
sighted Readers" noted "evident marks of a SMART genius stamp'd on my
last number."[10] This is important, because throughout the early phases of the
war, Smart himself was silent. Having launched *The Old Woman's Oratory*
on December 3, 1751, he probably had his hands full with production prob-
lems and Orator Henley's fulminations; but whatever the cause neither *The
Midwife* of January 7 (perhaps published just a bit too early) nor the printed
materials surviving from the relevant performances of the *Oratory* make
mention of the Fielding-Hill war. Thornton, on the other hand, continued to
strengthen the idea of partnership between the two journals. In his third is-
sue, he composed his pièce de résistance: a description of Mary Midnight and

Lady Pentweazle's (a reference to Smart's family of personae, the "Pentweazles") visit to Roxana Termagant at her chambers above a "rotting Chandler's shop" in Drury Lane. The three female authors (all products of irreverent male pens) have "a pot of half and half" and discuss their various virtues and productions. Eventually Pentweazle and Midnight get "into a chariot, and (determin'd to have a mob) bid the coachman drive us directly to Orator HENLEY'S."[11] While there is no evidence that Smart wrote this piece, Thornton's treatment of lower-class female personae clearly suggests the same cheeky irreverence toward grandees, males, and literary authority that, as I have suggested elsewhere, pervades Smart's *Midwife* during this period.[12] It is an attitude not likely to provoke sympathy for Fielding's posturing as Sir Alexander Drawcansir, the "Censor-General of Great Britain"; and certainly London audiences would not have missed the implication of Smart's involvement in Thornton's anti-Fielding project.

Smart, in any case, never seems to have disclaimed Thornton's publicity and praise. The connection between Thornton's Roxana Termagant and Smart's Mary Midnight was never disputed, and this may indicate that Smart was not entirely disinterested in Thornton's send-ups of Fielding and Drawcansir.[13] Indeed, despite his/her silence about the war, Smart's Mary Midnight became a central figure in its mythology. The January 29 pamphlet, *The March of the Lion,* for example, promised "all the Politeness of the INSPECTOR, all the Wit of the FOOL, and all the Smartness of MARY MIDNIGHT" and described Midnight gossiping at a "Night-house" and toasting a lass with golden locks (a reference to Smart's song "The Lass with the · Golden Locks)."[14] Similarly, when William Kenrick's "FUN and MUSICK" was advertised for performance at the Castle Tavern—the same venue where *The Old Woman's Oratory* got its start—his announcement in the *London Daily Advertiser* of February 12, 1752 seemed to draw directly on the idiom of Smart's ads for the oratory, promising "A Piece from the BRAZEN HEAD. A Solo by Minheer LEN ROOP, from the Antipodes. A Solo on the Jew's Harp, in Opposition to the Casuist" (compare with the Oratory's "A Solo in a new Taste, by Signor Piantofugo" and "A Declamatory Piece on the Jew's Harp, by a Casuist").[15] Smart, of course, had a long history with Kenrick, who during 1750-51 had mildly satirized him in various publications: *Kapelion, A Satirical Dialogue Between A Sea Captain and his Friend in Town,* "The Magazines Blown Up," and (stealing Smart's own title) *The Old Woman's Dunciad.* And Smart had hit back in *The Midwife* of August 21, 1751, with a satire on "Mr. Kendrico" (2:24-26). But, as Arthhur Sherbo points out, both Smart and Kendrick were part of Newbery's literary stable, and it may be that these productions were put-up affairs.[16]

In the case of "FUN and MUSICK," no such collusion seems likely since the entertainment was in direct competition with Smart's own show. Mary Midnight made this quite clear in a disclaimer in the *London Daily Advertiser* of February 13:

> As it has been reported, that I am the Author of the Entertainment advertised to be performed at the Castle-Tavern in Pater-noster-Row, this Evening, I must beg leave to assure my Friends, that I know nothing either of the People, or their Performance; and that I shall exhibit my own Entertainment at the New-Theatre in the Hay-market the same Evening.
>
> MARY MIDNIGHT

In the event, Kenrick's "FUN and MUSICK" was suppressed by a special order of the Lord Mayor—a prohibition that led Kenrick to accuse Smart/Midnight of colluding with Fielding (thus reversing Thornton's construction of Termagant and Midnight as enemies of Fielding). In the preface to the published version, *Fun: A Parodi-tragical-comical Satire,* Kenrick blamed the suppression on" a certain great Man" and claimed that he was "excited . . . to this Piece of Barbarity, by an Old Woman's Prophecy."[17] Whether Smart had any influence on Fielding, or Fielding any influence on the Lord Mayor, remains unknown, but Kenrick went on to complain that it was unfair for his entertainment to be suppressed when "the same Privilege had been permitted an old Woman of a very bad Character, one Mother Midnight"[18]—an accusation with some merit, particularly given the similarity of the two pieces.

Kenrick's *Fun* is something of a allegorical overview of the paper war and contains many of the parodic and performative elements of the *Old Woman's Oratory.* It seems precisely the kind of piece Smart might have written had he wished to comment on the war. The witches in the opening parody of *Macbeth* immediately bring Mary Midnight to mind, not only in their demeanor and magical ambiance, but when in weaving their spells they

> Sometimes unto the Salt-box play,
> Or to the Jews-harp dance away,
> To some old Saw or bardish Rhime
> With the Midwife and old Time.[19]

And, later, a major ingredient in their "literary" potion turns out to be a "Birth-strangled Babe, / . . . Child of Poverty and Spleen, / Mother Midnight's Magazine." Fun's central plot concerns the witches' prophecy that Drawcansir will never fall until "against him rise a mighty Hill" and "sexes change, and then thy Arm oppose" (a reference presumably to both Thornton and Smart). An interpolated parody of Orator Henley includes multiple references to "Old Women," "Smart Sayings," "Mother Midnight's Oratory," "Salt-boxes," and so on. And in the denouement, Roxana begs "Mountain" (Hill) for a potion to make Drawcansir love her, only to be betrayed when "Mountain" pours into the sleeping Drawcansir's ear a "Mixture of MID-NIGHT Weeds collected, / Works thrice damn'd and thrice neglected. / Journal in Drury-lane begun, / Poor Compound of Ribaldry and Pun"[20]—a concoction (combining works by Smart and Thornton) that makes Drawcansir hate Roxana.

What is intriguing about *Fun* is the way in which Mary Midnight, her witchlike associations, her magazine, and her show become something like defining tropes for the literary mayhem, crossdressing, and crossfertilization of a paper war. As in the paper war itself, Smart's Midnight appears in *Fun* not so much as a character with a voice, but more as a kind of pervasive referent, almost an atmosphere, redolent of all the madcap, transformative, irreverent subjects and goings-on that characterize Grub Street journalism.

This is the world epitomized in the next performative opus of the paper war, Charles Macklin's *The Covent Garden Theatre, or Pasquin Turn'd Drawcansir,* which played on April 8, 1752, for one night only. The opening speech by Pasquin (who also takes the role of Drawcansir) sums up the showmen's and journalists' London as "The Universal Rendevouz of all the Monsters produced by wagish Nature & fantastick Art"; a world in which

> Panopticons, Microcosms, Bears, Badgers, Lyons, Leapords, Tygers, Panthers, Ostriches and Unicorns,—Giants, dwarfs,—Hermaphrodites and Conjurers, Stateman [sic], Nostrums, Patriots and Corncutters! Quacks, Turks, Enthusiasts, and Fire eaters.—Mother Midnights, Termagants, Clare Market, and Robin Hood Orators, Drury Lane Journalists, Inspectors, Fools, and Drawcansirs, dayly Tax the Public.[21]

Mother Midnight's appearance (alongside "Termagants") in this catalogue of what might be called London's "whole show" is not surprising and sorts with my thesis that Smart while not yet in the paper war was certainly of it. But rather more unexpected is the subsequent appearance of a character actually called "Bob Smart" as one of the "dull disorderly Characters" making up the "Town."[22] He is introduced by "Hydra":

> "The first Character I have the Honour to introduce to your Highness is the facetious Bob Smart, a professed Wit and Critic; no Man knows the

Intrigues of the Court, the Theatres, or the City better. No Man has a first Taste in the Belle Letters, for he is deemed one of the best Gentlemen Harlequins in Europe, and is an Eminent Orator at the Robin Hood Society."[23]

Although this description is part of a more general satiric portrayal of a group called the "Smarts" (closely related to "wits" and "Town" in Grub Street jargon), Bob Smart seems individualized in ways that point directly to Kit Smart: most strikingly in combining a "Taste for the Belle Letters" with a taste for harlequinade and burlesque oratory. Later he introduces himself as "little Bob Smart"—certainly a reference to Smart's small stature—and announces that he has written a pantomime: "'I am to do the Harlequin in it, tidi, doldi, doldi, doldi, dee, tidi, doldi, doldi, doldi dee' (sings & dances the Harlequin)."[24] Kit Smart's propensity for burlesque writing and performance is certainly referenced here, as later when he sums up his relationship to competitors in those venues: "I gad I have more humour than Foot a Thousand times; and I'll lay a Chaldron of Guineas to a Nutshell that my Pantomime, is a better thing than his Taste. I think I have some Fun in me—demme."[25] Samuel Foote, of course, was known for his comic performances and burlesque productions; and I can't help but think that Bob Smart's "Fun" refers simultaneously to Kit Smart's personality and Kenrick's farce.

The inclusion of this Smartlike character in a play growing directly out of the paper war once again emphasizes Smart's symbolic importance in the struggle. But, more important, the response to Macklin's play seems to epitomize the kind of symbiotic authorial relationships that may form the deepest foundations of the war. For although clearly referring in mildly facetious ways to Fielding's "Drawcansir," the play was advertised repeatedly in *The Covent-Garden* Journal (March 14, 17, 21, and 28, 1752)—seemingly an indication of Fielding's approbation. And while Smart, as usual, had nothing to say about it, Thornton (writing as "THE TOWN") reviewed the play in *The Drury-Lane Journal* in a vein of ironic criticism that at least one scholar has mistaken for a negative assessment.[26] However, Thornton's "Condemnation, or (according to the Technical Term) DAMNATION of the Dramatic Satire, called PISCINE turned drawcansie" [*sic*] is a wholly ironic piece intended to praise Macklin's farce. In listing his complaints, for example, Thornton writes, "SECONDLY, 'tis a foolish affair, because I could not take it; that is, I could not at once see into the contrivance, but the stupid author led me on from one scene to another, and kept me in suspense all the while." And "THIRDLY, . . . he took away the free will and agency of the house by obliging us to play our parts his own way, and led us forcibly into a commendation of his piece."[27] Thus, both Fielding and Thornton (arch-enemies on paper) seem to join in supporting a play in which one of the characters is a satirical version of Smart—supposedly an ally to both.

II

In *The Midwife* of August 4, 1752, Smart himself finally joined the war when he wrote a parodic "Inspector" essay, presumably in answer to Hill's gloating over the supposed demise of *The Midwife* and *The Drury-Lane Journal:* "No more is heard of the Gossip or the Scold; the scattered Loading from each Blunderbuss has missed the Mark; nor is there anymore Trace left of their Passage through the Air, than if they succeeded."[28] Perhaps galled by Hill's failure to realize that *The Midwife* had never attacked him during the entire course of the war, Smart parodied the Inspector's well-known vanity and fondness for self-aggrandizement:

> It has ever given me great Pleasure, to find the Judgment of the Town concur with my own Opinion so intimately in this Point, that the Stile is the most pleasing and commendable Part of my Writing. I confess it is what I pride myself upon; and it was not long after I first undertook this Work, singly, without any kind of Assistance, what no Man ever had attempted before me, that I discovered there certainly is some Merit in easy Writing. My Dress has also been admired by many, imitated by some, and yet I cannot account for my Excellency in either, other than that I never trouble myself about them, judicious Nature acting upon these Occasions the double Part of an Amanuensis and Valet de Chambre, with her usual Grace and unaffected Simplicity. (3:84-85)[29]

Hill (presumably) answered this parody with *The Impertinent* (August 13, 1752), a paper that categorized authors in terms of their prevailing forms of inspiration: "There are men who write because they have wit; there are those who write because they are hungry; There are some of the modern authors who have a constant fund of both these causes; and there are who will write, although they are not instigated either by the one or by the other."[30] Hill found Smart to be one of those impelled wholly by hunger: "he wears a ridiculous comicalness of aspect, that makes people smile when they see him at a distance: His mouth opens, because he must be fed; and the world often joins with the philosopher in laughing at the insensibility and obstinacy that make him prick his lips with thistles." The essay, which included Fielding, Hill, and Smart (among others) in its analysis, was attributed by some to

Samuel Johnson, and disingenuously criticized by Hill himself in "The Inspector" No. 464 (August 25, 1752) as "a Piece that cruelly and unjustly attacked Mr. Smart."[31] Hill was subsequently exposed (perhaps by Johnson) as the author of both pieces: a "scribler who publish'd the load of personal abuse, that excited the indignation of the public, and produced the most pert assuming, and short-lived of all the periodical pieces that have lately appeared."[32] At the same time, Hill published a long review in *The Monthly Review* for August 1752 that both praised and critiqued Smart's *Poems,* but in a style, as Rizzo writes, "that managed to insult and degrade Smart with patronizing encouragement."[33] The exchanges of August 1752, then, seem something of a simulacrum of the transforming identities, loyalties, and tonalities that characterized the war; a war in which Smart/Midnight's early symbolic presence as something like the genius loci of a confusing and rather burlesque battlefield seems to have turned into a personal—and, one feels, rather heartfelt—fight with Hill.

In the meantime, the wider war continued and in fact expanded as the well-to-do returned to London and the Fall season began. On October 21, 1752, Arthur Murphy came out against Hill in his new *Gray's Inn Journal;* Thornton, whose *Drury-Lane Journal* had expired in April, reincarnated Roxana on November 16, 1752, in the form of her eighteen-year-old relation "Priscilla Termagant" in *The Spring-Garden Journal* and began to blaze away at Fielding and Hill. But the paper war itself was essentially transformed by the advent of a theater war between David Garrick and John Rich, one given physical form when on Friday, November 10, Thaddeus Fitzpatrick, resenting Garrick's parody of Rich's rope-dancer and animal acts, threw an apple from a Drury Lane stage box and hit Henry Woodward.[34] Over the next several days, "great Noise," "some blows in the pit," and Woodward's "saying I thank you to Fitzpatrick" punctuated Garrick's parody.[35] *The Gentleman's Magazine* reported that "The Inspector espoused the cause of the Gentleman; and the Covent Garden Journalist of the comedian," and, as Betty Rizzo has shown, the event had the effect of coalescing what heretofore had been a rather disparate group of writers into something like an anti-Hill coalition.[36] Hill's lashing out at his antagonists—whom he identified as Fielding, Smart, Murphy, Kennedy, and Woodward—appeared only to increase their activity. By December, a major anti-Hill opus was in production: Smart was reading aloud excerpts from his mock-epic, *The Hilliad,* "at Alehouses and Cyder Cellars."[37]

The Hilliad, though not the last shot fired in the war, was by far its loudest broadside.[38] The poem, published on February 1, 1753, seems to have been something of a collaborative effort, with Murphy probably supplying the reply to Smart's introductory letter and, according to Jesse Foot, writing the Notes Variorum: "Mr. Smart walking up and down the room, speaking the Verses, and Mr. Murphy writing the notes to them."[39] Rizzo makes a significant case for Fielding's contribution to the notes as well.[40] In light of this concerted anti-Hill effort, the poem itself has necessarily been read as an all-out attack on Hill, one which, if it did not silence him, at least sent him stinking down to posterity in the canon of one of the more important poets of the eighteenth century. But I would like to suggest here a supplementary reading, one that takes into greater account the confusion and expropriation of personae early in the war and the mock-mythical (or mock-magical) Grubean world in which they existed. The introductory matter and first half of the poem, I will contend, encodes Smart's self-implicating review of the economically driven, ethically neutral, and relentlessly transformative aesthetic of Grub Street, one that draws its imagery not only from previous mock-epics and anti-dunce satires, but from multifaceted allusions to the war of which it is a product.

Smart's PROLEGOMENA to the poem introduces the figural imperatives of what might be called the Grubean weltanschauung, when it quotes Hill's own analysis of the motive forces for writing as wit (redefined as caprice), hunger (redefined as laboriousness), or a shifting combination of the two. Hill (writing anonymously as "The Impertinent") names himself as the chief example of the third type, thereby engaging in precisely the kind of ambiguous (ranging from semi-serious to wholly hypocritical) self-depreciation or self-satire that so often powers the economic and imaginative engines of eighteenth-century commercial journalism.[41] Hill's "synthesis" (his persona acting as a critic not only of Fielding and Smart, but of himself) is immediately dismantled in the following excerpt from the *Gentleman's Magazine,* which not only exposes Hill as the author of "The Impertinent" but scolds him for writing the "Inspector" essay in which he hypocritically attacked his own production: "The man who thus resents the cruel treatment of Mr. Smart in the *Inspector,* and he who thus cruelly treated him in the *Impertinent,* is known to be the same."[42] This is Smart's world.

It is a world in which praise and abuse are often promiscuously distributed in order to keep the engines of commercial publication running—a practice quite specifically highlighted in the next section of *The Hilliad,* in which a dialectic eerily prophetic of the structure of *Jubilate Agno* presents excerpts of Hill's writings under a repeated pair of headings:

Mr. SMART Debtor to Dr. HILL,
for his PRAISES.

followed by
PER CONTRA, Creditor,
For his ABUSE.[43]

And concludes with the following "note":

Due on the Balance to the INSPECTOR
THE HILLIAD,
An Heroic POEM.
Bedford Coffee-House, Jan. 16, 1753.
Received then of one Smart, the first book of the HILLIAD, in part pay-
ment, for the many and great obligations he is under to me.

his
The   + INSPECTOR
mark

In the reversed world that so often characterizes Grub Street production, this seemingly satirical balance sheet on Hill emerges as something rather closer to the literal economic truth about paper wars. For it was precisely the exchange of praise and abuse, and the notoriety established by such exchanges, that generated sales that put shillings in capricious, hungry authors' pockets. In short, Smart actually was under "many and great obligations to Hill" and vice versa—a truth that Smart surely recognized and, I think, sought to convey in this ostensibly ironic "ACCOUNT."

The self-implication evident in the preliminary matter is carried over into the poem itself in perhaps a less conscious way—though the degree of intention is very difficult to determine. Whatever the case, Smart's opening address to Hill in his many roles—"Pimp! Poet! Puffer! 'Pothecary! Play'r!" (l. 8)—besides clearly deriving from Pope's address to Swift in *The Dunciad,* seems to skirt precariously close to Smart's own well-known propensity to wear many hats: Pentweazle! Poet! Mary Midnight! Player! (not to mention Student). The following request to Hill that he "Accept one part'ner thy own worth t'explore/ And in thy praise be singular no more" (ll.11-12), though a prelude to mock encomiums, posits a parallel between the author and his victim that is distinctly unmediated by an intervening persona. Quite the reverse, Smart ostentatiously writes the poem as himself and emphasizes that fact by signing his opening letter in large capitals.

As the poem enters the world of Grubean allegory, similar interesting equations occur: the "Sybil" who charms "Hillario" looks rather like Mary Midnight ("With age her back was double and awry, / Twain were her teeth, and single was her eye, / Cold palsy shook her head' [ll. 29-31]); her prophetic spell, although again deriving in part from Pope's Dulness, is also reminiscent of the witches' potion in Kenrick's *Fun*—a potion, we should remember, that included "Mother Midnight's Magazine" and that was intended to protect Drawcansir until "to fight against him, rise a mighty Hill"; and Hillario's transformation from apothecary to commercial writer seems rather too close for comfort to the career-change being undertaken precisely at that moment by Smart's close friend Bonnell Thornton (a.k.a. Roxana Termagant) who was earning a degree of Bachelor of Physic at Oxford to please his father, a prosperous apothecary, while spending most of his time scribbling within and without Newbery's stable of hacks. Thornton, of course, was the writer who, without the benefit of Smart's participation, had made Mary Midnight a major figure in the early stages of the war. My point here is that the sibyl's prophecy that "strange variety shall check thy life—/ Thou grand dictator of each publick show,/ Wit, moralist, quack, harlequin, and beau" (ll. 54-56) is in fact a rather precise description (were we to add "puppeteer," "magistrate," and "register office proprietor") of the multiple and shifting roles that characterize not only Hill but Hill's enemies (Smart, Thornton, Fielding, Murphy, as well as others) and all the Grub Street race. When Hillario, in the succeeding episode, is surrounded by the allegorical personifications of his various vices, Smart invents a wonderful phrase for the last member of the first group: "And neutral Nonsense, neither false nor true" (l. 84). It is a phrase that Murphy thought original enough to gloss at length:

> The train, here described, is worthy of Hillario, pertness, dulness, scandal and malice, &c. being the very constituents of an hero for the mock epic, and it is not without propriety that nonsense is introduced with the epithet, neutral, nonsense, being like a Dutchman, not only in an unmeaning stupidity, but in the art of preserving a strict neutrality. This neutrality may be aptly explained by the following epigram,
> Word-valiant wight, thou great he shrew,
> That wrangles to no end;
> Since nonsense is nor false nor true,
> Thou'rt no man's foe or friend.[44]

Murphy, of course, is wrong. The epigram he quotes does not describe "strict neutrality," but a form of written expression in which ostensible wrangling is a guise for emotional and factual relativism.[45] In this light, Smart's "neutral Nonsense" represents a rather precise analysis of many Grub Street paper wars and particularly the one in which he symbolically and actually participated in 1752-53. The succeeding definition of "Nonsense" as ethically and emotionally neutral "wrangling"—in which positions, personae, papers, allegiances, and authorship could transform in kaleidoscopic fashion—seems all the more corroborative in that the explanatory epigram was probably written by Smart himself: it first appeared in *The Midwife* of June 20, 1751.[46] Moreover, the phrase "he shrew" seems appropriate not only for the target of the epigram, but for the male-authored "female" fulminations of Smart's own Mary Midnight and later Thornton's Roxana Termagant.

In the magically transformative Nonsense world of the Fielding-Hill war, such hermaphroditic personae—along with witches, Inspectors, Drawcansirs, Mountains, and Orators—were among the commercialized protean figures whose antics seem to have imported into the "Enlightenment" world of eighteenth-century journalism the carnivalesque elements of a far older and murkier popular tradition.[47] And, perhaps more than any other eighteenth-century figure, Christopher Smart—scholar, poet, journalist, Old Woman, vaudeville performer, and religious maniac—seems not only to have written but to have lived the ambiguous allegories of the Grubean sages.

NOTES

1. Bertrand Goldgar misquotes the final phrase as "Advantage of Silence" in Henry Fielding, *The Covent-Garden Journal and A Plan of the Universal Register Office,* ed. Bertrand Goldgar (Middleton, CT: Wesleyan University Press, 1988), xxxviii. All earlier accounts, including Goldgar, CGJ, xxxvii, assign the date of Fielding's original proposition to January 8; but Martin Battestin proves that the proposition must have been made during Hill's original deposition on December 28. See Martin C. Battestin with Ruthe R. Battestin, *Henry Fielding: A Life* (London: Routledge, 1989), 556 and n. 296.

2. The most detailed accounts of the paper war are Goldgar's introduction and Gerard Jensen's introduction to *The Covent-Garden Journal,* ed. Gerard Jensen, 2 vols. (New Haven, CT: Yale University Press, 1915), 1: 1-129; supplemented by Betty Rizzo, "Notes on the War between Henry Fielding and John Hill, 1752-53," *The Library,* 6th ser., vii (1985): 338-53. The most complete account of Smart's role in the paper war is Sherbo, 88-92, et passim.

3. The best account of the Universal Register Office is found in Bertrand Goldgar's introduction to Henry Fielding, *The Covent-Garden Journal and A Plan for the Universal Register Office,* ed. Bertrand Goldgar (Middletown, CT: Wesleyan University Press, 1988), xv-xxviii.

4. *The Midwife; or the Old Woman's Magazine* (London, 1750-53), 1: 225-28. Hereafter, cited parenthetically by volume and page.

5. Ibid., title page.

6. For Smart's connection to the pamphlet *The Genuine Memoirs and Most Surprising Adventures of a Very Unfortunate Goose-Quill: With an Introductory Letter to Mrs. Midnight's Tye-Wig* and the succeeding epigram "The Physician and the Monkey," see Rizzo, "Notes," 343.

7. *The Covent-Garden Journal* was first advertised on October 31, 1751, although it did not appear until January 4, 1752. See Battestin, *Henry Fielding,* 531.

8. On the Smart-Thornton relationship, see Lance Bertelsen, *The Nonsense Club: Literature and Popular Culture, 1749-1764* (Oxford: Clarendon, 1986), 16-30.

9. *Have at You All, or The Drury-Lane Journal* (London: 1752), 10-11. Hereafter cited as DLJ. Smart was also included in the list of writers opposing Drawcansir in "A Journal of the Rout, Progress and defeat of the Forces under Sir Alexander Drawcansir" (DLJ, 15-19), but this hardly

represented a special relationship since Drawcansir had declared war on all of Grub Street.

10. Ibid., 27.

11. Ibid., 60-64. The Termagant-Midnight relationship continues intermittently in the DLJ in the form of the Female Disputant Society, of which both, as well as Lady Pentweazle, are members. See Robert Mahony and Betty Rizzo, *Christopher Smart: An Annotated Bibliography 1743-1983* (N.Y.: Garland, 1984), Items 1143, 1145, 1150.

12. Bertelsen, *Nonsense Club,* 25-27; Bertelsen, "Journalism, Carnival, and *Jubilate Agno,*" *ELH* 59 (1992), 364-67.

13. Sherbo is clearly wrong in thinking that Smart's parody of an "Inspector" essay appeared in "the second number of volume three of *The Midwife* . . . by January 20, 1752," and that it was a "reprint' (88). In fact it appeared in *The Midwife* vol. 3, no. 3, which was published on August 4, 1752. See Mahony and Rizzo, *Christopher Smart,* Item 460.

14. *London Daily Advertiser,* January 29, 1752. I have not seen this pamphlet and take my description of its contents from Mahony and Rizzo, *Christopher Smart,* Item 1142.

15. Ibid., February 12, 1752; compare with the *General Advertiser,* February 12, 1752.

16. Sherbo, 72.

17. William Kenrick, *Fun: A Parodi-tragical-comical Satire* (London: 1752), ii.

18. Ibid., iii. These accusations all are couched in the form of a birth allegory describing the conception and delivery of *Fun.*

19. Ibid., 3.

20. Ibid., 5, 22, 38.

21. Charles Macklin, *The Covent Garden Theatre, or Pasquin Turn'd Drawcansir* (1752), Larpent MS. 96, Augustan Reprint Society, No. 116, ed. Jean Kern (Los Angeles: 1965), 3-4.

22. Advertisement from the *London Daily Advertiser,* March 30, 1752.

23. Macklin, *The Covent Garden Theatre,* 17.

24. Ibid., 19.

25. Ibid., 20.

26. Jensen, *The Covent-Garden Journal,* 72.

27. DLJ, 282.

28. John Hill, "The Inspector" No. 422, *The London Daily Advertiser,* July 17, 752. As Rizzo points out, an anonymous anti-Hill epigram, "The Physician and the Monkey," which had originally appeared in *The Midwife* of May 16, 1751, had in June 1752 been reprinted in Smart's *Poems*

on Several Occasions, perhaps provoking Hill's attack (Rizzo, "Notes," 343).

29. Smart's parody focuses primarily on the "Inspector's" discussion of "Stile" and may have been the inspiration for an epigram by "SIMPLEX" appearing in *The Gentleman's Magazine* for September 1752, "On the New Stile, an EPIGRAM to the Inspector" (quoted by Jensen, *The Covent-Garden Journal,* 80):

> A change in our stile, our wise laws now decree;
> A hint, Great Inspector! to you!
> One line then of Sense, and we all will agree
> That your stile is entirely new.

30. *The Impertinent* No. 1 (August 13, 1752); Mahony and Rizzo, *Christopher Smart,* Item 1160.

31. The attribution to Johnson seems to have been intended by Hill, since the paper "appeared in the format of *The Rambler* and from its publisher" (Mahony and Rizzo, *Christopher Smart,* Item 1160).

32. *Gent. Mag.* 22 (August 1752): 387; Mahony and Rizzo, *Christopher Smart,* Item 1163. James Clifford denies Johnson's authorship in *Dictionary Johnson: Samuel Johnson's Middle Years* (N.Y.: McGraw-Hill, 1979), 106.

33. Rizzo, "Notes," 343.

34. Jensen records Fitzpatrick's name as "Richard" (Jensen, *The Covent-Garden Journal,* 84 n.5).

35. Notes by Richard Cross, Drury-Lane prompter, in *The London Stage 1660-1800,* Part 4: 1747-1776, ed. George Winchester Stone (Carbondale, IL: Southern Illinois University Press, 1962), 329-31.

36. Rizzo, "Notes," 344-45.

37. "The Inspector," December 7, 1752.

38. Most notably, the poem would be followed in March 20, 1753 by a revival of Fielding's *The Mock Doctor* at Drury Lane with Woodward in the lead role imitating Hill. Smart wrote the prologue for the play, only to have it "forbid by the Licencer." See *The London Stage,* 4:359; and note 45 below; and Betty Rizzo, "A New Prologue by Christopher Smart and a Forgotten Skirmish of the Theatre War," *PBSA,* 68 (1974): 305-10. According to Rizzo, Smart may also have had "the last riposte in the war of the wits against Hill" when on March 27, 1753 at the *Old Woman's Oratory* he recited an epilogue (from the back of an ass) that satirized Hill. See Rizzo, "Enter Epilogue on an Ass—By Christopher Smart," *PBSA,* 73 (1979): 343.

39. Jesse Foot, *Life of Arthur Murphy* (London: 1811), 106.

40. Rizzo, "Notes," 348-53.

41. On self-satire in the work of the Nonsense Club (a group with which Smart had dealings), see Bertelsen, *Nonsense Club,* 86-90, et passim.

42. *The Hilliad,* in *PW,* iv, 224.

43. Ibid., 225-38.

44. Ibid., 245.

45. Clement Hawes's comparison of eighteenth-century professional "paper wars" to modern professional "wrestling" seems rather appropriate here; with the proviso that a spark of anger instantly could transform burlesque blows to real ones. See the introduction to this volume, 14.

46. See Mahony and Rizzo, *Christopher Smart,* Items 400 and 134. This weird mixture of wrangling, neutrality, and transformative positionality is brilliantly engaged in the final lines of Smart's "Prologue" to *The Mock Doctor,* which was to have been spoken by Woodward:

> But let not wits mistake our true intent,
> Nor think that spleen, where only mirth is meant. . . .
> But if in this refin'd judicious age,
> There are MOCK-DOCTORS acting off the stage,
> We must be pleasant, and we must be free,
> And pay derision as their lawful fee;
> Whether they wait at Opulency's door,
> Or do they charitably kill the poor,
> To give them up to ridicule's our plan,
> But shou'd suspicion mark some single man,
> Let that same doctor in his turn be free,
> And as a brother-actor laugh at me.

47. On the conjunction of journalism and carnival, see Bertelsen, "Journalism, Carnival, and *Jubilate Agno,*" 357-69, 377, et passim.

CHAPTER 8

"Mary's Key" and the Poet's Conception: The Orphic versus the Mimetic Artist in Jubilate Agno

FRASER EASTON

For the hour of my felicity, like the womb of Sarah, shall come at the latter end.

***

For languages work into one another by their bearings.

—Jubilate Agno

THE PERSONA OF THE POET and the theory of art in *Jubilate Agno* are far from exhausted by studies of Smart's response to David as a divine psalmist or the contrast between music and the visual arts of sculpture or painting.[1] By setting Smart's verses on Orpheus (C52-56) beside those on the art of painting (B668-673) a contrast emerges between a reanimating Orphic artist, on the one hand, and a deadening mimetic artist on the other. This contrast goes to the heart of Smart's presentation of *Jubilate Agno* as a poem of praise: whereas the Orphic bard inspires and gives voice to the creature with a divine song, the mimetic painter despiritualizes and silences the creature in a static reproduction. In the context of Smart's revision of the Newtonian lexicon, which is central to his use of words such as "spirit," the dichotomy of the Orphic and the mimetic entails a kinetic measure.[2] But the "physics" of Orphic animation is also bound up with classical ideas of imitation (which call into question the strict opposition of the Orphic and the mimetic), and with Smart's views on the power of the fruitful female womb (through the virgin Mary, speaker of the Magnificat). We can thus extend Geoffrey Hartman's influential account of *Jubilate Agno* as a Magnificat: "Christopher" means Christ-bearer and Smart is as much a second Mary as a second David. Sexual generation may indeed, as Hartman argues, be bracketed from the analogy of the ark in Smart's poem, but the female matrix certainly is not.[3] On the contrary: Smart is acutely aware that, as a secondary creation like Noah's ark, the archetype of all human creation, sexual or not, is feminine. As we will discover, Smart uses archetypes of female speech and fertility to organize his ideas about poetry—and about enunciation in general.

Smart's rendition of the Orphic animation of creation lies at a point of intersection between sacred and secular artistic ideals. Orpheus is an artistic exemplar from classical culture with religious overtones (Orphism), and a figure that, due to the eighteenth-century identification of David and Orpheus, carried sacred authority. This Davidic Orpheus appears in the exordium to Smart's "On the Goodness of the Supreme Being" (1756):

> Orpheus, for so the Gentiles call'd thy name,
> Israel's sweet Psalmist, who alone couldst wake
> Th' inanimate to motion; who alone
> The joyful hillocks, the applauding rocks,
> And floods with musical persuasion drew;
> Thou who to hail and snow gav'st voice and sound,
> And mad'st the mute melodious! (*PW,* iv: 1-7)

In classical myth, the songs and melodies of Orpheus were so enchanting that no one and no thing could resist the rhythms of his verse and music—not even stones and streams and hills. What appeals to Smart about the legend of Orpheus is this image of the poet as an energizer of the creation. In Ovid's *Metamorphoses,* for example, Orpheus draws together a grove of trees in the midst of a barren green plain: "The shade came there to listen," and soon "the beasts / And birds made a circle all around him."[4] As the maker of a *locus amoenus,* this is a vision of the artist not as an imitator of nature, or even as a figure for "the coherence of the universe," but as the creator of a second nature in tune with humanity.[5]

To make the mute melodious is also an aim of *Jubilate Agno:* "Rejoice in God, O ye Tongues; give the glory to the Lord, and the Lamb" (A1). Smart urges all created things to praise God and Christ (A2-3), but it is the poet who gives the "tongues" for such praise to the mute creation. In an important insight, Hartman observes that this gift amounts to a supplement of the divine order—a potentially Satanic addition because of "the artist's sense that he is disturbing the 'holy Sabbath' of creation by his recreation . . ."(76). Of course, in "On the Goodness," Orpheus appears to be orthodox enough: more than a classical figure, he *is* the historical David by another name. But even in this poem, Smart's reference to the pagan bard has the effect of opening Christian doctrine (through the biblical David) to the poet as a powerful secondary creator—the Orphic animator.

The figure of Orpheus is considerably less orthodox in *Jubilate Agno,* which departs from classical legend by revisiting his instrumental technique:

> *For the story of Orpheus is of the truth.*
> *For there was such a person a cunning player on the harp.*
> *For he was a believer in the true God and assisted in the spirit.*
> *For he play'd upon the harp in the spirit by breathing upon the strings.*
> *For this will affect every thing that is sustaind by the spirit, even every thing in nature.* (C52-56)

Smart again asserts that the legend of Orpheus is true—or at least "of the truth." As in "On the Goodness," Orpheus is not merely a legendary individual: he is a historical "person" who was "a cunning player on the harp" and "a believer in the true God." The essential new fact is his unusual musical style—"he play'd upon the harp," which is not ordinarily a wind instrument, "by breathing upon the strings." This aeolian technique serves God "in the spirit." In part this is tautological: "*For H is a spirit and therefore he is God*" (C1). The *aitch* sound is an aspirate sound—"a spirit" sound according to Smart's pun—and Orphic art is an aspirate art, an art of breathing. Just as God breathes life into Adam, the Orphic artist breathes life into the creation at large ("every thing in nature").

Essentially, then, *Jubilate Agno* draws on the longstanding association of breath and spirit in Judeo-Christian doctrines of creation to explain Orphic animation. Smart thus enlarges on the power granted to Orpheus in classical legend: Orphic animation is not only "voice and sound" ("On the Goodness") but "the breath of Life" (A2) and life itself. At the heart of the matter is how we are to read the assertion that Orpheus "was a believer in the true God and assisted in the spirit" (C54). The repetition of "the spirit" in verses C54-56 invokes the spirit of God or the Holy Spirit as the sustainer of the creation. But the syntax of verse C54 is ambiguous: is it "in the spirit" of "the true God" (that is, as an agent of God) that Orpheus acts; or does the poet in some way sustain or assist God "in the spirit" (that is, with an aspirate art)?

The doubtful orthodoxy of the Orphic artist may be the reason that David, although identified as a harpist, is not directly linked to Orpheus in *Jubilate Agno.* On the contrary, David's tune is now an "*echo of the heavenly harp*" (A41, my emphasis)—a derivative rather than originary art. Yet Smart still maintains an implicit link between Orphic animation and Davidic praise: "*For the praise of God can give to a mute fish the notes of a nightingale* (B24)." Possibly Smart lost some of his enthusiasm for David as an artistic exemplar during the composition of *Jubilate Agno.*[6] But it is also possible that the Orphic harp is not Davidic at all: Smart gives Orpheus an instrument (a variation on the aeolian harp) that combines attributes of the Dionysian flute and the Orphic lyre. This novel apparatus would appear to highlight the ecstatic, Dionysian elements of Orphism.

It is difficult to know how seriously we should treat Smart's aeolian Orphism as an anticipation of romantic topoi of inspiration. The Orphic aeolianism of verses C52-56 does not derive from a power outside the poet, such as the depersonalized breath of the wind (a sort of automatic arche-writing): it depends on an explicitly human breath.[7] Of course, as the agent of a higher power, the wind may be recuperated in the phonocentrism of the divine Logos (as it is in B250ff, in stanza 67 of *A Song to David*, and in Coleridge's well-known poem on the aeolian harp). We should ask, then, if Smart's insistence on human breath as the agent of creaturely praise in *Jubilate Agno* is meant only to resist the pseudo-depersonalization of romantic aeolianism (and thereby to defend a phonocentric notion of art), or whether it is meant as the image of a genuine, as opposed to a feigned, arche-writing. The breath of the poet is always a secondary phenomenon, a wounded iteration: is its tacit priority here an example of the originary *différance* Derrida has described?

Compared with the Orphic animation of nature, the relations of primary and secondary appear much more certain in the mimetic arts. In his verses on the art of painting, for example, Smart describes how an animated original is "taken off" (B670) and immobilized through the power of iteration:

> For the blessing of God upon the grass is in shades of Green visible to a nice
>   observer as they light upon the surface of the earth.
> For the blessing of God unto perfection in all bloom and fruit is by colouring.
> For from hence something in the spirit may be taken off by painters.
> For Painting is a species of idolatry, tho' not so gross as statuary.
> For it is not good to look with earning upon any dead work.
> For by so doing something is lost in the spirit and given from life to death.
>   (B668-73)

Unlike the Orphic poet, whose song respiritualizes the creation, the mimetic painter despiritualizes it. Smart puns on "light" in verse B668 to suggest: first, a ray of light; second, the natural chiaroscuro of light and shade; and third, the appearance of colors such as green as they descend or alight on earth directly from God (rather than from the reflection of sunlight, as in Newton's theory). Far from a static visual field or image, Smart's pun presents light as a kinetic power, an idea that is explicit a few lines earlier (B662). As in the verses on Orpheus, Smart links "the spirit" to movement.

The theme of the descent of God's blessing on earthly creatures is a favorite of his, and in various passages he links rain, horns, and light in this way to God's direct intervention in existence (see C59-61; 110-13; and 118ff). Moreover, because "all bloom and fruit is by colouring," color is a factor in the sexual reproduction of the vegetable creation (supporting the role of flowers and fruits as lures for bees and other animal agents of fertilization). "Bloom" refers to both the flower that precedes a fruit and to the dusty white tint on fresh fruit such as plums. The (a)lighting of color animates and propagates, and invokes the striking connection between spirit and body in Smart's cosmology.

It is this principle of vitality that is lost, Smart claims, in a painting. The art of the painter halts the natural descent of color, freezing the play of living light and shade that is "visible to a nice observer." Literally, of course, the painting of a fruit or flower is lifeless: painting uses static materials such as canvas and paint as its medium. The French term for a still life is *nature morte*, something that Smart appears to have in mind in verse B673, where painting borders on murder. Painting is like the air-pump that Smart examines earlier in fragment B:

> For the AIR-PUMP *weakens and dispirits but cannot wholly exhaust.*
> For SUCKTION *is the withdrawing of the life, but life will follow as fast as it can.*
> For *there is infinite provision to keep up the life in all the parts of Creation.*
> (B218-20)

These lines identify air, life, and spirit. Suction creates a vacuum that withdraws life as well as air (Smart is thinking of a common experiment in which the air-pump was demonstrated on a bird or other small creature held captive in a glass jar).[8] The pump exhausts or removes the air in the jar, which Smart plays on as both physical (weakening) and mental (dispiriting) exhaustion, reinterpreting the principle that nature abhors a vacuum as the ongoing provision of life to the creation by God. The key point for the mimetic artist is that, unlike the breath of the Orphic artist, which animates otherwise static things, the already animated chiaroscuro of colors and shades is lost in the merely iconic art of the painter.

Smart develops two additional aspects of his concept of the artist in the verses on painting. First, he sutures classical and Christian doctrine by linking the Platonic criticism of imitation with the Protestant attack on iconographic art such as statuary. The painter is Plato's main example of the artist in book ten of *The Republic,* so Smart's definition of painting as "idolatry" serves to cross classical and Puritan notions, linking visual imitation to the worship of the image of a false God—unlike "the true God" of Orpheus.[9] The assertion that painting is not as idolatrous as statuary is a nod in the direction of the golden calf, or of the acceptance of stained glass by the English church. Second, Smart opens a specifically sexual criticism of visual art when he urges that "it is not good to look" longingly on a "dead work" (B672). The comment evokes the tradition of nude statuary, as represented by Michelangelo's David or the Venus de Milo. The implication is that in addition to idolatry, visual arts such as statuary invite an onanistic relationship between viewer and work. That Smart does not refer to the legend of Pygmalion in *Jubilate Agno* is significant: like Orpheus, the true artist animates and loves the creation, not his own work (or that of others).

Compared with the Orphic magnification of creation, then, painting is a reductive art, deadening its object and making the viewer an accomplice of this reduction. The key to all these relations lies in Smart's understanding of movement:

> For the PERPETUAL MOTION is in all the works of Almighty GOD.
> For it is not so in the engines of man, which are made of dead materials,
> neither indeed can be. (B186-87)

Like the "dead work" (B672) of the painter, "the engines of man" are "dead materials" without the perpetual motion of the "works of Almighty GOD"— such as the "perpetual moving spirits" (B501) of flowers, for example. In contrast, matter is a fully vital substance:

> For MATTER is the dust of the Earth, every atom of which is the life.
> For MOTION is as the quantity of life direct, and that which hath not motion,
> is resistance. (B160-61)

Smart's ideas about art flow directly from this decentering of the Newtonian lexicon: the premise of Newtonian mechanics (that everything is matter in motion) turns out to be pregnant with a very different message—that matter in motion is the agitated dust of the divine breath. Smart's theory of art is based, then, on this alternative materialism.

As a consequence, the dyad of sound and light (voice and image), with all its resonance for doctrines of logocentrism and phonocentrism, is a secondary opposition in *Jubilate Agno;* the primary dichotomy is between motion and stasis. The contrast of Orphic and mimetic artists comes down to the presence or absence of movement. First, the Orphic medium is air and the Orphic technique is the movement of air, entailing an art of the dynamic aspirate (voice or sound). The effect of Orphism is to impart this movement: thus Orphic art is the creation of a new experience. Second, the mimetic medium is light and the mimetic technique is a static reduction, entailing an art of the dead work (icon or image). The effect of imitation is paralysis: thus, mimetic art arrests the object as a visual inscription. It is impossible to know how Smart would classify the movement-image of the modern-day cinema (I will later examine his comments on the theater), but, as we have seen, it is the subtraction of movement that makes the art of the painter a deadening one. And it is through the addition of movement to the existing creation that the art of Orpheus is inspiriting.

The kinetic understanding of art in *Jubilate Agno* can help to put some new light on the role of translation in the poem. Alan Liu has drawn attention to Smart's interest in translation in verses B11 and B43, and linked it to the sequence on the Pauline "uncommunicated letters" (C44) early in the C fragment, arguing that *Jubilate Agno* is a "firmly logocentric" work.[10] But while Smart exhibits logocentric tendencies with his praise of the word of God (B195; B220), his interest in communication emphasizes the transmission of the letter, not the intuition of a meaning:

> Let Achsah rejoice with the Pigeon who is an antidote to malignity and
> will carry a letter.
> *For I bless God for the Postmaster general and all conveyancers of letters*
> *under his care especially Allen and Shelvock.* (B22)

Smart anticipates Marshall McLuhan's ideas on mediality in this verse: the meaning or semantic government of the word (Logos) is barely relevant; rather, Smart celebrates the agents of the pure movement of the word (lexis).[11] The theme of transportation puts the appearance of Hebrew letters in the seeds and veins of plants and animals and things (B477-491) in another light: the entire creation is a conveyancer of the letter. And the analogy of the *Jubilate* with Noah's ark means that the poem is a mover of names as well. This is a physics, rather than a metaphysics, of the word; a real, as opposed to feigned, arche-writing.

On this account of Smart's ideas about art, then, we are under no necessity to read *Jubilate Agno* as a fundamentally mystical text. Hartman has suggested that Smart's references to the role of the phonemes "mus" (mouse) in Latin, "ble" (bull) in English, and "cat" in Greek are part of his discovery that "language is a creature" and of "his feeling for the lost animal spirits of a language 'amerced' of its 'horn' (C118-62)."[12] But an "animal" is a mobile creature, and for Smart, as we have seen, spirit *is* matter in motion. Such a force or "spirit" is noncognitive: it can be experienced but not conceptualized, like the "ECHO," which is "the soul of the voice exerting itself in hollow places" (B235). According to Smart "an IDEA is the mental vision of an object" (B395), but unlike the reflective consciousness in all its modes (image, concept, Logos), Orphic art is mobile or rhythmic.

The contrast of mimetic and Orphic artists thus foreshadows Nietzsche's description of "a tremendous opposition, as regards both origins and aims, between the Apolline art of the sculptor, and the non-visual, Dionysian art of music."[13] As Amittai F. Aviram persuasively argues, the contrast of music and sculpture in Nietzsche is not fundamentally about alternative arts or modes of representation; rather, music stands for what lies beyond representational cognition.[14] Aviram develops these ideas in relation to poetry, arguing that rhythm is not reducible to an image of the meaning of the poem. On the contrary: a poem's meaning may be an attempt "to tell its rhythm—a paradox, since rhythm cannot be told, it can only be made" (6). In conjunction with Smart's artistic interest in movement, the idea of "telling rhythm" opens a new perspective on *Jubilate Agno,* beginning with the Let-For verse form. The repetition of these two words builds an emphatic beat (Let-Let-Let-... For-For-For-...), a beat that is told as a pure pulse to which the roll call of the poem comes as a response, perhaps. And as a general principle, movement can be understood in ways that go beyond Aviram's concentration on rhythm to embrace other lexical attributes such as paronomasia, musical setting, and enunciation in general.

Yet a question remains about the consistency of the opposition of the Orphic and the mimetic in *Jubilate Agno,* since some verses appear to upset a strict dichotomy between motion and stasis, or sound and image. Consider the following, a touchstone in studies of Smart's view of poetry:

> *For my talent is to give an impression upon words by punching, that when the reader casts his eye upon 'em, he takes up the image from the mould which I have made.* (B404)

Given Smart's interest in poetry as a spoken form, whether as prayer, hymn, oration, or oratorio, this is a surprising verse. The use of metaphors from the technology of type-founding (the visual reproduction of speech) and the appearance of the word *image* are striking: indeed, William Kumbier points out that the verse evokes the deadening repetitions of the painter, and he argues that it is only through verbalization that "the graphic medium" of poetry is redeemed for Smart.[15] Following the logic of the verse, however, it is the reader who imitates; the artist creates, making an impression or cavity in words—such as a lexical alteration—that is fertile, if not virile. The virile punch alters words by opening an empty space or womblike mold. The Orphic and the mimetic converge here, as do the sexes, in an image of conception that combines the vocabulary of imitation (eye, image) and of animation (punch, cast, take up).

It is hard, perhaps, to understand what Smart intends by treating the written word as a plastic medium, but he clearly describes himself typing *into* words. Words are made the support or passive medium of a diacritical activity, and we can grasp the novelty of this idea by contrast to classical ideas of imitation and typification, where a waxy medium supports the impression of words (as in Plato and Locke).[16] Perhaps even more puzzling is the way in which an optical or vision-based metaphor of imitation is used to model the properly lexical or discursive features of enunciation. Significantly, mimesis can be thought in terms of both vision and speech, as Philippe Lacoue-Labarthe has shown in his provocative study of *The Republic*, and, as we have already seen, Smart is particularly attuned in *Jubilate Agno* to the Platonic encounter with imitation.[17]

Considered in epistemological terms, the danger of mimetic art is the danger of untruth, of false images and ideas, a theme Smart develops in relation to the wiles of the devil:

> For the SHADOW is of death, which is the Devil, who can make false and faint images of the works of Almighty God. (B308)

Like the devil, the painter makes a false image (idol, *eidolon*) that substitutes for or replaces the animated creation with a dead work. The notion of art as a false copy springs from book ten of *The Republic,* where Plato calls into question the veracity of imitation per se. Plato's understanding of imitation in book ten is fundamentally visual: his example of a mimetic art is painting, and he draws instances of the unreliability of vision from the refraction of light.[18] (Smart clearly has this book of *The Republic* in mind in his treatment of painting, which he links to the science of light in Newton's *Opticks* [1704].) For Plato, mimesis is the iteration of a founding archetype or form (*eidos*) that is at an epistemological remove from the archetype, and it is this removal, rather than the infidelity of any particular copy, that falsifies: all copies, qua copies, are inauthentic—only the eidetic original is true. For this reason the maker of an actual bed is closer to the original idea (*eidos*) of "the bed" than the painter, whose two-dimensional representation of a bed is a copy of a copy.[19]

Smart invokes this epistemological critique of imitation when he attacks Newton's theory of light:

> For Newton's notion of colors is αλογοζ [alogos] unphilosophical.
> For the colors are spiritual. (B648-49)

The colors are spiritual in the sense that they proceed from God, and are a manifestation of God; the equation of *alogos* and unphilosophical is the equation of Logos (the divine fiat) and philosophy (the classical elevation of the idea). Smart presents the divine word as both a creative principle and a governing archetype or form:

> Let Barsabas rejoice with Cammarus—Newton is ignorant for if a man consult not the WORD how should he understand the WORK?
> —(B220)

The word precedes and governs the work in the same way that the form precedes and governs existence—whether the first creation of God or the secondary works of man: "*For [nothing] is so real as that which is spiritual*" (B258—brackets in original). For Smart, Newton's theory of colors deviates from both Platonic and Christian epistemology: the *Opticks* attends to deceptive images rather than divine originals, to the dead work rather than the living word.

Smart also indicts Newton for misconstruing the cognition of the creature, which is logically, not empirically, governed: "*For there is the model of every beast of the field in the height*" (B676). The word "BULL," for example, is a governing "word of Almighty God" (B674), unlike the idolatrous image of the sculptor (B671). The Adamic genera are forms of creation, like the Platonic idea, and are real, vital, spiritual archetypes. The empirical image or idea (*eidolon*) is only "the mental vision of an object" (B395), and as such fails to register the form (*eidos*) behind the object, merely copying the dead particularities of things. In this epistemological context, the Orphic artist would appear to resurrect the Logos after all.

Epistemological criteria do not, however, exhaust the bases of Plato's theory of art. In books two and three Plato offers an ontological critique of mimesis in which the voice is as unstable as the image, and it is in this context that he banishes the tragic poets.[20] Plato contrasts simple narration (*haple diegesis*) with dramatic representation (mimesis).[21] In a simple narration, the subject of the enunciation (speaker) and the subject of the enounced (person) properly coincide—for example, in the lyric, where the poet speaks in his or her own person.[22] In dramatic representation, however, the subject of the enunciation and the subject of the enounced diverge—for example, in tragedy, in which the poet speaks now as Oedipus, now as Antigone, and so on. As Lacoue-Labarthe points out, in books two and three of *The Republic* Plato conceptualizes falsehood (untruth) in two distinct ways: first as fiction (*pseudos*), when untruth is understood from the side of the content or Logos; and second as representation (mimesis), when untruth is understood from the side of the speech event or lexis.[23] Significantly, both mimesis and *pseudos* are linked by Plato to threats of feminization and impotence.

Plato dislikes impersonation, as found in dramatic works, because in the act of recitation speaker and person diverge. It is in this enunciative disjunction, seemingly born of a style of speech (but in fact a characteristic of all discourse), that the ontological threat to the self-identity of the mimetic speaker lies. Lacoue-Labarthe rereads *The Republic* in terms of this ontological threat, analyzing the fear of impersonation as a fear of depropriation (rather than of error).[24] Depropriation is the loss of self-identity and proper being; it is the threat of being double, of being doubled; a threat that springs from the spoken word; from sound—or recitation. In this context, far from reviving the Logos in the immediacy of living speech, the Orphic artist is exposed to the same derivative standing as the mimetic artist.

Jubilate Agno reactivates Plato's association of dramatic art and mimetic depropriation by mounting a sexual critique of theatrical impersonation and recitation, and by questioning the standing of the art of delivery more generally. Smart's concern with mimetic depropriation is linked, in terms of content, to fears of masculine degeneration in strength and height:

> *For men in David's time were ten feet high in general.*
> *For they had degenerated also from the strength of their fathers*
> *For I prophesy that players and mimes will not be named amongst us.*
> (C91-93)

Smart contrasts a virile past (associated with David) with a depleted present (associated with "mimes") and, like Plato, he hopes to banish the poet-actor. The notion that the theater has a devirilizing force was a traditional part of English attacks on the stage from the early seventeenth century, and the Puritan ideology that such critics drew upon.[25] Puritan critics before 1660 were, of course, especially concerned with the sexual implications of a travesty stage (where boys played women's roles, as men did in ancient Greece), but stage acting remained a site of suspect masculinity throughout the period.[26] Smart's own career as a female impersonator and mimic shows how the

sexual implications of the stage remained a vital issue long after the intro-
duction of actresses; and in passages like this Smart revisits his ambivalent
activities as Mary Midnight.[27] Indeed, as a midwife figure, Smart's "old
woman" links imitation, not with a generic femininity, but with the specifi-
cally maternal capacities of women.

Like Plato, Smart also connects the devirilizing effects of the theater to
the act of enunciation:

> For the Romans clipped their words in the Augustan thro idleness and ef-
> feminacy and paid foreign actors for speaking them out. (B417)

Here it is through recitation ("speaking")—rather than spectacle
("mimes")—that the threat of the theater is constituted. The voice (and sound
in general) is not exempt from the ill effects of mimesis ("clipping" echoes
"taking off" in the verses on painting). Elsewhere Smart differentiates be-
tween the clapping together of the hands in prayer (at worship) and applause
(at the theater) (B233; 343-45) in terms of enunciative criteria: God is prop-
erly (app)lauded in prayer, whereas clapping at the theater depropriates the
gesture. Clearly the problematic of imitation is not confined to visual media.

In many ways, Smart's interest in enunciation marks *Jubilate Agno* as a work
of the mid- eighteenth century. Nicholas Hudson has identified the rise of a "new
aural sensitivity" in this period: "Scholars of language and rhetoric in the mid-
century became far more aware of the special powers of speech—powers that
could never be captured in a written form."[28] Hudson has the so-called elocu-
tionists in mind: scholars who argued that the art of oral delivery had been ne-
glected in modern times, and who proposed to correct the deficiency with various
new pedagogies. Smart's imbrication of the *fiat lux* and classical oratory ("*For
Action and Speaking are one according to God and the Ancients*" [B562]) shows
him drawing the elocutionary interests of mid-century together with his religious
vocation (see also Chapter 2). And like other elocutionists, Smart approaches de-
livery as a pedagogical issue: for example, when introducing an alphabetical ex-
ercise that distinguishes between ordinary and "full" (B538) pronunciation:

> For in the education of children it is necessary to watch the words, which
> they pronounce with difficulty, for such are against them in their con-
> sequences. (B537)

Such concern for correct pronunciation and articulation could have come
from one of the elocutionary handbooks of John Walker or Gilbert Austin. It
is significant for emphasizing language as discourse, not hieroglyph.

Smart's interest in elocution may derive in part from theatrical milieux: from his quarrels, for example, with John "Orator" Henley (a target of Smart's stage impersonations), as well as from the ideas of the actor Thomas Sheridan (who lectured on elocution as *Jubilate Agno* was being composed). But unlike Sheridan, for whom the "consequences" of poor delivery include the unwanted expression of regional and class accents, Smart cares more for the generative role of sound: "full" pronunciations, for example, deliver a "secondary meaning" (B543):

> For C is a sense quick and penetrating. (B515)
> For C pronounced hard is ke importing to shut. (B540)

The same letter "C" is pregnant with at least two senses: "see" and "kee" (key). Pronunciation is a conveyancer of the letter and, since the spoken word is not an image of the written word, a mode of arche-writing. Significantly, given his views on women, Smart valorizes the voice as a feminine generative principle (in his verses on the echo [B234-38] and the Hebrew vowels [C39], for example), and gives scope to the ungovernable, doubling "feminine" elements of signification.

Understood as a mere repetition, "voice and sound" ("On the Goodness") are derivative and secondary. But Smart refuses to follow Plato's assimilation of enunciation to the paradigm of the mirror (and to the eidetic in general) in book ten of *The Republic*. On the contrary, Smart embraces enunciation as a generative power that animates and moves the word. The doubling that concerns Plato is what Smart celebrates: in contrast to the fertile doublings of "full" pronunciation, for example, "vicious pronuntiation" [sic] (B398) is a kind of verbal "clipping" (B579) or castration. Of course in the strictest sense Smart is inconsistent, since a clipped word is no less an act of lexical transportation (compare B333). Still, by linking the "clipping" of words to the clipping or "shaving" (B419) of a beard, which "was an invention of the people of Sodom to make men look like women" (B419), he connects mis-enunciation to the "effeminacy" (B417) of the stage and of mimesis (B419). If homosexuality is understood as a male principle in isolation from woman, then in this context the art of speech is potentially another dead work and the arts of prayer and music are reintroduced as problematic elements of worship. Even clapping or prayer (B343) threatens to become clipping (that is, lisping). The aeolian arts of voice and sound thus do not guarantee an Orphic animation. It is as enunciator, not mirrorer, that the aeolian artist is in danger of reducing the creation.

To clip or "amerce" the creation is, for Smart, an overtly sexual act—a threat to the proper or whole masculinity of his ideal husbandman-poet.[29]

The verses on the horn in fragment C reveal an intense preoccupation with heterosexual male virility; and the sexual agon between Smart and his wife is an important subtheme of this preoccupation. The link between Smart's sexual and poetic interests is especially clear in an evocative verse to which Clement Hawes draws attention:

> Let Japhia rejoice with Buteo who hath three testicles.
> *For I bless God in the strength of my loins and for the voice which he hath made sonorous.* (B80)

Hawes notes that "loins" and "lines" were homophones in the eighteenth century (214). Although the notion of a "manly" style is conventional, Smart literalizes poetic manliness in overtly sexual and physical terms by linking testicles, loins, lines, and a sonorous voice. He does the same thing with his inspiration as a sacred poet: "*For I bless the Lord JESUS for his very seed, which is in my body*" (B144). This "seed" marks Smart as a descendent of a virile Christ.

In the context of his concern for virility, Smart's use of metaphors drawn from female sexual experience strikes a dissonant note: "*For the hour of my felicity, like the womb of Sarah, shall come at the latter end*" (B16). Sarah's womb typifies the vindication of the believer, and it may reflect Smart's identification with the dispossessed in general. But the figure of the fruitful womb appears on several occasions in Smart's poetry and is linked to more than generalized states of vindication or dispossession. At the end of the verses on the Mosaic horn in fragment C, Smart uses the image of the horn of plenty to put male and female generative principles in a dynamic relationship. After his release from confinement in 1763, one of Smart's first publications was an Oratorio on Hannah's praise to God for her fruitful womb. More than a single dissonant note, the metaphor of the fruitful womb counterpoints the testosterone blare of male potency in *Jubilate Agno*. Indeed, by choosing to identify the Benedicite-like magnifications of the *Jubilate* with the Magnificat (B43), Smart puts the fruitful womb at the center of his poetry, and sets Mary with Orpheus and David as a type of the poet.

The poetic significance of the fruitful womb is clarified by Smart's hymn on "The Annunciation of the Blessed Virgin":

> Praise Hannah, of the three,
> That sang in Mary's key;
> With her that made her psalm
> Beneath the bow'ring palm;

With the dame—Bethulia's boast,
Honour'd o'er th' Assyrian host. (ix: 43-48)[30]

In these lines, Smart links three powerful Old Testament women, Hannah, Deborah, and Judith, with Mary as the mother of Christ. "Mary's key" refers, of course, to the Magnificat, her song in celebration of the annunciation. Like Mary, Hannah celebrated a divine conception with a song, while Deborah (under "the bow'ring palm") was a noted lawgiver and poet. The relevance of Judith ("Bethulia's boast"), who beheaded Holofernes, is clearer if we recall that Smart's Old Testament male heroes, such as David, have military and religious as well as artistic significance.[31] On the one hand, Smart imagines these women uniting their voices with Mary, so that their significance is Christianized (Mary's song celebrates the coming of Christ) and Hannah, Deborah, and Judith are reinterpreted as types of the Virgin Mary. But on the other hand, Smart puts Mary into an established tradition of female song and female heroism. Smart invokes this tradition in the first of his hymns, where Christian worshipers are urged to "Sing like David, or like Hannah" (I.37). The songs of Hannah (B458) and Mary (B43) thus exemplify sacred poetry for Smart just as much as those of Orpheus or David.

To see *Jubilate Agno* (or some part of it) as Smart's Magnificat is to accept that Mary's celebration of the divine conception is a suitable precedent for a male poet. The use of biblical women as literary precedents was common among female poets of the Restoration and eighteenth century. Women writers referred to Deborah and other Old Testament women to legitimate their own poetic aspirations. Aphra Behn, for example, wondered what had led Restoration women to be "Debarred from sense and sacred poetry" (6) by men when

> We once were famed in story, and could write
> Equal to men; could govern, nay could fight. (9-10)[32]

Behn could be alluding to the very trio of Hannah, Deborah, and Judith that Smart lists in his hymn. Anne Finch also draws on biblical women in the introductory verses to a volume of her poetry. Finch celebrates female singers such as Deborah, whose God-given ability refutes the view that "a woman that attempts the pen, / [is] an intruder on the rights of men" (9-10):

> Sure 'twas not ever thus, nor are we told
> Fables, of women that excelled of old;
> To whom, by the diffusive hand of Heaven
> Some share of wit and poetry was given. (21-24)[33]

Like other women writers of the period, both Finch and Behn are at pains to reclaim a female tradition of "sacred poetry" because it offers direct support for the premise that women poets can be "equal to men."

Unlike Behn and Finch, however, Smart foregrounds the biblical link between female song and female fertility in his poetry: he makes Hannah and Mary the exemplars of sacred female bards, and he puts Deborah and Judith in "Mary's key." It is Deborah (not Hannah or Mary) that Finch (directly) and Behn (indirectly) celebrate: the heroic female warrior and singer, not the childbearing woman; and neither poet analogizes female fertility and poetic creativity. It is surprising, of course, to find a male poet embracing this tradition in any form, even as a supplement to the figures of Orpheus and David. But Smart is less interested in legitimating women's capacity for poetry than he is in recasting the motif to justify the analogy of poetic creativity and the fruitful female womb. In *Jubilate Agno* the reference to a tradition of biblical poet-mothers brings us back to the distinction between an art of the dead work (mimesis) and an art of the living creation (Orphism).

"Mary's key" celebrates the quickening of her womb and the creation of a living being. Smart plays on "quick" as a word meaning life, speed, and intelligence, and links the fertility of Mary's womb to the animation associated with the Orphic poet:

> Let Mary rejoice with the Maid—blessed be the name of the immaculate CONCEPTION. (B139)
> For before the NATIVITY is the dead of the winter and after it the quick. (B305)
> For the propagation of light is quick as the divine Conception. (B325)

Smart conflates the virgin birth and the Immaculate Conception, but his intention is clear: the quickening of Mary's womb is a type of the return of life in the spring, and even of the *fiat lux*. Understood as propagation, Mary's Magnificat is moving as well as creative, like God's harp (B246-47); her "key" is Orphic, not mimetic; or, more accurately perhaps, the Orphic hymn, as a song of "the true God" (C54) like Hannah's, is an anticipation of the Christian Magnificat.

According to Christian doctrine, Mary's song celebrates an unprecedented arrival—the incarnation of God in human form. The product of Mary's womb is a new creation and, as Smart writes, "if the work be new, / So should the song be too" (ix: 25-26). As a new song, the analogy of the Magnificat comes into conflict with Smart's image of the Davidic "artist" whose tune is an "echo of the heavenly harp" (A41). The *idea* of the echoing artist dominates the opening of *Jubilate Agno:* the pairs of human and animal names analogize the poem as an act of preservation and as a secondary creation like Noah's ark (A4), which is linked to poetry through the ark of the testimony (A16). But the analogy with Mary extends the creative power of an extra-categorical, novel birth to the fertile womb celebrated by Hannah. Smart may bless *"the Lord JESUS for his very seed, which is in my body"* (B144); but since he, like Mary, authors a Magnificat, he is also an enunciator—bearer—of the divine, rather than merely its echoer. The reiterated command of *Jubilate* Agno's Let-verses echoes the fiat of Genesis as much as the Psalmic demand to praise, and as a result the *speaker* of the poem is put in the place of God or the divine artist as enunciator.[34] As we might expect of a poet who prayed in public and was confined for it, Smart has a fundamentally dramatic understanding of prayer as a speech genre. Far from simply "reiterating the jubilation of creation," as one critic describes it, when linked to Mary's womb as a generative principle "the voice of the poet" severs the pre-existing harmony of creation and creator by introducing something new.[35]

By embracing the metaphor of birth, Smart revisits both the Augustan consensus on art and his own adaptation of Pope's mother Dulness as the learned midwife Mrs. Midnight, and signals his approval of poetic innovation.[36] In *The Dunciad,* for example, the fruitful womb analogizes the hack writing of modern authors as a monstrous new birth. As Terry Castle has shown, the analogy of poetry and birth was consistently rejected by Augustan writers except for satiric purposes.[37] Castle relies on the work of M. H. Abrams to argue that this rejection reflects a poetics of skilled imitation defined against organic ideas of art: Abrams's mirror, rather than his lamp. Smart, however, is not really a writer of the organic governing idea or Logos, as we have seen, and in any case he shifts his attention in *Jubilate Agno* from print-mothers like Dulness to voice-mothers like Mary. Together, Mary and Orpheus provide a powerful justification for *Jubilate Agno* as a "NEW SONG" (B390) and a new way of writing (D84)—and even as a new New Testament (*"For the blessing of God hath been on my epistles, which I have written for the benefit of others"* [B125]). Like the Orphic theme of animation, the metaphor of birth in "Mary's key" appears to offer a release from art as copying, replicating, or repeating.

Yet the ultimate significance of the idea of the sacred poet-mother for Smart is as a way to rethink the possibilities of poetic creation as a new beginning. Smart's analogy of his poem with Noah's seaborne ark suggests a womblike empty vessel or *chora* filled by an external agent; and, like the ark, sexual generation per se reproduces rather than creates the species. As a secondary creation and Adam's helpmeet, woman in biblical myth is derivative, the copy of a copy of God. Smart is well aware that by invoking the Magnificat he raises the question of the maternal in general:

> Let Jubal rejoice with Caecilia, the woman and the slow-worm praise the name of the Lord.
> *For I pray the Lord Jesus to translate my magnificat into verse and represent it.* (B43)

In this oft-commented-upon verse, Jubal the first musician is paired with the slow-worm or Caecilian, a creature whose name evokes St. Caecilia, the patron saint of music. Eve, of course, is linked to Satan as the worm or serpent, and Jesus is described in the New Testament as the descendant promised by God to Eve to defeat the deceiving serpent (see B98).[38] In accord with Christian doctrine, the error of the general mother Eve is thus redeemed by the conception of the virgin mother Mary. But like all women Mary, too, is a daughter of Eve, and by drawing the two together in the verse that mentions the Magnificat, Smart is unable to surmount a fundamental ambivalence toward the female womb, which he both celebrates and fears.

The opposition between the Orphic and the mimetic artists in *Jubilate Agno* derives from this ambivalence toward the maternal. Far from an autonomous dyad, these figures are alternative conceptualizations of the female womb as an archetype of artistic creation. On the one hand, the Orphic gift of song can proceed directly from the female principle of the muse to the creation without a male-mediator or masculine artist: Melpomene herself, in Smart's addition to Horace's Book IV, Ode iii, "canst make the mute excel, / And ev'n the sea-born reptiles speak."[39] On the other hand, in *Jubilate Agno* Smart describes the maternal as a mimetic agency:

> For the Longing of Women is the operation of the Devil upon their conceptions.
> For the marking of their children is from the same cause both of which are to be parried by prayer. (B297-98)

Sexual reproduction should replicate the species and the father, but the maternal matrix is potentially self-actuated. The divine conception is governed by God; but the desires of women lead to their own conceptions ("the Devil" symbolizes the autonomy of this longing). There is no way, apart from the words of men, to guarantee the produce of a woman's womb; and when a woman is self-moved, when for example like Mary she sings her own song, it is the government of the act of creation by the husbandman-poet that is called into question. As Jacques Derrida observes, reversing a formula of Jacques Lacan, "the letter can always not arrive": the movement of the iter or mark can always exceed reproduction and open the possibility of a new creation or creature.[40]

Like Noah's ark, the female womb is a secondary creation. Yet unlike Noah's ark, it offers the possibility (or threat) of a new, perhaps diabolic, creation. It is by virtue of producing a living work that the Orphic poet threatens the stability of God's creation. "Mary's key" analogizes enunciation with the fruitful female womb. New poetic creation is an outcome of the mimetic modalities of speech (and of the lexical in general), not of the government of the Logos. For Smart, recitation is a lexical conveyance that quickens: it is a fertile new growth that acts by doubling and depropriating. The "female" (C39) spoken vowels quicken the written consonants of biblical Hebrew, for example, redirecting the letter through an act of verbal delivery (as seen in the fruitful confusion of *qeren* and *qaran* that undergirds Smart's meditation on the horn).[41] Thus the metaphor of the fruitful female womb opens up the Orphic register in Smart's poem to the same derivative status as the mimetic register.

It is the iterative element of speech that undergirds the two-in-one structure identified by Hartman as key to the poem (93). Positive recitation, like the echo, transports and magnifies via a lexical doubling; negative recitation, like painting, reduces an original. Smart's fear is not depropriation (the scattering of meaning in the channels of utterance) but de-citation or dis-iteration (the unification of utterance under the concept). We can see this, for example, in Smart's hieroglyphic exercise on the Hebrew letter *lamed* (see also Chapter 2):

> For the letter ל [lamed] *which signifies* GOD *by himself is on the fibre of* some leaf in every Tree. (B477)

According to the standard interpretation of this verse, Smart uses the alphabetical correspondence of the Hebrew *lamed* and the English *el* (L) to open an interlinguistic pun on the Hebrew word *El,* which means God in English.[42] But an English speaker who pronounces *lamed* will hear something else: lamb-èd. No wonder *lamed* "is on the fibre of some leaf in every Tree"—this is the wood of the cross, where the lamb Christ was sacrificed, like the "criminals" (B476) of the preceding verse who Smart hopes will be spared, presumably from Tyburn tree. This is how "languages work into one another by their bearings" (B624): what is borne *and* born in language is sound as an arche-writing that is not "Spelt" (B623) or written but pronounced; it is "the power of some animal" (B625), such as the "bear" sound of "bearings." What unites the animals, ultimately, is "bearing" or the matrix in general, and the "Bear" that David defeats to protect his father's flocks and initiate his heroic life returns in the "magnifical" (A41) resonances of Mary's bearing or delivery of the lamb or word as lexis (see also Chapter 11).

On a textual level the paradox of the new birth (both reproduction and creation) evokes the guilty conscience of the Christian dispensation. To Jewish believers, the "New" Testament lacks divine authority: it is the work of a heretical sect. For Christian believers, however, the Jewish Scriptures are an "Old" Testament to which the "New" comes as a fulfillment or "key." Just as the new man Christ is said to complete the creation and offer it a new life, his gospel reanimates the Jewish Scriptures with a new significance. As a new New Testament, *Jubilate Agno* seems to posit a similar relationship: only by way of a new work and a new song can the old one (in this case, the New Testament) be fulfilled or preserved. But Smart is skeptical of the pure new beginning. Departing from Christian hermeneutics, which finds anticipations of Christ throughout the Jewish Scriptures, Smart reactivates the Bible with lexical conveyances of all kinds, rather than with the allegorizing of Christian typology or a "Great Code."[43] The possibility that the letter may not arrive (but endlessly travel) is taken by Smart as the creative matrix for his own evangel. In the end it is not generation but the government or control of generation that Smart forgoes by uniting creatures across the species, a poignant resolution to both deeply personal and strictly artistic and religious concerns.

NOTES

I would like to thank Heesok Chang, Clement Hawes, and Camie Kim for their comments on an earlier version of this paper

1. John Block Friedman, "The Cosmology of Praise: Smart's *Jubilate Agno*," *PMLA*, 82 (1967): 250-56; Eli Mandel, "Theories of Voice in Eighteenth-Century Poetry: Thomas Gray and Christopher Smart," in James Downey and Ben Jones, eds., *Fearful Joy* (Montreal: McGill-Queen's University Press, 1974), 103-18; Thomas F. Dillingham, "'Blest Light': Christopher Smart's Myth of David," in Raymond-Jean Frontain and Jan Wojcik, eds., *The David Myth in Western Literature* (West Lafayette, IN: Purdue University Press, 1980), 120-33; Jeanne Murray Walker, "*Jubilate Agno* as Psalm," *Studies in English Literature*, 20 (1980): 449-59; Allan J. Gedalof, "The Rise and Fall of Smart's David," *Philological Quarterly*, 60 (1981): 369-86; William S. Kumbier, "Sound and Signification in Christopher Smart's *Jubilate Agno*," *Texas Studies in Language and Literature*, 24 (1982): 293-312.

2. On Smart's scientific ideas, see D. J. Greene, "Smart, Berkeley, The Scientists and the Poets," *Journal of the History of Ideas*, 14 (1953): 327-52; Karina Williamson, "Smart's *Principia*: Science and Anti-Science in *Jubilate Agno*," *Review of English Studies*, n. s. 30 (1979): 409-22; and Guest, 196-240.

3. Instead of "pairs of the same species," as in the legend of Noah, Smart brings together "unmateable *res creatae*" (Hartman, 96).

4. Ovid, *Metamorphoses*, trans. Rolfe Humphries (Bloomington: Indiana University Press, 1955), 237, 238.

5. Friedman, "The Cosmology of Praise," 252. One way to think of the significance of Orpheus is in contrast to Dionysus: where the flute of Dionysus evokes frenzy, the lyre of Orpheus harmonizes. This is Orpheus as an archetype of order and coherence. But from another point of view, Dionysus and Orpheus represent alternative *modes* of animation, and *both* must be contrasted to the stasis of the mimetic artist. On Orpheus as a disciple of Dionysus, see R. D. Stock, *The Flutes of Dionysus: Daemonic Enthrallment in Literature* (Lincoln: University of Nebraska Press, 1989), 19.

6. Gedalof, "Smart's David," dates the decline of Smart's interest in David to his translation of the Psalms, which appeared in 1765 (381). But Smart worked on the Psalms concurrently with *Jubilate Agno* and *A Song to David*.

7. Arche-writing is Jacques Derrida's coinage for the iterative nature of a representational process, where iteration is a nonfigurative, unmotivated stand-in for what is represented: "there is no *writing* as long as graphism keeps a relationship of natural figuration" (*Of Grammatology*, trans. Gayatri Chakravorty Spivak [Baltimore, MD: Johns Hopkins University Press, 1976], 32; the term *arche-writing* is defined on page 56).

8. See, for example, Joseph Wright's painting *An Experiment on a Bird in the Air Pump* (1768).

9. Smart follows Plato's belief that the painter imitates a "superficial appearance" and delineates "an apparition" rather than "the truth" (Plato, *The Republic*, trans. Desmond Lee, 2nd ed. revised [Harmondsworth: Penguin, 1987], 364). Unlike Smart, however, Plato uses the painter to explain the poet, equating them as mimetic artists (373).

10. Alan Liu, "Christopher Smart's 'Uncommunicated Letters': Translation and the Ethics of Literary History," *boundary 2*, 14 (1985-86): 118. See also Kumbier, "Sound and Signification," 306-7.

11. Marshall McLuhan, "Roads and Paper Routes," in *Understanding Media: The Extensions of Man* (Cambridge, MA.: MIT Press, 1994), 89-105. Following Philippe Lacoue-Labarthe (see note 17), I use the term *lexis* to describe the word in its non-conceptual or non-eidetic aspect (the term derives from the act of speech), in contrast with the word as Logos.

12. Hartman, 83.

13. Friedrich Nietzsche, *The Birth of Tragedy*, trans. Shaun Whiteside (Harmondsworth: Penguin, 1993), 33.

14. Amittai F. Aviram, *Telling Rhythm: Body and Meaning in Poetry* (Ann Arbor: University of Michigan Press, 1994), 109-34.

15. Kumbier, "Sound and Signification," 294.

16. Plato, *The Republic*, 72.

17. Philippe Lacoue-Labarthe, *Typography: Mimesis, Philosophy, Politics* (Cambridge, MA.: Harvard University Press, 1989), 43-138.

18. Plato, *The Republic*, 370.

19. In Plato's words, "the artist's representation stands at [a] third remove from reality," *The Republic, 363*.

20. Plato, *The Republic*, 98.

21. Lacoue-Labarthe, *Typography*, 132.

22. On enunciation (*énonciation*) and enounced (*énoncé*—usually translated as "statement"), see Antony Easthope, *Poetry as Discourse* (London: Routledge, 1983): 40-44.

23. Lacoue-Labarthe, *Typography*, 131, 133.

24. Ibid., 130, 133.

25. Laura Levine, *Men in Women's Clothing: Anti-Theatricality and Effeminization, 1579-1642* (Cambridge: Cambridge University Press, 1994).
26. Kristina Straub, *Sexual Suspects: Eighteenth-Century Players and Sexual Ideology* (Princeton, NJ: Princeton University Press, 1992).
27. Fraser Easton, "Christopher Smart's Cross-Dressing: Mimicry, Depropriation, and *Jubilate Agno*," forthcoming in *Genre*.
28. Nicholas Hudson, *Writing and European Thought, 1600-1830* (Cambridge: Cambridge University Press, 1994), 93.
29. See Albert J. Kuhn, "Christopher Smart: The Poet as Patriot of the Lord," *ELH*, 30:1 (1963): 126-27.
30. *PW*, ii; references to Smart's hymns appear parenthetically by hymn and line number.
31. Smart ties the power of the female womb and tongue to castration: behind Mary and Deborah are Salome (B140) and Jael (A30; B4), who, like Judith, were beheaders of men.
32. "Epilogue" to *Sir Patient Fancy* (1678); cited by line number from Aphra Behn, *Oroonoko, The Rover, and Other Works*, ed. Janet Todd (Harmondsworth: Penguin, 1992), 329-30.
33. "The Introduction"; cited by line number from Katharine M. Rogers and William McCarthy, eds., *The Meridian Anthology of Early Women Writers* (New York: Penguin, 1987), 78-79.
34. Walker is correct that the "subjunctive form of command *to praise* is common" in the Psalms ("'*Jubilate Agno*' as Psalm," 454, my italics); but its use in the command *to be* in Genesis is equally relevant here. See also Chapter 10, 205.
35. Guest, 239.
36. For an alternative view, see Lance Bertelsen, "Journalism, Carnival, and *Jubilate Agno*," *ELH*, 59 (1992), 357-384.
37. Terry Castle, "Lab'ring Bards: Birth *Topoi* and English Poetics 1660-1820," *Journal of English and Germanic Philology*, 78 (1979): 193-208.
38. See Hartman, 93.
39. *PW*, v:120 (ll. 27-28).
40. Jacques Derrida, *The Post Card: From Socrates to Freud and Beyond*, trans. Alan Bass (Chicago: University of Chicago Press, 1987), 444.
41. Hawes, 188.
42. Williamson, note to verse B477; Kumbier, "Sound and Signification," 303; for a reading of the exercise in terms of letter form or shape, see Guest, 171-72.
43. The phrase is Blake's; see Northrop Frye, *The Great Code: The Bible and Literature* (Toronto: Academic Press Canada, 1982), xvi.

CHAPTER 9

Johnson, Madness, and Smart

THOMAS KEYMER

YEARS AGO, I WAS ASKED to update some yellowing author-bibliographies that had passed serenely through the photocopier, year after year, without great scrutiny. There, under Smart, were all the classic sources of postwar criticism and scholarship. All were eclipsed, however, by a reference to a much earlier source: Samuel Johnson's "Life of Smart," in *Lives of the English Poets*, ed. George Birkbeck Hill (Oxford: Clarendon Press, 1905).

Needless to say, the library of the institution in question did not hold a unique copy of Hill's edition, complete with otherwise unknown appendix. There is, of course, no "Life of Smart" from Johnson's hand—although, as Robert Mahony and Betty Rizzo have demonstrated, the unknown compiler of my bibliography was not the first to have tried to will it into being. Francis Newbery materially shaped the posthumous *Poems* of 1791 as a covert addendum to the multivolume collection for which Johnson's *Prefaces, Biographical and Critical* had been written, describing it privately as "an Edition of his Poems in two small Volumes of the Size of Johnson's Poets, to which I trust it will not be deemed an unworthy Appendage," and couching newspaper advertisements in similar terms.[1] It was no doubt in the same spirit that he commissioned from Smart's nephew a prefatory life, structured on the Johnsonian model. The hint was soon taken by Robert Anderson, compiler of the rival *Works of the British Poets* (1795), who made room for Smart, supplied his own preface, and criticized Johnson's omission: editorial control had not been Johnson's own, but Anderson knew him to have argued successfully for several other inclusions, and insisted that Smart "had an equal claim to his notice, from piety, and from genius."[2] Complaints like this persisted even in the pre-Victorian nadir of Smart's reputation, and in one remarkable case a contributor to the *Gentleman's Magazine* for 1822 went so far as to construct a brief biography of Smart by analogy with Johnson's much earlier *Life of Savage*. Having quoted the opening sentence of that text, the author goes on to compare Smart and Savage as similar instances of blighted genius, and his essay is clearly an attempt to remedy in imagination the fact "that our great National Biographer, though he and our author were personally known to each other, has not deigned to take the smallest notice of him in his celebrated Lives of the English Poets."[3]

Various explanations have been offered for the exclusion of Smart's poems from *The Works of the English Poets* and the consequent nonexistence of a "Preface, Biographical and Critical" by Johnson. Anderson suggested merely practical impediments concerning copyright, but a century later Alexander Napier suspected a more deliberate exclusion, attributing the omission to "the irregularity of poor Smart's mind and life, in connection with which Johnson probably thought that his pious poems would rather scandalize than edify."[4] Rizzo and Mahony point to Johnson's friendship in the 1760s with Smart's estranged wife, and to Smart's own apparently Wilkesite politics, as further likely grounds for a disinclination on Johnson's part to press Smart's cause.[5] An alternative explanation is proposed later; but although the nonexistence of Johnson's "Life of Smart" can be explained away, it is impossible not to regret. It was a temptation to leave this bibliographical ghost to haunt my updated list, for here was a work that seemed on reflection to have no right *not* to exist, if only on some fantasy shelf of its own with Jane Austen's reflections on the slave trade, Laurence Sterne's critique of David Hume, and *A Checklist of the Works of Daniel Defoe, Written from His Own Memorandums* (1731). Johnson, after all, was on close terms with Smart by 1754 at the latest,[6] and, notwithstanding Arthur Sherbo's insistence to the contrary, it is more than likely that he visited him in the madhouse as *Jubilate Agno* was being written.[7] His "Life of Smart" would offer much more than lost biographical detail, however. Here we would find the leading arbiter of neoclassical taste compelled to encounter a body of poetry in which (even without the then unknown *Jubilate Agno*) the norms of the day were ingeniously challenged and strained. And here we would find—in a mind famously haunted by fears of its own estrangement—an encounter with a case-history in which Enlightenment constructions of insanity as the benighted Other, as well as older recognitions of the "near alliance" or "thin partitions" between wit and madness,[8] are inescapably forced into view. It has recently been written that Johnson's life of a comparable contemporary, William Collins, "lands us squarely in the middle of two quagmires of critical contention: 1) the issue of Johnson's attitude toward the poets of Sensibility and the rising Romanticism of his day; and 2) the issue of Johnson's attitude toward madness, as it affected Collins and as it affected him."[9] So, yet more squarely, might a "Life of Smart."

How, then, might it have run? No such question is answerable, of course, and even the *Gentleman's Magazine* enthusiast of 1822 had the wisdom to restrain his sense that the basic moves of the *Life of Savage* might somehow be co-opted to simulate an echoing "Life of Smart." The fact that Johnson wrote no such life, however, is far from meaning that he had nothing to say, or that it would waste our time to consider the troubling meanings he found in Smart's example. For there is a sense in which Johnson instead *spoke* his "Life of Smart," and spoke it copiously: the discontinuous, scattered, and murkily transmitted medium of his reported conversation yields up an intriguing set of responses, and one made all the more intriguing by its failure to smooth away its own anxieties and contradictions in the polished prose that typifies the *Prefaces, Biographical and Critical*. Indeed, it is perhaps in the more volatile medium of posthumously recorded anecdote and table-talk—almost Ossianic in its residual state of fragmentariness and uncertainty—that the characteristic evasiveness and uncertainty with which Johnson confronted Smart's case are most appropriately caught. Articulated in a variety of contexts, circles, and periods, his comments eloquently convey not only the importance to him of Smart's example, but also the conflicted nature of his ongoing response.

So what, in the first place, does Johnson seem to have thought of Smart as a poet? A well-known passage from Boswell's *Life of Johnson* would seem to offer the simplest of answers: "Johnson, for sport perhaps, or from the spirit of contradiction, eagerly maintained that Derrick had merit as a writer. Mr. Morgann argued with him directly, in vain. At length he had recourse to this device. 'Pray, Sir, (said he,) whether do you reckon Derrick or Smart the best poet?' Johnson at once felt himself rouzed; and answered, 'Sir, there is no settling the point of precedency between a louse and a flea.'"[10] On the face of it, Johnson's attitude here is simple contempt, coupled perhaps with the allegation of derivativeness. A louse being "a small animal, of which different species live on the bodies of men," and a flea being "a small red insect remarkable for its agility in leaping, which sucks the blood of larger animals,"[11] the implication would seem to go beyond an identification of Smart and Samuel Derrick as the lowest conceivable forms of poetic life. More damaging is that both are parasites, sucking what vigor their poetry has from richer veins. To distinguish between them at all would be mere nit-picking.

There are, however, some curious features to this exchange (which Boswell had from Morgann and placed in the 1783 section of the *Life*, though the conversation may have happened in the 1760s).[12] In the first place, if Johnson really does think Smart such a lousy poet, Morgann's conversational tactics become hard to explain. The comparison between Derrick and Smart seems already to have been a commonplace (used much to Smart's advantage in a reference by his friend Bonnell Thornton to "poets of every magnitude from Sm—t to De-r—ck"),[13] and for that reason it may have come into his mind. Yet the only kind of comparison that would have posed problems for Johnson's perverse pro-Derrick position would have been with a manifestly *superior* writer, not with another parasite: he would then have had to argue an impossible relative case or abandon it altogether. Morgann's gambit only makes sense, in fact, if he suspected or knew that Johnson thought *well* of Smart's verse. As for Johnson's rejoinder, the general problem of assessing his reported conversation (the textual trace of an utterance whose meaning would be conditioned by "lost" factors like tone and gesture) is particularly acute here, given his stated mood of "sport" or "contradiction." Clearly he does not mean what he says about Derrick, and it would be rash to base too many assumptions on what he appears to say about Smart. What is clear is that he and Morgann are sparring intensively here, and that the need not to lose a dispute may be more prominent in Johnson's mind than the merits or otherwise of *A Song to David*. It is not irrelevant that Morgann's only other anecdote of the same occasion has Johnson make a reluctant and highly unusual admission of conversational defeat; and on this occasion he avoids further defeat only by shifting his ground. It has recently been noted that John Eachard's *Grounds and Occasions of the Contempt of the Clergy* (1670) offers the relative nobility of lice and fleas as a comic example of pointless rhetorical exercise:[14] recalling the passage, Johnson is laughing off a challenge that if accepted would leave him checkmated, and instead invites Morgann to acknowledge the merely conventional nature, irrespective of subject, of any such task. The poetry of Derrick and Smart is no longer at issue. Nor, to confuse matters further, may it ever have been: as the Hill-Powell edition notes at this point, another witness maintained that the conversation in question had actually concerned Derrick and Samuel Boyce.

An individual anecdote can be explained away. But problems remain for any attempt to argue that Johnson had, or would have been likely to have had, any grasp at all of Smart's importance as a poet. His reference to *The Hop-Garden* as evidence that "one could say a great deal about cabbage" is hardly auspicious,[15] yet beyond this it is impossible to demonstrate his acquaintance with, let alone esteem for, any of Smart's poems in English. Edmund Blunden once lamented that he had left no judgment of *A Song to David*, but this was a poem so alien to contemporary tastes that it was omitted from the 1791 *Poems* on the now notorious grounds that it seemed to demonstrate "the recent estrangement of his mind," and it is hard to imagine even Johnson grasping its force.[16] No doubt his verdict would have been less cheap and catty than Mason's notorious view ("I have seen his Song to David & from thence conclude him as mad as ever"), but it probably would have added little to that of James Boswell (who may or may not been influenced by Johnson, whom he had recently met), when calling the poem "a strange mixture of dun obscure and glowing genius at times."[17]

Moreover, although Johnson cannot have had access to the masterpiece that in our own day has replaced *A Song to David* as Smart's major work, it is hard to imagine him viewing it as anything but anathema. "Only a few years after the long labours of Samuel Johnson to catalogue with precision in his *Dictionary* the definitions of English," writes Allan Ingram of *Jubilate Agno*, "Smart achieved a dramatic dissolution of the capacity of words to be and mean through the linguistic resources of insanity."[18] That may be to underestimate the sophisticated tentativeness of Johnson's theory and practice in the *Dictionary*, as well as the extent to which *Jubilate Agno*'s linguistic playfulness rests on an assumption that there are meanings in place on which to play. The divergent impulses are striking, however, and they are further clarified by Clement Hawes's account of Smart's wordplay in *Jubilate Agno* as strategically disruptive of the Enlightenment impulse toward linguistic standardization: Hawes cites Johnson's famous intolerance of Shakespearian quibbles and punning, and notes by contrast that "few authors are 'seduced' into more puns per line than Christopher Smart" (197). Even as Johnson was at work on his edition of Shakespeare, it would seem, the "fatal Cleopatra"[19] was alive and well in Bethnal Green, enfeebling another victim.

There are moments at which *Jubilate Agno* almost begs to be read as direct repudiation of Johnsonian poetics. Where *The Vanity of Human Wishes* strives for an authoritative mode of lofty and lucid omniscience, *Jubilate Agno* turns instead to a kind of fractured opacity in which all pretensions to didactic coherence and connectedness are relinquished. The poem, indeed, could hardly be less like Johnson's. It is a work identified by its very history of slow, incremental composition as more a flexible process than a finished product; it is a work fragmentary and volatile in its mode of utterance, characterized as it is by rapid unexplained transition; and it is a work explicitly committed to fragmentation and diversity as the nearest possible approach to valid description of the created world. "Let observation with extensive view, / Survey mankind, from China to Peru," Johnson famously begins; and in "On the Immensity of the Supreme Being" (written two years later) Smart expresses a comparable desire to advance "Up to the mountain's summit, there t' indulge / Th' ambition of the comprehensive eye."[20] Even in this early poem, however, we find a complicating sense of postlapsarian limits to vision ("'tis Man's dim eye / That makes th' obscurity"),[21] and by the time of *Jubilate Agno* no such claim to eagle-eyed omniscience seems tenable: "*For nature is more various than observation tho' observers be innumerable*"

(B53). To see creation whole is to falsify its plenitude and resistance to generalization; instead one must rely on more minute and mobile perspectives, responsive to detail and variety, patiently (and in theory endlessly) alert to the finest distinction. Where Johnson's Imlac insists on the need to distill a generalized essence from nature's "inexhaustible variety" (famously, the poet's task "is to examine, not the individual, but the species; to remark general properties and large appearances: he does not number the streaks of the tulip, or describe the different shades in the verdure of the forest"),[22] there seems something rather pointed about the section of *Jubilate Agno* that Smart was writing shortly after *Rasselas* appeared. Even the more conventional *Song to David* is nothing if not eccentrically individualizing in vision: the specificity of nature is crystallized in all its variable strangeness, and general properties or large appearances are never more than secondary to the kind of "minuter discriminations" that Imlac forbids. But in Fragment B of *Jubilate Agno* we enter a poetic world in which streaks must be numbered and different shades described with all the perceptual and verbal resources at the poet's disposal. Now verdure comes in *"ten thousand distinct sorts"* (B654), and observation must descend to ground level: *"For the blessing of God upon the grass is in shades of Green visible to a nice observer as they light upon the surface of the earth"* (B668). If tulips have general properties in this world, moreover, it is hard to see them as ones acceptable to Johnsonian reason: *"For Flowers can see, and Pope's Carnations knew him"* (B568).

Writing of the "Life of Collins," Nicholas Williams claims to find in Johnson "an underlying sympathy with and understanding of pre-Romantic conventions."[23] Yet there is a marked reluctance in this "Life" to engage with Collins's poetry at all, and the cool praise that Johnson bestows on its occasional moments of "sublimity and splendour" are far outweighed by his distaste for its anomalous features: "peculiar habits of thought . . . flights of imagination which pass the bounds of nature . . . harshness and obscurity . . . deviation in quest of mistaken beauties."[24] Such clear distaste for Collins's deviant muse hardly increases the likelihood of an appreciation of Smart's, and it is hard not to be put in mind at this point of the following passage in Boswell: "I was somewhat disappointed in finding that the edition of the English Poets, for which he was to write Prefaces and Lives, was not an undertaking directed by him: but that he was to furnish a Preface and Life to any poet the booksellers pleased. I asked him if he would do this to any dunce's works, if they should ask him. JOHNSON. 'Yes, Sir; and *say* that he was a dunce.'"[25]

Whatever Johnson may or may not have thought of Smart's English poems, however, there is strong evidence that he found something much more estimable than this in the intellect that produced them. By Smart's own account he and Johnson had shared animated conversations (the first of which "was of such variety and length, that it began with poetry and ended at fluxions"),[26] and a clear sense emerges elsewhere that on Johnson's part such conversations were founded on an admiration, even fascination, for the mind of his interlocutor. The anonymous discreditor of the louse/flea anecdote called Smart "a man of genius, a poet, and one of whose abilities Dr. Johnson entertained the highest respect," and this view is vividly supported in the glimpse given by another minor anecdotist of Johnson holding court in 1765: "He then proceeded to speak highly of the parts and scholarship of poor Kit; and to our great surprise, recited a number of lines out of one of Smart's Latin Triposes; and added, 'Kit Smart was mad, Sir.'"[27] As this last anecdote suggests, however, Smart's fascination for Johnson lay not only in his intellectual accomplishments or in the memorability of his Latin verse: it lay in the coexistence of these qualities with something quite else. This readiness to make simultaneous yet apparently contradictory points about the acuteness and derangement of Smart's mind chimes interestingly with Hester Piozzi's testimony that Smart "was both a wit and a scholar, and visited as such while under confinement for MADNESS";[28] and it is in this paradox that we find the key to the vexed scrutiny that Johnson repeatedly turned, in conversation if not in writing, on Smart's case.

Notwithstanding Michel Foucault's categorization of the eighteenth century as the age of a "great confinement," in which conduct offensive to rational sensibilities was newly demonized and systematically quarantined,[29] it has long been clear that the particular period of Smart's confinement was one in which simple assumptions about madness as a stable natural category—unproblematically distinct from, and therefore a validation of, normative sanity—were being interrogated and rethought. Smart was admitted to St. Luke's Hospital in May 1757 and released from Potter's in January 1763, but he later recalls spending "Seven years in Madhouses," and his admission to St. Luke's was probably preceded by confinement in a private institution.[30] In his own writings of the 1760s the category of madness is insistently relativized, and made to seem little more than the invention of a society strategically concerned to discredit all utterance or conduct that threatens its interests and norms. Modifying the third commandment, he forbids such arbitrary strategies in *A Song to David*: "Thou shalt not call thy brother fool."[31] In *Jubilate Agno* he aligns himself with Christ, for whom he is *"willing to be called a fool"* (B51), in suffering the same hostile interpretation of his challenge to conventional decorums: *"For I am under the same accusation with my Saviour—for they said, he is besides himself"* (B151). Looking forward to a time in which the habits of prayer for which he was confined (*"For I blessed God in St James's Park till I routed all the company,"* B89) will themselves be normative, and in which the deviant will be those who neglect to pray, he strongly implies a notion of madness as time-bound and socially constructed: *"For I prophecy that the praise of God will be in every man's mouth in the Publick streets"* (C62). In the mean time he must suffer a punitive incarceration, at once Hogarthian and Foucauldian in character, in which the repressive apparatus of the confining institution subjects him to scapegoating (*"For silly fellow! silly fellow! is against me,"* B60), spectacle (*"For they pass by me in their tour,"* B63), and punishment (*"For they work me with their harping-irons, which is a barbarous instrument,"* B124).[32] In these conditions, moreover, a vicious circle begins to work, in which the resentment of the incarcerated victim only generates further evidence to validate incarceration: *"For where Accusation takes the place of encouragement a man of Genius is driven to act the vices of a fool"* (B365).

Taken together, we may read such passages as constituting a sustained denial on Smart's part not only of his own alleged insanity, but also of the status of insanity as a coherent notion, as an absolute or given, or indeed as anything more than a socially convenient fiction. Later Smart makes much of the Stoic paradox that all who fall short of perfect virtue or wisdom might strictly speaking themselves be defined as mad, and he uses Horace's playful reworking of the idea to turn the tables on an incarcerating world: "Now hear how those, that give to you / The name of madman, are so too."[33] While Smart was extreme in this respect, however, he was far from alone, and we may find in others a similar readiness to challenge or problematize their culture's assumptions. In his *Treatise on Madness* of 1758, William Battie (the pioneering psychiatrist who the same year discharged Smart "uncured" in his capacity as first physician at St. Luke's), vigorously attacked the standard views of madness as an undifferentiated category of incurable otherness, and extended his attack to the abuses that followed from such a view, including madhouse tourism and punitive incarceration (as opposed to the asylum of protective confinement). "We . . . find that Madness is, contrary to the opinion of some unthinking persons, as manageable as many other distempers, which are equally dreadful and obstinate, and yet are not looked upon as incurable," Battie insisted; "and that such unhappy objects ought by no means to be abandoned, much less shut up in loathsome prisons as criminals or nusances [*sic*] to the society."[34] Johnson himself was more radical and unsettling in *Rasselas* the following year, in which a superficially sane astronomer discloses a madness that has passed undetected for half a decade. In the analysis that follows, Imlac's observation that "of the uncertainties of our present state, the most dreadful and alarming is the uncertain continuance of reason" is chillingly juxtaposed with his insistence that insanity is not a condition apart but a universal affliction, conspicuous only in those whose ability to "control and repress" the affliction breaks down: "Perhaps, if we speak with rigorous exactness, no human mind is in its right state."[35] Much of Tobias Smollett's *Sir Launcelot Greaves* (1760-61) turns on the apparent insanity, by the depraved standards of a world run mad, of traditional notions of virtue; the novel culminates in the double bind of Sir Launcelot's wrongful incarceration in a London madhouse, surrounded by other victims of arbitrary or malicious diagnosis, and "knowing that every violent transport would be interpreted into an undeniable symptom of insanity."[36] The abuses represented in Battie's *Treatise, Sir Launcelot Greaves,* and elsewhere came under legislative scrutiny with the constitution of a parliamentary committee of enquiry in 1763 and the eventual passage, in 1774, of the Act for Regulating Private Madhouses;[37] and while the surrounding debates of course stop short of any Foucauldian critique of confinement and silencing as perverse expressions of cultural fear, or any Szaszian view of madness as an arbitrarily constructed and cynically medicalized category,[38] they certainly constitute a radical problematization of standard eighteenth-century assumptions. The mad might exist, and be essentially unlike the sane; but the boundaries were looking increasingly unstable, and the grounds for judgment uncertain.

Decades later, Hester Piozzi could remain confident in madness as a coherent category, but found diagnosis more problematic. Her account of Smart's obsession with spontaneous public prayer, and of his otherwise entirely sound judgment, is familiar to scholars, but the significance of the context needs emphasis. Considering the proper usage of the term *madness* and its cognates, she sees insanity as the silent companion of everyday life, detectable only in cases that erupt into public display: "A friend once told me in confidence, that for two years he durst not ever eat an apple, for fear it should make him drunk; but as he took care to consign no reason for his forbearance, and as no man is much solicited to eat apples, the oddity escaped notice; and would not have been known at this hour, but that he told me many years after he had recovered his senses to perfection, and told it as an instance of concealed INSANITY." Only then does Piozzi give her description of Smart, before returning again to her original point of reference, the anonymous abstainer from apples:

> The famous Christopher Smart, who was both a wit and a scholar, and visited as such while under confinement for MADNESS, would never have had a commission of LUNACY taken out against him, had he managed with equal ingenuity—for Smart's melancholy shewed itself only in a preternatural

excitement to prayer, which he held it as a duty not to controul or repress—taking *au pied de la lettre* our blessed Saviour's injunction to *pray without ceasing*.—So that beginning by regular addresses at stated times to the Almighty, he went on to call his friends from their dinners, or beds, or places of recreation, whenever that impulse towards prayer pressed upon his mind. In every other transaction of his life no man's wits could be more regular than those of Smart; for this prevalence of one idea pertinaciously keeping the first place in his head, had in no sense except what immediately related to itself, perverted his judgment at all: his opinions were unchanged as before, nor did he seem more likely to fall into a state of DISTRACTION than any other man; less so perhaps, as he calmed every start of violent passion by prayer. Now, had this eminently unhappy patient been equally seized by the precept of *praying in secret;* as no one would then have been disturbed by his irregularities, it would have been no one's interest to watch over or cure them; and the absurdity would possibly have consumed itself in private, like that of my friend who feared an apple should intoxicate him.[39]

Here Piozzi stops short of arguing that Smart was sane (though by the end of her analysis his insanity diminishes to mere "irregularities" or "absurdity").[40] Equally, she resists any conclusion that, if Smart was sane in all other respects, and if others live with the reputation of sanity while equally mad in the privacy of our own minds, the concept of insanity becomes incoherent. The consequence as she represents it, however, is scarcely less unsettling: that for practical purposes the only distinction available to us is not between the sane and the insane, but merely between concealment and display.

Evidently, Johnson was in Piozzi's mind as she wrote her essay on madness and Smart. It is not simply that she takes as her starting-point and guiding assumption the astronomer episode from *Rasselas*, and specifically Imlac's relativistic insistence on the unavailability of any ideal human "right state" of uncompromised sanity. In her *Anecdotes* of 1786, she had made public Johnson's fears of running mad himself, and she is now known to have been custodian of the notorious "Fetters & Padlocks" that Johnson seems to have acquired as more than merely symbolic tokens of his status as potential Bedlamite.[41] Her memorandum that "our stern Philosopher Johnson trusted me about the Years 1767 or 1768 . . . with a Secret far dearer to him than his Life" has been widely interpreted as a confession of self-diagnosed madness, and of even greater relevance in the present context is the further note that she committed to her journal during the crisis surrounding George III's delirium in 1788-89: "I don't believe the King has ever been much worse than poor Dr Johnson was, when he fancied that eating an Apple would make him drunk."[42] At once intellectual authority and case study, sane author of *Rasselas* and deranged abstainer from apples, Johnson is as central to Piozzi's argument as Smart himself. Combining localized insanities with otherwise uncorrupted eminence in learning and wit, both problematize the assumption that madness is a category apart. All that distinguishes mad poet from sage philosopher is the element of visibility.

Johnson's own personal take on Smart was probably a further influence on Piozzi. Mahony and Rizzo put it beautifully when they write that Johnson "was of several minds about Smart's condition";[43] but there are significant constant features to his recorded comments, most of which anticipate Piozzi's account. First there is his tendency to move from Smart's case toward a more general reflection, skeptical or satirical, on his culture's discriminations between the sane and the mad. Second is his identification between Smart's case and his own, characteristically jocular in tone, but nonetheless significant for its implication that little separates one of the most notorious lunatics of the day from the most eminent rationalist. Sometimes he suggests nothing more radical than Piozzi's point about concealment and display, as in the following remark, which clearly refers to Smart: "Many a man is mad in certain instances, and goes through life without having it perceived:—for example, a madness has seized a person of supposing himself obliged literally to pray continually—had the madness turned the opposite way and the person thought it a crime ever to pray, it might not improbably have continued unobserved."[44] Here Smart's madness is apparently accepted as objective (though limited) fact, rather than as a problematic or culturally determined diagnosis: Johnson anticipates Piozzi's arguments about the difficulty of detecting insanity, and about the possibility of localized madness coexisting with localized reason, but fails to ask further questions. But in another version of this same speech (which seems to have been something of a party piece), more unsettling implications are on show: "Madness frequently discovers itself merely by unnecessary deviation from the usual modes of the world. My poor friend Smart shewed the disturbance of his mind, by falling upon his knees, and saying his prayers in the street, or in any other unusual place. Now although, rationally speaking, it is greater madness not to pray at all, than to pray as Smart did, I am afraid there are so many who do not pray, that their understanding is not called in question."[45] Here we are closer to a view of madness as a cultural construct (though not all the way there, since Johnson is describing a madness that *discovers itself* by deviation from social norms, as opposed to being, in the Szaszian view, *no more than* such deviation). Now Smart's confinement is attributed primarily to his public violation of polite codes, and only indirectly to his state of mind. What defines his insanity, or at least renders it observable, is not its opposition to sanity as such, but its opposition to social convention—and a convention whose polite upholders, if believers, are more insane than the deviants they scapegoat and shackle. The deviants, moreover, include Johnson himself, as another conversation (with Charles Burney) makes clear: "I did not think he ought to be shut up. His infirmities were not noxious to society. He insisted on people praying with him; and I'd as lief pray with Kit Smart as any one else. Another charge was, that he did not love clean linen; and I have no passion for it."[46] Again we find the implied view of madness as a label used to scapegoat crimes against politeness; again the acknowledgment that Johnson himself is complicit in the same offense.

All these conversations suggest skepticism on Johnson's part, both about Smart's madness as an objective fact, and about the larger assumptions about madness and sanity to which he had fallen victim. Elsewhere he satirically exposes the arbitrariness of the term by using it in shifting and unstable senses, as though deliberately emptying it of secure signification: when he recalls contributing to the *Universal Visiter* "for poor Smart, while he was mad, not then knowing the terms on which he was engaged to write," he seems initially to be taking Smart's madness for granted in the conventional sense. As the anecdote continues, however, the madness that Smart and (more fleetingly) he himself share is constituted by nothing more than the inability to recognize an exploitative contract: "I hoped his wits would return to him. Mine returned to me, and I wrote in "The Universal Visitor" no longer."[47] The anecdote is casually told, and at Smart's expense. Inherent in it, however, is a redefinition of madness just as perverse as the famous *Dictionary* definitions of "Patron" or "Pension," and just as unsettling in its implications about the capacity of the word (or any other) to denote a meaning that is constant and agreed.

The last anecdote, not from Boswell but from Baptist Noel Turner, describes Johnson's visit to Cambridge of 1765. Turner dwells here on Johnson's outlandish appearance, and describes how he walked through Cambridge, "or rather, perhaps rolled or waddled, in a manner not much unlike Pope's idea of 'A dab chick waddling through the copse."[48] Later, as seems to have been the way in Johnson's presence, we find "Kit Smart happening to be mentioned." First Johnson comments cynically on claims that at the time of his escape from the madhouse those responsible for his confinement were planning to release him anyway. Then comes his praise (cited earlier) for Smart's "parts and scholarship," and then the incongruous afterthought "Kit Smart was mad." Pressed to define his terms, Johnson then produces an unexpected reply: "Why, Sir, he could not walk the streets without the boys running after him." Again Johnson refuses to validate Smart's incarceration or the diagnosis behind it, and turns instead to his wry but now familiar sense of madness as an allegation that accompanies conspicuous unconventionality, or any refusal to observe the niceties of deportment, rather than simply a matter of clinical fact. Again, moreover, he includes himself. This time he leaves the point implicit, but in light of his recent dab-chick performance his companions are able to grasp it: "On Johnson's leaving the room, Beauclerk said to us, 'What he says of Smart is true of himself;' which well agrees with my observations during the walk I took with him that very morning."[49]

All such anecdotes cut two ways, of course. At one level they wittily subvert the category of madness, redefining our sense of it (in partial anticipation of the modern critiques of Foucault or Thomas Szasz) as above all a strategy for marginalizing and scapegoating deviant conduct or threatening thought. If Smart is mad, Johnson seems to be insisting, then so is he, the most strenuous upholder of reason; the lesson perhaps being that contemporary views of Smart as mad should not be accepted as having any objective or transhistorical status. Yet what if Johnson saw himself, as Piozzi would have us believe, as *truly* deranged? What if, as has been suggested more recently, he and Smart were both similarly mad (specifically cyclothymic) by the measures of modern psychiatry?[50] At another level, it is hard not to sense a more heartfelt side to even the most playful of Johnson's remarks, as though in contemplating Smart's misfortunes he sees a terrible glimpse of his own potential future self, his battle with unreason lost.

"Of all the calamities to which the condition of mortality exposes mankind," writes Adam Smith, "the loss of reason appears, to those who have the least spark of humanity, by far the most dreadful, and they behold that last stage of human wretchedness with deeper commiseration than any other." Yet the madman may laugh and sing, and the sentiments of the commiserating beholder cannot be taken for reflections of the madman's own. "The compassion of the spectator must arise altogether from the consideration of what he himself would feel if he was reduced to the same unhappy situation, and, what is perhaps impossible, was at the same time able to regard it with his present reason and judgment."[51] It is worth remembering these words when we read Boswell's plain yet moving observation that Smart was a man "with whose unhappy vacillation of mind [Johnson] sincerely sympathised,"or when we combine it with Boswell's earlier admission that "insanity . . . was the object of his most dismal apprehension."[52] To sympathize was for Johnson "to feel with another,"[53] and it is in a peculiarly acute version of this response—pity grounded in identification, an imaginative entry into another's lot—that we must see him as feeling with Smart. It would not be unreasonable to speculate, moreover, that it was precisely because of this acute sympathy, and not because of any more hostile response to Smart as either a poet or a man, that Johnson failed to press for his inclusion in the multivolume collection for which his *Prefaces, Biographical and Critical* were written. Those who have argued that Johnson failed to make Smart's case because of some more hostile response to him as either man or poet have been looking in the wrong direction. He failed to press the case for the poems because he would then have had to produce a preface. None of the indirection and irony that mark his conversation about Smart would have been admissible, and he would have had to confront directly (to return to Smith's words) "what he himself would feel if he was reduced to the same unhappy situation, and . . . able to regard it with his present reason and judgment." It would have driven him mad.

NOTES

1. Francis Newbery to Sir Joseph Banks, Nov. 4, 1791, quoted by Robert Mahony and Betty Rizzo, *Christopher Smart: An Annotated Bibliography 1743-1983* (N.Y.: Garland, 1984; hereafter cited as *Annotated Bibliography*, entry 178); Mahony and Rizzo also cite a *Times* advertisement (Dec. 23, 1791).

2. *The Works of the British Poets*, ed. Robert Anderson, 13 vols. (Edinburgh: 1795), 11: 122, quoted in *Letters*, 151.

3. *Gent. Mag.*, 92 Pt. 2 (Dec. 1822): 500. "Omicron's" contribution is noted in *Annotated Bibliography* as entry 1333; see also entries 1341 (George Dyer in 1824) and 1355 (Richard Gooch in 1834).

4. *Works of the British Poets*, ed. Anderson, 11: 122; James Boswell, *The Life of Samuel Johnson*, ed. Alexander Napier (London: George Bell and Sons, 1884), 1: 324 n., quoted in *Annotated Bibliography*, entry 1389.

5. *Letters*, 152-53.

6. Thomas Tyers, "Biographical Sketch of Dr. Samuel Johnson," in *Johnsonian Miscellanies*, ed. G. B. Hill, 2 vols (Oxford: Clarendon, 1897), 2: 364. The friendship may have begun earlier: Smart was actively promoting the *Rambler* in 1750, recommending it to Charles Burney soon after its launch (Boswell's *Life*, 1: 208 n.), and probably supplying the introductory compliment to the *Rambler* in the *Student* for Oct. 16, 1750 (*Annotated Bibliography*, entries 112, 326).

7. Sherbo, p. 125. Sherbo assumes a short memory on Smart's part when he argues that the prayer for Johnson in *Jubilate Agno* (B74, composed circa Aug. 24, 1762) cannot be evidence of a recent visit on the grounds that Johnson left London for Devon on August 16. Nor is it clear, if Sherbo is right that Johnson's well-known report of Smart digging the madhouse garden "need be no more than hearsay," why Burney should have elicited the report in a form of words implying a recent meeting ("How does poor Smart do, Sir; is he likely to recover?"), or why Johnson should have responded with such a strong sense of personal impression, and with an occasion-specific pluperfect: "It seems as if his mind had ceased to struggle with the disease; for he grows fat upon it" (Boswell's *Life*, 1: 397). Sherbo is right that Johnson's known visit to Bedlam at about this time is an irrelevance, as Smart was never there—though it is an irrelevance that hardly reduces the likelihood of his desire to visit a madhouse elsewhere.

8. "Great Wits are sure to Madness near ally'd; / And thin Partitions do their Bounds divide" (*Absalom and Achitophel*, ll. 163-4, in *John*

Dryden: Selected Works, ed. William Frost [San Francisco, CA.: Rinehart, 1953], 26): for other instances of the trope see Roy Porter, *Mind-Forged Manacles: A History of Madness in England from the Restoration to the Regency* (London: Penguin, 1990): 21-2.

9. Nicholas Williams, "The Discourse of Madness: Samuel Johnson's 'Life of Collins,'" *Eighteenth-Century Life*, 14 (May 1990): 18.

10. Boswell's *Life*, 4: 192-93.

11. Johnson, *Dictionary of the English Language* (London: 1755), s. v.

12. Boswell's *Life*, 4: 191 n. and 513-15.

13. *Spring-Garden Journal*, 2 (Nov. 23, 1752): 34, quoted in *Annotated Bibliography*, entry 1167; see also entry 1200.

14. Marcus Walsh, "Samuel Johnson on Poetic Lice and Fleas," *Notes and Queries*, 234 No. 4 (Dec. 1989): 470.

15. Boswell's *Life*, 2: 454-55.

16. "Friends of Samuel Johnson," *Johnson Society Transactions* (Dec. 1967): 33-34; *The Poems of the Late Christopher Smart*, 2 vols (Reading: 1791), 1: xliii n.

17. William Mason to Thomas Gray, June 28, 1763, *Correspondence of Thomas Gray*, eds. P. Toynbee and L. Whibley (Oxford: Clarendon, 1935), 802; James Boswell to Sir David Dalrymple, July 30, 1763, quoted in *Annotated Bibliography*, entry 1234.

18. Allan Ingram, *The Madhouse of Language: Writing and Reading Madness in the Eighteenth Century* (London: Routledge, 1991), 173.

19. Samuel Johnson, "Preface to Shakespeare," in *The Oxford Authors: Samuel Johnson*, ed. Donald Greene (Oxford: Oxford University Press, 1984), 429.

20. Samuel Johnson, *The Vanity of Human Wishes*, ll. 1-2, in *The Oxford Authors: Samuel Johnson*, 12; Christopher Smart, *On the Immensity of the Supreme Being*, ll. 83-86, in *PW*, v: 187.

21. *On the Immensity of the Supreme Being*, ll. 25-26.

22. Samuel Johnson, *Rasselas*, in *The Oxford Authors: Samuel Johnson*, 352. For more about "numbering the streaks of the tulip," see also Chapter 12.

23. Williams, "Discourse of Madness," 21.

24. *Lives of the English Poets*, ed. G. B. Hill, 3 vols. (Oxford: Clarendon, 1905), 3: 337-38.

25. Boswell's *Life*, 3: 137.

26. Quoted by Tyers, "Biographical Sketch," in *Johnsonian Miscellanies*, 2: 365. *Fluxions* is a term in Newtonian mathematics—exactly the subject to which Johnson would reportedly turn in moments of fear for his own sanity (*Johnsonian Miscellanies*, 1: 200).

27. Quoted in *Annotated Bibliography*, entry 1303; Baptist Noel Turner, in *Illustrations of the Literary History of the Eighteenth Century*, ed. John Nichols (1817-58), 6:156.

28. Hester Lynch Piozzi, *British Synonymy*, 2 vols. (London: 1794), 2: 3.

29. Michel Foucault, *Madness and Civilization: A History of Insanity in the Age of Reason*, trans. Richard Howard (London: Routledge, 1989). For the case against "Foucault's prose poem," see Andrew Scull, *The Most Solitary of Afflictions: Madness and Society in Britain 1700-1900* (New Haven: Yale University Press, 1993), 6 and passim.

30. *Letters*, 132, xxxv.

31. *A Song to David*, l. 244, in *PW*, ii: 137.

32. Sherbo writes that Smart was "fortunate" to be at St. Luke's and Potter's as opposed to other madhouses (114, 125), given their enlightened practices, and perhaps in these lines Smart does not so much reflect his actual experience as imaginatively construct himself in the role of victimized Bedlamite. Casual tourism of the kind undertaken by Johnson at Bedlam was forbidden at St. Luke's (Scull, *Most Solitary of Afflictions*, 53 n.), and the regime at Potter's enabled Smart to exercise in the garden and teach Latin. Yet even St. Luke's, a "model institution" created in "a bright new image free of Bedlam's tarnish" (Porter, *Mind-Forg'd Manacles*, 129-30), was coercive enough to consume its fair share of iron: Scull cites a bulk order for chain, chain benches, handcuffs, and stock locks from the hospital's minute-book for Oct. 12, 1764 (66).

33. *Satires* 2.3, ll. 93-4, in *PW*, v: 228. On the Stoic claim and Horace's use of it, see Christopher Gill, "Passion as Madness in Roman Poetry," in *The Passions in Roman Thought and Literature*, eds. Susanna Morton Braund and Christopher Gill (Cambridge: Cambridge University Press, 1997), 230-32.

34. William Battie, *A Treatise on Madness* (1758), 93. For Smart's record at St Luke's, see Sherbo, 112-13.

35. Samuel Johnson, *Rasselas*, in *The Oxford Authors: Samuel Johnson*, 405-6. See John Wiltshire's analysis of the episode in light of mid-eighteenth-century assumptions about madness, *Samuel Johnson in the Medical World* (Cambridge: Cambridge University Press, 1991), ch. 5.

36. Tobias Smollett, *Sir Launcelot Greaves*, ed. David Evans (London: Oxford University Press, 1973), 187.

37. Porter, *Mind-Forg'd Manacles*, 151-52.

38. Thomas S. Szasz, *The Manufacture of Madness* (London: Paladin, 1972).

39. Hester Piozzi, *British Synonymy*, 2: 4-5.

40. Elsewhere Piozzi writes of Smart's public prayers that "this indecorous Conduct obliged his Friends to place him in a Confinement whence many mad as he remain excluded, only because their *Delusion* is not known" (*Thraliana*, ed. Katharine C. Balderston [Oxford: Clarendon, 1942]: 728). "*Indecorous* Conduct *obliged*": as good an acknowledgment as any (though doubtless inadvertent) that Smart's incarceration had as much to do with violation of bourgeois proprieties as with insanity objectively defined.

41. *Thraliana*, 415 n.; see Wiltshire, *Samuel Johnson in the Medical World*, 43-49.

42. *Thraliana*, 384 (May 1, 1779), 724 (Dec. 26, 1788).

43. *Letters*, 152.

44. Boswell's *Life*, 4: 31.

45. Ibid., 2: 397.

46. Ibid., 2: 397.

47. Ibid., 2: 345.

48. Turner, *Illustrations of the Literary History of the Eighteenth Century*, 6: 154; compare with *Dunciad*, II, line 63, in *The Poems of Alexander Pope*, ed. John Butt (New Haven: Yale University Press, 1963), 738.

49. Ibid., 6: 156.

50. Russell Brain, *Some Reflections on Genius* (Philadelphia: Lippincott, 1960), 20, 113-22.

51. Adam Smith, *The Theory of Moral Sentiments*, eds. D. D. Raphael and A. L. Macfie (Oxford: Clarendon, 1976), 12.

52. Boswell's *Life*, 1: 306; 1: 66.

53. Johnson, *Dictionary*, s. v.

CHAPTER 10

The Utopian Public Sphere: Intersubjectivity in Jubilate Agno

CLEMENT HAWES

For a man cannot have publick spirit, who is void of private benevolence.

—Jubilate Agno

CHRISTOPHER SMART'S *Jubilate Agno,* written between 1759 and 1763, remained unpublished until 1939. The poem had been privately preserved, for some 170 years after it was written, as a case study in "religious mania" rather than as a poem. Few poems have had a more circuitous route to publication; among published poems, fewer still have been more often received as the document of a strictly private experience. The question of Smart's authorship as such—of the subject who writes, and in what manner—thus informs much of the literary and scholarly tradition surrounding the *Jubilate.* To this day, the single best-known fact about the *Jubilate* remains that it expresses an aberrant or exorbitant subjectivity.

The concept of the sublime has been central to critical efforts to come to terms with the extravagant subjectivity of *Jubilate Agno.* For sublimity has traditionally involved a suddenly altered mode of subjectivity for the individual: the sublime, as Peter de Bolla and Andrew Ashfield point out, is *transformational.*[1] One approach has confronted Smart's transformed subjectivity in the *Jubilate* by way of the religious sublime: a reflection, that is, of his God-soaked absorption in an otherworldly spirituality. For R. D. Stock, this sublimity primarily concerns Smart's mood of pious awe—what Stock terms "religious love or fear"—which is closely allied to Burkean understandings of the sublime's dependence on terror. Stock traces this sublime effect in the *Jubilate* to a Hebraicizing turn in Smart's work: a turn, more specifically, toward a psalm-based poetics of repetition and parallelism widely assumed to derive from the influence of Bishop Robert Lowth's *Lectures on the Sacred Poetry of the Hebrews* (1753; English translation 1787).[2] David B. Morris usefully sophisticates such an account by suggesting, in effect, that Smart Christianizes the Hebraic sublime, creating thereby a sublimity that is "cumulative and stilling, not passionate and abrupt."[3] Like Christopher Devlin[4], Morris emphasizes, above all, Smart's otherworldly or Franciscan vision of "a profound spiritual unity comprehending the diverse and fractured phenomena of existence."[5] While this approach does restore a public context and quasi-prophetic role to Smart as author, it tends to underestimate his investment in the politics of here and now.

If one approach to the *Jubilate*'s altered subjectivity has been to emphasize the poem's public—if otherworldly—dimensions, another has been to emphasize its secular, but seemingly cryptic and hermetically private, aspects. This latter approach has addressed the question of transformed subjectivity through the biographical theme of "madness." Poets, critics, and physicians—notably William Ober and Sir Russell Brain[6]—have elaborated extensively on a diagnosis of religious mania. This slant thus attempts to account, albeit now in psychomedical terms, for the altered textual subjectivity of the *Jubilate*. It has been common since Robert Browning revived interest in "A Song to David" in 1887, moreover, to understand Smart as "liberated" from convention by his supposed madness.[7] The aberrant subjectivity of "madness," then, can likewise be recuperated as "genius" within the aesthetics of the sublime that we have inherited from Immanuel Kant. For the Kantian sublime genius is a transgressive or aberrant individual—one who breaks the aesthetic rules in order to give new ones: a seeming aberration that nevertheless becomes exemplary and paradigmatic.[8] Both of these approaches to the aberrant subjectivity of *Jubilate Agno*—the spiritual and the psychomedical—derive from a polarized understanding of public and private spheres of meaning.

Indeed, what both of these approaches fail to address adequately, despite their otherwise valuable contributions to Smart studies, is the specifically eighteenth-century configuration of public-private relations that constituted the historical terrain on which Smart operated. That is why neither an exclusively privatizing language (that seeks to map the contours of Smart's psychopathology) nor an exclusively publicizing one (that seeks to render his appropriation of a long-standing spiritual tradition) can adequately explain the peculiar mode of authorship projected by *Jubilate Agno*. The theme of individual pathology, as I argued in *Mania and Literary Style,* has served to obscure the public significance of Smart's selective affiliation with a Scripture-based "manic style."[9] The specific theological terms in which Smart claims in the *Jubilate* to be a divinely inspired "reviver of ADORATION amongst ENGLISH-MEN" (B332) reopened a dialogue, in refurbished language, with the rhetoric of the Civil War era. Smart's mid-eighteenth-century moment, however, was also different from the acknowledged high-water mark of enthusiasm in the mid-seventeenth century.[10] For the sort of public tradition that Smart inherited from an earlier radical religious movement had by this time been increasingly reinvested in the space of the private individual. The implications of Smart's historical moment—his status, above all, as an early Enlightenment author—thus shapes his particular negotiations in *Jubilate Agno* with the configuration of public and private.

Smart writes well after seventeenth-century religious hegemony had yielded to that lengthy "crisis of representation" described in the introduction to this volume, and well after the bourgeois articulation of separate spheres had begun to emerge. The appearance in 1714 of Bernard Mandeville's *The Fable of the Bees* conveniently marks a widely noted breach between traditional morality, which continued to decry "luxury," and the emerging science of political economy: for Mandeville scandalized his contemporaries by contending that the private vice of greed provided public benefits to the economy. Authorship itself, moreover, had entered into a markedly transitional period characterized by the "overlapping economies" of patronage and marketplace (see 12-15). Smart thus lived, breathed, and wrote within the prevailing eighteenth-century assumptions about the public sphere of coffeehouse sociability (with its worldly ethos of periodical essays, sober conversation, and "productive leisure"[11]) and that which was increasingly understood to ground it: the private realm, seen as a prepolitical enclave of commercial exchange, on the one hand, and of bourgeois domestic intimacy, on the other. The emergence of this distinction itself begins to differentiate *Jubilate Agno* from premodern modes of spirituality, such as the Franciscan tradition into which Smart has been repeatedly assimilated.

At the same time, however, one must firmly resist the powerful temptation to assimilate Smart to harshly individualistic models of authorship that were neither fully consolidated nor unquestionably dominant. *Jubilate Agno* simply does not belong to the romantic problematic of the lone artistic hero confronting a society that is so inertly conformist or narrowly utilitarian that it refuses to pay attention. The eighteenth-century individualism of Smart, while constituted within the developing liberal dichotomy of public and private spheres, nevertheless belongs to a softer and less rugged individualism than that which eventually triumphed during the nineteenth century. As Kathleen Wilson points out, the "ideal political subject" produced by the emerging print culture of this moment "was not the private, isolated individual but the public man willing to renounce all selfish interests in order to promote the public welfare."[12] Similarly, Dena Goodman has pointed out in a different context that the public and private remain profoundly and explicitly enmeshed in the eighteenth century. There was thus a significant difference in this regard between Smart's moment and that of, say, William Wordsworth— a difference that, following Goodman, one might name "associational individualism": "In the eighteenth century, individualism was not a simple assertion of autonomy, but was framed within theories of natural sociability and gender complementarity, as well by practices of voluntary association which shaped eighteenth-century culture. The individual was not simply cut loose from all ties to brave it alone in the world, as romantics would later represent him; rather individuality and sociability went hand in hand, just as it was individuality that made the public more than just a mass and publicity that allowed individuality to be enacted and experienced."[13] It is only by way of a familiar false teleology—above all, through the spurious notion of pre-Romanticism—that the specific and unique dynamics of the eighteenth-century public sphere can be conflated with the nineteenth-century antagonism between the atomized "individual" and an equally reified "society."

Poised on the cusp of modernity, *Jubilate Agno* belongs instead to a more complex and layered history of the developing public sphere in Britain. As a conspicuous participant in the building of mid-eighteenth-century British public culture, Smart had both coedited and contributed to *The Student* (1750-51); had edited and done virtually all of the writing for *The Midwife* (1751-53); had skirmished with John Hill in the rowdy Paper War (1752-53) described by Lance Bertelsen in Chapter 7; and had regularly contributed verse to the leading periodical of the day, *The Gentleman's Magazine* (1754-55). Smart inherited the uniquely transitional nature of authorship in the eighteenth-century moment. A peculiar range of formal and generic possibilities was made available to him by the mutual interference of religiously motivated, patronage-based, and market-driven varieties of textual production. Smart's self-fashioning as an author straddled these swirling crosscurrents in a charged fashion. And so it was, then—writing from a poignant condition of involuntary solitude—that Smart elaborated in *Jubilate Agno* a utopian version of the Enlightenment's "associational individualism." Indeed, one of the striking achievements of the *Jubilate* is precisely his invention, in the rhetorical sense, of a utopian subjectivity based on a new understanding of the relation between public and private.

Smart's innovation as regards the emerging public-private polarity thus involves considerably more than a mere confessional disclosure of his private experience: the fresh revelation of hidden subjective depths arguably achieved by, for example, a great epistolary novel such as Samuel Richardson's *Clarissa*.[14] For the *Jubilate* is a poem that sets out to reimagine that cultural space where the public, in the phrase of Jürgen Habermas, mirrored its own existence by "entering itself into 'literature' as an object."[15] *Jubilate Agno* accomplishes this act of imagination by means of a root-like and endlessly ramifying structure of enunciation that is designed, above all, to mobilize novel infiltrations between the space of private subjectivity and that of public reflection.

The most telling illustration of Smart's reconfiguration of public and private in *Jubilate Agno* is perhaps found in the arrangement of the poem itself on the page. Indeed, Smart's call-and-response form is so unusual in the original manuscript, in which lines beginning with "Let" and "For" are linked across discrete folio pages, that it constitutes a notable crux of editorial presentation.[16] Although *Jubilate Agno* survives only in fragments, the intact portions of Fragments B and C are evidently organized by Smart's pairing of a line beginning with "Let" with an answering versicle beginning with "For." The "Let" lines ritually juxtapose an individual human being with another of God's species so that the pair can rejoice together: "Let man and beast appear before him, and magnify his name together" (A5). *Jubilate Agno* thus strives to imagine an entire cosmos of God's creatures—animals no less than people—worshiping together. "Let Huz bless with Polypus," Smart writes a bit later—"a lively subtlety is acceptable to the Lord" (A84). It is a line that envisions the deity's response to the creatures—and, presumably, to *Jubilate Agno* itself—precisely in terms of a playful aesthetics of performance, display, and gratitude.

The "Let" line in the *Jubilate* usually comments on attributes of the nonhuman creature that make appropriate the coupling with its human counterpart. The answering "For" line, then, generally moves from this public world of rejoicing creatures to related particularities in Smart's experience: to themes that usually seem more private, meditative, and autobiographical. The free-verse poem of some 1700 lines is evidently based on the liturgical ideal of antiphonal performance—on the public language, that is, of *The Book of Common Prayer*—and is almost certainly intended by the audacious Smart as a revision of the Anglican liturgy. The naming of creatures in *Jubilate Agno,* however, is "common" in quite a different sense: for it is cosmopolitan rather than popular and local, evoking the international language of a more learned scientific subculture. Having *"glorified God in GREEK and LATIN"* (B6), as he says—languages also consecrated as vehicles of Holy Scripture—Smart largely eschews the charms of vernacular English names for the creatures.[17] He draws instead on the sonorous and stately nomenclature established by the Swedish botanist Carolus Linnaeus: a Latin-based "public sphere of science," as Lisbet Koerner puts it.[18] This cosmopolitan bookishness serves to temper and sophisticate his version of enthusiasm: a leavening that produces a texture described by John Hollander as both learned and ecstatic.[19] Indeed, Smart's use of natural history enables him to imagine a public sphere in which "nature" is not external to "culture." He offers, as Geoffrey Hartman puts it, "a visionary representation of the restored human link with the *res creatae. . . .*"[20] At the same time, his ritual coupling device, which pointedly celebrates the possibility of interspecies communication, can be seen as a remarkable attempt to reimagine bourgeois domesticity.

The "Let" and "For" lines, especially in the broadsheet folios of the original manuscript, might initially seem to conjure up public and private spirituality as strictly separate domains. That, indeed, is why William Force Stead, who first published the *Jubilate,* consigned the "Let" and "For" pages to discrete sections of his edition. In the breakthrough edition by W. H. Bond, however, the connection between interlinked "Let" and "For" lines is restored. And this connection is emphasized even more firmly in Karina Williamson's edition of the *Jubilate* for the standard Oxford edition of Smart's poetry. The Oxford edition joins "Let" lines (in roman type) to "For" lines (in italics) in vertically arranged doublets. Williamson's arrangement, undoubtedly the best for most purposes, maximizes the poem's accessibility while still highlighting its antiphonal structure.

In Bond's bicolumnar edition, nevertheless, the *Jubilate* more obviously manifests a remarkable "cross-wording" dimension. Reading horizontally across two facing pages, one sees the call-and-response structure: lines beginning with "Let" and their antiphonal answer by those beginning with "For." Reading vertically down the verso, one sees, simultaneously, a formal and thematic parallelism connecting one "Let" line to the next; or, on the facing recto, one "For" line to the next. Zigzag patterns emerge as well, as material in the right column kindles sparks further down in the left, and so on. It is a formal arrangement that bears comparison with such experimental texts as John Ashbery's "Litany" (the two columns of which are "meant to be read as simultaneous but independent monologues"[21]) and Jacques Derrida's bicolumnar *Glas.*

To be sure, Harriet Guest has argued that while the "For" lines form a private commentary on the "Let" lines—and thus directly depend upon them—the "Let" lines have no corresponding dependence on the "For" lines. While the "Let" lines might have been intended for liturgical performance by a congregation, she contends that the poem's overall structure is not, strictly speaking, antiphonal: the "For" lines, rather, are intended to be read in meditative silence while the "Let" lines are performed aloud.[22] This finely nuanced solution to the dilemmas posed by *Jubilate Agno* suggests again how strongly its form raises for contemporary readers the question of the relation between public and private. Consider, however, the following bicolumnar sequence of Let: For versicles:

Let Ibhar rejoice with the Pochard—a child born in prosperity is the chiefest blessing of peace.	For I bless God for my retreat at CANBURY, as it was the place of the nativity of my children.

(Bond, B^{1}75)

Let Elishua rejoice with Cantharis—God send bread and milk to the children.	For I pray God to give them food which I cannot earn for them any otherwise than by prayer.

(Bond, B^{1}76)

There is clearly a transverse relationship between the "For" line in B75 and the B76 "Let" line, which depends directly upon it. Such diagonal ramifications in fact pervade *Jubilate Agno*. By dramatically increasing the number of dimensions in which reading occurs, Smart figures a knot-like interlacing of public and private.

This crisscrossing formal arrangement permits the poem to rework the public-private split from both sides at once. And indeed, what makes *Jubilate Agno* such a uniquely prolonged exercise in threshold effects is precisely the way that it straddles both the public and the private domains simultaneously. As a result, the public mode in *Jubilate Agno* tends to rewrite Smart's private reality in surprising ways. Indeed, the effervescent quality of the private "I" in *Jubilate Agno*—Smart's unwillingness to write in terms of a merely pedestrian and workaday self—belies the poem's seeming connections with private genres. Hence the significance of a muted allusion to Milton's prayer at the opening of *Paradise Lost* for the heavenly muse to aid his "advent'rous Song / That with no middle flight intends to soar /Above th' *Aeonian* Mount. . . ."[23] Compare Smart, who writes as follows: "*For I have adventured myself in the name of the Lord, and he hath mark'd me for his own*" (B21): an echo that highlights the lofty aspirations that inform Smart's far-from-quotidian diary.

Smart's supposedly private spiritual diary[24] constantly conjures up a public context of meaning and imagined reception. Despite his stigmatization as a madman, Smart hopes to become acceptable, even beautiful, in the eyes of posterity. Indeed, the portmanteau and nonce word *existimation* enables a conception of identity that entirely subsumes, in the name of a higher beauty, the dailiness of private life: everything that is nonlinguistic, bodily, personal. The fluent beauty of a swan, Olor, and its punning link to the Latin for "to smell of," *olere,* thus become the site of an affiliation for Smart, who pairs Olor with a priest whose sacrificial offerings unto the Lord (Numbers 7:36) are of a sort the Bible describes as sweet and savory:

> Let Shelumiel rejoice with Olor, who is of a goodly savour, and the very look of him harmonizes the mind.
> *For my existimation* [sic] *is good even amongst the slanderers and my memory shall arise for a sweet savour unto the Lord.* (B3)

Here Smart identifies his living, breathing, embodied self entirely with the words of his own text. For what he calls his "existimation," borrowing from Latin *existimatio* and fusing "existence" with "estimation," means a self, an "I," seen entirely as an object of discourse. It is an "I" already viewed, already judged, already estimated, already esteemed. Smart's "existimation" thus foretells his posthumous translation into a *name,* a specular or mirrored identity, linked with praise. Smart thus becomes, at the very instant of his writing, what he imagines he will have been to his readers in the future. While the private life is effectively nullified, Smart "existimates" already as an object of public remembrance.

A similar double inscription of public and private informs the oft-noted themes of quantitative scale and enumerative listing in Smart's poem. Although these themes are in fact related to a broader matrix of enthusiastic *topoi* dating back to the seventeenth-century revolutionary moment, they have very seldom been seen as more than echoes of Smart's individual biography. Yet Smart's insistence on celebrating even the most seemingly insignificant creature, with no privileging of tame over wild, beautiful over ugly, clean over unclean, or mammals over reptiles and insects, is precisely an extension of a tradition of politically "leveling" catalogues from the revolutionary era. *Jubilate Agno* pointedly juxtaposes Moses with a Lizard, Cornelius with a Swine, Mary with a Carp, Boaz with a Rat, and so on, with a leveling effect that is both stunning and sublime.[25] What Smart proposes is, in effect, a revisionary expansion of the biblical covenant to include all of creation. A verse-pair that celebrates a worm is quite typical:

> Let Magdiel rejoice with Ascarides, which is the life of the bowels—the worm hath a part in our frame.
> *For I rejoice like a worm in the rain in him that cherishes and from him that tramples.* (B37)

It is precisely the smallness and lowness of "Ascarides," in every conceivable sense, that Smart celebrates here: not just a worm, indeed, but an *in-*

testinal worm. In refusing to exclude the worm from his company of celebrants, Smart insistently displaces humankind from its traditionally unique place in the rest of the natural world. The juxtapositions in *Jubilate Agno* thus contribute to a movement from vertical transcendence in the other world to horizontal immanence in this one: a modernizing project that marks Smart's affiliation with the radical ethos of the seventeenth-century millenarians, for whom leveling was both a political and a divine agenda.[26]

So, on the one hand, the "public" in Smart reinscribes what is often taken to be "private." Smart can discover who he is only in the process of imagining himself as constituted with and through others.[27] These elements of quasi-theatrical performance and self-making point to an enlarged understanding of intersubjective dynamics. "To speak at all," according to a psychoanalyst of the Lacanian school, "is to express the desire for recognition, whether the speech is in the form of a demand or not."[28] The divine addressee imagined by Smart obviously belies the state of compulsory solitude in which he writes; but that interlocutor stands in as well for an ideal human public—a posterity yet to arrive. Indeed, for such an ambitious poet as Smart, wounded by what he perceived as slander, existence itself is inseparable from the sphere of public audibility and cultural longevity. Conceived thus, the public institutions of cultural memory have the function of forming identities, rather than merely disclosing them.[29]

On the other hand, however, Smart's supposedly private experience is likewise authorized in *Jubilate Agno*—through its remarkable structures of address—to rewrite public modes of worship. To grasp how these structures of address serve to privatize the public, however, an excursion into the seemingly pallid realm of pronouns is necessary. The *Jubilate*, as Tom Keymer observes, "invokes the largest implied (if not actual) audience, a universal community embracing ancient Hebrews, primitive Christians, modern Britons, and all the species of creation, undivided by time or place."[30] As the posterity addressed by Smart, we who now read the poem likewise join the universal community. However, our place, or places, in this vast chorus of praise must be specified with care: for intersubjectivity in *Jubilate Agno* operates to transgress the grammatical foundations of personhood that subtend discourse in the bourgeois public sphere.

The classic public sphere instantiated a historically new form of intersubjectivity: a purely formal leveling of identities that nevertheless registers the democratizing impact of the English Revolution. The ideal of uncoerced dialogue entailed a stripping away of "polite" forms of the second person: above all, perhaps, the nonreciprocal use of *thou* and *you*. The *tu-vous* or T/V distinction, as linguists term it in cross-language comparisons, is a mediation signaling relations of deference. Used nonreciprocally, it permits a given exchange to be saturated by impersonal elements of irrational social mystique. The seventeenth-century Quakers' notorious practice of addressing everyone as "friend" or "thee" (the latter being a grammatically perverse twisting of the nominative *thou*) was precisely an egalitarian repudiation of the discursive pragmatics that had supported late-feudal social stratification.[31] This repudiation became much more general in the eighteenth century. The eighteenth-century abandonment of *thou* in Britain, as Peter Burke points out, marks a very early manifestation of a more general and continent-wide modernizing process involving an egalitarian trend toward reciprocity.[32] The eighteenth-century public sphere thus produced an egalitarian pragmatics as the secularized norm of civil society. Indeed, according to Habermas, the major achievement of this emerging public sphere was the formulation, as a regulative ideal, of the "ideal speech situation"[33]: a communicative ethics in which "parochial" private identities are temporarily bracketed in favor of impartial reason.

This purely formal suspension of explicit social inequalities enables a streamlined pragmatics of discursive sociability: a conversational encounter of the plain "I" and "you" in which no one's appropriation of subjectivity is overtly or grossly compromised. "I" and "you" are interdependent concepts, structured around a dialectic of mutual recognition, or specular "echoing," summed up as follows by Emile Benveniste:"Language is possible only because each speaker sets himself up as a *subject* by referring to himself as *I* in his discourse. Because of this, *I* posits another person, the one who, being, as he is, completely exterior to 'me,' becomes my echo to whom I say *you* and who says *you* to me."[34] It is in this sense that the discursive basis of the bourgeois public sphere rests upon the flexible reversibility of pronouns: the ideal of reciprocal accountability between "I" and "you."[35]

It is precisely this person- or subject-based foundation that is submitted in the *Jubilate* to a further utopian elaboration: a sublime exchange in which these grammatical shifters are transposed. In thus transposing what it is fashionable to call subject-positions, Smart transfigures the usual liberal dilemmas around the opposition of private autonomy and public solidarity. Like a kinetic sculpture, a whirling mobile, *Jubilate Agno* spirals upward and outward even as one enters into it. What circulates within its enunciative structure are precisely those seemingly fixed positions of "interiority" and "exteriority" established by pronouns. This accounts for the peculiarly intersubjective mode of Smart's sublimity. According to Longinian speculations, the sublime can be achieved by sudden changes in the number and person of pronouns.[36] If Longinus can be read as an early theorist of enunciation, as Suzanne Guerlac argues, then the *Jubilate* may be the ultimate poetic consummation of such Longinian anticipations: "a kind of imprinting process," as she says of the Longinian sublime, "which includes moments of expropriation and identification."[37]

So it is that pronouns become a crucial vehicle for Smart's private rearticulation of public genres such as the liturgy: for there is an implied *fusion of the first and second persons* in his structures of address. This produces a leveling that is ontological rather than merely formal. A further complexity arises, moreover, from the way Smart both praises and addresses God simultaneously.[38] In the imperative mode of his "Let" lines, "I" can also mean "you"; "you," moreover, can also mean "God." When Smart commands "Let so-and-so rejoice," it means both "(I) let" and "(You, O God) let." For God is indeed an implied auditor—perhaps, indeed, even an implied *reader* of *Jubilate Agno.* Thus, outrageous as it may seem, both Smart and the implied reader are, in some sense, *in God.* Both are occupying, that is to say, God's discursive position as interlocutor. This enthusiastic fusion is enacted formally: Smart's position in his own devotional discourse, as the triumphant composer of cosmic praise, echoes God's divine fiat in Genesis with its reiterated "Let . . .Let . . .Let."

This fusion of "I" and "you" in the "Let" or supposedly public line has the necessary effect of threatening to implode the poem's Let-For structure. Their apparent partial autonomy, while asserted by the poem's format on the page, is complicated by Smart's ability to make even the deep structure of pronouns a pattern where public and private interpenetrate. Smart thus extends the poem's leveling dynamics into the topology that normally differentiates "I" from "you." To quote Benveniste again: "This polarity of persons . . . offers a type of opposition whose equivalent is encountered nowhere else outside of language. This polarity does not mean either equality or symmetry: 'ego' always has a position of transcendence with regard to *you*" (225). Such transcendence, however—based on the opposition of "interior" to "exterior"—is precisely what the *Jubilate* cancels by creating what Guerlac calls "an identification across the positions of enunciation" (283).

Smart's rearticulation of public modes of worship is even more apparent when one considers the reversal of ordinary causal relationships that occurs between the lines that begin with "Let" and those that, answering antiphonally, begin with "For." The "Let" lines, which invoke a public realm of rejoicing creatures, are, despite their serial priority to the "For" lines, made to depend on them logically. Since the "For" lines usually refer to Smart's private circumstances, the public world is made to depend on Smart himself: Magdiel must rejoice with Ascarides *because* Smart rejoices like a worm in the rain. The sly inversion by which Smart invokes the "effect" (the rejoicing) before the cause to which it is subsequently traced (his own circumstances) cannot be read as an indication of causal priority. The reversal, rather, enables Smart to straddle the divide between two genres: the scripted program of liturgical worship and the meditative informality of private devotion. The new authorial subjectivity he strives to create is neither a private caprice, nor an ascribed public role, but precisely a double inscription—shuttling back and forth across that seeming divide—of both simultaneously.

It must also be observed that Smart's antiphonal form is self-referential in a way that bears on the ontology of fictional worlds (see also the treatment of enunciation and mimesis in Chapter 8). The form of *Jubilate Agno* makes a "strange loop" or "tangled hierarchy" that mingles different logical levels, as when a Pirandellian author becomes a character in his own play.[39] Specifically, there is a recursive loop in that Smart (as maker of the poetic utterance) *invokes* the scene of rejoicing in which Smart (the "I," the subject of the enunciation) is imaginatively positioned as the suffering or rejoicing cynosure of the public events. *Jubilate Agno* thus threatens to subvert its public dimension by "translating" acts of liturgical rejoicing into so many contingent consequences of the "private" author's existence.

The challenge, then, of Smart's recursive interlacing of private and public devotional modes is that it constitutes an intersubjective "we" in which individual selves overlap, mingle, and even swap places. The core of Smart's sublime rhetoric, indeed, lies in its hybridization of the pronominal positions established in the very process of enunciation. His poem formally transgresses the relations between text and reader, intrinsic and extrinsic, producing slippages between the positions constituted by pronouns. One of the most justly famous verse-pairs in *Jubilate Agno*—often used to epitomize Smart's sublime—will serve to illustrate this pronominal slippage:

> Let Hushim rejoice with the King's Fisher, who is of royal beauty, tho' plebeian size.
> *For in my nature I quested for beauty, but God, God hath sent me to sea for pearls.* (B30)

These lines, at first glance, would seem to respond well to the traditional scale-based thematics of the sublime. One can say, without venturing upon an exhaustive analysis of them,[40] that they play upon a juxtaposition of the ocean's vastness with the comparative smallness of the King's Fisher—and of Smart himself, analogously overwhelmed by God. The lines thus juxtapose the smallness of Smart with the awful sublimity of his quest for pearls: a quest that, as in the parable of the merchant in Matthew 13: 45-46, has cost him everything. Indeed, Smart's divinely enforced quest is, like the sublime, beyond mere "beauty." And, because this quest is contrary to his own nature, it necessarily implies a radical decentering of his own identity. It is now an identity centered, as the placement and stuttering repetition of "God" suggest, around an ineffable experience of infinitude.

The need to take this analysis further, however, becomes apparent if we ponder the relationship between the "me" (whose questing script is, as it were, written by God) and the "Let" line conjoining Hushim and the King's Fisher. Consider: Smart *asks* God, as in a prayer, to let Hushim and the King's Fisher rejoice. And we as readers are then strongly positioned *with* the divine interlocutor, for it is as if the poet asks us at the same time. Consider again: Smart himself, as the maker of the poem, *wills* their joint appearance, as in the *fiat lux* with which creation itself begins. So we, the readers, are likewise "with," or "in," Smart as author and orchestrator. And what about the force of that "For," which posits the dependence of the public program of rejoicing on Smart's quest? Who, indeed, is ventriloquizing whom? Such considerations lead inexorably back to the conclusion that pronouns in *Jubilate Agno* are not strictly separate zones of subjectivity, but, rather, intersubjective nodes where the stability of that seemingly self-evident separation is profoundly challenged. Smart's "I" in the *Jubilate*, like the staging of the first-person singular in enthusiastic rhetoric more generally, is not to be confined by a literalism that circumscribes it with mere empirical details about the author's biography.

It is, of course, Christopher Smart the biographical author who does finally stand "behind" or "above" all the intricately braided loops and tangles described earlier. Given the onslaught of pathologizing language that has greeted his supremely imaginative poem, moreover, it is crucial—however unfashionable it may be—to assert his authorial agency in its composition. The remarkable impact of Smart's poetry on twentieth-century artists, moreover, as confirmed in Chapters 11 and 12, certainly does demand a consideration of Smart in terms of his exemplary importance to literary and cultural history. Smart is, in fact, an author, and a major one, in precisely that exemplary and generative sense. The innovations he proposed as a poet have now been registered and significantly replicated in the poetics of later generations. His voice, whether or not we have yet fully acknowledged the fact, is now an inescapable feature of the shared idiom of the Anglophone poetic tradition. One suspects, indeed, after learning of Smart's impact on Allen Ginsberg (see Chapter 12), that Ginsberg's great chant in the third part of *Howl*—"Carl Solomon! I'm with you in Rockland"[41]—could perhaps be varied without distortion as "Kit Smart! I'm with you at Bethnal Green." One need not subscribe to a cult of genius to insist on Smart's courageous and hard-won originality across an impressive range of genres.

Although in that sense Smart's work is his own, the real power of the *Jubilate* lies elsewhere than merely in an untrammeled celebration of the private. Indeed, Smart's symbiotic reworking of interiority and exteriority in the *Jubilate* would seem to problematize any attempt to approach his work sheerly in terms of "self-expression." By reading Smart's "altered subjectivity" in historical terms, however—through the problematic of authorship and the eighteenth-century public sphere—one can recognize that it is, rather, an alternative intersubjectivity that motivates his sublime rhetoric. And it is exactly here, then, in Smart's defamiliarization of the emerging contours of a world recently dividing into private and public dimensions, that *Jubilate Agno* is perhaps most radical, most a crucial event in literary and cultural history. This defamiliarization entails, first of all, a sharply heightened reflexivity about the violent reifications often involved in the proprietary settling of identities: in the rivalrous determination of what is mine and thine. To the trademark and brand-name approach to poetic originality, Smart replies, almost in advance, that "there is no invention but the gift of God. . ."(B82). He casts himself more as permeable medium than as literary proprietor, and it is truth-telling rather than a commodified novelty that he asserts in claiming, for example, that *"I preach the very gospel of christ without comment. . ."* (B9). In looking back to *Jubilate Agno,* we glimpse possibilities—later to be foreclosed—other than that of the proprietary and autonomous author.

The peculiar achievement of Smart's reinvention of authorship, then, lies in its utopian rendering of the "associational individualism" of the eighteenth century. The exorbitant subjectivity of *Jubilate Agno* inhabits fully the logic of the eighteenth-century public sphere. The poem's justly celebrated spirituality, therefore, is not so much otherworldly as it is a daring extension of the possibilities opened up within that historical moment. The point, moreover, of recovering the utopian achievement of the *Jubilate* now is to point to alternative possibilities for the trajectory of modernity: possibilities, indeed, that serve to challenge the halo of "the natural" and "the inevitable" that surround our particular experience of modernity. Smart's poem demands of us, perhaps above all, that we recognize the contingency of our own arrangements of public and private: for the *Jubilate,* by compelling us to revise our sense of the usable past, resonates as well with alternative versions of the here and now. It speaks to alternative historical pasts that drew upon, and cultivated, a less violent polarization of public and private than that which happened to become the basis not only of our modernity but of our so-called postmodernity as well.[42] Smart's act of utopian imagining in *Jubilate Agno* thus conjures up an apparition seldom entirely welcome in contemporary versions of the history of modernity: the specter, that is, of an *alternative modernity.*

Notes

I wish to thank Mrinalini Sinha for thinking through the argument and structure of this chapter with me.

1. Peter de Bolla and Andrew Ashfield, Introduction, *The Sublime: A Reader in Eighteenth-Century Aesthetic Theory,* eds. Peter de Bolla and Andrew Ashfield (Cambridge: Cambridge University Press, 1996), 11.
2. R. D. Stock, *The Holy and the Daemonic from Sir Thomas Browne to William Blake* (Princeton, NJ: Princeton University Press, 1982), 314-25.
3. David B. Morris, *The Religious Sublime: Christian Poetry and Critical Tradition in 18th-Century England* (Lexington: University Press of Kentucky, 1972), 178.
4. Devlin, 17.
5. Morris, *Religious Sublime,* 171.
6. See Sir Russell Brain, "Christopher Smart: The Flea That Became an Eagle," in *Some Reflections on Genius* (Philadelphia, PA: J.B. Lippincott Co., 1961), 113-22; William Ober, "Madness and Poetry: A Note on Collins, Cowper, and Smart," in *Boswell's Clap and Other Essays: Medical Analyses of Literary Men's Afflictions* (NY: Perennial Library, 1988), 137-92; and Gordon Claridge, Ruth Pryor, and Gwen Watkins, "The Powers of Night: Christopher Smart," in *Sounds from the Belljar: Ten Psychotic Authors* (NY: St. Martin's Press, 1990), 71-87.
7. See, for a recent example, Pat Rogers, "Literature," in *The Cambridge Cultural History of Britain,* ed. Boris Ford, 9 vols. (Cambridge: Cambridge University Press, 1988-91), V: *Eighteenth-Century Britain,* 168.
8. See Henry Sussman, *The Aesthetic Contract: Statutes of Art and Intellectual Work in Modernity* (Stanford, CA: Stanford University Press, 1997), 150-55.
9. I am attempting in this chapter, sometimes with close paraphrase, to develop fully an argument intimated in chapter 5 of *Mania and Literary Style.*
10. Kathleen Wilson, however, notes a certain revival of Civil War political rhetoric by about 1770. The radical Whig followers of John Wilkes, though eschewing enthusiasm, engaged in "a sustained effort to reinvent the events of the Civil War and Revolution as part of a legitimate indigenous radical tradition that justified the people's right to resist tyranny in the present." See her *The Sense of the People: Politics, Culture and Imperialism in England, 1715-1785* (Cambridge: Cambridge University Press, 1995), 215.

11. See Peter Stallybrass and Allon White, *The Politics and Poetics of Transgression* (Ithaca, NY: Cornell University Press, 1986), 98.

12. Wilson, *Sense of the People,* 44.

13. See Dena Goodman, "More Than Paradoxes to Offer: Feminist History as Critical Practice," in *History and Theory: Studies in the Philosophy of History,* 36: 3 (1997): 401-2. Goodman's observation, though based on French history, applies in equal measure to eighteenth-century British history.

14. For a sophisticated account of the eighteenth-century novel's formal and thematic relationship to the public sphere, see John Richetti, "The Public Sphere and the Eighteenth-Century Novel: Social Criticism and Narrative Enactment," in *Eighteenth-Century Life,* 16 (1992): 114-29.

15. Jürgen Habermas, *The Structural Transformation of the Public Sphere: An Inquiry into a Category of Bourgeois Society,* trans. Thomas Burger (Cambridge, MA: MIT Press, 1991), 43.

16. Each of its three twentieth-century editors has thus chosen to present the poem in a significantly different format. See Bond, Introduction, 11-25; Guest, 123-32; Tom Keymer, "Presenting Jeopardy: Language, Authority, and the Voice of Smart in *Jubilate Agno,*" in *Presenting Poetry: Composition, Publication, Reception,* eds. Howard Erskine-Hill and Richard A. McCabe (Cambridge: Cambridge University Press, 1995), 97-103; and Hawes, 172-73.

17. See Hartman, 98.

18. Lisbet Koerner, "Purposes of Linnaean Travel: A Preliminary Research Report," in *Visions of Empire: Voyages, Botany, and Representations of Nature,* eds. David Philip Miller and Peter Hans Reill (Cambridge: Cambridge University Press, 1996), 119.

19. John Hollander, *The Work of Poetry* (N.Y.: Columbia University Press, 1997), 210.

20. Geoffrey Hartman, *The Fateful Question of Culture* (N.Y.: Columbia University Press, 1997), 65

21. John Ashbery, "Author's Note" [to "Litany"], in *As We Know: Poems by John Ashbery* (Manchester, NH: Carcanet New Press, 1979), 2.

22. Guest, 142-45.

23. John Milton, *Paradise Lost,* in *Complete Poems and Major Prose,* ed. Merritt Hughes (N.Y.: The Odyssey Press, 1957), 211-212.

24. I borrow this description from Devlin, 100.

25. See Hawes, 54-55, 161-164.

26. See Hawes, Chapter 2.

27. See Eli Zaretsky, "Hannah Arendt and the Meaning of the Public/Private Distinction," in *Hannah Arendt and the Meaning of Politics,* eds. Craig Calhoun and John McGowan (Minneapolis: University of Minnesota Press, 1997), 226-28.

28. Stanley A. Leavy, *The Psychoanalytic Dialogue* (New Haven, CT: Yale University Press, 1980), 80.

29. See Craig Calhoun, "Plurality, Promises, and Public Spaces," in *Hannah Arendt and the Meaning of Politics,* 246-47.

30. Keymer, "Presenting Jeopardy," 97.

31. See Hawes, 51-52; and Richard Bauman, *Let Your Words Be Few: Symbolism of Speaking and Silence among Seventeenth-Century Quakers* (Cambridge: Cambridge University Press, 1983), 43-62.

32. Peter Burke, "Introduction," *The Social History of Language,* eds. Peter Burke and Roy Porter (Cambridge: Cambridge University Press, 1987), 11.

33. See Stephen K. White, *The Recent Work of Jürgen Habermas: Reason, Justice, and Modernity* (Cambridge: Cambridge University Press, 1988), 55-58.

34. Emile Benveniste, *Problems in General Linguistics,* trans. Mary Elizabeth Meek, 1966 (Coral Gables, FL: University of Miami Press, 1971), 225.

35. See Seyla Benhabib, *Critique, Norm, and Utopia: A Study of the Foundations of Critical Theory* (NY: Columbia University Press, 1986), 285-86.

36. Longinus, *On the Sublime,* trans. James A. Arieti and John M. Crossett (NY: The Edwin Mellen Press, 1985), 128-39.

37. See Suzanne Guerlac, "Longinus and the Subject of the Sublime," in *New Literary History,* 16:2 (1985): 275.

38. Edward Katz has argued that the sublime achievement of the author of *Jubilate Agno* is precisely a mode in which Smart places himself in dialogical relationship to that immanent divinity which he also purports to describe. See "Transcendent Dialogic: Madness, Prophecy, and the Sublime in Christopher Smart," in *Compendious Conversations: The Method of Dialogue in the Early Enlightenment,* ed. Kevin Cope (Frankfurt: Peter Lang, 1992), 151-64.

39. These terms for self-referentiality I have borrowed from Douglas Hofstadter's *Gödel, Escher, Bach: An Eternal Golden Braid* (NY: Vintage Books, 1980). See Chapter XX, "Strange Loops, or Tangled Hierarchies," 684-742.

40. These lines, often quoted by subsequent poets, are also discussed in Chapter 12.

41. Allen Ginsberg, "Howl," in *Howl and Other Poems* (San Francisco, CA: City Lights Books, 1956), 24.

42. For a thoroughly "postmodern" view that public and private are forever incommensurable, see Richard Rorty, *Contingency, Irony, and Solidarity* (Cambridge: Cambridge University Press, 1989).

PART III

PARLEYING WITH THE EIGHTEENTH CENTURY

CHAPTER 11

Benjamin Britten's Rejoice in the Lamb: Figural Invention, "Impression" and the Open Text

WILLIAM KUMBIER

I

BY 1943, WHEN BENJAMIN BRITTEN accepted the invitation from the Reverend Walter Hussey to compose a choral work for the Jubilee of St. Matthew's Church, Northampton, he had already distinguished himself in the setting of traditional texts, notably in *A Ceremony of Carols*, Op. 28 (1942) and, more strikingly, in the setting of non-English poetry, as in the stunning presentations of Rimbaud's poems, *Les Illuminations*, Op. 18 (1939) and Michelangelo's sonnets (*Seven Sonnets of Michelangelo,* Op. 22 [1940]). As commentators have noted, even Britten's early settings are marked by an eclectic choice of texts that shows a cosmopolitan literary awareness and by treatments of those texts that, while often surprising, idiosyncratic, and not readily transparent, always strike one as both emotionally charged and thoroughly thought-out, assured, and accomplished.[1]

Moreover, in these vocal settings Britten's musical rhetoric diversely animates the texts he chooses, displaying a range of resources for enhancing the significance of a text through music. His strategies of text setting sometimes recall those traditionally associated with conventional musical rhetoric; for example, a setting may evoke a familiar affect that corresponds to what might be perceived as a predominant affect in the text, essentially a baroque strategy, as in virtually any of the Michelangelo sonnets. Or the setting may opt for incidental pictorialism, as in the figurations of the "Marine" section of *Les Illuminations* (for example, on "tourbillons"), a device that goes back at least to early Renaissance vocal music, exploiting what music rhetoricians referred to as hypotypotic figuration, or arrangements of notes that vividly bring a picture to the listener's imagination.[2] Yet Britten's settings also enlarge one's conception of what musical rhetoric can entail because, for each of the texts or text cycles Britten chose to set, he *invented* appropriate musical approaches from qualities peculiar to the text. Britten's capacity to discover and deploy figurative inventions may not differ essentially from what baroque composers drew on when called to set a text, but one senses that routine or formulaic recourse to rhetorical paradigms or variations on them, through commonplaces such as one comes to expect, say, from baroque arias or settings of liturgical texts, is less a possibility for Britten. This is due partly, of course, to the greater scope of musical resources open to a twentieth-century composer, but also to the idiosyncrasies of each new text Britten came to set. It is therefore difficult to discuss his settings in any detail without exploring the particular concerns, the stylistic and substantive turns of the texts themselves. By studying closely Britten's setting of selected verses from Christopher Smart's *Jubilate Agno* in the festival cantata *Rejoice in the Lamb*, Op. 30 (1943), I hope to show how unusually perceptive and responsive a reader of Smart Britten was and how thoroughly his musical setting represents the poem, not only in a limited, mimetic way but also through its creation of a pervasively figured musical text whose play at once invokes and illuminates the play of Smart's poem.

II

Britten's most recent biographer, Humphrey Carpenter, reports that Britten came upon Smart's poem almost as soon after its publication as anyone could have. In a letter to Elizabeth Mayer, Britten wrote that "Wystan [that is, W. H. Auden] introduced me to [it (Smart's poem)] in the states" when Britten and Peter Pears were visiting there from 1939-42.[3] Britten read Smart's poem in the only form it was then publicly available, the 1939 edition by W. F. Stead published under the title *Rejoice in the Lamb: A Song from Bedlam*. From among the hundreds of verses of the poem Britten selected 48 to set (two of which he repeats, for a total setting of 50 lines) for chorus (Treble, Alto, Tenor, and Bass or, alternately, S, A, T, B) and organ.

Perhaps the most notable feature of Britten's arrangement of the text is his grouping of Smart's verses into thematic "clusters," which, though reflecting key preoccupations of the poem, do not correspond exactly to groupings of the verses by any editor other than Britten himself. [4] It must be stressed that Britten made his selection and constructed his arrangement of verses years before Bond published his seminal reconstruction of Smart's poem in 1954, with its now accepted antiphonal pairings of "Let" and "For" verses in Fragments B and C. Of course, for practical reasons Britten's sections are generally shorter than the corresponding segments of *Jubilate Agno*, involving far fewer verses, but the number of verses set is less significant than the fact that Britten decided to make the groupings in the first place. That is, the first intriguing achievement of Britten's setting is his re-creation of Smart's text as a collage, as an anthology of Smart's anthology, arranged into discrete and concise sections, each of which will have its distinctive character; a remarkable degree of diversity given the approximately 16 minutes it takes to perform the cantata.

But just what are the text's sections and how are they ordered? The first, brief description of the cantata, provided by Walter Hussey, who commissioned it, states that the cantata has ten sections, though he does not specifically demarcate them. [5] In the only article-length study of the cantata to date,[6] Peter Le Page divides the cantata into seven sections, reducing the number of sections from ten by counting the first three choral sections as one section and the last two as one. In doing so, however, Le Page blurs distinctions between what clearly emerge even on first hearing of the cantata as discrete sections, distinctive in both character and function. On the other hand, identifying a new section with each shift in musical character also may mislead because such a division responds *only* to differences from section to section. It may miss the relative structural functions of the sections and much of the text's symmetry and parallelism, which Britten elicits through his ordering of thematic clusters and the repetition of verbal and musical units.

Though much of the rationale for my own view of the cantata's structure will be given in the section-by-section reading of the cantata in the next part of this chapter, I suggest the following as a more fruitful way of seeing the cantata's organization. Verse fragment and line number designations are from the 1980 Oxford edition of Smart's poem, though it should be noted that, with the B and C verses, Britten sets only what are now known as the "For" parts.

Introduction	(A1, A2, A3)
Section 1	(A9, A10, A11, A13, A18, A67, A41[a]7)
Response	(A41[b])
Section 2	(B695, B696, B697, B698, B737, B763, B738, B68)
Section 3	(B638, B639, B640, B638, B641)
Section 4	(B493, B500, B499, B503, B506)
Section 5	(B151, B90, B60)
Counterresponse	(B139)
Transition	(C1, C3, C4, C5)

Section 6   ([B584][8], B586, B587, B588, B589, B592, B593,
                       B591, B585, B245, B246, B248, B249)
Response/Conclusion   (A41[b])

One advantage of this division is that it distinguishes three categories of the cantata's sections: first, those that, while certainly displaying a distinctive character, are primarily functional, such as the introduction and the transition between Sections 5 and 6; second, those that are primarily characteristic and secondarily functional, such as the "cat," "mouse," and "flower" sections; and third, the one-verse response and counterresponse, both highly characteristic and highly functional. Also, this division manifests possible pairings that are only slightly latent in the cantata: Section 1 and the first response, the praise by biblical figures and animals, for example, is balanced by Section 6, the praise and power of instruments, and the reprise of the response. Sections 2 and 3, "cat" and "mouse," antithetically parallel each other while their subjects, taken together as images of divinity, oppose Section 5, which deal with Smart's victimization by his mockers and accusers, his persecution by the "adversary." The central Section 4, on "flowers," itself centrally turning on the opposition of "flower" and "root"—and on the very verse opposing them, B499—reflects the divinity represented in the sections that preceded it while anticipating, or "parrying," the verses on the force of the adversary and Smart's enemies that follow. The counterresponse following Section 5, which Le Page identified not only as related to the "musical idea" of the Hallelujah response but as the "structural climax" of the cantata, can be seen as the point of an arrow or wedge whose wing tips are the response and its reprise, defining the overarching, concentric, almost mirror-structure of the cantata as a whole. [9] The following analysis, therefore, aims to respond both to the diverse, characteristic musical features of each section while also tracing the figurative motives that work throughout the cantata toward its unified effect.

III

Under the marking "Measured and mysterious" the cantata opens with the choral voices intoning the verse in unison on C pitches.[10] Along with the organ pedal on c1, the chanting establishes C as a tonal base for this section, though that is challenged by staccato eighth-note chord figures in the organ that hint at alternate tonalities. As Evans noted, these figures combine a step up of a whole tone with a step down of a fourth (see figure 11.1). [11]

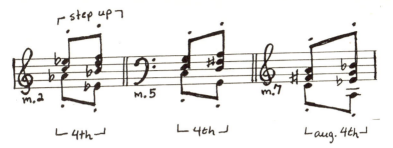

Figure 11.1. Benjamin Britten. *Rejoice in the Lamb.* **Step-Up and Descending Fourth Figures from the Introduction.**
©Copyright 1943 by Boosey & Co. Ltd. Copyright Renewed,
Reprinted by permission of Boosey & Hawkes, Inc.

Also, each presents *in nuce* the tonic/dominant/subdominant cluster of a given key; in the example above, the A-flat triad of m. 2 steps up to a B-flat triad and simultaneously down to e-flat[1]. Britten repeats this figure at mm. 5, 8, and 9-10; with each repetition, the figure highlights the step progression and the interval of the fourth, a seminal one in the cantata. Only once is the pattern significantly varied, at m. 7, where the triad on d[1] steps up to one on e-flat[1], against a step down from d[1] to a. In this instance the figure moves down not to the fourth but to the tritone or augmented fourth, since A is the tritone of E-flat. Tritones will appear more pointedly later in the cantata but this incidental one should be noted because tritones can be understood *both* as augmentations and as dissonances that, traditionally in music, were to be avoided; which were, in fact, referred to as *diabolus in musica* (the devil in music).

At m. 12 ("Let man and beast appear. . . .") the tonality moves from C to F minor, and the step figure smooths into alternating F minor and E-flat quarter-note chords against alternating quarter-notes on F and C in the organ's lower manual, with a crescendo to "magnify" at m. 14. Britten's setting of this word is striking, first in its unexpected turn—the expansive A major organ chord is harmonically distant from both the E-flat and F minor chords that preceded it and from the organ pedal on C—and second in that the E-flat pitches to which the unison voices rise and which they repeat glare as the tritone of A: if the tritone is heard as an augmentation in this case, the setting is mimetically appropriate for "magnify," and the slurred rise from C through D-flat to E-flat in the voices suggests a telescopic zoom. This is also the first instance in the cantata of Britten's finding a musical analogue for Smart's conception of his poem as a "Magnificat": "For I pray the Lord Jesus to translate my MAGNIFICAT into verse and represent it" (B43).

Section 1: "Let Nimrod, the mighty hunter . . . "

A quick echo of the introduction's steps from C to F in the organ pedal line sparks the cantata's first major section, marked "With vigour" and impressive at once in the rhythmic vitality of its variously shifting compound meters (alternately 7/8, 6/8, 9/8, 5/8, 4/8, and 11/8). Britten stresses the inherent syncopation of these meters with accent and staccatissimo markings, typically in the pattern shown below:

For this section, which sets verses invoking mainly the praise of God by biblical figures paired with animals, culminating in the "dance" of David and the bear, Britten exploits the use of metrical units that amplify—or "magnify"—each other. Rhythmic variety is matched by the range of the section's tonality—from the initial F tonality it migrates to C (at "Let Balaam . . ."), to B-flat (at "Let Ithamar . . . ") and to E-flat (at "Let Jakim" before returning to and climaxing at F ("Let David . . ."). In the course of this stunning sequence, particularly arresting is the brief leap into the modality of Aeolian A at "Let Daniel" (m. 18): for Britten, the "procession to the altar" is a progression of modalities that include but are not limited to the more common major and minor modes. [12] Moreover, the pitches in the treble line at which the first clause of each "Let" verse is set, themselves accumulate in an extended ascent from c^2 to f^2, as diagramed in figure 11.3.

Figure 11.3. Benjamin Britten. *Rejoice in the Lamb.* **Section 1: Initial Pitches of "Let" Verses.**
©Copyright 1943 by Boosey & Co. Ltd. Copyright Renewed,
Reprinted by permission of Boosey & Hawkes, Inc.

The last three notes of this trajectory may even be heard as an extension and echo of the melodic progression of half-step/whole step that Britten used to set "magnify" in the introduction.

This ascent overarches the briefer, more compressed and accelerated runs up the scale that Britten uses typically to set the second clause of each "Let" verse, as in mm. 5-6, 10-11, 16, 20-21 and 28-30. In the context of the section's prevalent syncopation—"syncope" can also signify shortness of breath—these figures display an especially 'breathless' quality when the quick ascents are reduplicated and one succeeds another seemingly before the first can finish, as if one figure explodes from another. The bursts of sixteenth-note arc or circle figures in the organ's upper manual, first heard in mm. 30-31 and elaborated in mm. 33, 35, and especially mm. 37-38, are flourishes that enhance David's dance but might also bear the "crown" or "laurel wreath" connotations that similar "circle" figures sometimes carried in baroque settings. [13] Overall, this section's rhythmic, harmonic, and melodic strategies unite to evoke the ethos of a highly charged song of ascents, the unabashed vitality of David's dancing before the ark.

Response: "Hallelujah"
Directly counter to the excitation of Section 1 is the "gently moving" pace of the "Hallelujah," in 3/4 as opposed to the prevailing 6/8 and 7/8 of that section. Still, the response's characteristic dotted-eighth-note figuration and the melodic contours of the canon for the voices clearly devolve from the quicker ascents of Section 1 (see figure 11.4).

Figure 11.4. Benjamin Britten. *Rejoice in the Lamb.* **Section 1 Motif and "Hallelujah" Derivation.**
©Copyright 1943 by Boosey & Co. Ltd. Copyright Renewed,
Reprinted by permission of Boosey & Hawkes, Inc.

Beneath the canonic voices, deliberate, quarter-note step progressions in the organ's pedal line unroll, clearly elongations of the staccato eighth-note steps of that line in the preceding section. Both the canon of voices and the progression directed by the pedal line peak at m. 7, where the pedal rises to a syncope of tied quarter-notes on b-flat and the voices fall off from each other, each paradoxically imitating the preceding on the text "inimitable," dovetailing into the settings of "echo of the heavenly harp" that, in turn, reduplicate echoes of each other. Yet one could argue that the exquisitely wrought internal echoes of the response—echoes of the significance of the text in the figures of the setting, echoes of one voice's tendency in those of the others and the organ—are ultimately secondary to the broader function of the response as an echo or mirror of the concerns and contours already cast in Section 1 of the cantata, an antiphon to them, and that in framing the response in this manner Britten recalls both Smart's antiphonies and his concern with the play of sound and its reverberation in his poem. Though, intriguingly, Britten chose not to set any of Smart's verses that deal directly with Echo, the *idea* of "echo" both informs particular moments in Britten's setting and becomes a generally formative strategy in the setting. As with the earlier setting of "magnify," in the setting of "echo" and "—imitable" and "magnifical"!— in this section, an initially mimetic gesture becomes a *metamimetic* one, generating intertextual ramifications beyond its immediate occasion, or other modes of magnifying. That the response also, according to Peter Evans, shows the influence of Henry Purcell merely enhances its musically intertextual status. [14]

Section 2: "For I will consider my Cat Jeoffry . . ."

This section, "quietly moving" in 4/4 and devoted to presenting a few of Smart's familiar verses on his cat, focuses the question of the setting's mimetic potentialities. The key of the section is ostensibly A, but the insistence throughout of incidental D-sharps—A's augmented fourth—in addition to reintroducing the tritone, marks the actual modality of the section as Lydian A. In both the treble solo and the upper organ line, d-sharp^2 accents the melody's turns, especially in the sixteenth-note triplet figurations Britten uses to capture the "variety" of Jeoffry's movements. These figures interplay with others that seem mainly mimetic: creeping parallel sixths in the organ's bass line (as in mm. 6-8), staccatissimo leaping eighth-notes (as at mm. 7, 9, 17), numerous extended trills, and chromatic windings, especially the long, sinuous, chromatic descent at m. 15. A remarkable concentration of the "cat" figures occurs in the setting of "wreathing his body seven times round with elegant quickness" (mm. 11-13), where Britten deploys seven sixteenth-note figures in succession, three quick, rising figures followed by four circle or "wreath" figures. Evocative as these figures are, they are not only locally mimetic; the tropes of the setting respond to tropes of the earlier sections and anticipate ones to come (especially in Section 5). The extended arc of the treble solo at mm. 8-10, with its measured ascents and descents, echoes the steps and long arcs of praise in Section 1 and the response, as well as thematically the praise by animals. Moreover, the tonality of the "Jeoffry" section should be heard as both a reflection and a transmutation of the predominant F major tonalities of those sections: though A is the third of F, the key of A major is distant from F, and the Lydian A tonality even more distant. Hence, the sudden move from A to C-sharp to E-sharp at mm. 12-14 sounds like a turn toward an extremely exotic key, but, because E-sharp can be read enharmonically, the modulation really takes us no further than the familiar tonality of F. Britten's modulation is a manner of making the familiar strange, revisiting the F tonality from a fresh perspective. As Smart's poem frequently surprises with its multiple perspectives on a subject, Britten's invention discovers diverse ways of looking at the same thing, another form of magnification.

Section 3: "For the Mouse is a creature of great personal valour"

Obviously, this brief section, marked "fast and light" and set in D-flat, counters the "cat" section. Its characteristic features—notably the eighth- and sixteenth-note triplet figure in the organ's upper manual—have been heard not merely as mimetic but mocking. The tenor's recitative of the section's middle portion (mm. 9-20), with its exaggerated declamation, startling melodic leaps and banter with the accompaniment, is not only mock-operatic but possibly *mock*-mock-operatic; Humphrey Carpenter suggests that it may recall the "melodramatic cat-and-mouse cartoon films [Britten] had loved in the thirties" (perhaps the pseudo-opera of the Mighty Mouse cartoons?). [15] There are also echoes of Claude Debussy's pianism (for example, his *Children's Corner Suite*) in the light and lightly dissonant triplet figures but more subtly in the whole-tone descent of the melodic turn at m. 9, a modulation from D-flat to Aeolian D-flat, with the melody in both the tenor line and the organ bass line built on the scale shown in figure 11.5.

Figure 11.5. Aeolian D-flat Scale.
©**Copyright 1943 by Boosey & Co. Ltd. Copyright Renewed,**
Reprinted by permission of Boosey & Hawkes, Inc.

Again, it is important to hear this tonality as both responding to and mocking that of the "cat" section, especially in instances such as mm. 13-14, where chords built on B-flat-*flat* parody enharmonically the "cat" section's A major. Cat and mouse may be traditionally inimical but in the universe of Smart's poem and the cantata they emerge as twin embodiments of divine traits.

Section 4: "For the flowers are great blessings"

This central section of the cantata is a slow, pianissimo, gently rocking berceuse, alternating 4/4 and 3/4 with an occasional measure in 5/4. Immediately notable here is the independence of the three lines: the tenor line devolves in increasingly longer, heliotropic arcs of slurred quarter-notes that faintly echo the revolutions of Jeoffry's praises in Section 2; rocking thirds of the organ's upper line continue with only the briefest interruptions throughout the section's 29 measures; and, except in the sequence of mm. 18-23, the pedal line shows almost no movement at all, lingering mainly on tones of the A major or minor triad as, for example, when it repeats several times the hesitant drop of a fourth from A to E . At the same time, the tonality that emerges from the concurrence of the three lines is ambiguous, continually shifting. Though in the opening bars, for example, the thirds of the organ's upper line seem to play E minor against B minor, they do so over sustained A and E pedal tones, so that, once again, the tonality is modal, moving between major and minor; in this case, Aeolian B for the first twelve bars and then, with the insinuation of G-sharps starting at measure 11, shading into Dorian B, with yet another hushed but crucial modal shift at m. 17—for the setting of "adversary." Here Britten plays F against C tonalities, but the modality approaches Mixolydian C because of the prevalence of B-flat tones and Britten's remarkable use of F mainly as a passing rather than a resting or home tone. As in the cantata's earlier sections, the familiar F tonality is worked to appear foreign.

Moreover, when one considers the text set through these shifting modalities, one sees that the modality changes first on "God's Creation" (mm. 11-12) and next on "adversary" (m. 17); the modulation, in other words, frames verse B499, the middle verse of the section but, more important, the verse that opposes "flower" to "root" and "God" to "adversary" in antithetical parallelism. One might imagine this opposition's branching into the musical lines, with the tenor and upper organ lines as the "flower" and the pedal line as the "root"; there is considerable play with "rootless" chords in the section and the lower organ line grows notably more active in the six measures under the text immediately following "parry the adversary" (mm. 18-22). As stated earlier, the lines entwine only once in this section, at m. 23, for the setting of "poetry [of Christ]" (see figure 11.6).

Figure 11.6. Benjamin Britten. *Rejoice in the Lamb.* **Figuration on "poetry" from Section 4, mm. 23-24.**
©**Copyright 1943 by Boosey & Co. Ltd. Copyright Renewed,**
Reprinted by permission of Boosey & Hawkes, Inc.

Here, a gently curving fall and rise in the organ's thirds is succeeded by a complementary rise and fall in the tenor line; taken together, the lines describe, literally around the -*o*- of "poetry," an undulant S-curve, a variant of the successive half-circle or sine curve figuration that in music—as in graphic art, at least from the time William Hogarth expressly designated it so—has been associated with the "line of beauty," the serpentine line. [16] Britten's use of the figure here may be mimetic, tracing the flower's tendrils as the whole section may trace its heliotropics, but because of its particular instance in the setting, it also suggests the power of poetry to focus opposing tendencies and the power of Christ to mediate.

Section 5: "For I am under the same accusation with my Saviour"
The ambivalent closing e^1 of Section 4 leads directly into the opening E minor tonality of this section, a brief but intensely harrowing setting of four of Smart's verses dealing with his persecution, marked "slow and passionate." The chorus chants the first verse a cappella in open minor fifths, settling on an unexpected, inverted C minor chord at "Saviour" (m. 3), underscored by the organ. Britten then disorients further the sense of the section's tonality by moving to an alternate minor harmony about every three measures: to B minor at m. 6, G minor at m. 9, E-flat minor at m. 12, and back to C minor with the seventh superimposed at m. 14. Answering the chorus' declamation of each verse and over the minor chords in the lower organ line, Britten interjects a characteristic four-note organ figure, first sounding on the pitches f-sharp^2—g^2—e^2—d-sharp^2, as in mm. 3, 12, and 14, but later transposed. This figure strikes first in its snaking chromaticism, and in that respect it suggests a sinister parody of Jeoffry's "pranks" in Section 2. But the figure is also marked by its piercing insistence on f-sharp^2, which, as it initially sounds over C in the bass, signals the reappearance of the devilish tritone. Though the F-sharp resolves up to the fifth, G^2, Britten's obsessive repetition of the figure drives home the F-sharp's force, perhaps most acutely at m. 12, when the same motto is repeated, fortissimo, this time over E-flat minor. Appropriately for a

section that harps on Smart's accusers' claim that he is "beside himself," the motto is usually doubled whenever it sounds, and its significance is sharpened when, for verse B60, it sets the accusers' very words, "Silly fellow! Silly fellow!" (m. 14). A second striking figuration of this section is the series of quarter-notes falling into a "stutter" of eighth-notes, on "he is beside himself" at mm. 5-6 and "neither to me nor to my family" at mm. 16-18. Descending steeply rather than smoothly ascending, this figure suggests collapse and contraction rather than augmentation and expansion: it seems the antithesis of the rising figures of praise heard earlier in the cantata, perhaps most pointedly of the setting of "magnify" itself in the introduction.

Counterresponse: "For I am in twelve hardships . . . "

At Number 21, just after the setting of B60, Britten moves into the setting of B139. He treats the verse canonically, breaking it into three clauses—first, "For I am in twelve HARDSHIPS"; second, "but he that was born of a virgin"; and third, "shall deliver me out of all"—that each of the four choral lines moves through once, each extending the last clause. That is, the four lines move through three sections each, in a 4-by-3 patterning, the canonical equivalent of the "twelve hardships." The canon builds in intensity to its climax on "deliver" in the treble line at m. 25. It is crucial to see the protracted arc of the melody here precisely as a drawing out of the figure for "Silly fellow!," an ironic counterpart to the Hallelujah response's drawing out of its characteristic figuration from the praises of Section 1. Structurally this dark canon certainly shadows the response, as Le Page points out, and since it is so distinctly the response's antithesis it makes sense to see it as he does as the cantata's "structural climax." As the charge of the counterresponse is diffused, the setting stumbles from a-flat^2 down to e^1 through the organ's pathetic prolongation and dismantling of the persecution figure (mm. 30-31).

Transition and Section 6: "For the instruments are by their rhimes"

Starting from the *ppp* E minor at the close of the counterresponse, Britten sets four of Smart's verses on the spiritual significance of letters as a transition to Section 6. The settings for each verse, sung as a bass solo recitative, spring from E minor to alternate tonalities, only to fall back each time to E minor for the setting of the subsequent verse. These impulses toward alternate tonalities resemble what in another context have been described as the successive "casts" of Smart's verses toward his object, as if the poet were fishing or angling. [17] On the setting of C5 ("For M is musick and therefore he is God") the cast arcs into an F major arpeggio and catches, and the arpeggio is repeated fortissimo by the entire chorus, introducing the fanfares of Section 6.

Though it takes only slightly under three minutes to perform, this section, marked "Very gay and fast," achieves a grandeur and spaciousness, a "stupendous magnitude and melody," whose sublimity mirrors the praises of Section 1, complements the beauty of Section 4 and counters the dark grotesqueries of Section 5. It does so mainly through breathtaking transformations of an extremely elastic "fanfare" motif first used to set the catalogue of instruments and their rhymes (verses [B584] through B585), and then stretched to set the closing four verses. This figure consists of a "trumpet call" followed by sharply accented hammering on the same note; with each repetition this figuration strengthens. In its deployment over the choir Britten makes greater use of antiphonies between lower and higher voices than previously in the cantata, and this antiphonal patterning stands out as distinct from the earlier, close canonic treatments of the chorus, or those passages where all the voices progress isorhythmically. This spreading out of the voices quickly expands the setting's height and breadth. The voices are reined in, yoked together in a stretto-like sequence just before Number 27, where they enter successively under increasingly pitched half-notes in the treble, which ascends from d^2 to e^2 to f^2 over 16 bars, until they are forcefully unified, *fff*, for the setting of B245 at Number 28. The organ accompaniment echoes the fanfare motif but supplements it with brilliant, trill-like, eighth- note triplet figures, and, at two points, plummeting triplet scales (just before Numbers 24 and 28), in the second instance descending from b-flat^2 to G, a span of more than three octaves in a split second.

When the voices unify at Number 28, quarter-note triplets alternate with half-notes to press the limits of the 2/4 meter, and that stress is pressed further by the triplet arpeggios that gradually ascend the scale over eight bars in the organ's pedal line. As these peak, the treble line soars in an arc from e^1 up to a^2 and back down to d^2, which is reinforced with similar arcs in the other voices but which also culminates the cantata's earlier arcs of praise. At this point, the tonality also moves from F to Lydian B-flat, casting a special radiance over the texture.

At Number 29, Britten begins an extended deceleration, *poco a poco rallentando*, marked by growing quietude and the gradual relaxation of the fanfare motif as it is recast in quarter-notes at Number 30, in measures of 6/4 and 9/4. The organ accompaniment deflates to waverings of the trill figure over an F pedal; notably, at the close of each trill figure the adjacent tones of C and B-flat are sustained over F, another instance of Britten's predilection for ambivalent modalities but also a recollection of the prevalence of tonal clusters in the harmonies of the introduction and Section 1. The portion of Section 6 that runs from Numbers 30 to 31, in fact, mirrors in slow motion the energized activity of the catalogue of instruments, much as the first appearance of the Hallelujah response echoed the animated praise of Section 1. But in this case Britten reinforces the closing serenity of the cantata, assures its quelling of the devils, by reprising the response after the close of Section 6, as a sort of conclusion or coda that redoubles the effect of slowing down and coming to rest, an echo of an echo as well as an echo of the cantata as a whole.

IV

In a frequently cited verse from *Jublilate Agno* not included in the cantata, Smart speaks of his talent for impression: *"For my talent is to give an impression upon words by punching, that when the reader casts his eye upon 'em, he takes up the image from the mould w[hi]ch I have made"* (B404). Smart also refers to impression in the introduction to his translation of Horace, calling it a "talent or gift of Almighty God, by which a Genius is empowered to throw an emphasis upon a word or sentence in such wise, that it cannot escape any reader of good sense, and true critical sagacity" (*PW*, v: 6). Much has been written about how this talent displays itself in the poem, and on the strategies Smart uses to "throw an emphasis" on not only individual words but also on their constituent syllables and letters. By now it should be clear that the cantata displays a comparable musical talent of Britten's, a talent for *impressing* the significance of the text with characteristic musical figurations. With the most striking and memorable of these instances, it is not difficult to detect a particular verbal stimulus for the musical figure, and in sparking his setting from particular words Britten employs an approach to text-setting that composers had long practiced and, at least in the eighteenth century, had been urged expressly to exploit. One notable instance of such advice is the late baroque treatise by Johann David Heinichen entitled *Der General-Bass in der Composition* (Dresden: 1728).[18] In this manual Heinichen provides a "practical demonstration" of how composers who must come up with a setting for an aria, for example, can mine the text for gem words likely to yield multifaceted possibilities for musical figuration. Words like *accusare* or *gridere* could lead to "quarrelsome" or "concerted inventions," or, to represent the "burning fire of love" the composer might invent a rapidly rising sixteenth-note figure (a picture of ascending flames). Heinichen offers numerous examples of musically correct settings for aria texts, and, in fact, his treatise probably reflects and codifies as much as it prescribes, for baroque operas, oratorios, and cantatas—both before and after the date Heinichen's treatise appeared—were saturated with what seem to be instances of the sometimes ingenious but often commonplace results of the procedure Heinichen recommends.

Britten's setting of Smart's poem has, of course been praised for its resourcefulness, especially its mimetic resourcefulness: "The major impulse of the music is mimetic, the music in free verse, so to speak, determined by the sense of the words," says Le Page in his laudatory article on the cantata.[19] Yet if the setting did not do more than repeat a traditional text-setting routine it would not be the match for Smart's text that it is. For Britten's setting wants to invent not only figures for particular words and their referents in Smart's text; it seeks also a global invention, aiming to discover musical analogues for the activities Smart's poem enacts, activities such as imitation, magnification, echoing, and antiphonal response, to the point that engagement of these in the setting becomes intensively metamimetic, calling attention to the activities, the manifold articulation of their gestures, as much as or more than it does to the particular verbal text represented. That is, Britten's setting, within its limitations of scope and time, becomes a musical text as self-consciously reflective and reflexive as Smart's poem. It interestingly pushes the center of gravity for musical signification away from the signifieds of the set text and toward the play of its own figures, using the text as a springboard for its own ramifications, what Laurence Dreyfus recently referred to as the "sheer breadth and detail within a musical experience."[20]

Dreyfus's remark appears in a discussion of how Bach's music—both text-setting and textless music—challenged the received Enlightenment aesthetic that privileged the imitation of nature and "desired the representation of nature to be as effortless as possible. In other words, art was to be produced and judged according to how well it offered direct access to the mental representations that lay behind the work, its signifying ideas. . . . Words, music, gestures, pictures—all were there not to draw attention to themselves as signs but to be as transparent as possible."[21] As Laurence Draftees points out, such a theory "spells big trouble for music, particularly music that is dedicated to thinking through its own materials," as he persuasively argues Bach's music does.[22]

It is intriguing that the inventions Draftees claims Bach was working out, in a forward-looking and not reactionary way, inventions that ultimately enable the "emancipation" of music from text, to use John Knobbier's term,[23] were being discovered during Smart's time. In other words, the inventions Draftees attributes to Bach emerge contemporaneously with—and against—tenacious theoretical assertions, by Germans such as Johann Christoph Gottsched and Johann Adolph Scheibe and Frenchmen such as Jean-Jacques Rousseau, that music without words is meaningless. Draftees cites

Gottsched, who writes in 1754 that "music without text and dance is only a dead thing, only a body without a soul. Why? [Because] one understands only half of what is played when either gestures or words are not added which explain more clearly that which the notes wanted to say."[24] Untexted music, that is, makes incomprehensible demands on the listener; hence Rousseau's famous exasperation, "Sonata, what do you want of me?" Specifically, it is the *excess* of musical figures that is seen as dangerous. Draftees refers to Scheibe's view that, while a composer "cannot arouse and express feelings without figures," too many metaphors, as, for example, in overornamented melodies, will yield confusion: ". . . this obscurity and turgidity increase when [composers] set many metaphors on top of one another, in that they namely write metaphorically in all parts of a many-voice piece."[25]

Perhaps the main reason that Britten's setting is such an appropriate match for Smart's text is precisely that it takes its cue from the metaphorical or figural "excess" of Smart's "many-voiced piece." While certainly responding to and re-presenting Smart's text, it develops a figural life of its own, and, in its launching of metamimetic play from ostensibly mimetic sites, it deftly situates the cantata so as to recall and reignite a moment in eighteenth-century music history and theory when the representational status of music expressly was at stake. As Kevin Barry has argued, eighteenth-century English poets and aestheticians were attracted increasingly to music and its "signs," which, unlike the signs of language, can be suggestive precisely because they were seen as not representational, not bound to an external referent or signified, though their play and texture certainly can engage the listener's imagination: musical signs were perceived as "constituted first by their relative emptiness, and second by their intention toward a response that is relatively uncertain."[26] Although what Barry says of music's "empty" signs relates mainly to instrumental, nontexted music, and although much of the richness of Britten's setting derives from its play with all the resonances of Smart's text, certainly the shift in emphasis toward the imaginative freedom generated in the musical texture is exemplified in the cantata.

Moreover, just as Smart's poem had to wait until the twentieth century to be disseminated, the sort of setting that Britten invents for it probably could not have been realized without twentieth-century musical resources. Most notable among these is the cantata's reliance on modes other than the conventional major and minor. Britten's Lydian, Dorian, and Aeolian modes can impart the sense of being not entirely in either major or minor and can even hint at bitonality; thus, they are apt musical resources for illuminating Smart's unique mode of metaphoric, double vision, his capacity to see one thing from manifold perspectives. More precisely, particular musical devices

Britten uses, whether on a microlevel, as with the pointed instances of the tritone/augmented fourth, or on a macrolevel, as with the use of parallel canonic structures in the response and counterresponse, aptly convey the proximity of demonic to divine, the thin line between Jeoffry's celebratory "wreathing" and the asylum inmate's besieged writhing in Smart's writing. The chameleon fluidity of Britten's figuration seems always equally receptive to lighter or darker casts: it allows the sublime to slide into the silly and back, the magnificat to magnify the cat, the masterful to squeak into the mousterful, psalm to trip to pratfall and stupendous sound to slip to silence, in seconds. As Evans said of the cantata, "motivic principles forge subtle connections between the most unlike contexts."[27]

In other words, far from being restricted by the poem's "incoherence" or heterogeneity,[28] Britten's setting urges listeners constantly to hear and see one verse or conception of Smart's in terms of another, much as Smart's poem irrepressibly urges, through all the associative play at the poet's disposal, the reader to realize and re-create links from world to word and word to word—and both to Word—in an ongoing exercise of translation. As Smart claimed languages work into one another by their "bearings" (verse B624), musical figure and text work into each other as well. In that sense, both the poem and its setting are "open" texts, each evoking trumpets but never sounding the decisive blast of the Last Trumpet, the final troping of which St. Paul speaks, that which would redeem Babel and remove the need for the perpetual translation in which both music and text are engaged.[29] Remarkably, Britten closes the cantata by leaving it open: though the tonality of the Hallelujah response is F major, it ends with a fermata on C, the tonality in which the cantata began, implying the possibility that the cantata could again loop back on itself or take other trajectories. Britten's *Rejoice in the Lamb* may not be exactly the representation or "translation" of his Magnificat that Smart prayed for or could even have dreamed of, but it resonates as an example of the applause that *Jubilate Agno* asserts is the "*natural action of a man on the descent of the glory of God*" (B233).

NOTES

1. Seminal appraisals of Britten's vocal music are to be found in *Benjamin Britten: a Commentary on his works from a group of specialists*, eds. Donald Mitchell and Hans Keller (London: Rockliff, 1952), especially the articles by Peter Pears and by H. F. Redlich; in Peter Evans, *The Music of Benjamin Britten* (Minneapolis: University of Minnesota Press, 1979), and in Evans's article on Britten in Sir George Grove, *The New Grove Dictionary of Music and Musicians*, ed. Stanley Sadie (London: Macmillan Publishers, 1980).

2. On the nature and role of hypotypotic figuration in musical rhetoric, see George J. Buelow, "Rhetoric and Music," *New Grove Dictionary of Music and Musicians*, XV, 793-803. Further discussion and examples of such figuration may be found in William Kumbier, "A 'New Quickening': Haydn's *The Creation*, Wordsworth and the Pictorialist Imagination," *Studies in Romanticism,* 30 (1991): 535-63.

3. Humphrey Carpenter, *Benjamin Britten* (New York: Charles Scribners' Sons, 1992), 188.

4. Peter V. Le Page, "Benjamin Britten's *Rejoice in the Lamb,*" *Music Review,* 33 (1972): 122-37. Le Page remarks on Britten's selection of "Smart's best lines" and "his capturing as no one else has the great spirit of Christopher Smart in the range, flavour and economy of his [that is, Britten's] selections."

5. See Hussey's preferatory note to the vocal score.

6. Le Page, "Benjamin Britten," 124-126.

7. Britten extends his setting of Smart's A41 over the end of Section 1 and into the Response.

8. Britten adapts Smart's "For the rest of the stops are by their rhimes" to For the instruments are by their rhimes."

9. Le Page, "Benjamin Britten," 129n10.

10. All citations of the text and music of the cantata are to the vocal score (London: Boosey and Hawkes, 1943). In this analysis, measure numbers, counted from the beginning of each section of the cantata, are provided, although, unfortunately, they are not indicated in the published score. To identify particular pitches, I have used an upper- or lower-case letter, in some cases with a superscript numeral: 'middle' C is designated c^1, the C an octave higher c^2, the next higher c^3, and so on, while the C an octave below middle C is designated c, the next lower as C, the next lower as C^1, and so on. This scheme holds as well for the

other pitches within an octave, for example, e-flat[1] for the E-flat just above middle C (c[1]).

11. Evans, *Music of Benjamin Britten*, 88.

12. Evans frequently draws attention to Britten's predilection for modal writing. For a concise and clear overview of the modes, see Leonard Bernstein, "What is a Mode?" *Leonard Bernstein's Young People's Concerts*, Jack Gottlieb, ed. (New York: Doubleday/Anchor Books, 1992), 287-315.

13. On the varieties and significance of such circle (*circulatio*) figures, see Warren Kirkendale, "'*Circulatio*'-Tradition, *Maria Lactans*, and Josquin as Musical Orator," *Acta Musicologica* 56 (1984), 69-92, especially pages 72 and 80.

14. Evans, *Music of Benjamin Britten*, 90.

15. Carpenter, *Benjamin Britten*, 189. I thank Jeremy Lynn for bringing to my attention, from the cat-and-mouse musical cartoon genre, the incomparable "Hep Cat Symphony," a Famous Studios Release (dir. Seymour Kneitel, n.d.) that depicts a frenetic competition between a jazz-jamming feline and an orchestra of mice with a malicious zeal for Rossini.

16. William Hogarth, *The Analysis of Beauty*. 1753. Reprint (Hildesheim: Georg Olms, 1974). For a more detailed discussion of the "beautiful" and the "sublime" in music see William Kumbier, "Rhetoric and Expression in Haydn's *Applausus* Cantata," *Haydn Yearbook,* 18 (1993): 213-65, especially pages 239-242.

17. Hartman, 89: "Smart's verses are, as he implies, a 'conjecture' (B173), a 'cast' of the line or tongue whose outcome is uncertain enough to be the object of a wager like that between God and the Accuser (Satan) in the Book of Job."

18. On Heinichen's treatise see George J. Buelow, "The *Loci Topici* and Affect in late Baroque Music: Heinichen's practical Demonstration," *Music Review,* 27 (1966): 161-76.

19. Le Page, "Benjamin Britten," 137.

20. Laurence Draftees, *Bach and the Patterns of Invention* (Cambridge, MA: Harvard University Press, 1996), 234.

21. Ibid., 233.

22. Ibid., 234.

23. John Knobbier, *The Emancipation of Music from Language* (New Haven, CT: Yale University Press, 1986).

24. Cited in Draftees, *Bach*, 234.

25. Ibid., 236.

26. Kevin Barry, *Language, Music and the Sign* (Cambridge: Cambridge University Press, 1987). See especially Barry's introduction and the discussion of Barry in Kumbier, "A 'New Quickening,'" 558-59.

27. Evans, "Britten," *New Grove*.

28. H. F. Redlich states that the cantata seems "to suffer somewhat from the text's lack of coherence." See his "The Choral Music," in *Benjamin Britten*, 96.

29. On the trumpet in Smart and St. Paul, see William Kumbier, "Sound and Signification in *Jubilate Agno*," *Texas Studies in Language and Literature,* 24 (1982): 307.

CHAPTER 12

Surfing the Intertext: Smart among the Moderns

KARINA WILLIAMSON

Christopher Smart's energy
*   originality*
innate resourcefulness
in choice of diction
and rhythm
Make him one of my favorite poets.
                    —Marianne Moore

IN MAY 1957, Allen Ginsberg and Gregory Corso visited London, where Edith Sitwell took them to lunch at her club. The unlikely encounter between two young American Beat poets and a seventy-year-old English aristocrat was a great success. As Ginsberg recalled in 1984, they discussed their poetry with Sitwell and found her in complete sympathy: "She appreciated the poetry—-understood the language. The whole key was the inventiveness of words—-putting two words together that were unusual—-she could see that in our poetry. And we liked Christopher Smart and Whitman, and few English poets had any strong appreciation of that kind of stuff. And Blake, of course. The English thing was, Blake was still not considered 'mature,' so to speak, by the wits of Oxford."[1]

This chapter examines a diverse range of responses to Smart's writings by poets from his own time up to the present, but with the main focus on the second half of the twentieth century. It is not an intervention into discussion of the theory of intertextuality. Smart, however, provides empirical evidence of unusual interest because of another peculiarity about his place in intertextual history. He was extravagantly eclectic in his own textual borrowings and, as the checklist that concludes Part III shows, his writings have entered with surprising frequency into the texts of modern poets. What makes his position unusual is not these facts, but the unmediated nature of his impact on later poets. Unlike the writings of mainstream poets from Homer to T.S. Eliot, Smart's poems failed to gain textual currency by being handed down through successive generations of poets and readers. Consequently even his most anthologized poem, *A Song to David*, did not carry into the twentieth century the multiple resonances that poems contemporary with it, like Thomas Gray's *Elegy* or Oliver Goldsmith's *Deserted Village*, brought with them. In this respect Smart's situation is comparable to that of poets such as Thomas Traherne, John Clare, William Blake and Gerard Manley Hopkins who had to wait until the modern period for canonization, except that, unlike them, Smart did not lack applause in his own lifetime. He is singular in that his writings have undergone successive waves of acclaim, alternating with troughs of neglect, each wave bringing different texts into prominence.

The term *intertextuality* is not used in this chapter in its broadest Kristevan sense, as a precondition of all textual reading. It is used simply to mean any involvement of literary texts with other literary texts by imitation, parody, quotation, or other kinds of relationship. Many of my examples indeed are not "intertextual" by Michael Riffaterre's rigorous definition. Riffaterre distinguishes between the *obligatory* relation between texts that constitutes intertextuality ("when words signify by presupposing an intertext either potential in language or already actualized in literature") and the *aleatory* relation set up by allusion or quotation (in which "identification [of pre-text] depends upon the reader's culture"); "literary passages are collocable and comparable as text and intertext only if they are variants of the same structure."[2] Important though this distinction is for semiotics, from a literary-historical standpoint it is unduly restrictive and I have ignored it.

The different forms of intertextual engagement examined here fall into three broad divisions, which may be labeled "intersubjective," "imitative," and "allusive." *Intersubjective* texts are those, such as the poems listed by Edward Hirsch, Jeremy Reed, and John Williams, which engage with "Christopher Smart" as author and biographical subject. The *imitative* class covers a wide spectrum of textual assimilation, ranging from close imitation or parody of Smart's matter, style and verse form, to free, generic imitation as in Ralph Hodgson's "Song of Honour" and Anne Sexton's "O Ye Tongues." *Allusive* texts are those in which a pre-text, identified by quotation, allusion, or other means, generates or feeds into a more independent new text, as in the listed poems by Theodore Roethke, Donald Davie, W.S. Merwin, and others (in these, relation to the intertext is usually *aleatory*). These categories are convenient rather than watertight: intersubjective texts may also be imitative, as are those by Anne Sexton, John Heath-Stubbs, and Joseph Stroud, or allusive, or all three, as with Edward Hirsch's "Wild Gratitude."

In the first section, I briefly trace the first stages of Smart's intertextual history, down to 1939. The second section is concerned with Smart in England from the 1940s onwards; the third section follows him into twentieth-century North American poetry. "Cat Jeoffry" imitations, English and American, are discussed as a group in the final section.

I

In the eighteenth century, Smart was valued principally for his early religious verse, the "Poetical Essays" on the divine attributes, which earned him the Seatonian Prize annually from 1750 ("On the Eternity of the Supreme Being") to 1755 ("On the Goodness of the Supreme Being"). The Seatonian poems are the main focus of a cluster of verse tributes to Smart dating from 1759 while he was imprisoned in the madhouse.[3] William Woty, in one of these pieces, laments the breaking of Smart's "harp coelestial," foreboding that "no more . . . its tuneful strings, / Touch'd by his hand, will praise the *King of Kings.*" Richard Rolt rhapsodizes about his "elevated genius" which "soar'd divine." Arthur Murphy assures him that angels themselves incline their heads to listen when "To the All Good thy Muse attunes her lay." So firmly was Smart at this time defined as poet by his Seatonian compositions that they served as cannon-fodder for his detractors as well: in 1755 Francis Gentleman sneered that Smart "Tho' devoted to wine, sings the glories of God," and that he writes "for the sake of a legacy."[4]

These intersubjective poems mark Smart's first though least enduring entry into the web of intertextuality. The commendatory verses adopt the diction and imagery of his Seatonian poems, just as the Seatonian poems themselves are draped in the biblical-Miltonic rhetoric of earlier eighteenth-century exercises in the religious sublime. The writers regard Smart's achievement as awesome but dangerous. In their texts the poet is presented as a tragic hero whose fall comes about through *hubris*: Apollo's "fav'rite bard," he drew "Celestial science" from the sacred fountain of the gods and "quaff'd his fill"; but then, says this anonymous admirer, "seeking more, like Phaëton, he fell"[5] (Phaëton, son of Apollo, attempted to drive his father's sun-chariot but lost control; Jove killed him with a thunderbolt and he fell into the river Eridanus). Or, as John Lockman writes:

> Wrapt in a vision, he presum'd to sing
> The attributes of Heav'n's eternal King:
> But O! approaching tow'rds the Throne of light,
> Its flashing splendors overpow'r'd his sight.[6]

The other pre-text here is Milton's *Paradise Lost* Book VIII, in which Raphael cautions Adam against aspiring to forbidden knowledge, warning him that

> God to remove his ways from human sense,
> Placed heaven from earth so far, that earthly sight,
> If it presume, might err in things too high,
> And no advantage gain. (VIII.119-22)

Reading Lockman's allusion to Milton from a Romantic perspective (to thicken the intertexture still further) emphasizes the tragic nature of Smart's transgression. The tributes of 1759 do not quite glorify Smart as a proto-Romantic rebel against divine authority like Satan or Prometheus—Phaëton, after all, was more the victim of his own folly than heroically defiant—but they come close to it. The effect is to alert the modern reader to an element of audacity in Smart's rhetoric that makes his Seatonian poems stand out from the ordinary run of physico-theological verse to which they generically belong.

The sharp decline in Smart's reputation after his brief heyday in the 1750s, the century-long period of neglect that followed his death, and the second phase of partial recognition in which *A Song to David* was raised to solitary eminence, is all familiar history.[7] Yet although Smart's *Song* has been acclaimed by poets from Browning onward, the text itself has remained peculiarly unassimilable. In the half century between 1880 and 1930, Browning himself and two other authors, Edmund Blunden and Ralph Hodgson, wrote poems concerned with this text, but only Hodgson used it as a model. Both Browning and Blunden turn *A Song to David* into an icon, demonstrating the poet's unique power to transcend the material limits of the human condition, "his triumph over time" as Blunden puts it.[8]

In Browning's "With Christopher Smart" (from *Parleyings with Certain People of Importance*, 1887), it is initially the visual and architectonic qualities of the *Song* that are emphasized, by means of an extended metaphor representing it as a richly ornamented rococo Chapel (lines 36-63).[9] But the paramount value of the poem to Browning appears later, in part VI. He stations Smart momentarily (words like "once," "one," "moment," "only," occurring ten times in forty lines) on a level with Milton and Keats, and above all other poets of the period in between, on the strength of this single, "supreme" achievement:

> Smart, solely of such songmen, pierced the screen
> 'Twixt thing and word, lit language straight from soul.

A Song to David thus becomes a new site for Browning's perpetual struggle against the constrictions of language. It demonstrates the magical capacity of words in "song" to transcend the limits of mere "speech" and achieve real presence; an achievement like that of Browning's own "Mage," John of Halberstadt, who "vents a brace of rhymes, / And in there breaks the sudden rose herself."[10]

Ralph Hodgson's "Song of Honour" (1913), a now forgotten poem, was much admired in its time.[11] It imitates Smart's *Song* both in its structure and language and in its vision of a universal harmony of nature. Hodgson's text is divided into 24 sections of varying length that are based metrically on Smart's tail-rhyme stanza. It also borrows certain features of Smart's style, such as use of alliterative word-pairs, metonymic triplets (for example, "leopard, lark, and rose"), syntactic repetition, and a rhapsodic vocabulary ("sublime," "exalt," "hosannas"). But the gulf between the two poems is vast. This is not merely a measure of the difference between writers of very unequal endowments; it also has to do with the genre and the conditions for its success. *A Song to David* belongs to the tradition of the high sacred ode, the great exemplars of which for Smart were Milton's *Nativity Ode* and John Dryden's *Song for St Cecilia's Day*. Such poems reflect and sustain an ideology of order based on the conception of a divine harmony binding the whole of creation.[12] The poet's role in this highly public genre was as celebrant, not subject. Under Romantic ideology the genre was transformed in function and nature. The ode was appropriated by Wordsworth and Coleridge to proclaim the *loss* of harmony, and the authorial ego became central; for in the poet's subjectivity alone, according to their philosophy, lay the hope that the pristine bond between man and nature might be restored. Unsurprisingly, the high sacred ode did not survive the decline of Romanticism, and Hodgson's attempt to renew it by harnessing an apocalyptic rhetoric associated with failure and loss to a hopeful, democratic idealism inevitably rings hollow.

Blunden, in his edition of *A Song to David* with other poems (1924), attempted to interest readers in Smart's other writings, but in spite of his efforts the *Song* remained the only text by which Smart was generally known until 1939. The breakthrough came with the discovery and publication by W. F. Stead of the manuscript of *Jubilate Agno*, under the title *Rejoice in the Lamb*.[13] The immediate response in England to this literary event now seems curiously muted, but reasons for the delayed reaction are not far to seek: Stead's book was published in February, within a few months of the outbreak of war. Moreover, in Britain (though not in America) it was sold only in an expensive limited edition that put it beyond the reach of ordinary readers and penurious poets.

That is one possible reason, but a relatively trivial one, why *Jubilate Agno* has had a greater impact in America than in England. A far more important factor is the difference in the patterns of development in poetry in the two countries in the postwar period. The 1950s were "the formative decade of postwar American poetry";[14] a climate of political protest and social, moral and sexual "liberation" was reflected in poetry by rejection of tradition and New Critical values, rediscovery of Whitman and the Romantic ethos, and adoption of "open" forms of verse. It was an era obviously favorable to the reception of revolutionary poets such as Blake and Smart. In England, by contrast, the trend in the 1950s was in the opposite direction. The decade was dominated by poetry of the so-called Movement, which developed as a reaction against the neo-Romanticism of poets in the 1940s such as Dylan Thomas and George Barker: against precisely those wild, energetic, apocalyptic modes of writing that American poets in the same period were embracing.[15]

Primary credit for awakening readers on both sides of the Atlantic to Smart's newly discovered work lies with W. H. Auden. Auden must have read Stead's edition almost as soon as it was published, for he quoted three verses in a work he was writing in the summer of 1939.[16] Another four lines were quoted soon afterward in Auden's notes to the first edition of *New Year Letter* (1941). Auden quoted, as the note to Part III, lines 1643-64 ("We need to love all since we are / Each a unique particular"), the following verses:

> For I bless God for the Postmaster general and all conveyancers of letters
> under his care especially Allen and Shelvock.
> For my grounds in New Canaan shall infinitely compensate for the flats
> and maynes of Staindrop Moor.
> For the praise of God can give to a mute fish the notes of a nightingale.
> For I have seen the White Raven and Thomas Hall of Willingham and am
> my self a greater curiosity than both. (Stead, VII:22-25: *Jubilate Agno*,
> B22-25)[17]

Auden's increasing commitment to Christianity, his interest in metrics and diction, and his philosophical attachment to "particulars," must all have made him responsive to Smart's religious verse. Yet Auden's own poetry bears no imprint of Smart that I can discern.[18] His imperviousness perhaps stems from the attachment to the rational and commonsensical that made him impatient with Surrealist poetry: "No, Surrealists, no! No, even the wildest of poems / must, like prose, have a firm basis in staid common-sense."[19]

Nevertheless, Auden's interest in Smart had wide repercussions. It was he who introduced Benjamin Britten to *Rejoice in the Lamb*,[20] and it was through him (courtesy of William H. Bond) that the text in its antiphonal form first reached the reading public. Four years before publication of Bond's 1954 edition, substantial excerpts from his rearranged text, together with one of Smart's hymns ("The Nativity of Our Lord") and *A Song to David*, were included in a widely used anthology, *Poets of the English Language*, compiled by Auden with Norman Pearson and published in 1950.[21]

II

In England, publication of *Jubilate Agno* (as *Rejoice in the Lamb*) did not arouse any general response among poets or alter Smart's status in the popular view as a literary-historical oddity; it was not until the 1980s that the potential for the modern poet of Smart's most innovative work began to be more widely recognized. Long before then, however, *Rejoice in the Lamb* had made a significant impact on two poets of very dissimilar age and literary outlook, Edith Sitwell and Peter Porter.

Edith Sitwell was already an admirer of *A Song to David*. She included it in her personal anthology, *The Pleasures of Poetry* (1930), introducing it as a "beautiful and neglected work" and praising its spiritual qualities. She commented also on the distinctiveness of its style: the "solemn piling of adjective upon adjective," the "curious modernity . . . at once strange and deeply touching" of Smart's syntax (citing lines 249-52), and "the extreme strangeness of the imagery; all natural objects are seen with such clarity that, for the moment, nothing else exists."[22] Despite her interest, however, the *Song* left no discernible traces on her poetry. It was only in the last, prophetic phase of her writing, during the war and after her encounter with *Rejoice in the Lamb*, that the fabric of her writing began to show the impress of Smart. In *A Poet's Notebook* (1943) Sitwell quoted several scattered lines from *Rejoice in the Lamb* together with some stanzas from *A Song to David*. On stanza lii, she commented: "The colour is so rich as to be not of this world."

The line misquoted here, in what looks like an act of creative misprision rather than carelessness, is from *Jubilate Agno* A47 (II:22 in Stead): "Let Esdras bless Christ Jesus with the Rose and his people, which is a nation of living sweetness."[23] Sitwell used this line two or three times in other contexts, though not elsewhere in conjunction with the *Song*. At this point she seems to have been drawn to the sacramental element in Smart's writing; seeing in his "Rose" the same intersection of the earthly and the transcendental, real flower and Christian symbol, that characterized the imagery of her own early poems.[24]

Rejoice in the Lamb had an important influence on Sitwell's writing prior to this, however. According to the account she gave in 1952 of her poetic development, Smart was instrumental in her return to poetry after a silence of several years before the war: in 1940, she says, "I began to write again—of the state of the world, of the terrible rain." The phrase "terrible rain" alludes to her most famous war poem, "Still Falls the Rain," a lament for the bombing of London, in which the blitz is envisioned as a reenactment of the Crucifixion. In this dark mood she saw civilization descending into bestiality: "In one poem, I wrote of the world reduced to the Ape, . . . But, too, with poor Christopher Smart, I blessed Jesus Christ with the Rose and his people, which is a nation of living sweetness."[25]

The most obvious interpretation of the last sentence is as a reference to the redemptive ending of "Still Falls the Rain," in which the crucified Christ speaks ("Still do I love, still shed my innocent light, my Blood, for thee"). But Smart's poem is also associated by implication with technical changes in Sitwell's poetry. The quotation from *Rejoice in the Lamb* in the preface is followed immediately by the statement, "My time of experiments was done," and a description of Sitwell's adoption of long-line verse under the influence of Whitman (quoting the famous passage from his 1855 preface to *Leaves of Grass* in which "perfect poems" are said to be those whose metrical form grows out of the natural laws of their being "as unerringly and loosely as lilacs or roses on a bush.")[26] The seamless transition in Sitwell's text from Smart to Whitman is noteworthy as an anticipation of Ginsberg's recruitment of Smart into the Whitman patriarchy in the 1950s. What seems clear is that Sitwell (like Ginsberg and other American poets later) found strict metrical patterns inappropriate at a time of cataclysm; an apocalyptic reading of events called for a new poetics, and for this she turned to the oracular verse of Smart and Whitman.

One poem that shows the impact of Smart directly is "The Two Loves," written in 1944 and dedicated to the neo-Romantic painter, Pavel Tchelitchev, whose surreal mergings of human and vegetable forms inform the imagery of the first half of the text. The poem expresses Sitwell's conception of love as a natural force, a "Universal Fire" nourishing the whole physical creation, and her fear of its extinction. The second half begins: "Gone is that heat," to be replaced by other, baser "loves": the false warmth of "brotherhood" (in money-grubbing), and the "monstrous Life-force" of blind procreativeness. In a move common in Sitwell's wartime poetry, she turns in the final section towards Christian atonement for renewal of the primordial fire of love.

> I thought of the umbilical cords that bind us to strange suns
> And causes . . . of Smart the madman who was born

To bless Christ with the Rose and his people, a nation
Of living sweetness . . .Of Harvey who blessed Christ with
the solar fire in the veins,
And Linnaeus praising Him with the wingèd seed!—
[. . .] Of terrestrial nature generated far
From heaven . . . the argillaceous clays, the zircon and
    sapphire
Bright as the tears of heaven, but deep in earth -
[. . .] And of One who contracted His Immensity
And shut Himself in the scope of a small flower
Whose root is clasped in darkness . . . God in the span
Of the root and light-seeking corolla . . .with the voice of
Fire I cry—Will He disdain that flower of the world, the heart of Man?

It is not the long-line verse, or even the recourse through Smart to Christian
hope, that is distinctively Smartian in "The Two Loves" but the method of in-
sinuating metaphysical ideas. Throughout the poem scientific terms and con-
cepts (here, Harvey's discovery of the circulation of the blood and Linnaeus's
theory of plant generation) are absorbed into the eschatological and cosmo-
logical scheme of the poem, in the same way as they are in Smart's text in
Fragment B.

Sitwell's favorite line from *Jubilate Agno* and its rose symbolism played
a vital role in the composition of her Hiroshima trilogy, *Three Poems for an
Atomic Age*. By her own account, Smart's prophecy enabled her once more
to move beyond despair to reaffirmation of "the glory of Life" in the final
poem of the trilogy, "The Canticle of the Rose."[27] Smart also provided the
pretext for a late poem, "Praise We Great Men," which was written for Ben-
jamin Britten in 1959 in celebration of Purcell's tercentenary. She wanted the
poem to be "extremely triumphant and full of pomp, like one of Christopher
Smart's paeans," she told Britten, "something like this:

    Praise with the purple trumpet
    Praise with the trumpet flower."[28]

There is no single pretext here. Smart quotes "praise him upon the sound of
the trumpet" (from Psalm 150) in *Jubilate Agno* D177, but the rhythm and
syntactic patterning of Sitwell's specimen lines are closer to Smart's metri-
cal versions of Psalms 147-150, while the wordplay uniting flowers and mu-
sic is in the manner of Smart's Hymn 12 ("Pull up the bell-flowers of the
spring, / And let the budding greenwood ring.") The poem in its published

form[29] attempts to marry the variable line-lengths and rhyme-scheme of a Pindaric ode to the rhapsodic but tightly controlled movement of *A Song to David*, but it is not a success; not so much through failure in the management of rhythm and sound, but through lack of that "clarity" that Sitwell herself recognized in Smart's *Song*; the power to project images that are at once "strange"—new, exotic, mysterious—and yet so distinct that they appear instantaneously real and self-sufficient. Sitwell's comment accurately identifies the singularity of Smart's images in the *Song*: they are not metaphors, nor are they exactly metonyms. Although word-pictures like "the beaver plods his task" or "Her cave the mining coney scoops" (stanza xxv) do indeed have a metonymic function within the logical structure of the poem, perceptually they stand for nothing but themselves. Sitwell's images in "Praise We Great Men," by contrast, come trailing clouds of meaning—a signifying fuzz of symbolism, resemblance, representation—as if she lost her nerve after writing to Britten. Her treatment of the sample lines she sent him is salutary. Instead of leaving them in their Smart-like bareness, allowing the pun on "trumpet" alone to forge the link between flowers and music, she laboriously spun them out into this piece of grotesquery:

> Praise with the trumpet's purple sound—
> Praise with the trumpet flower
> And with that flower the long five-petalled hand
> That sweeps the strings.

The only other poet writing in England in the 1950s whose work was palpably affected by *Jubilate Agno* was the young Australian, Peter Porter. Porter was and is an intensely allusive poet; so much so that, as Peter Steele remarks, he "would be a paradigm case for anyone wanting to press the claims of intertextuality, of language speaking us rather than our speaking the language, if it were not for the matter of tone, of voice."[30] But Smart occupies a special place in his mental world; *Jubilate Agno* he describes as "a key work in my interior map."[31] He first encountered it in 1951 through a recording of Britten's *Rejoice in the Lamb*, was "haunted" by the passages in the cantata, and went on to read the work in full, first in Stead's version and later in Bond's.[32]

He was influenced also by Auden's interest in Smart's poem. Auden and Smart came together early in Porter's writing, as tutelary geniuses of *The Losing Chance*, a play in blank verse written in 1952, during a deeply troubled period in the author's personal life. The play explores despair and mental breakdown through the experiences of its chief protagonist, Peter

Mainchance. Peter is threatened by a mysterious, offstage "Adversary" (deriving from Auden); Smart figures in the text as a police inspector who comes to investigate when Peter attempts suicide. Inspector Smart tries to restore Peter's will to live, exhorts him to accept his "madness" as a constructive state of mind, and utters a speech in the oracular manner of *Jubilate Agno*.[33] The play was never performed or published, but it had productive results. Inspector Smart was reborn later as Porter's dramatic persona in two monologues, *Inspector Christopher Smart Calls* (1964) and *The Return of Christopher Smart* (1969), pronouncing uncomfortable words to a decadent age. The poems are written in the "exuberantly rough satirical mode" that is one of Porter's many styles.[34] Scattered allusions to and quotations from Smart are embedded in the text but Porter makes no attempt at direct imitation; nevertheless the poems have a distinctly Smartlike "voice," in the broader sense in which Porter himself uses the word. "Voice"—the poet's individual "way of saying"—is paramount for Porter. Poetry he thinks is perpetually involved in a struggle with its own medium, language: it "has to put up a fight against meaning," that is, against the propensity of words to *signify*, to be "mere symbols, not their own creatures." "Voice" resists this drift towards interpretation, towards reading *through*: it "underlies and subverts meaning in poetry."[35] This may look like a recapitulation of the issue of *différance*, but Porter's ideas about language are closer to Browning than to Derrida.

In the Inspector Smart poems, the intertextual voice is a composite utterance representing different facets of Smart: the boisterous comic figure of the *Midwife* writings, and the indignant, sorrowful, visionary evangelist of *Jubilate Agno*. Through this voice, Porter like Smart assembles wildly disparate orders of being and experience, placing them all on the same plane. Porter commented on the egalitarian habit of Smart's mind, as shown in *Jubilate Agno* and *A Song to David*, in a radio talk on "Poetry and Madness" in 1976. Smart, he says, "was mentally deranged only in the sense that he connected all the multifarious activities of the world and put them on equal terms in the mind of God."[36] The human mind is less capacious than God's, however, and Porter's Inspector poems, like Smart's, now need explication to make their tissue of allusions accessible to the present-day reader.

Porter returned to Smart in three later poems: glancingly in "Cat's Fugue" (1975) and centrally in "Sunday" (1970), and "Pope's Carnations Knew Him" (1981). The quotation from *Jubilate Agno* (B568) from which the title of the last is taken, provides the fulcrum for a beautifully poised consideration of the principle of "order." Pope was "a gardener who never put a foot wrong," he "had such a way with the symmetry / of petals, he could make a flower yield an epic from its one-day siege." But for him, the flowers were always "on duty," they "bowed, they kneeled, / they curtseyed, and so stood up for prosody"—

> No wonder Smart learned from their expansive
> hearts that they loved the ordered, the well-heeled
> and ornate, the little poet with the giant stride.
>
> Each gossipy morning he sniffed their centres
> and they saw him: the lines of paradise revealed.
> *God make gardeners better nomenclators.*[37]

"Sunday" is a less successful poem, but a revealing example of Porter's intertextual habits. The poem reflects sardonically on modern modes of Christian worship, initially in contrast to George Herbert, but later using Smart's manic enthusiasm for public prayer to highlight the vacuous pieties of the 1960s. The poem ends with a reverie, in which

> the Holy Nuisance of
> St. James's Park stands in St. Crud—
> the—Great in the twenty-four colours of love
> Chanting the *Song of David* to birds
> And beasts and flowers and I wake up
> To Sunday in London, to comfortable words
> And the Grail filled with orange cup.[38]

Porter's habitual allusiveness is almost too compact for comfort here: a reader unfamiliar with *Jubilate Agno* would be in difficulties. Without naming him, the lines conflate Smart as "Holy Nuisance" (who "routed all the company" by blessing God in St James's Park, *Jubilate Agno* B89), with his philosophy of colors (B649-69: *"For the colors are spiritual. . . . For the blessing of God upon all things descends in colour,"* and so on). This hieratic figure in his technicolor dreamcoat is then merged with the author of *A Song to David*, a Franciscan singer at one with birds and beasts and flowers. It is notable that the image of Smart comes to the writer in a dream: Smart's mind, Porter says, "was the perfect storehouse for the dreaming intelligence." Dreams also are important in Porter's scheme of ideas. The "dreaming imagination," he believes, is of value to poetry, not as a means of penetrating the recesses of the unconscious but as a release from the constraints of waking reason, an alternative method of ordering perception and experience; for dreams, he points out, "are inevitable in their unfolding but not logical—they are seamless but full of non sequiturs."[39]

The configuration of Porter's "interior map" and Smart's key position in it begins to become clearer. The principle of dream-order is instantiated alike in the flickering sequences of images in *A Song to David* and in what Steele calls the "kaleidoscopic rapidity and virtuosity" of Porter's own writing.[40] The concrete or *dinglich* quality of Porter's poetry too can be related to the pre-eminence of *things* (Auden's "unique particulars") within the schema of both *Jubilate Agno* and the *Song*. Even the tonal shifts from scornfulness, humor, and ridicule to tragedy and pathos, which are so distinctive a feature of Porter's anatomy of the twentieth-century world, have their counterpart in the oscillations between arrogance and pathos, "innocence" (Porter's word) and satirical perspicacity, with which Smart anatomizes the world of his own time.

Two other English poets have engaged with Smart in recent years, both intertextually and critically: Donald Davie and Jeremy Reed. They differ widely, however, in their approach. Jeremy Reed is mainly interested in Smart as a "mad" poet. In his study, *Madness: The Price of Poetry* (1989), he discusses Smart's asylum poetry at length, explaining its "obscurantism" and "weirdness," alongside its flashes of intense "luminosity," entirely as reflections of Smart's life and psychology.[41] These interests also predominate in his poem, "Christopher Smart in Madness" (1984: see checklist). Reed assembles a *bricolage* of fragments from *Jubilate Agno* and external biographical sources in order to construct an imaginary self-portrait of the poet in confinement in St. Luke's.

Davie's championship of Smart in the 1950s was instrumental in turning the attention of readers in England to Smart's neglected lyrical poems, and to the end of his life Davie continued to uphold the merits of Smart's work, especially the *Psalms* and *Hymns*.[42] His interest is thus focused on Smart's text, not his life. "The Creature David" appeared in Davie's last collection of new poems, *To Scorch or Freeze* (1988, see checklist). The Psalms of David, in Coverdale's translation, provide the main pretext for these poems but they are interwoven with quotations and allusions to other poets, ancient and modern. Two themes, "song" (again) and voyaging—by sea, land and air—run through them. Smart appears in "The Creature David" in relation to both: as a "main poet," one whose song is about the sea and seafaring.

> *The disposings of the heart in man,*
> *and the answer of the tongue . . .*
> Not the domain of any
> main poet's song;

> not the halcyon, the mid-ocean range
> where Ceteosaurus spouts, and Christopher Smart
> numbers the streaks of the mollusc, where
> the Spaniard is challenged for the Main,
> comradely, and Drake takes on the world,
> a hirsute pirate. None of this
> is documented history, it is not
> fastidious, but dreadnought David's song.
>
> Speech murmurs, and is always
> forked, but this is song.
> Nothing in this is talked.
>
> *There goe the shippes; there is*
> *that Leviathan, whom Thou hast made*
> *to play therein*
>
> upon the harp.

The opening quotation is part of a sentence, from Proverbs 16:1, which ends "is from the Lord." Davie's poem juggles with ideas of creature and creator through the concept of the poet as God-like "maker," a time-honored trope which Smart himself uses.[43] The psalmist David is at once creator and created being; even his utterance ("tongue") is "from the Lord." Through his renderings of "dreadnought David's song," Smart in turn replicates this creator/creature duality. Like Browning, Davie presents "song" as a paradigm of verbal creativity; in opposition both to "speech" or "documented history," and to neo-classical generalization (Smart "numbers the streaks of the mollusc" in defiance of Johnson's famous definition of the poet's task in *Rasselas*).

The maritime puns ("main" and "dreadnought"), the allusions to the halcyon, Drake, and Leviathan, are all reverberations from Smart's poetry,[44] but the crucial intertextual link is the final reference to God/David playing "upon the harp" (the second biblical quotation is from Psalm 104, verse 26). Harp-playing is the primal act of creation as Smart envisions it in *Jubilate Agno* ("For GOD the father Almighty plays upon the HARP [. . .] and his tune is a work of creation," B246-7).[45] The syntactic slippage that invites us to read that Leviathan too "play[s . . .] upon the harp" has a comic propriety in keeping with Smart's "Great Flabber Dabber Flat Clapping Fish with hands" (*Jubilate Agno* D11). The intertexture here gets even denser, for both Anson's *Voyage* and Psalm 98 ("Let the floods clap their hands") are cited by Smart himself as sources for his fantastic image.

Davie, with his lifelong devotion to precision and elegance of diction and form, did not prize Smart for his "mad," oracular qualities. *Jubilate Agno*, he found, was redeemed from its "apparent waywardness," by the "intricate and rationally coherent plan" revealed by Bond. *A Song to David*, similarly, is "distinguished by an astonishingly intricate and logical order, not by any sublimely disjointed afflatus."[46] Nothing could more clearly show the distance between Davie and most of Smart's American admirers than his preference for rational coherence and logical order to "afflatus."

III

In the United States, as in England, *Jubilate Agno* has been the main focus for poets interested in Smart in the last 50 years, but *A Song to David* had a significant impact on three poets who came of age before mid-century: Robert Frost, Marianne Moore, and Theodore Roethke. All three, apparently quite independently, found stanza lxxvii particularly inspirational:

> But stronger still, in earth and air,
> And in the sea, the man of pray'r;
> And far beneath the tide;
> And in the seat to faith assign'd,
> Where ask is have, where seek is find,
> Where knock is open wide. (*PW,* ii: 145)

Frost seems an unlikely admirer of Smart, yet according to a biographer, *A Song to David* was one of Frost's favorite poems.[47] In old age, he was in the habit of quoting from it, apparently by heart, at meetings of the Bread Loaf School of English at Middlebury College in Vermont. Frost's attachment to a poem once regarded as a jewel in the pre-Romantic crown may seem at odds with his rejection of the visionary aspirations and grand gestures of high Romanticism, but it is in line with his beliefs about style. Freedom, boldness, and spontaneity were for him the hallmarks of poetic utterance: the best poetry, he thought, is "a kind of mischief." At Middlebury in 1947 he reportedly praised Smart for his "cavalierness with words" and for making "free with the English language," quoting the lines, "Where ask is have, where seek is find, / Where knock is open wide" as an example.[48]

The relationship between Frost and Smart is one of affinity rather than influence or imitation. Reginald Cook finds general resemblances between the two poets in those qualities of verbal "mischief" and "cavalierness" that Frost picks out in Smart, and more specifically in their command of "the bounding line"; that is, a technique that makes the poetic sentence seem to "leap and bound toward the completion of its idea and form" under the impetus of "its own autonomous joy."[49] In other respects, Frost's attachment to Smart seems to be an attraction of opposites. Frost admired in Smart an exuberant certainty of faith quite unlike the skeptical and ironic cast of his own writing. In 1960, he expatiated to the Bread Loaf students on "glory," an underrated value, he thought, not to be confused with the "vainglory" of military achievement. By way of illustration he quoted the final two stanzas of *A Song to David*, adding: "All glory, you see, great glory, glory, glory. And those last three lines are the kind of things you wish on the world all the time. You wish for it now—now 'that stupendous truth believ'd.' See that stupendous truth believer. Nothing like that line anywhere."[50] Nothing of that kind, certainly, in Frost's handful of religious poems.

Marianne Moore is a less surprising devotee of Smart: the qualities cited in her epigraph to this chapter[51] are qualities also possessed by her own poetry. Conversely, Smart is as much a "literalist of the imagination" as Moore herself. They have in common a precise, vivid and idiosyncratic perception of the particularity of things—animals, birds, fishes, objects of all kinds—and comparable habits of wordplay and linguistic compression. If one didn't know the source of Smart's phrase "quick peculiar quince" one might justifiably guess that it was coined by Moore. Perhaps their most striking affinity is a fascination with armored or armed creatures: snails, porcupines, hedgehogs, crocodiles, the rhinoceros, the scaly anteater ("another armed animal" in "The Pangolin," Moore's most famous poem on this subject). Randall Jarrell, the first to comment on this aspect of Moore's poetry, related it to her love of "exactness" and "concision"—qualities which she shares with Smart—but also to her irony, restraint, and fastidious "untouchableness," qualities untypical of Smart.[52] Armor and weapons in his poetry are connected with innocence and vulnerability. "Open, and naked of offence, / Man's made of mercy, soul, and sense; / God arm'd the snail and wilk" (*A Song to David*, stanza xlii): the armor of virtue protects the man of mercy, as the snail and wilk (whelk) are protected by their shells. Moore's snail, conversely, epitomizes "virtue," the stylistic grace of "contractility" ("To a Snail").

Moore voiced her interest in Smart in public in 1948 in a lecture on "Humility, Concentration, and Gusto."[53] Smart is cited both for his insight into "gusto" (she quotes his theory of "Impression") and for his practice of it: "Gusto, in Smart, authorized as oddities what in someone else might seem effrontery," she says, quoting a line from Smart's version of Psalm 147: "He [Jehovah] deals the beasts their food." Among further examples, she too quotes *A Song to David*, stanza lxxvii.

By "gusto" Moore seems to mean a combination of verbal energy and the capacity to surprise by unexpected words and grammar. But in a draft version of this passage she also remarked that "in Christopher Smart himself there is an EFFLATUS [*sic*] that APATHY CAN'T RESIST." Bonnie Costello takes this to mean that Moore "identifies gusto as the opposite of ennui"[54] but "afflatus" has a more specific connotation than that. Peter Porter also fastens on this quality in Smart, observing that "he was always able at his best to rise from the concrete to the sublime in a single gesture—and this is the only way poetical afflatus can be achieved if it isn't to be corrupt or fulsome."[55] Porter's distrust of "afflatus," like Davie's, reflects the anti-Romantic bias of poets in England, but in Renaissance critical terminology it was an honorific concept, synonymous with "inspiration": the power claimed for poetry to communicate knowledge "breathed in" from supernatural sources. *Afflatus* in this sense has always been a hallmark of oracular rhetoric; Whitman in *Song of Myself*, for example, declares with typical self-confidence "Through me the afflatus surging and surging, through me the current and index" (24:9). Moore does not mention Smart's most oracular poem, *Jubilate Agno*, and may not have known it at this time, but she recognizes in Smart a quality that was of prime importance to the rising generation of American poets.

Theodore Roethke's interest in Smart was more personal and intense than that of Frost and Moore. He used the now familiar line from *A Song to David*, "Where knock is open wide" as the title of the first poem in his volume, *Praise to the End!* (1951). How this five-part poem, the first stage of Roethke's journey into the interior of childhood, relates to the pretext is debatable, since "Where Knock Is Open Wide" bears no obvious resemblance in subject matter or style to *A Song to David*. Ralph J. Mills, Jr. notes merely that Roethke "seems to use the line from Smart to imply birth and entry into the world."[56] It is a safe guess that one reason why Roethke chose it was because of its compression. As he explained in 1950, he was aiming in his poetry at this time at a "compressed" language capable of expressing simultaneously the immediacy of a child's perspective and the intensity of the adult poet's vision.[57] But Roethke's interest in Smart certainly went deeper than that.

Roethke told Mills that the titles in *Praise to the End!* were "little quotes from those I think of as ancestors."[58] Roethke suffered from a chronic anxiety of influence about literary "ancestors," but Smart, along with Blake and John Clare, were benign forefathers in his genealogy. In a late poem, "Heard in the Violent Ward" the speaker/patient takes comfort in the thought of sharing his hardships with these three poets:

> In heaven, too,
> You'd be institutionalized.
> But that's all right,—
> If they let you eat and swear
> With the likes of Blake,
> And Christopher Smart,
> And that sweet man, John Clare.[59]
>
> * * * * *
>
> Christopher, help me love this loose thing.
> I think of you now, kneeling in London muck,
> Praying for grace to descend.[60]

Roethke's repeated allusions to Smart lend credence to an intertextual reading of "Where Knock Is Open Wide" by one critic that might otherwise seem overstrained. Jenijoy La Belle argues that the poem is based on *A Song to David* as a whole, finding common ground in its structure (the unification of a multiplicity of creatures and things through "methods of musical arrangement"), its style (breaking away from "conventional patterns of logic and discourse"), and its psychological motivation. The grounds of belief, however, are different: "Smart and Roethke use 'where knock is open wide' to image a psychic state where the normal kinds of relationships are collapsed and where the usual disjunction between desire and gratification does not occur. To Smart, this state of a complete identification between desire and fulfillment exists for the man of prayer; to Roethke, it exists for the child."[61] Roethke, in short, puts Freudian psychoanalysis in the place occupied by Christian theology in Smart's scheme of things.[62] *Praise to the End!* was a sequel to Roethke's previous sequence of poems, *The Lost Son* (1948). Psychoanalytical interpreters might ponder the fact that Smart too was a "lost son" in Roethke's sense: a boy who suffered the loss of his father during his formative years.

Roethke's poetry in these two volumes represents a personal break away from his earlier work, but his turn toward Romantic models (Blake, Wordsworth, Dylan Thomas) is typical of radical changes in postwar American poetry generally. Whether the key date is seen as the publication of Charles Olson's "Projective Verse" manifesto in 1950,[63] or the famous poetry reading by Allen Ginsberg and others at the Six Gallery in San Francisco on October 13, 1955, the "Renaissance" of American poetry in the post-war, post-Holocaust, post-Hiroshima era is recognized as an epoch in American cultural history. Out of a period of profound anxiety, disaffection and alienation among American intellectuals came a poetry of countercultural protest which started in San Francisco and swept throughout the United States.[64] Geoffrey Thurley argues further that the mid-1950s represent the "American moment": that is, the moment when American culture at last broke decisively with the past, and poetry, freeing itself from the prison-house of canonical English Literature, began to be "wholly and authentically American without being in the slightest degree provincial."[65]

This was the stage on which Smart entered when, as Allen Ginsberg tells it, *Jubilate Agno* became one of the "model texts" for *Howl* (1955-56) and was thus involved directly in the birth of Beat poetry and the countercultural movement at large. But the whole picture, both of postwar developments and of Smart's contribution to them, is more complicated. In 1960, in the preface to *The New American Poetry: 1945-1960*, Donald Allen proclaimed the emergence of a younger generation of American poets with a new poetics. Allen recognized five groups of "new poets," emanating from Berkeley, San Francisco, Boston, Black Mountain, and New York City. While differing from one another in many ways they were united in one aim: "a total rejection of all those qualities typical of academic verse."[66] "Academic verse" meant poetry approved by the New Critics: using traditional meters and verse forms and showing the irony, wit, coolness, and restraint privileged by the prevailing critical code. Rebellion against those values entailed a reaction against mainstream English poets, and a return to earlier American writers, especially Whitman, Ezra Pound, and William Carlos Williams. The English poets to whom the new generation was now attracted were subversives like Blake, Shelley, and D.H. Lawrence, or neo-Romantic "apocalyptic" writers like Dylan Thomas. And Christopher Smart.

Allen's selection of "new poets" staked a claim in effect for the counter-cultural writings of the Beat poets and their fellow travelers as the true vanguard of New American poetry. In so doing, his *New American Poetry* laid down the gauntlet to an earlier anthology, *New Poets of England and America* (1957), compiled by Donald Hall and others.[67] Allen's definition of the new as a radical alternative to "academic verse" excluded several gifted "new" poets, such as Richard Wilbur, Anthony Hecht, James Wright, and W.S. Merwin, who appeared in Hall's anthology. These writers, too, were critical of American postwar culture and by no means slavishly conventional in their poetry, but their aim, at that time, was to revitalize poetic forms and traditions, not to break with them altogether. Some of these poets also admired Smart.

Smart was thus involved in both kinds of "new" writing in the same way, if not to the same degree, as other neglected or rediscovered authors such as Blake and Whitman. The extent of interest shown in him by American poets since 1950 is remarkable, especially in contrast to the relative lack of institutional recognition of his poetry. In addition to the poets whose intertextual links with Smart are demonstrable, many others registered his impact in different ways. From the sum of all these testimonies it is clear that, for the postwar generation, Smart had the same vital contemporaneity as certain other poets of the past, English and American. Yet he remains the invisible man of literary history. In particular, while the influence of Blake, Shelley, Whitman, and others on the development of long-line, "open" verse and an oracular, anti-rational rhetoric has been widely acknowledged by academic historians, Smart's contribution has been almost universally ignored.[68]

Hence what American poets themselves have said about Smart deserves particular attention. Two closely related aspects were most frequently singled out in the 1950s: his "madness" and his unconventional verse form. Louise Bogan fastened on the first of these when she discovered Smart in Auden and Pearson's *Poets of the English Language*. Reviewing the anthology in 1951, she acclaimed it as "a peculiarly modern achievement," commending it especially for including "the unexpected and the neglected" alongside canonical English texts. Examples she gave were the "two great 'mad' poets, John Clare and Christopher Smart" whose poetry, she said, "brilliantly set off the works of their more reasonable contemporaries."[69] Bogan recognized as "modern" both the swerve away from mainstream literary tradition and the rejection of Enlightenment rationality. In a private letter some years later she linked Smart through his "madness" with the Beat poets: "O the madness of poets! How carefully we must tread! For that McClure guy, who writes out of a 'peyote depression,' may yet connect with the sacred fire in no uncertain way: look at Clare, look at Hölderlin, et al. And Chris Smart. . . .[her punctuation]"[70]

James Dickey , too, attributed the unique qualities of Smart's poetry to his "madness." "A Song to David," he wrote, might be "the ultimate mad song, combining reason and unreason, inspiration and the strictest of forms"; it might give us what we have always wanted from the insane: the life-extending, life-deepening insight, the ultimate symbolic sanity."[71] This was written in 1966, but Dickey's recently published notebooks show that he was already thinking about Smart's poetry in the early 1950s, at a time when he was struggling to work out a personal poetics. Dickey was occupied with the idea of composition as an unwilled, unconscious process, depending on a kind of secular *afflatus*. He wanted "a poetry which proceeds naturally (or *is* from the situation or encounter, which is the *essence* of its make-up, its being, . . . as it utters itself through me." Like Porter, Dickey is troubled by the drift of language toward "meaning": "the too-meaningful and so meaningless words," he says, "are cracks in the mirror" and need to be excised. Smart figures as one of a string of poets exemplifying Dickey's belief that "You must allow the poem to invent itself and its meaning simultaneously: Blake, [Hart] Crane, [W. S.] Graham, Smart, [Dylan] Thomas, Clare, [Friedrich] Hölderlin."[72] His exemplars are a somewhat motley cohort, but they were all in one way or another "deranged" (visionary, alcoholic, or clinically insane) and hence uninhibited by "normal" conventions of meaning-making.

With John Hollander, a poet-critic like Bogan, Smart's "madness" and his verse form come together. Hollander's interest in *Jubilate Agno* dates from his preoccupation with language and metrics in the 1950s. In *Vision and Resonance*, which came out of these studies (though published later),[73] he placed Smart ahead of Blake, Hopkins, and Whitman in a line of poets who foreshadowed the "metrical crisis" in twentieth-century American poetry. *Jubilate Agno* represented "a complete break with accentual-syllabism in English" but it was unreadable as a poem in its own time. Because of its "methodical madness, prophetic bursts of energy, obsessive learning, and almost symbolist associative coherence" it could be read with recognition only in "the literary bedlam of the twentieth century" and by "an audience with the Romantics, Whitman, and Pound's *Cantos* behind it."[74]

It was at this very juncture, in 1956, that Northrop Frye attacked conventional literary history and doctrine in his famous essay, "Towards Defining an Age of Sensibility."[75] One of Frye's main objectives was to redefine the poetry of the second half of the eighteenth century, rejecting the concept of pre-Romanticism and nominating *Jubilate Agno* as a representative of what he called "the poetry of process" or "oracular poetry." As defined by Frye, oracular poetry of the eighteenth century uncannily anticipates the "new American poetry" of the twentieth. Frye himself commented that "contemporary poetry is still deeply concerned with the problems and techniques of the age of sensibility." Oracular poetry, he notes, is loose in structure, often taking the form of "a series of utterances, irregular in rhythm but strongly marked off one from the other"; he cites Whitman's verse as an example.[76] The oracular poet writes in an "ecstatic, trance-like state: autonomous voices seem to speak through him"—*afflatus* again. Such poetry is often tragically "personal and biographical" (Frye quotes *Jubilate Agno* B30, "For in my nature I quested for beauty, but God, God, hath sent me to sea for pearls"); and its language typically represents assumed or actual mental breakdown, through "free association of words" and a "radical" use of metaphor. Thus, Frye says (quoting Rimbaud), "poetry of the associative or oracular type requires a 'dérèglement de tous les sens.'"

This is close to Peter Porter's definition of the mentality of poets like Smart as a "creative derangement of sensibility which is unsought but unavoidable."[77] It was just such a state of mind that the Beat poets cultivated deliberately in San Francisco in the 1950s, experimenting with drugs to induce it in the belief that, as Ginsberg claimed, the poet "becomes a seer through a long, immense, and reasoned derangement of the senses. All shapes of love, suffering, madness."[78] In short, some years ahead of the moment when "madness" was reconceptualized as a cultural and sociological phenomenon, by R.D. Laing and Michel Foucault simultaneously, the discourse of Unreason was being actively revalorized by poets.

Howl was the main channel through which *Jubilate Agno* entered the bloodstream of "new American poetry," but this was not the first of Ginsberg's own intertextual encounters with Smart. The jokey, jazz-inspired "Bop Lyrics" he wrote in 1949[79] have as refrain "Smart went crazy, Smart went crazy." Smart's "craziness" is used to authorize Ginsberg's own defiance of social and cultural norms: "All the doctors think I'm crazy," but what they take for psychosis is a canny evasion: "I made visions to beguile 'em / Till they put me in th' asylum." At the end, like Smart, he claims God as his ultimate author: "I'm a pot and God's a potter, / And my head's a piece of putty. [. . .] I'm so lucky to be nutty." Louis Simpson remarks that Ginsberg found in *Jubilate Agno* a precedent for the Surrealists' belief that anything could be admitted into the poem, no matter how "crazy" it seemed: "Smart had included everything he knew in his locality together with the City of God; there was no dividing line of here and there, life and vision—everything that lives is holy."[80]

The bearing of this on the writing of *Howl* is obvious, but in his 1986 account of the composition of the poem Ginsberg focused on Smart's innovative verse technique as the formative influence:[81] The elasticity of the long verse line of Christopher Smart is the immediate inspiration *by ear*. No other English verse plays with humorous quantitative delicacy of line, variably long or short, counterpointed to its neighbors in such accurate balance. Smart's aural intelligence tends to the appropriate syncopated whip crack of a definite self-enclosed rhythm. With typical eclecticism Ginsberg allies Smart with a long list of other sources—Blake, Shelley, Whitman, Kurt Schwitters, Vladimir Mayakovsky, Antonin Artaud, Federigo García Lorca, Williams, Hart Crane—claiming Guillaume Apollinaire's "Zone" also as a Modernist version of "the variable breath-stop line of Smart." That Smart is only one ingredient in this transhistorical stew-pot makes his presence more not less significant; he joins the rest as a generative "precursor" of Ginsberg's new poetics, not a revered but dead "influence" on it. All his models, Ginsberg says, exemplify Whitman's principle of "expansion of breath, inspiration as in unobstructed breath, 'unchecked original impulse'" as the basis of meter (by this date Ginsberg had absorbed Olson's breath-based metrical theory, though whether it was already in his mind in 1955 is questionable). Barry Miles pinpoints the feature of Smart's verse in *Jubilate Agno* that makes it stand out from that of Ginsberg's other models:[82] that is, the pattern of repeated "statement" and "counterstatement," which Ginsberg adopts in the Rockland section of *Howl* (Part III), as in:

> I'm with you in Rockland
>> where we are great writers on the same dreadful typewriter
> I'm with you in Rockland
>> where your condition has become serious and is reported on
>> the radio [etc.]

There are numerous parallels of other kinds, besides verse form, between *Howl* and *Jubilate Agno*, as Bruce Hunsberger has shown,[83] though many of the features they share—prophetic stance, spontaneous style, ego-centered viewpoint, use of Hebraic symbolism and liturgical style, and so forth—are characteristic of oracular poetry generally. Ginsberg's own word "humorous" points to a more specific affinity. Both Smart and Ginsberg have the ability to pass unexpectedly from lament to mockery and from earnestness to absurdity, bringing an element of playfulness to a rhetoric otherwise prone to be oppressively passionate, indignant, wrathful, or plaintive. Ginsberg's "Psalm III,"[84] another poem from the 1950s influenced by *Jubilate Agno*, suffers from lack of this saving grace. Both its attempted elevation from mundane to sublime and its imitation of Smart's conception of self-identity sound labored and artificial.

A late poem by Ginsberg, "London Dream Doors" (1986)[85] returns to Smart in a more interesting way. Beginning, "On London's Tavern's wooden table, been reading Kit Smart—/ God sent him to sea for pearls—till eyes heavy must sleep—" the poem goes on to describe a sexual encounter with an unknown boy in a rooming-house, its farcical interruption by the landlord, the transformation of wishful dream into nightmarish comedy, and the writer's final awakening to solitary reality. The poem is not an imitation of Smart's text but relates to it intersubjectively. The lonely poet of *Jubilate Agno*, imprisoned in an English madhouse and "sent to sea" for wish-fulfillment, is reincarnated in 1980s New York as a lonely poet entrapped in a dreamworld of erotic fantasy and tragi-comic frustration.

From *Howl*, the cadences and rhetoric of *Jubilate Agno* spread in turn to Jack Kerouac and Philip Lamantia.[86] Delmore Schwartz, no admirer of the Beat poets (the "San Francisco Howlers" as he called them), picked it up independently. He had discovered Smart by 1954, and the influence of the verse and style of *Jubilate Agno* shows in two of his poems, "Love and Marilyn Monroe" (the second paragraph of which appears to be an imitation of the Cat Jeoffry verses) and "The Kingdom of Poetry."[87] The second reads like a secularized, intoxicated version of *Jubilate Agno*, cross-fertilized by Marianne Moore and neo-Romanticism. It endows poetry with the powers that Smart assigns to supernatural agency. Poetry, it says, "magnifies and heightens reality," it is "in a way, omnipotent" and endowed with miraculous powers of transformation and invention,

> For it is true that poetry invented the unicorn, the centaur and the phoenix.
> Hence it is true that poetry is an everlasting Ark,
> An omnibus containing, bearing and begetting all the mind's animals. [. . .]
> Poetry is quick as tigers, clever as cats, vivid as oranges,

—and so on. What makes Schwartz's rambling piece intertextually interesting is its oscillation between levity and grandiosity. While not achieving the fine balance of humor and vatic elevation of Ginsberg at his best, it confirms the impression that the element of "play" was one of Smart's distinctive legacies to twentieth-century oracular poetry.

It is difficult otherwise, if not impossible, to disentangle Smart's contribution from that of other precursors to the spread of oracular rhetoric in the 1950s, and pointless to try. As Clement Hawes's recent book on the rhetoric of "Enthusiasm" from the Ranters up to Smart, and earlier studies of Blake by E.P. Thompson and others have shown,[88] the transmission of rhetorical styles is a complex process which cannot be adequately explained through a machinery of specific "sources" and "influences." The evidence suggests that a "rhetoric of enthusiasm," developed by radical religious writers in the turbulent years during and after the English Civil War went underground, as it were, at the end of the seventeenth century, to surface again whenever the configuration of social, cultural and material conditions favored its reemergence. The "Age of Revolution" in England in the 1790s provided just such a context, as did the 1950s in America, in which it was "the social traumas of reconstruction and disaffiliation following World War II" that fueled the San Francisco Renaissance.[89]Smart's place in this ideological pattern is, on the face of it, surprising. He did not, like Blake, live in revolutionary times, or become involved in movements of radical dissent, nor was he either democratic or anarchic in his principles. His political and social professions are orthodox; despite his compassion and fellow-feeling for the poor and underprivileged victims of society, he did not challenge the class system as such. On the contrary, his touchy concern about his own claims to gentlemanly status, and the whiff of sycophancy that hangs about his personal relations with the aristocracy, show a wholly conventional attachment to social hierarchy. Smart's revolutionary spirit emerges openly in his metaphysics and poetics. In the counter-Enlightenment attitudes voiced in *Jubilate Agno*, notably the replacement of mechanical and materialist natural philosophy by a spiritual understanding of nature, is manifest a radical countercultural impulse, engendering or renewing a rhetoric of enthusiasm.

This brings us to a third aspect of Smart's poetry that was important to American writers in the postwar period: his celebration of natural creatures and things. Here one has to tread with particular care, for two reasons: firstly because the turn to the natural world among American poets took differing forms, and secondly because Smart's poetry was only one among several factors contributing to this turn. Others include nineteenth-century Romantic nature philosophy, the writings of D. H. Lawrence and English neo-Romantic poets, and Buddhism with its emphasis on compassion for all sentient beings.[90] Some writers however, such as James Dickey, Galway Kinnell, and W.S. Merwin, directly associate Smart with their attitude towards natural life.

These poets seek in nature not beauty or solace or evidence of divine benevolence, but self-knowledge, leading on to self-transcendence or grounding in a deeper "reality" through identification with natural creatures and things. "Each creature or thing you write about brings out some aspect of yourself," Kinnell says.[91] The movement from creature back to self is prefigured by Smart in *Jubilate Agno*, Fragment B, where observations on the creature in the "Let" verse are regularly applied to the poet's own nature or condition in the corresponding "For" verse. The most poignant example, quoted by Frye and by many poets since, is B30, where description of the kingfisher ("of royal beauty, tho' plebeian size") is answered by, *"For in my nature I quested for beauty, but God, God, hath sent me to sea for pearls."*

Smart's feeling for creatures has been described as "Franciscan."[92] Shorn of its sentimental accretions, "Franciscan" does usefully differentiate Smart's sacramental understanding of nature from Romantic "One Life" nature philosophy. Its foundation is not pantheism but a belief that the variety and plenitude of nature are direct manifestations of divine goodness and omnipotence. Among later writers, the poet whom Smart most resembles in this is Gerard Manley Hopkins, whose sacramentalism owes much to the Franciscan philosopher Duns Scotus. Its special quality is recognition of individual "essences" of natural things and creatures (their earthly "selves" in Smart's and Hopkins's terms) as equal not subordinate in value to their value as "signs" of a supernatural reality. Dickey, Kinnell and Merwin, however, reading Smart through the lens of Wordsworthian romanticism, seek a closer identification with forms of natural life than the empathy shown in Smart's writing. "If you could keep going deeper and deeper, you'd finally not be a person," Kinnell says, "you'd be an animal; and if you kept going deeper and deeper, you'd be a blade of grass or ultimately perhaps a stone. And if a stone could read poetry would speak for it."[93]

In the early 1970s, James Dickey was one of a number of contemporary poets asked by Richard Howard to nominate one poem from the past of special importance to them, to accompany one of their own, for a collection titled *Preferences*.[94] Dickey chose the Cat Jeoffry sequence from *Jubilate Agno*, and his own poem, "The Sheep Child."[95] For Dickey, the physical "reality" of nature is paramount. He said in the early notebooks that he wanted to "write 'out of' the brute and animal nature of reality, to deal with essences, entelechies [. . .] *as if I were* a stone, frond, tiger, kiss."[96] In spite of his terminology, Dickey is more interested in a Wordsworthian unity of natural life than in individual "essences." "The Sheep Child," he said, is "a poem about the universal need for contact between living creatures that runs through all of sentient nature and recognizes no boundaries of species."[97] Hence intertextual links between "The Sheep Child" and Smart's Cat Jeoffry are tenuous; partly because of the lack of creaturely *haecceitas* in Dickey's poem, partly also (as Howard remarks) because Dickey "cannot apostrophize his sheep child" in the same way as Smart praises his cat because "his is the imagination of metamorphosis, and he must *become* what [Smart] addresses."[98]

Philip Levine, a poet of the same generation as Dickey, also nominated an excerpt from *Jubilate Agno* for *Preferences*. The passage he chose, B224-30 ("For" verses only), is specifically about human and creaturely self-identity: through prayer, "*a man speaks himself from the crown of his head to the sole of his feet,*" as "*a lion roars himself compleat from head to tail.*" Levine chose, for his own text, "They Feed They Lion."[99] As Howard points out, this poem, like Smart's, depends on the conviction that the power to act and the power to pray and bless are one, a concept embodied by both poets in the biblical figure of the lion.[100] The biblical lion commonly symbolizes the wrath of God against human impieties and the oppression of His chosen people; but also, in Revelation 5:5, it represents the power that will eventually redeem them. Levine's poem transfers the prophecy on to the deprived and suffering people of working class America.

Galway Kinnell's "Franciscan" sympathies, wittily demonstrated in "Saint Francis and the Sow," are evident also in the sacramental view of nature he has expressed in interviews.[101] Animal life, he has said, offers the only assurance of "mystery" in the terrestrial world: "If the things and creatures that live on earth don't possess mystery, then there isn't any. To touch this mystery requires, I think, love of the things and creatures that surround us: the capacity to go out to them so that they enter us, so that they are transformed within us, and so that our inner life finds expression through them."[102] For Kinnell the supreme precursor-poet is Whitman, but a small cluster of other poets, including Ranier Maria Rilke, Blake, Ginsberg, and Smart, have been hardly less important to him. Critics who discuss his understanding of nature are too ready to associate it with Whitman alone. "Both are poets of empathy," as Thomas Gardner remarks, but the delicate balance characteristic of Kinnell's animal poems, between symbolism and a keenly observant naturalism, is closer to certain other poets, including Lawrence and Smart, than to Whitman.[103] Of Lawrence's poetry Kinnell remarks, "I like it that the animals remain animals yet take on a symbolic character too," adding that "John Clare's ladybug" and "Christopher Smart with his cat" show the same quality.[104]

Kinnell, like others, values Smart's so-called madness as a fundamental aspect of his creativity. In an interview given in 1976 he placed Smart and Clare, both "supposedly mad," among "the handful of poets I like most": in their poems, "you find an incredibly intense clarity and selflessness, divine madness and divine sanity both at once." He quoted the long flower passage from *Jubilate Agno* (B493-509) as an example.[105] As far as I know, Kinnell refers openly to Smart only once in his poetry, (in "Flies"), but Smart also provides a pretext for one of his best- known poems, "The Porcupine" (1968; see checklist). The second section is surely modeled on the Cat Jeoffry verses:

> In character
> he resembles us in seven ways:
> he puts his mark on outhouses,
> he alchemizes by moonlight,
> he shits on the run,
> he uses his tail for climbing,
> he chuckles softly to himself when scared,
> he's overcrowded if there's more than one of him per five
>   acres,
> his eyes have their own inner redness.

The combination of magical and realistic attributes, listed under the mystic number seven, makes Kinnell's porcupine close kin to Smart's cat, who worships by "wreathing his body seven times round," before he "performs in ten degrees" his duty to himself.[106] Gardner refers to Kinnell's passage as a "rather light-hearted catalogue of resemblances," but as with Smart, levity is only half the equation.[107] Like Jeoffry (who is "a mixture of gravity and waggery"), Kinnell's porcupine is no less sacred for not being solemn. Gardner's recognition of section 2 as incongruous is, in Riffaterre's terms, an "ungrammaticality" that *obliges* the reader to complete the meaning by reference to the intertext.[108] This section is not a digression, it is vital to the economy of Kinnell's poem as a whole, anticipating the spiritual references (Zoroastrian and Christian) in sections five and six, contrasted with the palpably physical description of animal and human behavior in other sections.

Kinnell's "Flies" (see checklist) depends intimately on intertextual play, using a string of quotations from different authors as triggers for autobiographical reflection. The series begins with Whitman and includes, among others Karl Shapiro, Miroslav Horub, Emily Dickinson, Clare, Blake, and Luther. Smart appears in the lines,

> When so many vibrate together, the murmur
> Christopher Smart called "the honey of the air"
> becomes a howl.

The quotation, prised out of its context in *Jubilate Agno* (A95), is textually accurate but acquires a new frame of reference. Smart says, "Let Hashum bless with the Fly, whose health is the honey of the air, but he feeds upon the thing strangled, and perisheth." The fly is "healthy" while it feeds on air, but becomes mortal by feeding on dead matter. Kinnell keeps the health-sickness opposition but transfers it from feeding habits to sound: flies, innocent as a single "murmur," become a threatening "howl" in their multitudinousness. If "howl" is read as a reference to Ginsberg's text with its cast of millions, the frame expands. The "many vibrat[ing] together" are now linked with Ginsberg's "lost battalions" whose individual existences are warped or destroyed by capitalist society. Kinnell talks about the feeding habits of flies later in the poem; by then the fly has been internalized and associated with his mother's death, as the "fly inside me" who feeds on "a filth-heap" of guilt and humiliation.

The progression toward total identification in Kinnell's poems is similar to the path followed by W.S. Merwin (a friend of Kinnell) in "Lemuel's Blessing" (1962). This powerful and enigmatic poem belongs to a period of change in Merwin's outlook; an intensified awareness of social, cultural and environmental danger was reflected in his poetry by conversion to open form and a different rhetoric. "Lemuel's Blessing" begins with an epigraph from *Jubilate Agno*, "Let Lemuel bless with the wolf, which is a dog without a master, but the Lord hears his cries and feeds him in the desert" (A76). The poem has been interpreted as a recoil from Merwin's earlier writing self, a "willful rebirth," Edward Brunner calls it, in response to a new consciousness of the deathly effect of the conventional proprieties and responsibilities which define human existence. The wolf to whom it appears to be addressed ("You that know the way / Spirit / I bless your ears which are like cypruses on a mountain") is a creature whose mode of living requires obedience to nothing but the laws of its own being. Brunner claims that the poem in its "deeper form" has "little to do with literary predecessors" such as *Jubilate Agno*; it seems to me, on the contrary, to be vitally in dialogue with Smart's text.[109] Smart's verse is predicated on the belief that to be masterless is to be unnurtured and uncomforted. Merwin's poem emphasizes the converse: that the price of nurture and comfort is subservience to a spirit or being not oneself.

Self-determination becomes the sole imperative, overriding all other values. But the choice for Merwin is neither painless nor unequivocal. An eloquent passage at the center of the poem both acknowledges the hard consequences of independence ("Let fatigue, weather, habitation, the old bones finally, / Be nothing to me"), and prays for relief, using the immemorial words of the twenty-third psalm, "But lead me at times beside the still waters." The poem ends by returning to the pretext with the plea

> And sustain me for my time in the desert
> On what is essential to me.

Paradoxically, independence itself needs some external power to sustain it; alternatively, the "Spirit" may be a power *within* the supplicant.

Close in time to Merwin's poem but distant in kind is "A Garland for Christopher Smart" by Mona Van Duyn. She was attracted to Smart's poetry, she says, by "the startling quirkiness and freshness of Smart's details, observations, juxtapositions and diction."[110] "A Garland" is a set of five meditations, each based on a verse or verses from *Jubilate Agno*, but connected by the title also with Smart's religious lyrics (called a "wreathed garland" in *Hymns and Spiritual Songs*, I:10). The text marries the two kinds. It imitates the diction of *Jubilate Agno*, and is like it in the mingling of earthy detail and global vision, humor, tenderness, and philosophical reflection; but the four-line stanzas and use of rhyme, pararhyme, and consonance bring it closer to lyrical form. Van Duyn does not seek identification with nature but cherishes its particularities. Moreover the world of her poem, like Smart's, is sustained by the man-made as well as the natural: "soapflake coupons," "drainage ditches," "prefabricated houses," as well as "snapdragon and candytuft and rue,"

> And the world is lifted up with even more humble words,
> snail-scum and limey droppings and fly-blow
> and gold loops that dogs have wetted on snow—
> all coming and going of beasts and bugs and birds.

Like Mona Van Duyn, Anthony Hecht was one of the "new" American poets of the 1950s who resisted the movement away from formal tradition. Hecht evidently knew *Jubilate Agno* at this stage, for there are clear allusions to Fragment B in his "Divination by a Cat" (1954: see checklist). The poem is in ten-line stanzas made up of pentameters and trimeters, with an intricate rhyme pattern. In the second stanza, Hecht (addressing the cat) admires the agility and "Athenian equipoise" with which he leaps from a height to "End up unerringly on your feet." The echo of Smart's pun ("For the Greek is thrown from heaven and falls upon its feet," B632) is unmistakable. Smart uses it airily to illustrate the proposition that "the power of some animal is predominant in every language," the Cat being the spirit of Greek (B625-6). "O this is Greek to all of us," Hecht comments. "You are the lesser Tiger," he continues in the next stanza (see B722). Smart's cat then merges into Blake's Tyger, whose blazing intensity of vision even the lesser cat possesses, so that "we, in our imperfect symmetry, . . . / Can see mirrored in your chatoyant gaze / Our fire, slight, diminished." The cat/human contrast strikes a serious note, but only momentarily. Hecht's witticisms, puns, metrical ingenuity, and teasing allusiveness sustain an effect of intellectual play rather than philosophical or personal commitment.

The poetic current, however, as Louis Simpson saw later, appeared to be driving inexorably towards poetry of the vatic and "confessional" kind. He saw "an accelerating movement away from rationalistic verse toward poetry that releases the unconscious, the irrational, or, if your mind runs that way, magic. . . . Donne is out; Blake is in."[111] Anne Sexton found her voice as a poet within this movement, but it was to Smart's *Jubilate Agno* rather than Blake that she turned.

Mental instability is the most obvious and least interesting connection between Sexton and Smart. As poets they share a quality that Sexton called "exuberance" ("Saints have no moderation, / nor do poets, / just exuberance").[112] Sexton imitated the style of *Jubilate Agno* in the 1960s, but "O Ye Tongues," a sequence of ten "Psalms," written in 1971-72 and published in the last year of Sexton's life, is her boldest appropriation of Smart's text.[113] It not only imitates *Jubilate Agno* formally, incorporating many phrases and details, but also integrates Smart himself into the whole apparatus of supplication, praise, and self-inscription. "Christopher" becomes alter ego of "Anne," first as co-subject in the Third Psalm ("Let Anne and Christopher kneel," "appear," "rejoice"), then in the Fourth Psalm as symbiotic Other:

> For Anne and Christopher were born in my head as I howled at the grave of the roses, [. . .]
> For Christopher, my imaginary brother, my twin holding his baby cock like a minnow.
> For I became a we and this imaginary we became a kind company [. . .]

Thereafter, "Christopher" assumes multiple roles: as loving parent-figure ("For I shat and Christopher smiled and said let the air be sweet with your soil"); the co-deliverer of "Anne" from the "disease" of biological generation ("For birth was a disease and Christopher and I invented the cure. / For we swallow magic and we deliver Anne") in the Fourth Psalm; later, in the Eighth Psalm, the somewhat sinister controller of a nameless woman's pregnancy ("For she is stuffed by Christopher into a neat package that will not undo until the weeks pass"), and perhaps the baby's father ("For the baby grows and the mother places her giggle-jog on her knee and sings a song of Christopher and Anne"). The baby is destined to supplant its mother ("For the baby lives. The mother will die"), but Christopher, now identified as impregnator, will die also ("and when she does Christopher will go with her. Christopher who stabbed his kisses and cried up to make two out of one"). The sequence concludes with an elaboration of this prophecy, in which their death becomes both a joyful termination of their psychic journey and an affirmation of God (the last verse echoes the opening of the First Psalm: "Let there be a God as large as a sunlamp to laugh his heat at you").[114]

> For Anne sat down with the blood of a hammer and built a tombstone for herself and Christopher sat beside her and was well pleased with their red shadow. [. . .]
> For God did not forsake them but put the blood angel to look after them until such a time as they would enter their star. [. . .]
> For God was as large as a sunlamp and laughed his heat at us and therefore we did not cringe at the death hole.

Whether or not Sexton's fantasies of union between "Christopher" and "Anne" consciously replicate Smart's own fantasies about "Anne" (Hope) in

Jubilate Agno (B534, B666-67, D186),[115] they show an uncanny enmeshing of the two texts. A new dimension of intertextuality, beyond the intersubjective and imitative, seems to be involved.

I have left for last the most radical of all reworkings of Smart in North American writing. In 1963 the Canadian poet, Eli Mandel, wrote a one-act verse drama, *Mary Midnight*, which he described as "a farcical re-invention" of "The Old Woman's Oratory."[116] In Mandel's surreal fantasy, 1763 London is merged with 1963 Toronto, and Mary Midnight herself, Christopher Smart, and the "Author" have speaking roles, along with Blake, Henry Fuseli and others. The drama is about the making of poetry, and poetry as "making," subjects that mattered intensely to Mandel. Smart's poetry was important to his scheme of ideas from the start: his doctoral thesis was on Smart's poetic theory and he later wrote a closely argued essay on theories of "voice" in Smart and Gray.[117] But this was not solely an academic preoccupation for Mandel. He suffered to an acute degree the postwar trauma that affected so many poets of his generation; the Holocaust especially haunted him for more than 20 years before he was able write about it in his most famous poem, "On the 25th Anniversary of the Liberation of Auschwitz" (1970). The metaphysical, religious, and political implications of the death camps, he said, touched "on the very nature of writing itself," compelling him to find a new poetics for the "unsayable poem."[118] *Mary Midnight* belongs to an early stage of this long search, but already in 1961 Mandel (a disciple of Frye) saw in poetry a violent subversive energy that gave it a significant role in resistance against tyranny and conformity. "Against the witless rigidities of society and personality," he wrote, poetry "employs the strategies of the lively mind: ironic perspectives, the masks of comedy, tragedy and anarchy, new dramas of voice and imagery."[119] In a broadcast talk a few years later, he spoke of the power of poetry to "dissolve the structures by which we form ourselves in the daylight world" and force us to confront "not the assumed images of ourselves but those genuine and terrifying ones of the night world and the world of imagination." Insofar as it is "the language of the unconscious," poetry is "the language of darkness, of chaos, of the impossible, . . . of madness."[120]

It is to this somber, yet vitally creative, domain of poetry that Smart's "Mary Midnight" gives access. As mother-midwife, she is the procreator of poetry: "My uterus is seminal with rhymes," as she proclaims in her prologue. "I unpage the universal heart / Of continental tears and provinces of hurt."

> Do not be afraid of my vulvular mouth.
> Such darkness was before the dust.

> Such darkness will be after wrath.
> In such darkness will be after birth.

Mandel's drama is intentionally hard to understand: "Mary is always obscure, and tonight she's darker than ever," says a mysterious "Shape." It involves changes of shape, sexuality and identity, and layers of intertextuality. Smart himself appears in various guises, including woman's dress and the robes of Macbeth, and his speech echoes Milton and Shakespeare; recalling (Mandel's preface tells us), Smart's own parodies of other writers. Through such means it dismantles the rational "daylight" structures of signification Mandel speaks of, anticipating the discovery that enabled him to write his Auschwitz poem: that, "Not reality but *derealization* might now be the necessary subject or mode itself of poetry."[121] Where the Prologue stressed the creative process, in the Epilogue the Author declares the power of the poet (Prospero-like) to *unmake*:

> Shadows and phantoms
> read yourself into darkness again.
> I have dreamed you to undream you.
> Making you I am the unmaker.
> Read yourself into your rest.

To this, Mary Midnight replies that "They will not be unmade though they will be hidden. . . . They are my death / And my birth. / I am the cave." The "darkness" and pessimism of Mandel's poetry have received more than enough critical attention. The Freudian language here points to the other side of his undeniably bleak vision, or at least the possibility of relief from it. Descent into the "cave" of poetry appears to hold out the promise of psychoanalytical catharsis, even though it leads ultimately (in the final line) to the "breathless ecstasy of death." Robert Kroetsch has commented that it is not fortuitous that a poet as radical as Mandel should have found a model in Christopher Smart: "indeed, Mandel's violent reading of that mad eighteenth-century Londoner transforms him into a North American poet, into a father (mother?)-figure for the poets of the New World."[122]

IV

Two factual observations come out of a survey of Smart among the moderns. One is that the range of texts involved is very narrow. With rare exceptions, twentieth-century poets have been interested only in *A Song to David* and *Jubilate Agno*. The second is that in the last 20 years the Cat Jeoffry sequence from *Jubilate Agno* has easily surpassed any other of Smart's writings in popularity as a model for imitation and adaptation. These facts give rise to a disquieting thought. From the nineteenth century up to the middle of the twentieth Smart was in the invidious class of authors whose reputation rested on a single poem. The danger now appears to be that the Jeoffry verses, already his most frequently anthologized text, will simply replace the *Song* as that one poem.

However that may be, it is no mean achievement to establish a new genre, as Smart's Cat Jeoffry verses have effectively done. Alistair Fowler observes that it "will often be [an author's] successors who first see the potential for genre and recognize, retrospectively, that assembly for a new form has taken place."[123] This is clearly what has happened with the Jeoffry verses. Modern versions make the generic features of the new form quite distinct: perhaps Geoffrey Hartman's coinage, "magnifi-cat," should be its label.[124] Formally, a magnifi-cat is a short poem consisting of a series of nonmetrical lines, end-stopped and of variable length, similar in syntactic structure and usually beginning with the word "For." In mode it is descriptive-eulogistic, drawing up a catalogue of discrete attributes to delineate the subject (creature, person, or object). A personal relationship between poet and subject is normally established from the outset by formulae such as "I will consider my x" or "I will praise my x." Tightly defined though it is, the genre lends itself nevertheless to a range of subjects: apart from cats, modern imitations celebrate a dog, a lover, a school, a porcupine, a film-star, and Christopher Smart himself.[125]

It also serves a variety of purposes. Smart's own magnifi-cat is more than merely celebratory. As Marcus Walsh points out, the Jeoffry verses demonstrate a basic postulate of Smart's religious poetry: that "every creature worships God simply by being itself." Each of the cat's actions is part of a "ritual of praise" ("For he is the servant of the Living God duly and daily serving him," B696).[126] Edward Hirsch's "Wild Gratitude," though not a strict imitation, is centered on Cat Jeoffry and reaffirms Smart's (and Hopkins') principle of self-being as the ultimate form of service. Whereas his earlier "Christopher Smart" (1981) had been, like Jeremy Reed's poem, a dramatization of Smart's madhouse experiences by means of *bricolage*, "Wild Gratitude" is a meditation. Kneeling down with his cat "Zooey," the author thinks of Smart: his passion for kneeling in prayer, "his sad religious mania and his wild gratitude," his blessings on lunatics, postmen, and gardeners (alluding to various verses in Fragment B). Holiness by this showing manifests itself in the practice of humane virtues: "compassion," "warm humanity," "benevolence." But then he wakes up to a sense of what it means beyond this to call a cat a servant of God: watching Zooey being her cat-self, he reenacts Smart's intimate observation of Jeoffry,

> And only then did I understand
> It is Jeoffry—and every creature like him—
> Who can teach us how to praise—purring
> In their own language,
> Wreathing themselves in the living fire.

For human beings to achieve this state, however, the equation (self-being = worship) has to be reversed: Smart's poetry of the 1760s insists that it is only *by* serving God—through prayer, gratitude, "Christian heroism," and so forth—that "man" can attain a state of unified being, "speak himself" wholly. John Heath-Stubbs in "Jeoffrey" (which gives a cat's-eye view of Smart himself), and Joseph Stroud in "To Christopher Smart," are concerned with this side of the equation. Both claim integrity of being for "Christopher Smart" himself. Addressing the paradox of his life, the contradiction between his drunkenness, grubby habits, and manic behavior and the beauty of his spiritual vision, they resolve it by showing Smart's faith manifested *through*, not in spite of, his actions: "For he saw the Lord daily and drank with him often" (Stroud).

Susan Schaeffer and Erica Jong in their magnifi-cats refer sporadically to God as universal creator, but their outlook is essentially humanist rather than religious. Schaeffer's "Jubilate Agno: Thomas Cat" is a hymn to "love," demonstrated by Thomas both in the body ("He is love in his fur") and by his actions. Jong's magnifi-cat is more elaborate. It is one of a number of poems in which Jong reflects on the human condition through the medium of doggish behavior. In "Jubilate Canis" she celebrates her dog Poochkin's egalitarian relish for all foods and odors ("For to him, all smells are created equal by God—both turds and perfumes"), his androgynous body ("For though he is male, he has pink nipples on his belly like the female"), his joy in activity and his unfastidious contentment with basic comforts. He is thus a model for humankind: "For though he is canine, he is more humane than most humans."[127] Gay Clifford, in "I will consider my cat Thisbe" keeps Smart at arm's length with the disclaimer "And I fear she does not fear the Lord," while still, like Smart, capturing the cat's feline *haecceitas*, her fierceness, grace, independence and companionability. The impulse behind Clifford's poetry is an intense feeling for the reality of things, especially living things, which comes close to Smart's ontological principle. One of her last poems,

"Happiness" (1984), is explicit on this subject, and the intertexture of biblical and colloquial language is distinctly Smartlike, though Smart is not mentioned: "It is happiness / Knowing the real exists," for that is the ground of joyful "song." This happiness, again,

> Is to have under your feet the song of things
> The song of the hump-backed whale.
> So enter then her gates with praise,
> Approach with joy her courts unto;
> The happiest thing is to know that
> A fact is greater than its definition.[128]

The poems by Gavin Ewart, Wendy Cope, and Isaac Raine exploit the potential of the genre for comedy and realism, with no overarching purpose beyond entertainment. Ewart's "Jubilate Matteo" parodies Smart's magnifi-cat with cheerful irreverence: instead of the "Living God," Ewart's cat Matty duly and daily serves his London neighborhood, "For he sleeps and washes himself and walks warily in the ways of Putney." Raine is engagingly candid and funny about his school, and Cope nails her lover with the accuracy of a lepidopterist pinning down a butterfly, though with unscientific hilarity and wit. All three are affectionate rather than satirical; hence these poems are not parodies (mock-magnificats) in a debunking sense, for magnanimity, like humor, is a modal feature of the genre. The only way in which the genre could be effectively "mocked" would be by making it serve a malicious or mean-spirited purpose.

When the poet Richard Eberhart was asked in 1969 if Smart had had any influence on him he replied, "If I had encountered Smart first he might have influenced me but Blake got there first. So did Wordsworth. And later Hopkins meant more to me than Smart . . . but I gloried in him as a paean-maker, a great celebrant, cataloguer and sender of revelations. He exemplified the notion that the mad are sane enough to see the truth."[129] The distinction between Smart's "influence" and what Smart "exemplified" returns us to that moment in 1957 when Edith Sitwell and Allen Ginsberg agreed that Christopher Smart and Whitman and Blake were the "kind of stuff" they liked. If "intertext" is defined as "the corpus of texts the reader may legitimately connect with the one before his eyes,"[130] this survey shows that intertextual readings of modern poetry cannot afford to leave Smart out of the reckoning. The "kind of stuff" his texts represent is not reducible to a tidy formula, however. Syncretic vision, "creative derangement," "afflatus," subversive anger and scorn, innovative verse form and rhythms, peculiarity and precision of diction and imagery, humor, sacramentalism, empathy with creatures, self-awareness, and carnivalesque shape-shifting: these are some of the different aspects of Smart's poetry that modern poets have fastened on. Yet, though diverse, they are not wholly separable. Smart's voice remains one and distinctive; not just as a style, but in Porter's sense of "voice," as a way of saying that is thereby a way of bringing into being. In *Jubilate Agno* (B80) Smart rejoices in his sonorous voice, significantly coupling it with his sexual vigor: *"For I bless God in the strength of my loins and for the voice which he hath made sonorous"* (the "Let" verse refers to the buzzard's legendary three testicles). It is the procreative energy of Smart's poetry, above all, I believe, that explains the potency of his appeal to modern writers.

NOTES

This essay could not have been written without the help of poets, colleagues, and others who generously responded to my requests for information. I am grateful especially to Peter Porter, Mona Van Duyn, Ann Mandel, Germaine Warkentin, Richard Greene, Roger Savage, Jane Goldman, and Marni Stanley; finally but not least, to Clement Hawes who gave invaluable assistance and whose own intertext-surfing turned up many poems that were new to me.

1. Allen Ginsberg, *Journals Mid-Fifties 1954-1958*, ed. Gordon Ball (London: Viking, 1995), 344. Other American poets of Ginsberg's generation were interested in Sitwell, but mainly for her early, modernist verse. Her post-Hiroshima apocalyptic poems seem not to have attracted much notice.

2. Michael Riffaterre, "Syllepsis," *Critical Inquiry,* 6 (1979-80), 626-28; for discussion of Riffaterre, see the introduction to Michael Worton and Judith Still, eds., *Intertextuality: Theories and Practices* (Manchester: Manchester University Press, 1990), 24-27.

3. They are printed in *PW*, iv: 405-8. The poems are discussed in Devlin, 102-3.

4. *PW*, iv: 405.

5. "On Mr. Garrick's appearing in a new Entertainment for the Benefit of Mr. Smart," *PW*, iv: 406.

6. *PW*, iv: 406.

7. See *PW*, ii: 100-3.

8. Edmund Blunden, "On receiving from the Clarendon Press the new Facsimile of Christopher Smart's 'Song to David'" (see checklist).

9. See *Robert Browning: The Poems*, ed. J. Pettigrew (Harmondsworth: Penguin Books, 1981), II: 796-802.

10. Robert Browning, "Transcendentalism: A Poem in Twelve Books," from *Men and Women* (1855), in Pettigrew, I: 735-36.

11. It was awarded the Polignac Prize of the Royal Society of Literature, and highly regarded by A. E. Housman, among others. See checklist for details of publication.

12. See David B. Morris, *The Religious Sublime* (Lexington: University of Kentucky, 1972), 104-14, and *PW*, ii:112-15.

13. *Rejoice in the Lamb: A Song of Bedlam,* ed. W.F. Stead (London: Jonathan Cape, 1939).

14. David Perkins, *A History of Modern Poetry: Modernism and After* (Cambridge, MA: Harvard University Press, 1987), 350.

15. See A. Alvarez, "The New Poetry or Beyond the Gentility Principle" in *The New Poetry* (Harmondsworth: Penguin Books, 1966), 19-32, and Perkins, *A History*, 349.

16. W. H. Auden, *The Prolific and the Devourer* (Hopewell, NJ: Ecco Press, 1976), verses XXIII: 20-22 (*Jubilate Agno* C20-22, "For" lines only are used as epigraph to Part II, 27).

17. W. H. Auden, *New Year Letter* (London: Faber and Faber, 1941), 157.

18. Edward Callan in *Auden: A Carnival of Intellect* (New York and Oxford: Oxford University Press, 1983), 118-19, quotes Paul Fussell's suggestion of links between *A Song to David* and Auden's "A Summer Night," but the supposed resemblances seem to me weak. They include Auden's use of the *Song* stanza, but tail-rhyme was used frequently by other poets, notably Burns and Wordsworth.

19. W. H. Auden, "Shorts II," *Collected Poems*, ed. E. Mendelson (London: Faber and Faber, 1976), 643. See also Auden's note on *New Year Letter*, l.1378.

20. Benjamin Britten to Elizabeth Mayer, *Letters from a Life: Selected Letters and Diaries of Benjamin Britten*, eds. Donald Mitchell and Philip Reed (London: Faber and Faber, 1991), II: 1172. Norman Nicholson, an admirer of Auden, may also have been alerted to *Rejoice in the Lamb* by him (see checklist).

21. W. H. Auden and Norman Holmes Pearson, eds., *Poets of the English Language* III: *Milton to Goldsmith* (New York: Viking Press, 1950. London: Eyre & Spottiswoode, 1952).

22. Edith Sitwell, *The Pleasures of Poetry, First Series*: *Milton and the Augustan Age* (London: Duckworth, 1930), 76-78.

23. Edith Sitwell, "Notes on Smart," in *A Poet's Notebook* (London: Macmillan, 1943), 91-93.

24. See "Some Notes on My Own Poetry" in *Edith Sitwell: A Selection by the Author* (Harmondsworth: Penguin Books, 1952), xxvii-xxx. Quotations from Sitwell's poems are from this edition unless otherwise noted.

25. Edith Sitwell, "Some Notes," xxxiii-iv. "Lullaby" is the poem Sitwell refers to.

26. Walt Whitman, *Walt Whitman's Leaves of Grass: The First (1855) Edition*, ed. Malcolm Cowley (New York: Viking, 1959), 10.

27. *The Canticle of the Rose: Selected Poems 1920-1947* (London: Macmillan, 1949); see "Some Notes," xxxviii. Sitwell went on reading Smart to the end of her life: see *Selected Letters*, eds. John Lehmann and Derek Parker (London: Macmillan, 1970), 221; Edith Sitwell, *Taken Care Of: An Autobiography* (London: Hutchinson, 1965), 59-60.

28. Edith Sitwell to Benjamin Britten (March 6, 1959). Britten's setting of the poem was still uncompleted at his death: see *Selected Letters of Edith Sitwell*, ed. Richard Greene, Revised edition. (London: Virago, 1998), 415-16 and 493 n.16.

29. Edith Sitwell, *The Outcasts* (London: Macmillan, 1962), 19-20. (First published in *The Listener*, June 18, 1959).

30. Peter Steele, *Oxford Australian Writers: Peter Porter* (Melbourne: Oxford University Press, 1992), 43.

31. Peter Porter, "Composer and Poet," in *The Britten Companion*, ed. Christopher Palmer (London: Faber and Faber, 1984), 275.

32. Privately communicated.

33. For a full account of this unpublished work, see Bruce Bennett, *Spirit in Exile: Peter Porter and his Poetry* (Oxford: Oxford University Press, 1991), 48-50. The direct source for the "Inspector" figure was J.B. Priestley's *An Inspector Calls* (1947), but Porter perhaps also remembered Auden's notion of poet as "inspector" investigating "vast spiritual disorders" in *New Year Letter* I, 233-66.

34. Anthony Thwaite, *Poetry Today: A Critical Guide to British Poetry 1960-1984* (N.Y.: Longman, 1985), 69. See checklist for bibliographical details of the poems discussed.

35. Peter Porter, "Recording Angels and Answering Machines" (Warton Lecture, 1991), *Proceedings of the British Academy* 80 (1993), 1-18.

36. Peter Porter, "Poetry and Madness," *Australian Broadcasting Commission*, published in *Southerly* No.4 (December 1976): 385-405 (my quotations are from the typescript, by courtesy of Philip Lewin).

37. Text from *Collected Poems* (Oxford: Oxford University Press, 1983), 300. The last line is from *Jubilate Agno* (B509).

38. Text from *Collected Poems*, 134.

39. Porter, "Poetry and Madness."

40. Peter Steele, *Oxford Australian Writers,* 59.

41. Jeremy Reed, *Madness: The Price of Poetry* (London: Peter Owen, 1989), 155-69.

42. See, for example, Donald Davie, *The Late Augustans: Longer Poems of the Later Eighteenth Century* (London: Heinemann, 1958), introduction, xxvii-viii; "Christopher Smart: Some Neglected Poems," *Eighteenth-Century Studies,* 3 (1959), 242-64; *The Eighteenth-Century Hymn in England* (Cambridge: Cambridge University Press, 1993), 95-120.

43. See Christopher Smart, "On the Eternity of the Supreme Being," l. 21 (*PW*, iv: 148). Smart inverts the trope by addressing God as "Great Poet of the Universe."

44. For Drake and other naval references, see especially Christopher Smart, *Hymns* 17 and 21 (*PW*, ii: 65-8, 73-5); and "Ode to Admiral Sir George Pocock" (*PW*, iv: 339-42). For Leviathan see "On the Immensity of the Supreme Being," ll. 56-9 (*PW*, iv: 186) and *Jubilate Agno* B227. The Halcyon is referred to in B36, but Davie may also be alluding to B30, the King's Fisher (often identified with the halcyon), and Smart's quest for "pearls," giving further significance to his interest in "the mollusc."

45. For the harp as a central image of creativity for Smart, see Christopher M. Dennis, "A Structural Conceit in Smart's *Song to David*," *Review of English Studies,* n.s. 29 (1978): 257-66.

46. Davie, *The Late Augustans*, xxvii-viii.

47. Lawrance Thompson, *Robert Frost: The Years of Triumph 1915-1938* (London: Jonathan Cape, 1971), 484.

48. See Reginald L. Cook, *The Dimensions of Robert Frost* (New York: Rinehart, 1958), 49-50.

49. Ibid., 49.

50. Reginald Cook, ed., *Robert Frost: A Living Voice* (Amherst: University of Massachusetts Press, 1974), 143-44.

51. Written in 1967; see Frances E. Anderson, *Christopher Smart* (NY: Twayne, 1974), 123. Reprinted in Marianne Moore, *The Complete Prose of Marianne Moore*, ed. Patricia C. Willis (London: Faber and Faber, 1987), 667.

52. Randall Jarrell, "Her Shield," in *Poetry and the Age* (London: Faber and Faber, 1955), 167-86. For "The Pangolin" and "To a Snail," see *The Complete Poems of Marianne Moore* (London: Faber and Faber, 1955), 117-20 and 85.

53. Marianne Moore, *Complete Prose*, 420-26: read at the Grolier Club in Manhattan, December, 1948, and subsequently published as an essay in 1949. Moore presumably used Blunden's edition of *A Song to David* with other poems (London: Richard Cobden-Sanderson, 1924). Blunden quotes the "Impression" passage, from the preface to Smart's verse translation of Horace, and includes his Psalm 147 among "other poems."

54. *Marianne Moore: Imaginary Possessions* (Cambridge, MA: Harvard University Press, 1981), 275, n.7.

55. Peter Porter, "Poetry and Madness."

56. Ralph J. Mills, Jr. *Theodore Roethke* (NY, 1963), reprinted in *Seven American Poets from Macleish to Nemerov*, ed. Denis Donoghue (Minneapolis: University of Minnesota Press, 1975), 104. Mills goes on to find a more significant intertext in Dylan Thomas's "Before I Knocked and Flesh Let Enter."

57. Theodore Roethke to Ralph J. Mills, Jr., *Selected Letters of Theodore Roethke*, ed. Ralph J. Mills, Jr. (London: Faber and Faber, 1970), 230.

58. Theodore Roethke, in *Selected Letters of Theodore Roethke,* ed. Ralph J. Mills, Jr. (London: Faber and Faber, 1970), 230.

59. Theodore Roethke, *Collected Poems* (London: Faber and Faber, 1985), 220.

60. Theodore Roethke, "The Dark Angel" (1950-53), *Straw for the Fire: From the Notebooks of Theodore Roethke 1943-63,* ed. David Wagoner (Garden City, NY: Doubleday, 1972), 61. The fragment could have been inspired by *A Song to David* plus biographical knowledge; I have seen no evidence that Roethke knew *Jubilate Agno* at this date.

61. Jennijoy La Belle, *The Echoing Wood of Theodore Roethke* (Princeton, NJ: Princeton University Press, 1975), 51-56.

62. Geoffrey Thurley notes that "an inward orientation, not towards God or Christ or Man, but towards Dr. Freud" is characteristic of "Confessional" poetry. See *The American Moment: American Poetry in the Mid-Century* (London: Arnold, 1977), 64.

63. Printed in *Poetry New York*, No.3 (1950); reprinted in *The New American Poetry 1945-1960*, ed. Donald M. Allen (NY: Grove Press, 1960), 386-97. For Olson, "projective" and "open" verse are synonymous terms.

64. See Perkins, *A History of Modern Poetry*, 331-53; Richard Gray, *American Poetry of the Twentieth Century* (London and New York: Longman, 1990), 214-18; Michael Davidson, *The San Francisco Renaissance: Poetics and Community at Mid-Century* (Cambridge: Cambridge University Press, 1989), 6-7.

65. Thurley, *The American Moment*, 29-30.

66. Allen, *The New American Poetry: 1945-1960*, xi-xiv.

67. *New Poets of England and America*, eds. Donald Hall, Robert Pack, and Louis Simpson (Cleveland and New York: Meridian Books, 1957).

68. Geoffrey Thurley is an exception; see *The American Moment*, 98, 146, 182, 197-98.

69. Louise Bogan, *Selected Criticism* (London: Peter Owen, 1958, 373; compare her comments on the "general sifting out and rearrangement of values" at mid-century, leading to recovery of neglected writers such as Beddoes, Smart, and Clare "whose work has bearing on the present," in *Achievement in American Poetry 1900-1950* (Chicago, IL: Henry Regnery, 1951), 94-5.

70. Louise Bogan to Ruth Limmer, November 23, 1961, *What the Woman Lived: Selected Letters of Louise Bogan 1920-1970*, ed. Ruth Limmer (NY: Harcourt Brace Jovanovich, 1973), 336.

71. James Dickey, *Master Poems of the English Language*, ed. Oscar Williams (NY: Trident Press, 1966), 339-40.

72. James Dickey, *Striking In: The Early Notebooks of James Dickey*, ed. Gordon Van Ness (Columbia, MO: University of Missouri Press, 1996), Notebook III, 118-19. The notebooks are not chronologically arranged, but these notes appear to belong to the 1950s. "*Poems—Christopher Smart* (2 vol.)" is on a 1951 list of books to read or buy (page 67).

73. John Hollander, *Vision and Resonance: Two Senses of Poetic Form* (New York: Oxford: Oxford University Press, 1975); the first chapter was originally published as an essay in 1956.

74. Ibid., 203-5.

75. Northrop Frye, "Towards Defining an Age of Sensibility" (*ELH*, June 1956), reprinted in *Eighteenth Century English Literature: Modern Essays in Criticism*, ed. J. L. Clifford (NY: Oxford University Press, 1967), 311-18.

76. Compare Hollander's emphasis on end-stopping in oracular verse: "the sense of line terminus is crucial; each line has become a larger unit of utterance. . . . There can be no enjambment in oracular poetry." (*Vision and Resonance*, 231-32); see also Ginsberg on Smart's "self-enclosed rhythm," note 81.

77. Porter, "Poetry and Madness."

78. Quoted by Ann Charters, introduction to Jack Kerouac, *On the Road* (Harmondsworth: Penguin Books, 1991), xi.

79. See checklist for details.

80. Louis Simpson, *Studies of Dylan Thomas, Allen Ginsberg, Sylvia Plath and Robert Lowell* (London: Macmillan, 1978), 64. Simpson says Ginsberg "tried writing like Smart" in "Hymn," another early poem (*Collected Poems*, 36).

81. Allen Ginsberg, *Howl: Original Draft Facsimile*, ed. Barry Miles (NY: Harper, 1986), Appendix IV, "Model Texts: Inspirations Precursor to HOWL, 175. *Jubilate Agno*, B1-44, is printed as one of the "model texts." Ginsberg gave different versions over the years of the evolution of *Howl*, not always mentioning Smart, but his own list of "forms and sources" for his "Beat-hip-gnostic-imagist" phase (that is, up to 1970) is headed, "Bible and Kit Smart, parallelism and litany"; see *Contemporary Poets*, 6th edition., ed. Thomas Riggs (NY: St. James Press, 1996), 387.

82. Barry Miles, *Ginsberg: A Biography* (New York: Viking Press, 1990), 197-98.

83. Bruce Hunsberger, "Kit Smart's Howl," *On the Poetry of Allen Ginsberg*, ed. Lewis Hyde (Ann Arbor: University of Michigan Press, 1984), 158-70.

84. It is dated "Seattle, June, 1956." See checklist for details.

85. See checklist.

86. See, for example, Jack Kerouac, "228th Chorus" from *Mexico City Blues* (1955) and Lamantia, "Still Poem 9" (1959); both are included in *New American Poetry 1945-1960* (175-76 and 157).

87. For Schwartz's opinion of the Beat poets, see "The Present State of Poetry" (1958) in *Selected Essays of Delmore Schwartz,* eds. Donald A. Dike and David H. Zucker (Chicago: University of Chicago Press, 1970), 44-6. He refers to Smart in "T.S. Eliot's Voice and His Voices" (1954-5), *Selected Essays*, 142. See checklist for details of the poems discussed.

88. See especially Hawes; and E. P. Thompson, *Witness Against the Beast: William Blake and the Moral Law* (Cambridge: Cambridge University Press, 1993).

89. Davidson, *The San Francisco Renaissance*, 7.

90. The danger of attributing too much "influence" to Smart can be exemplified by "A Canticle to the Waterbirds" (1950) by William Everson (Brother Antoninus), *New American Poetry 1945-1960*: 118-21. Everson's Franciscan vision, enthusiastic inventory of species, biblical diction, and psalm cadences make "Canticle" sound distinctly Smartian, but he appears not to have known Smart's poetry at this date: see *William Everson: On Writing the Waterbirds and Other Presentations*, ed. Lee Bartlett (Metuchen, NJ: Scarecrow Press, 1983), 57-60.

91. Thomas Gardener, "An Interview with Galway Kinnell," *Contemporary Literature* 20 (1979), 428-9.

92. See Devlin, 151.

93. Galway Kinnell, *Walking Down the Stairs: Selections from Interviews* (Ann Arbor: University of Michigan Press, 1978), 79.

94. *Preferences: 51 American poets choose poems from their own work and from the past*, ed. Richard Howard (NY: Viking Press, 1974). Only six "past" poets, including Smart, were chosen more than once.

95. James Dickey, *Collected Poems 1957-1967* (Middletown, CT: Wesleyan University Press, 1967), 252-53.

96. Ibid., 119.

97. *Self-Interviews*, eds. Barbara and James Reiss (Garden City, N.Y.: Doubleday, 1970), 183.

98. *Preferences*, 58.
99. *They Feed They Lion* (New York: Atheneum, 1972); *Selected Poems* (London: Secker and Warburg, 1984), 81. First published in 1968.
100. Howard, *Preferences,* 166.
101. Levine, *Selected Poems* (Boston: Houghton Mifflin, 1982), 126.
102. Kinnell, *Walking Down the Stairs*, 52.
103. Gardener, "An Interview with Galway Kinnell," 423. Joseph Bruchac notes the combination of naturalism and symbolism, but he too compares Kinnell's attitude toward animals with Whitman's; see "I Have Come to Myself Empty: Galway Kinnell's Bear and Porcupine," in *On the Poetry of Galway Kinnell: The Wages of Dying,* ed. Howard Nelson (Ann Arbor: University of Michigan Press, 1987), 203-9.
104. Kinnell, *Walking Down the Stairs*, 55.
105. Ibid., 101-2. In "Poetry and Madness," Peter Porter names Kinnell himself as a distinguished "heir" to one kind of writing inaugurated by Smart.
106. Bruchac says "seven is a significant number for Kinnell, full of magical associations" (the poem is divided into seven sections): see "I Have Come to Myself Empty," 207.
107. Gardner, "An Interview with Galway Kinnell," 425. Neither he nor Bruchac notes any connection with Smart in this poem.
108. See Riffaterre, "Syllepsis"; and Worton and Still, *Intertextuality*, 25.
109. Edward J. Brunner, *Poetry as Labor and Privilege: The Writings of W.S. Merwin* (Urbana: University of Illinois Press, 1991), 90-110. Lack of space compels me to pass over the ambiguous identity of the "Spirit," but see Paul Carroll's detailed interpretation of this text in *The Poem in its Skin* (Chicago and New York: Follett Publishing Company, 1968), 143-50.
110. Privately communicated. Van Duyn first read Smart in graduate school (1943-46), later acquiring Callan's edition of his complete poems and Bond's *Jubilate Agno*. "A Garland" was written in the late 1950s or 1960; see checklist for other details.
111. Louis Simpson, "Dead Horses and Live Issues," in *A Company of Poets* (Ann Arbor: University of Michigan Press, 1981), 27-29. First published in *Nation* 204 (April 24, 1967).
112. From Anne Sexton, "The Saints Come Marching In," *The Complete Poems*, ed. Linda Gray Sexton (Boston: Houghton Mifflin, 1981), 470. Anthony Hecht finds in Sexton's early poem, "Her Kind," the same "curious mixture of pride, self-consciousness, and vulnerability" as Smart shows in *Jubilate Agno*; see *On the Laws of the Poetic Art* (Princeton, NJ: Princeton University Press, 1995), 112-17.

113. Diana Wood Middlebrook says Sexton's unpublished play *Mercy Street* (1961-69) contains "a psalm like litany" modeled on Smart's poetry and the Song of Songs; see *Anne Sexton: A Biography* (London: Virago, 1991), 323. See checklist for "O Ye Tongues."

114. See Middlebrook, *Anne Sexton*, 353-5, and "Poet of Weird Abundance," in *Anne Sexton: Telling the Tale*, ed. Steven E. Colburn (Ann Arbor: University of Michigan Press, 1988), 462- 64.

115. The "virgin" in B666-67 is identified as Anne Hope in both Stead's and Bond's notes.

116. All quotations are from *Mary Midnight*, New Draft (Toronto: Coach House Press MS Editions, 1979). I am very grateful to Ann Mandel and Germaine Warkentin for supplying me with a photocopy of this rare work.

117. Eli Mandel, "Christopher Smart: Scholar of the Lord. A Study of his Poetic Theory and its Eighteenth-Century Background" (Ph.D. diss., University of Toronto, 1957); "Theories of Voice in Eighteenth-Century Poetry: Thomas Gray and Christopher Smart," in *Fearful Joy: Papers from the Thomas Gray Bicentenary Conference at Carleton University*, eds. James Downey and Ben Jones (Montreal: McGill-Queen's University Press, 1974), 103-18.

118. Eli Mandel, "Auschwitz and Poetry," in *The Family Romance: Critical Essays by Eli Mandel* (Winnipeg: Turnstone Press, 1986), 3-10. The poem was written in 1970, published in revised form in Mandel's *Stony Plain* (Victoria: Press Porcépic, 1972), and frequently anthologized.

119. See Mandel's preface to *Poetry*, 62, eds. Eli Mandel and Jean-Guy Pilon (Toronto: Ryerson Press, 1961), n.p.

120. Eli Mandel, *Criticism: The Silent-Speaking Words* (Toronto: Canadian Broadcasting Corporation, 1966), 10-11, 23.

121. Mandel, "Auschwitz and Poetry," 8.

122. Preface to *Dreaming Backwards: The Selected Poetry of Eli Mandel* (Don Mills, Ontario: General Publishing Co., 1981), n.p. Kroetsch refers in particular to Mandel's "Two Dream Songs for John Berryman," saying that "Smart is the picture behind the picture" of Berryman's suicide in "Dream Songs." For extended criticism of *Mary Midnight*, see Andrew Stubbs, *Myth, Origins, Magic: A Study of Form in Eli Mandel's Writing* (Winnipeg: Turnstone Press, 1993), 209-22.

123. Alistair Fowler, *Kinds of Literature: An Introduction to the Theory of Genres and Modes* (Oxford: Clarendon Press, 1982), 159.

124. See Hartman, 74-98.

125. For bibliographical details of the poems discussed, see checklist.

126. Marcus Walsh, introduction to *Christopher Smart: The Religious Poetry* (Manchester: Carcanet, 1988), 11.

127. Benjamin Franklin V discusses this poem in "Erica Jong," *Dictionary of Literary Biography* 5: *American Poets since World War II*, ed. D.J. Greiner (Detroit: Bruccoli Clark, 1980), 380-86.

128. *Poems by Gay Clifford,* ed. Germaine Greer (London: Hamish Hamilton, 1990), 179-80. The fifth and sixth lines are a quotation, with pronominal gender altered, from the metrical version of Psalm 100 that begins, "All people that on earth do dwell, / Sing to the Lord with cheerful voice."

129. Anderson, *Christopher Smart*, 123.

130. Riffaterre, "Syllepsis," 626.

CHAPTER 13

Poetic Envoi:
Epistle of Mrs. Frances Burney to Dr. Samuel Johnson Regarding the Most Unfortunate Mr. Christopher Smart

AMITTAI F. AVIRAM

Dear Dr. Johnson,

> Patience, first, I pray,
> As my unruly Fancy runs astray
> So far as to attempt a Verse or two—
> Something my feeble Wit can scarcely do—
> Indulge this Lady Scribbler of Prose
> To correspond in verse—though well she knows
> What you already think of Ladies preaching—
> Like dancing Dogs, their canine Kens o'erreaching—
> We marvel not how well, but that they can,
> You say, do aught at all that doth a Man.
> I just return'd from poor, dear Mr. Smart,
> Bearing a Burden heavy on my Heart
> That Verse than Prose might better chance to lift.
> I find, moreover, that the Visit's Drift
> Of Conversation now inspires a *Muse*
> In me, whose Strains I durst not straight refuse,
> Though she might better rest restrain'd and mute
> Than suffer me to trammel her Repute.
> Dear Sir! The View of this ingenious Wight
> Made wretched *Fortune's* Victim as for Spite—
> 'Twas most affecting! Yea, I knew the sad
> Rumor that Mr. Smart was lately mad,
> But I had not made ready to regard
> The face of Genius so by Furies scarr'd.

His manner was now grave, now almost wild,
As if prophetick Rage his Sense despoil'd.
He would not long with any Subject stay,
But interrupt his Discourse oft to pray,
In Terms so learned and sublime, they led
Where Logick follow'd not, nor would my Head.
Intent, he hied, as, to a Race devote,
Swift Runners disappear in Paths remote.
'Twas tiring to this feeble Auditor,
I own—my Eyes did stray toward the Door.
We talked but half an Hour, before, o'ercome,
I fain would leave, full weary and quite dumb.
The worst was, whilst he hath been thus confin'd,
Dire Poverty hath with his suff'rings join'd.
To think, he was constrain'd to beg this Ninny
To bid my Father lend him but a Guinea!—
This Mr. Smart, who lately had won Fame
From out the hands of miserly acclaim,
Whilst even Poets, jealous, hard to please,
Admitted, privily, that, when at Ease,
They pass'd their Hours in reading o'er his Lines,
Hoping to steal some elegant Designs!
So, likewise, Sir, if you should think of aught
That one might do to help this poor Distraught,
Do tell it me, and if, perchance, you can,
Do what you might for this good, wretched Man.

Whilst I was there, he read to me aloud
From some new Verses, seeming almost proud
In Fancy's quaint and busy Wandering—
He seem'd, for Moments, to begin to sing.
They sounded strange to my too simple Wit,
'Twixt Reason and enthusiastick Fit,
Hallow'd with Cadences of Psalmistry,
. With classick and new-found Sublimity—
And, most surprising for the Theme he sounded:
His Cat-Companion, Jeoffry, who had bounded
Sleekly into the Chamber just before,
Purring as loudly as a Drunk might snore,
And, as to take what Honors were new scrawl'd,

Close by his Master's feet in Langour sprawl'd—
A meagre Fellow, not in perfect Bloom,
Yet bearing some bright Spirit into the Gloom.
Still, I these curious Verses much admir'd,
And came away, though sad, perhaps inspir'd.
These Lines were but a Portion of his Work,
Praising all Things that fly or creep or lurk.
His Verse is wrought with wondrous strange Conceipt,
Most learned, with Allusions quite replete—
He English'd several Sentences in Greek,
Latin, and Hebrew, for his List'ner meek—
And though forgetting most, I caught, good Sir,
Some Praises for Yourself and then—a Bur!
Devis'd of an Imagination wild,
These antick Lines belied their Author mild.

If I may be so bold, it seems the Task
May lie beyond what God of Men would ask,
To make fit Verse to magnify His Throne,
And such high Matter sing in blameless Tone:
The more, bending to hard perfection's Toil,
We strive for Truth, the more appeareth Guile;
'Tis vain to hope mere Verse God's Truth might bear,
Since Musick's Nature doth beguile the Ear.
Thus Mortals' Figures oft to Falsehood tend,
Whilst Notes divine we cannot comprehend.
I wonder, might our Poet's long Pursuit
To press in Service to the Absolute
The wanton Words of Art have tir'd his Sense,
And tried his Faith without Faith's recompense?
Alas, God's faithful Bard is thus dismay'd,
The *Muse's* Lover by the *Muse* betray'd!

No more! I wander where I durst not tread,
And warn my Fancy not to scape my Head.
Meanwhile, I hope, with all my silly Heart,
His latest Work will comfort Mr. Smart.
God willing, all his exercise of Mind,
At least, will let him straight his Senses find;
And whilst he praiseth creatures high and low,

May God His peace on this his humble Child bestow!

[Ed.: *desunt nonnulli versus.*]

As I from out that dismal House withdrew,
Through Tears, I saw, in Front, a gnarled Yew,
Beneath which, in a sweet, angelick Voice,
A Boy sang out a Strain, and sang it twice.
I conn'd the novel Air as best I could;
It clos'd the Scene, as I, sole Audience, stood.
Its melancholy Conceit seem'd strangely fit—
Unwitting Sense its Sentence could admit;
To homely Words mere Hap its Genius lent,
And made weak Memory strong—for thus it went:—

> *Come Darkness, come! My Love is gone,*
> *And Days have lost their Light;*
> *The Sun doth mourn his life alone,*
> *And weary worn hath hardly shone,*
> *Since fled was all Delight.*

> *Come Darkness, that of Love alone*
> *My dreams might fill the Night;*
> *Asleep, I'll gaze upon the one*
> *Who once my Days did shine upon,*
> *And dwell upon that Sight.*

It seem'd a happy Chance, as I dare say,
The Song should treat of Dreams, Sight, Night, and Day,
As if to give a Gloss, the House without,
For inward Poetry, Madness, Faith, and Doubt;
Behold a Figure for God's hidden Light
That most appeareth when 'tis out of Sight:
Poetick prayer, as you, dear Poet, know,
Can shine but darkly with God's obscure Glow;
Yet Poetry may spark the Soul's desire
To build—or con—or mock—God's brighter Fire.—
Belike such thoughts drove not my Singer sweet,
Who pass'd the Time 'til Latin Hour should meet.
He seem'd a likely Student of our Friend,

Whom e'en in Madness studious Youths attend.

Again, dear Friend, forgive my artless Script,
My pen too oft in *Dullness'* Inkwell dipt.
Should you, perchance, find Time to pay a Call
To Mr. Smart, 'twould lift his Spirits withal.
If so, I send you Godspeed on your Journey—
Wisheth,

       Your humble Servant,

           Frances Burney.

CHAPTER 14

Annotated Checklist:
Twentieth-Century Poetic Encounters with
Christopher Smart

KARINA WILLIAMSON

THIS IS NOT A COMPLETE INVENTORY; our search has been unsystematic and confined mainly to English and American poetry. Only those poems for which there is good internal and/or external evidence of a link with Smart are included. Length of text is indicated if it occupies one page or less.

1. Aviram, Amittai F. (b. 1957), "Epistle of Mrs. Frances Burney to Dr. Samuel Johnson Regarding the Most Unfortunate Mr. Christopher Smart," in *Christopher Smart and the Enlightenment*, ed. Clement Hawes (NY: St. Martin's Press, 1999), 283-287.
2. Blunden, Edmund (b. 1896), "On receiving from the Clarendon Press the new Facsimile of Christopher Smart's 'Song to David'" (14-line sonnet), separately printed (Oxford: John Johnson at the Clarendon Press, 1927), signed "Edmund Blunden Tokyo December 1926"; titled "'Song to David' 1763" in *The Poems of Edmund Blunden* (London: Cobden-Sanderson, 1930), 313. In praise of the *Song* and the press.
3. Clifford, Gay (b. 1943), "I will consider my cat Thisbe" (23 lines), in *Poems,* introduction by Germaine Greer (London: Hamish Hamilton, 1990), 100, dated "1982." Imitation of "my Cat Jeoffry" verses.
4. Cope, Wendy (b. 1945), "My Lover," in *Making Cocoa for Kingsley Amis* (London: Faber and Faber, 1986), 36-38. Imitation of "my Cat Jeoffry" verses.
5. Davie, Donald (b. 1922), "The Creature David" (19 lines), *To Scorch or Freeze: Poems about the Sacred* (Chicago, IL: University of Chicago Press, 1988), 24. Alludes to Smart's poetry.
6. Ewart, Gavin (b. 1916), "Jubilate Matteo," *Collected Poems 1980-1990* (London: Hutchinson, 1991), 68-69, from the 1980-82 section; *Selected Poems 1933-1993* (London: Hutchinson, 1994), 105-6. Imitation of "my Cat Jeoffry" verses.

7. Ginsberg, Allen (b. 1926), "Bop Lyrics," *Collected Poems 1947-1980* (Harmondsworth: Viking, 1985), 42-3, dated "New York, March-December 1949." Alludes to Smart's madness.

8. ———"Howl," *Howl and Other Poems* (San Francisco, CA: City Lights, 1956); *Collected Poems*: 126-33, dated "San Francisco, 1955-1956." Verse form modeled on *Jubilate Agno*. The title page of *Howl: Original Draft Facsimile*, ed. Barry Miles (NY: Harper, 1986), quotes verse B32 as epigraph: "For the mighty Visitor is at the window of the impenitent, while I sing a psalm of my own composing."

9. ———"Psalm III" (11 lines), in *Reality Sandwiches* (San Francisco, CA: City Lights, 1963); *Collected Poems,* 155, dated "Seattle, June 1956." Imitates form and style of *Jubilate Agno*.

10. ———"London Dream Doors," in *Cosmopolitan Greetings: Poems 1986-1992,* 1994. (NY: HarperCollins, 1995), 10-11; dated "May 6, 1986, 3:10 A.M." Alludes to Smart and quotes *Jubilate Agno* B30.

11. Heath-Stubbs, John (b. 1918), "Jeoffrey" (18 lines), in *Cats' Parnassus* (London: Hearing Eye Books, 1987), n.p. Imitation of "my Cat Jeoffry" verses.

12. Hecht, Anthony (b. 1923), "Divination by a Cat," *A Summoning of Stones* (NY: Macmillan, 1954): 46-47. Alludes to *Jubilate Agno,* B625-32 and B722. A103 is quoted as an epigraph.

13. ——— Verse A103 from *Jubilate Agno* is quoted as an epigraph to *Flight Among the Tombs* (Oxford: Oxford University Press, 1997), but these sardonic, death-haunted poems do not otherwise show any sign of Smart's influence.

14. Hirsch, Edward (b. 1950), "Christopher Smart," in *For the Sleepwalkers* (NY: Knopf, 1981), 32-33. Soliloquy by "Christopher Smart," based on *Jubilate Agno*.

15. ———"Wild Gratitude," in *Wild Gratitude* (NY: Knopf, 1986): 17-18. Alludes to "my Cat Jeoffry" verses.

16. Hodgson, Ralph (b. 1871), "The Song of Honour," in *Poems* (London: Macmillan, 1917), 12-24. First published in the *Saturday Review* (October 11, 1913). Loosely modeled on *A Song to David*.

17. Jong, Erica (b. 1942), "Jubilate Canis," *At the Edge of the Body* (NY: Holt, Rinehart and Winston, 1979), 40-41. Imitation of "my Cat Jeoffry" verses.

18. Kinnell, Galway (b. 1927), "The Porcupine," in *Body Rags* (Boston: Houghton Mifflin, 1968); *Selected Poems* (Boston: Houghton Mifflin, 1982), 88-91. Second section imitates "my Cat Jeoffry" verses.

19. ———"Flies," *Imperfect Thirst* (Boston: Houghton Mifflin, 1994), 68-73. Quotes *Jubilate Agno* A95.

20. Mandel, Eli (b. 1922), *Mary Midnight,* new draft (Toronto: Coach House Press MS Editions, July 1979); first written in 1963. One-act drama centered

on Smart's "Mary Midnight" persona and writings. The prologue was published as "Mary Midnight's Prologue" in *Black and Secret Man* (Toronto: Ryerson Press, 1964), 2-3.

21. Merwin, W.S. (b. 1927), "Lemuel's Blessing,"in *Selected Poems* (NY: Atheneum, 1988), 85-86. First published in *The New Yorker*, Dec. 8, 1962. Based on *Jubilate Agno,* A76.

22. Nicholson, Norman (b. 1914), "The Bow in the Cloud," *Collected Poems*, ed. Neil Curry (London: Faber and Faber, 1994), 103-11 (from *Five Rivers*, 1944). The final section (iv) contains seven "Let" verses followed by thirteen "For" verses, modeled in form, language, and Christian theology on *Jubilate Agno* (Stead's text). The "For" verses link virtues with colors of the rainbow (compare with B649-69; Stead XIX: 5-25). Nicholson's imitation is vital to the effect of his fine verse sequence, but Smart has no discernible influence on his other poetry.

23. Porter, Peter (b. 1929), "Inspector Christopher Smart Calls," *Poems Ancient & Modern* (Lowestoft, Suffolk: Scorpion Press, 1964); *Collected Poems* (Oxford: Oxford University Press, 1983), 75-76. Soliloquy: alludes to Mrs Midnight and quotes *Jubilate Agno,* B30 and B139 ("For" verses).

24. ———"The Return of Inspector Christopher Smart," *A Porter Folio: New Poems* (Lowestoft, Suffolk: Scorpion Press, 1969); *Collected Poems*: 93-96. Soliloquy: several quotations from *Jubilate Agno.*

25. ———"Sunday" (27 lines), in *The Last of England* (London: Oxford University Press, 1970); *Collected Poems*, 134. Alludes to the *Song to David* and to Smart's reputation for public prayer.

26. ———"Cat's Fugue," *Living in a Calm Country* (London: Oxford University Press, 1975); *Collected Poems*, 228-9. Alludes to "Jeoffry."

27. ———"Pope's Carnations Knew Him" (15 lines), in *English Subtitles* (Oxford: Oxford University Press, 1981); *Collected Poems,* 300. Based on *Jubilate Agno,* B568, also quotes B509. Peter Porter informs me that some stanzas from *A Song to David* were incorporated, in the form of a congregational hymn, in an unpublished opera text for children: *The Wolf of Gubbio,* performed in 1979.

28. Raine, Isaac (b. 1979), "My Dragon School" (72 lines; subtitled "after Christopher Smart"), *London Review of Books* (July 23, 1992), 6. Imitation of "my Cat Jeoffry" verses.

29. Reed, Jeremy (b. 1951), "Christopher Smart in Madness," in *By The Fisheries* (London: Jonathan Cape, 1984), 12-14. Soliloquy by "Christopher Smart," based on *Jubilate Agno.*

30. Roethke, Theodore (b. 1908), "Where Knock Is Open Wide," *Praise to the End!* (Garden City, NY: Doubleday, 1951); *Collected Poems* (London: Faber and Faber, 1966), 71-74. Based on *A Song to David,* stanza lxxvii.

31. ———"Christopher, help me love this loose thing" (three-line fragment), in *Straw for the Fire: From the Notebooks of Theodore Roethke 1943-63,* ed. David Waggoner (Garden City, NY: Doubleday, 1972), 61. Alludes to Smart.

32. ———"Heard in a Violent Ward" (seven lines), in *The Far Field* (Garden City, NY: Doubleday, 1964); *Collected Poems* (London: Faber and Faber, 1966), 228. Alludes to Smart.

33. Schaeffer, Susan Fromberg (b. 1941), "Jubilate Agno: Thomas Cat" (subtitled "for Christopher Smart and his Geoffrey"), in *The Bible of the Beasts of the Little Field* (NY: E.P. Dutton, 1980), 60-63. Imitation of "my Cat Jeoffry" verses.

34. Schwartz, Delmore (b. 1913), "Love and Marilyn Monroe," *Summer Knowledge: New and Selected Poems 1938-1958* (Garden City, NY: Doubleday, 1959), 23-24, dated "1955?" Partly imitative of "my Cat Jeoffry" verses.

35. ———"The Kingdom of Poetry," in *Last and Lost Poems of Delmore Schwartz,* ed. Robert Phillips (NY: Vanguard Press, 1979), 187-89. Partly imitative of *Jubilate Agno.*

36. Sexton, Anne (b. 1928), "O Ye Tongues," in *The Death Notebooks* (Boston: Houghton Mifflin, 1974); *Anne Sexton: The Complete Poems*, ed. Linda Gray Sexton (Boston: Houghton Mifflin, 1981), 396-413. Imitation of *Jubilate Agno*: "Let" and "For" verses are used *en bloc* in alternate Psalms. The sixth psalm appears to be based on Ginsberg's "America" (published in *Howl and Other Poems*).

37. Sitwell, Edith (b. 1887), "The Two Loves" (subtitled "To Pavel Tchelitchew and his work in progress"), in *The Song of the Cold* (1945); *Edith Sitwell: A Selection* (Harmondsworth: Penguin Books, 1952); *Collected Poems* (London: Macmillan, 1957), 332-35. Quotes *Jubilate Agno,* A47.

38. ———"Praise We Great Men," in *The Outcasts* (London: Macmillan, 1962), 19-20. First published in *The Listener* (June 18, 1959). Imitates Smart's "paean" mode.

39. Stroud, Joseph (b. 1943), "To Christopher Smart" (ten lines), in *In the Sleep of Rivers* (Santa Barbara, CA: Capra Press, 1974), 32. Reprinted in *19 New American Poets of the Golden Gate*, ed. Philip Dow (San Diego, NY, London: Harcourt Brace Jovanovich, 1984), 326. Imitation of "my Cat Jeoffry" verses.

40. Van Duyn, Mona (b. 1921), "A Garland for Christopher Smart," in *If It Be Not I: Collected Poems 1959-1982* (NY: Knopf, 1993), 68-71. Quotes and reflects on several verses from *Jubilate Agno.*

41. Wellman, Mac (b. 1945), Act Two of *The Hyacinth Macaw* in *Two Plays: A Murder of Crows and The Hyacinth Macaw* (Los Angeles, CA: Sun and Moon Press, 1994), 159. Speech in the form and style of *Jubilate Agno* (14 lines, beginning "Let" and "For" alternatively).

42. Williams, John (b. 1922), "A History" (eight lines), in *The Necessary Lie* (Denver, CO: Verb Publications, 1965), 38. About Smart's life, quoting exchange between Burney and Johnson ("How does poor Smart do? . . . ," "It seems as if his mind had ceased to struggle with the disease; for he grows fat upon it"), from Boswell's *Life*, May 24, 1763.

Notes on Contributors

AMITTAI F. AVIRAM is associate professor of English and Comparative Literature at the University of South Carolina, where he teaches literary theory and poetics. His *Telling Rhythm: Body and Meaning in Poetry* (1994) presents an original theory of poetry. He has published essays on the works of such poets as Countee Cullen, Claude McKay, Allen Ginsberg, Judy Grahn, Audre Lorde, and Walt Whitman. His own poems have appeared in magazines and anthologies and in his chapbook, *Tender Phrases, Brassy Moans* (1994).

LANCE BERTELSEN is associate professor in the Department of English at the University of Texas at Austin. He took his undergraduate degree at Dartmouth College and his Ph.D. at the University of Washington. He is the author of *The Nonsense Club: Literature and Popular Culture, 1749-1764* (1986) and of numerous essays on eighteenth-century writers, including Christopher Smart. He has also published several articles on World War II and the media, one of which was awarded the 1990 Texas Institute of Letters O. Henry Award. Professor Bertelsen is currently completing a book entitled *Fielding's Last Offices: Magistracy, Business, and Writing*.

MARK BOOTH is currently associate dean, College of Arts and Sciences, at the University of Wyoming. He received his B.A. from Rice University in 1965 and his Ph.D. from Harvard in 1971. He has written essays on Samuel Johnson's criticism and on lyric poets of the eighteenth century, including Christopher Smart. His book about song verse, *The Experience of Songs*, which explores songs as a distinctive art and experience of language, was published in 1981.

FRASER EASTON is assistant professor of English at the University of Waterloo, Ontario. He received his B.A. from the University of British Columbia and his Ph.D. from Princeton University. In 1990-92 he held a Killiam Postdoctoral Fellowship in the History Department at the University of British Columbia. He is the author of articles on Defoe, Davies, Smart, Austen, Foucault, and others (including "The Political Economy of *Mansfield Park*: Fanny Price and the Atlantic Working-Class," recently published in *Textual Practice*). He is currently writing a book on plebeian life in eighteenth-century British literature.

CLEMENT HAWES is currently associate professor of English at Southern Illinois University, Carbondale. He received his B.A. from Hendrix College (1978) and his Ph.D. from Yale University (1986). His publications include *Mania and Literary Style: The Rhetoric of Enthusiasm from the Ranters to Christopher Smart* (1996) and essays on Smart, Johnson, "Ranter" Abiezer Coppe, Sterne, and Gay. He is currently at work on a new book, tentatively titled *Cannibalizing History*, that will analyze the significance of the eighteenth-century moment for the project of postcolonial revision.

EDWARD J. KATZ is currently assistant professor of Literature and Language at the University of North Carolina at Asheville. He received his B.A. from the University of Washington (1986) and his Ph.D. from the University of Rochester (1992). He is the author of an essay dealing with madness, prophecy, and the sublime in Smart's work. His other published works include an essay on Jewish-African-American relations and numerous book reviews. Katz is currently at work on a book-length manuscript, *Transcending Origins: Ethics and the Idea of the Sublime in Eighteenth-Century England*.

THOMAS KEYMER was born in Greenwich in 1962. Educated at Gonville and Caius College, Cambridge, he has held a research fellowship at Emmanuel College, Cambridge, and a lectureship at the University of London (Royal Holloway and Bedford New College). He is now Elmore Fellow and tutor in English Language and Literature at St Anne's College, Oxford, and a lecturer in the faculty of English at Oxford. His publications include *Richardson's Clarissa and the Eighteenth-Century Reader* (1992), editions of Sterne's *A Sentimental Journey and Other Writings* (1994) and Fielding's *The Journal of a Voyage to Lisbon* (1996), and numerous essays on poets of the eighteenth century, including Macpherson, Pope, and Smart. Among his most recent publications is a general introduction to the 16-volume facsimile edition of *The Gentleman's Magazine* published in 1998 (Pickering & Chatto).

WILLIAM KUMBIER (B.A., Michigan State University; Ph.D., S.U.N.Y. Buffalo) is associate professor of English at Missouri Southern State College, where he teaches writing and comparative literature. He is the author of articles on William Blake's prosody, sound and signification in Smart's *Jubilate Agno*, and on the interrelation of text and music in the compositions of Joseph Haydn. Recently, he coedited, with Ann Colley, a volume of essays and poetry entitled: *Afterimages: A Festschrift in Honor of Irving Massey* (1996). A native of Michigan, he currently resides in Joplin, Missouri.

ERIC MILLER was a Mellon Fellow at the University of Virginia, where he completed his Ph.D. in 1997. His dissertation, entitled "System and Nemesis: Christopher Smart, Jean-Jacques Rousseau, John Clare and the Legacy of Linnaeus," examined the uses to which a number of writers, including Smart, put the taxonomical work of Carolus Linnaeus. His recent essay in *SEL* pursues these themes further. Miller has published prose and poetry widely in nonacademic venues. His most recent publication is an elegy-cum-memoir of the ornithologist Roger Tory Peterson in *Brick Magazine*. Miller is currently visiting assistant professor at Saint Thomas University in Fredericton, New Brunswick.

TODD C. PARKER was born in Albuquerque, New Mexico, in 1965. He attended the University of New Mexico and graduated in 1987. In 1988, he was a Fulbright Scholar at Oxford University, where he worked on Christopher Smart's poetry with Karina Williamson. He completed his Ph.D. from Cornell University in 1994, and has been assistant professor of English at DePaul University in Chicago since Fall 1995. He has published articles on the female body and female sexuality in early eighteenth-century medical discourses and on scatology and epistemology in Swift's description poetry. His book, *The Rhetoric of Sexual Difference in British Literature 1700-1750,* is forthcoming.

BETTY RIZZO is a professor of English at the City College of New York and the Graduate Center of the City University. Her dissertation was on the canon of Christopher Smart, to which she added numerous poems, and was followed by *Christopher Smart: An Annotated Bibliography, 1743-1983* (1984) and *The Annotated Letters of Christopher Smart* (1991), both volumes coedited by Robert Mahony. Her other works include writing texts; many essays on eighteenth-century writers; the monograph *Companions without Vows: Relationships among Eighteenth-Century British Women* (1994); an edition of Sarah Scott's *The History of Sir George Ellison* (1995); and a forthcoming volume of the McGill University journals and letters of Frances Burney.

MARCUS WALSH, who is a reader in English Literature at the University of Birmingham, has edited with Karina Williamson the Oxford *Poetical Works of Christopher Smart* (1980-1996), and has written extensively on Smart, Swift, Johnson, and Sterne, on the history and theory of editing, and on biblical interpretation and scholarship in the seventeenth and eighteenth centuries. His book *Shakespeare, Milton and Eighteenth-Century Literary Editing: The Beginnings of Interpretative Scholarship* appeared in 1997.

KARINA WILLIAMSON is principal editor of *The Poetical Works of Christopher Smart* (Oxford, 1980-1996), for which she was awarded the Rose Mary Crashaw Prize in 1997. She has been a lecturer at the universities of Uppsala, Oxford, and Edinburgh, and visiting professor at the University of New Mexico. She is now supernumerary fellow of St. Hilda's College, Oxford, and senior teaching fellow at the University of Edinburgh. Her publications also include numerous articles on English and Caribbean literature.

INDEX